TO CATCH A FASCIST

TO CATCH A FASCIST

THE FIGHT TO EXPOSE THE RADICAL RIGHT

CHRISTOPHER MATHIAS

ATRIA BOOKS

NEW YORK AMSTERDAM/ANTWERP LONDON TORONTO SYDNEY/MELBOURNE NEW DELHI

Let's stay in touch! Scan here to get book recommendations, exclusive offers, and more delivered to your inbox.

For Mom and Dad.
For M. and the kid about to be born.

Contents

TO CATCH A FASCIST

Introduction

did not know much about antifa when I arrived in Charlottesville, Virginia, to report on the "Unite the Right" rally on August 12, 2017. Like a lot of Americans, I mostly associated antifa with viral videos on my timeline of Nazis getting punched. The recent rise of President Donald Trump to the White House had engendered an explosion of new white supremacist groups taking to the streets across America. In response, it seemed, there was a new generation of leftist activists who wanted to take these fascists down.

I did not yet realize that Nazi-punching makes up but a fraction of a percentage of the work antifa does in America. I did not know that in the years to come I would see antifa's research into the far right and its intelligence-gathering capabilities at times outstrip any media organization or think tank or law enforcement entity; that I would see antifa go on to unmask, or "dox," thousands of modern American fascists hiding behind pseudonyms and usernames online. I did not know antifa had *spies* either, or that even before I arrived in Charlottesville, one such spy had obtained private messages fascists sent to each other ahead of the Unite the Right rally, messages that laid bare their murderous intent for the event—including memes about driving cars through counterprotesters. Antifa had shown these messages to government officials, warning them that the white supremacists coming to town wanted to kill people, and that their rally permit needed to be revoked.

Many Americans now know the historical significance of those warnings going unheeded.

It's been eight years, but some of my memories are still vivid. I remember the silent white militiamen in bulletproof vests carrying long guns. The loud hordes of neo-Nazis shouting slurs as they charged at counterprotesters. The racist chants emanating from Emancipation Park mixing with the screams from scattered melees in the surrounding streets.

A short walk from the park, in a parking garage, I remember running toward a gang of white men beating DeAndre Harris, a young Black man lying prone, covering his head with his arms. Suddenly I found myself staring down the barrel of a pistol, a neo-Nazi swinging the firearm from side to side. I ducked behind a car, standing seconds later to see Harris stumbling away from his assailants, leaving behind a pool of blood on the pavement. Then, right outside the parking garage, I stared in disbelief at dozens of police officers just standing there, doing nothing.

A few blocks away, I interviewed a young, trembling woman, struggling through sobs to recount what she'd just witnessed: one of the Nazis had just deliberately driven his muscle car into a crowd of her friends and comrades. He'd then sped into reverse and fled, leaving the street littered with dozens of bloody and broken bodies, including the now-lifeless body of a thirty-two-year-old woman. The next day, I walked to the street corner where the attack took place, finding it overlaid with flowers and messages drawn in chalk, all memorializing this woman, her name—Heather Heyer—already known around the world.

That evening, I went to a bar downtown with a group of other reporters, where we started chatting with a bride and groom married in a ceremony just hours earlier. We toasted their marriage, salvaging some joy from an otherwise ominous weekend, drinking and talking late into the night. Eventually, a friend of the newlyweds recounted how earlier that day, fearful of the Nazis in town, she thought it wise to conceal the Star of David on her necklace, tucking it beneath the fabric of her bridesmaid dress.

As I walked back to the hotel that night, the breeze gently pushed a small piece of paper across the sidewalk. It was a political flyer, likely dropped or discarded during the weekend's mayhem, with big black letters declaring simply: ALWAYS ANTI-FASCIST.

* * *

By the time I got back to New York, the whole world was talking about Charlottesville, not only because of the live-streamed footage of racist violence, but because of what the president of the United States had said afterward. Trump had asserted there were "very fine people" among the Nazis in Charlottesville, the remark instantly becoming emblematic of an emergency in American politics, the country's "liberal democracy" teetering on a precipice, with mainstream pundits pontificating whether "it"—fascism—could be happening here.

I was shaken by what I saw in Charlottesville, too, beginning a nearly decade-long journey as a reporter to investigate a movement that had felt emboldened enough to hold the largest white supremacist gathering in a generation. It was my job to identify the members and leaders of this movement, which at the time branded itself the "alt-right." I set forth to unearth their influence in society, mapping their connections to people in power, to document their crimes.

Through this work, I learned very quickly there was a network of people investigating fascists with great success, only they weren't journalists working for recognizable news outlets, like me. They were underground activists who saw researching the far right as an integral part of protecting their communities. These activists, simply put, were doing the best research about fascist groups and movements in the country. There was a name sometimes used for this network, a word seldom used in America before, but that in the years to come became ubiquitous: antifa, short for anti-fascist. It was a term imported from Europe, pronounced "an-tee-fa" there, but in the American twang it was quickly recast as "an-teef-uh."

Today, antifa refers to a radical, decentralized, and localized network of militant leftists dedicated to disrupting and defeating fascist groups wherever they go, by any means necessary.

Antifa was not created out of thin air, but emerged from preexisting networks of anarchists, socialists, and communists that chased previous generations of fascists off the streets of America. Although these leftists do not agree on everything, what they do agree on is that fascists sometimes need to be violently confronted in the streets; that they should be given "no platform" to speak or organize; and that the state and police cannot be trusted in this fight. This modern iteration of antifa, like the iterations before it, is often recognizable for the symbols, slogans, and songs it uses, borrowed from early twentieth-century anti-fascist movements in Europe—the two flags of Antifaschiste Aktion, the three arrows of the German Iron Front, the Spanish anti-fascist cry "no pasaran" (meaning "you shall not pass"), and the Italian anti-fascist anthem "Bella Ciao."

If you live in America, you are likely not far from an antifa group—though that group might consist of just a handful of people, their presence announced perhaps only with some antifa stickers placed on lampposts, or a blog, or a social media account. These small, autonomous political formations operate as "affinity groups," often sharing tactics and intelligence with each other, or coordinating direct actions, like a counterdemonstration at a neo-Nazi rally. Antifa, in other words, is not an official organization. There are no national headquarters. No leaders. No formal structure. No official spokespeople. In its current incarnation, antifa is not a mass movement, but a fundamentally underground phenomenon or subculture whose adherents largely keep their identities a secret to prevent reprisals from the fascists they fight, and to forestall state prosecution for some extralegal tactics they employ, including occasional acts of violence, sabotage, and computer hacking.

Its decentralized structure also means that antifa doesn't adhere to a single definition of "fascism." When antifa sets out to confront fascists in America today, its activists are not busy making sure their opponents meet strict academic definitions of fascism. Rather, they target far-right actors who they see as *fascistic*; who they see as a threat; or those they see as especially racist, sexist, antisemitic, Islamophobic, homophobic, or anti-trans. This is not to say, however, that antifa would dox everyone at a Trump rally, where many attendees might display those bigotries. No, for the most part antifa is targeting the worst of the worst, the most explicit and extreme bigots— those who may be on the cusp of committing violence if they haven't already. Each anti-fascist activist and group uses their own discretion to decide who to target and will generally provide plenty of evidence to make their case.

Fascism, after all, is a notoriously hard term to pin down, and "fascist" is often used colloquially, in a loosely defined fashion, as a casual pejorative for anyone demonstrating authoritarian tendencies or just acting like an asshole. But scholars of fascism have worked hard to provide us some precise definitions. Perhaps the most cited is the historian Robert Paxton's. In his book *The Anatomy of Fascism*, he defines fascism, in part, as "a form of political behavior . . . in which a mass-based party of committed nationalist militants, working in uneasy but effective collaboration with traditional elites, abandons democratic liberties and pursues with redemptive violence and without ethical or legal restraints goals of internal cleansing and external expansion."[1]

I won't list other definitions here but will mention perhaps the most common word they share is "violence." While every form of politics obviously has a relationship to violence, fascism is exceptional for its fetishization of violence, for its brutality and cruelty.

In my years covering the far right, I've come to formulate my own working definition of fascism in my head, borrowing heavily from all the academic definitions I've read before. I'm not an academic, of course, but it's just how I've made it a little more legible for myself: I think of fascism as a right-wing politics of *domination* that is hostile to democracy, often taking the form of ultranationalism, situating a particular group of people atop a social hierarchy, while targeting already marginalized groups for death, violence, and expulsion, in order to "cleanse" or "purify" the nation, restoring it to a mythical past of ethnic and cultural homogeneity.

In the American context in particular, "fascist" is often synonymous with "white supremacist," the two terms essentially joined at the hip. In 1937, Langston Hughes, the famous Black writer and poet, brought home this point while speaking in Paris to the International Writers Congress.[2] "We Negroes in America do not have to be told what fascism is in action," he said. "We know. Its theories of Nordic supremacy and economic suppression have long been realities to us."

*   *   *

In the years after Unite the Right, I came to rely on the intelligence antifa was gathering about the far right for my own investigations, along the way unmasking white supremacist soldiers, cops, teachers, and politicians. Eventually, I earned rare access to these leftist activists who were often wary of, or outright hostile to, the press. As I became familiar with the personalities in antifa, understanding the ideologies and personal motivations driving them to do this work, I witnessed "antifa" become a scare word among conservatives and liberals alike, a shorthand for "extremists" who should be considered outside the realm of political respectability. These pundits were quick to denounce anti-fascists when they were seen in viral videos punching the likes of Richard Spencer, the alt-right leader who liked to wear suits and ties, smiling on TV while advocating that the US be ethnically cleansed of everyone but white people. Trump himself appeared to savor screeching "anteeeeefuh," in his speeches—threatening at multiple points to designate antifa a "domestic terror" group. And by the summer of 2020, when massive anti-racist uprisings swept the country, Trump and the wider MAGA movement became fixated on blaming the unrest on antifa—even though antifa groups represented a vanishingly small percentage of those taking part. Baseless conspiracy theories flourished online, implicating antifa in nearly every disaster or mass shooting.

I watched the public perception of antifa grow wildly out of step with the activists I met at rallies or exchanged messages with over encrypted apps. Colored by these news cycles and viral images of antifa members punching neo-Nazis on the street, Americans today most often associate antifa with militancy. But the centrality of political violence in the discourse about antifa obscured the bulk of the work antifa was actually doing. "Physical confrontation comes very late in anti-fascist organizing, though it often draws a disproportionate amount of media attention," the philosopher Devin Zane Shaw notes.[3] "Most anti-fascist work is much less spectacular, often beginning and ending as letter-writing or educational campaigns to raise awareness about or prevent Far Right organizing and recruitment in public spaces."

This nonviolent work often involves getting far-right activists deplatformed from social media; mounting pressure campaigns to force venues—hotels, conference centers, bars, concert halls—to cancel scheduled fascist gatherings; getting city governments to revoke permits for neo-Nazi rallies; and finding and removing fascist propaganda from the streets. But perhaps the most significant, underappreciated, and often unseen aspect of antifa's work—and the focus of this book—is that of intelligence gathering and, more specifically, doxing.

To "dox" means to publish identifying information about a previously anonymous person online. Although it often refers to posting someone's home address or contact information as a means of inviting harassment, in the anti-fascist context, and for the purposes of this book, doxing refers to the practice of naming and shaming pseudonymous white supremacists or other far-right activists—the digital equivalent of ripping the white hood off a Klansman.

In the pre-internet era, exposing the identities of fascists would often entail tactics like surveillance, secretly photographing a militia group meeting; skulking around a parking lot near a Klan rally, writing down license plate numbers; or rummaging through dumpsters outside a suspected neo-Nazi's house, looking for discarded mail. Those tactics are still in use, but in the last ten years a lot of anti-fascist sleuthing moved online. Across America today there is a hidden army of antifa researchers quietly transcribing every far-right podcast, archiving every tweet from white supremacist accounts, and infiltrating every far-right message board, collecting clues to uncover fascists' real, offline identities.

This book tells the stories of anti-fascist spies who infiltrated white supremacist groups in the Trump era, collecting invaluable intelligence in the form of photos, videos, secretly recorded audio, and millions of fascist groups' internal messages. It also tells the stories of the anti-fascist researchers who then sorted through all this intelligence, doing remarkable investigative journalism to unmask hundreds upon hundreds of modern American fascists. Their research was the hidden hand behind thousands and thousands of mainstream news stories since 2015—their anti-fascist detective work shaping the way many Americans understood this perilous moment in our politics.

I found these anti-fascists compelling because of a certain selflessness they displayed—they did this work anonymously, unpaid, neither for glory nor acclaim. They just earnestly believed the work was vital to protecting their families, their neighbors, themselves. Many told stories of personal brushes with fascists in their communities, of white supremacists threatening people they knew and loved.

In reporting this book, I interviewed roughly sixty anti-fascists, almost all of them using pseudonyms to hide their identities. I also created a spreadsheet of nearly one thousand doxes they published from 2015 to 2025—an incomplete sampling but still breathtaking in its scope. These doxes, in the form of articles, blog posts, and Twitter threads, identified white Americans, often people in real positions of power, who were leading secret double lives as neo-Nazis or other far-right activists, hiding behind usernames and pseudonyms online. Anti-fascists unmasked these people because they see them as an urgent threat, not only promoting a genocidal ideology, but always at risk of committing real-world violence. The doxes were also published in hopes of creating a social cost for being a fascist, to create pressure for racists and other bigots to face consequences for their actions, in the process dissuading other Americans from joining their ranks.

This book names dozens of fascists unmasked by antifa in the Trump era, roughly from 2015 to 2025. Unless otherwise noted, these fascists either did not respond to requests for comment or could not be reached.

Taken together, the thousands of doxes published by antifa over the last ten years offer an urgent and alarming portrait of a rapidly radicalizing American right, a chronicle of hate crimes, murder plots, and terror plots. The people anti-fascists helped unmask were neo-Nazi podcasters with high-ranking jobs in the State Department or at the local university, or men with their name downballot in a congressional race. The doxes included white supremacist doctors, prison guards, teachers, a therapist. They included veterans, suffering PTSD from America's conquests abroad, finding brotherhood in fascist paramilitaries back home. The doxes seemed to lay bare a country rife with angry, bitter white people often suffering a vengeful loneliness that found a reprieve only in cruelty; they showed America veering toward a dark place.

Examined independently, each dox was its own universe, each one revealing or setting into motion intimate dramas. Doxes led to grieving parents desperately trying to save lost sons, but also revealed parents who were proud of what their sons had become. The doxes saw friends and family members suddenly finding themselves navigating the painful quandary of whether they should excommunicate someone they love from their life. There were towns that came together to fight the newly unmasked fascists in their midst, but also towns where people seemed indifferent to, or even perfectly content with, having Nazis as neighbors.

It is my hope for this book to humanize the anti-fascists who compiled these doxes, and to demystify "antifa" for the wider public. I believe they have an urgent and compelling story, one with real lessons for us all. Over the last decade, these American anti-fascists have frequently felt like canaries in the coal mine, constantly screaming that the far right wasn't actually "far" at all, that it wasn't "fringe." They felt like Cassandra, too, prophesying that this insurgent far right was poised to grow and grow, that it would gain the kind of elite support that would help it metastasize into a bigger, mass populist movement—a movement with the power to roll back whatever meager democratic gains the most marginalized in American society have fought tooth and nail to procure. Again and again, these anti-fascists felt their prophecies were disregarded, finding themselves dismissed by the chattering classes as hysterics, radicals, extremists.

It feels urgent to tell American antifa's story because in so many ways: *Antifa was right.*

*   *   *

Finally, on a personal note, my far-right detractors have often taken to labeling me antifa, so it feels important to address that claim briefly here. I'm a journalist who believes in militant anti-fascism. I'm not a part of an anti-fascist group, and I don't keep an antifa flag in my apartment. From my decade reporting on the far right in America, however, I've had a front-row seat to the growth of this new generation of fascists. I've seen up close how dangerous they are, and I've watched the alarming speed with which they have gained real power. This experience has instilled in me the belief, as the Spanish anti-fascist José Buenaventura Durruti once put it, that "fascism isn't to be debated, it is to be destroyed!"[4]

I refuse to pretend that I'm somehow unbiased or "objective" regarding what's happening in America right now, in 2025, when a lot of my friends and neighbors are at risk. I refuse to say I don't have a stake in all this. We all do.

That it sounds like an admission or confession to state that I believe in militant anti-fascism underscores how dangerous America is right now— how far beyond the Rubicon our politics have crossed when being militantly opposed to a genocidal ideology still feels risky. That by saying this I could be labeled a radical or extremist myself.

None of this is to say, of course, that I've somehow abandoned the core tenets of journalism, like fairness and accuracy. It's just to say that I have a perspective, like we all do, and it feels right to be honest about that.

Not for nothing, I'm about to have a kid, and I'm invested in that kid living in a world that is less fascist than it is today. I won't pretend I'm not a part of this fight.

—*July 28, 2025*
Rockaway Beach, New York

PART I
THE INFILTRATOR

CHAPTER 1

Those Guys Aren't My Friends

F ive white guys squeezed into a high-backed leather booth at 13 Coins, an upscale diner just across International Boulevard from SeaTac Airport. The restaurant had an open kitchen, and the sounds of clattering plates and servers barking orders at line cooks felt like a reprieve from the constant drone of jets taking off and landing nearby. The guys didn't know each other's real names, only the pseudonyms they used online. Normal American white guy names. John, David, Vincent, Charles, Anthony. Four of them were ardent white supremacists. One of them was just pretending to be.

This group was led by John, the director of Network 8, the Pacific Northwest chapter of the organization to which they all belonged. Less than a year earlier, four members of the Joint Terrorism Task Force—a Seattle police officer, two Kings County sheriff's deputies, and an FBI agent—had knocked on John's door.[1] They had questioned him about Network 8 and some related vandalism in the area, but John had kept his mouth shut, opening it only to ask for an attorney. He'd still caught charges, but the prosecutor dropped them, prompting John to brag to Network 8 about beating the rap, reminding members to always mask up during missions. "No face, no case," he'd told them.

John was feeling emboldened. Only two weeks earlier, in late July 2021, he and four other masked men, under the cover of darkness, had defaced a mural down in Portland, Oregon, that had honored the lives of George Floyd, Breonna Taylor, and Ahmaud Arbery—all Black Americans murdered by white cops and vigilantes. Afterward, to the organization's delight, the crestfallen artist behind the mural had lamented that there could still be so much "hate and ignorance" in the world.[2] Newspapers published the quote in stories about the vandalism—the kind of stories the organization often proudly posted in a chat group devoted to its "trophies," news article after news article documenting its hate crimes and flash-mob-style marches. Cops were investigating the Portland incident, maybe hot on John's trail again, but he didn't seem worried, just indignant.

"Funny how BLM and Antifa can get away with literal riots, murder, and arson, but some white guys put paint on the side of a building and it's suddenly a big deal . . ."[3] he'd written in a message.

Here and now at 13 Coins, John was determined to make Network 8 one of the best in the nation. He wanted to gather as many "trophies" as possible, to ensure more and more Americans knew their organization by name. He wanted to recruit more and more white men to meetings like this.

John was also desperate to get back in the good graces of national leadership down in Texas. He'd run afoul of the organization's rules about firearms, designed to prevent unwanted attention from the feds—no online discussion of guns, no guns on missions, no group trips to the shooting range—and had served a one-month suspension as punishment. But he was back now—even if he and Network 8 were still flagrantly breaking the firearms rules. (One member had recently posted a video of himself using a shotgun to blast a stolen Black Lives Matter sign to bits).[4] He trusted his subordinates to keep these transgressions a secret.

Subordinates like David, hopelessly loyal and devoted to John, who sat quietly at the table. A baby-faced twentysomething, he lived with his parents a couple hours east across the Cascades and kept a copy of *Eastern Front: Memoirs of a Waffen SS Volunteer*[5] in his car. Rumor had it he once peed into a bottle on the highway rather than be a few minutes late to a Network 8 meeting. Anxious and intensely shy, he hated talking to people with a passion, a passion equal only to the way he threw himself into missions, the kind they often carried out while wearing gaiter masks pulled up over their pale faces.

The three other men at the table were newer to the organization. Vincent was taller and a little older than the rest, with glasses and a shaved head. He did mixed martial arts, he'd said during the vetting process, so he knew how to handle himself.[6] He wasn't worried about clashing with antifa, if need be, dismissing them as a bunch of "skinny or fat trans people." Vincent believed other races were "parasitic," and he hated that society wanted him to feel guilty about being white. He was from a conservative Christian family up in Snohomish County but wasn't too religious these days, even if he still knew Bible verses by heart. His favorite, he'd told John, was Proverbs 27:17: "As iron sharpens iron, so one person sharpens another."

Charles, from Bellingham, was too young to be at this table. Just seventeen years old. The rules were clear on this point: You had to be eighteen to join up, but John needed new recruits so had looked the other way. There was another problem with Charles, though: his skin was suspiciously dark, owing to some traces of Filipino heritage, he explained. The rules were clear here, too: You had to be at least 75 percent white. Charles had assured everyone he was, tossing in some anti-Asian slurs for good measure, and quipping, "At least I'm not part Black."[7] He'd kill himself if he was part Black, he said.

Anthony was a 100 percent white college-aged kid from Mount Vernon. He didn't think Charles belonged at this table. He didn't want to work with anyone with any Asian phenotypes whatsoever.[8] He had no time for ch*nks or go*ks, he'd said. He griped to John about this privately, and John was mulling whether Charles should take a DNA test.

Sitting here now, staring down at their menus, their muscles were sore. The organization they belonged to was always training for violence, so earlier that day, before reassembling at the diner, they'd gathered at Pat Ryan Field for a group workout. The field was typically bustling on the weekends, home to a local rugby league, but that afternoon, it'd been empty, save for a man up on the hill above picking blackberries.

To start their session, they'd fastened a Betsy Ross American flag to the field goal post—that symbol of the country's founding, those thirteen stars in a perfect circle, signifying a purer time in American history—and then dropped to the ground to do push-ups. John insisted everyone do sets of fourteen push-ups, a little inside joke, a reference to something called the "fourteen words," a mantra they all knew that goes: "We must secure the existence of our people and a future for White children." It had been coined in the 1980s by the leader of another secretive organization for white men, a predecessor to theirs, that was perhaps best known for assassinating a Jewish talk show host.[9]

They moved on to other exercises, John overseeing it all in black Adidas pants and a black T-shirt emblazoned with the words FREE OUR POLITICAL PRISONERS: RISE ABOVE MOVEMENT, a reference to some other white men he admired, part of a fight club, who'd been arrested by the feds for roughing up lefties at rallies across the country.[10] John had the guys do burpees—jumping with arms outstretched, dropping to the grass for a push-up, then rising to their feet again. They would surely get in fights, too, ones in the street during their missions, but also maybe that grand Manichean fight one glorious day soon, that final battle imagined in their favorite novels, when everything went to shit and they got their chance to vanquish their enemies, take absolute power, make a nation reborn. They needed to be prepared, so for now John was setting some bare minimum standards for Network 8: They each had to be able to do five pull-ups, a plank for three minutes, and run a mile in under ten minutes.

After the workout, they'd walked back to their cars and put on masks—time for a quick mission before heading to the diner. They drove to a nearby highway overpass, parked, and removed a large piece of cloth from John's car. They quickly got to work fastening the cloth to the pedestrian railings on the overpass with string, then tossing it down toward the highway.

Driving back to the highway, they had gotten a good look at their work. It was glorious: a massive banner, twenty feet by ten feet, declaring RECLAIM AMERICA in red and blue lettering, with the URL for the organization's website visible for all of Seattle rush-hour traffic to see. Vincent snapped photos as they drove past—John was auditioning him to be the Network 8 photographer. Leadership was going to love these.

Sitting at 13 Coins, waiting for their food, they shot the breeze. Anthony spoke about drinking raw milk as a way of building muscle mass. They enjoyed some lighthearted banter about Anthony's shaved chest—he'd gone shirtless during the workout—with everyone laughing that he was a "femboy."

But there were more serious, urgent topics to discuss, too. Anthony had a proposal: He thought national leadership should make a rule requiring every recruit to say "n***er" during the vetting process. He said the word loud and clear, rising above the clatter of the crowded restaurant, maybe loud enough even for their Latina waitress to hear.

The requirement, Anthony explained, would help weed out any infiltrators. The sheer force of that word—those two syllables that, when spoken in succession from a white man's tongue, instantly invoked centuries of slavery, lynchings, and burning crosses—would make any "anti-fascist" spy squirm in their seat, he argued.

The fear of infiltrators was real. It was why national leadership encouraged members not to know each other's real names, to stick to pseudonyms. Were an infiltrator to discover anyone's actual identity, they'd be liable to lose their jobs, their scholarships, their girlfriends, be kicked out of their homes. Some might go to prison. Every member knew they stood to lose it all. "The enemy cannot attack you if they do not know who you are,"[11] leadership had stressed.

There had been spies in their midst before, anti-fascists who posed as patriots to gather intelligence about the organization. Twice, in 2017 and 2018, anti-fascists had gone through the vetting process before gaining access to the group's online chat server, which they then hacked, exposing members' unseemly private messages to the public. Messages like "gas the kikes race war now,"[12] and another that argued raping women is fine "as long as you're raping, like, people in your own race."[13] One of the hacks had even exposed the identity of an erstwhile member, his real name ending up in the news: He'd been arrested for shooting a Black man in Maryland.[14] "Go back to Africa!" he'd screamed before opening fire.

There'd also been the infiltrator in 2019 who national leadership had trusted enough to bring to Europe, to be the photographer for their meetings with far-right groups in Italy, Germany, Sweden, and Latvia. This infiltrator had even joined them in Warsaw for Poland's Independence Day celebration, snapping photos as these American fascists marched alongside thousands of their European counterparts, lighting red flares and chanting in the streets. But leadership never got many of the photos and videos he had taken, which would've been used for the group's propaganda reels. The spy had handed off that footage to journalists instead.[15]

And then finally, in 2020, there'd been "Gabriel" in California, the infiltrator who everyone really liked. They had been heartbroken to learn Gabriel, an Iraq War vet built like a brick shithouse, was a secret anti-fascist. Looking back, it made some sense: Gabriel, after all, had always insisted on leading combat trainings, using group sparring sessions as a ruse to beat the shit out of different members, giving some concussions.

The legacy of these anti-fascist infiltrations ran deep, sowing mistrust in the organization—everyone always on the lookout for the next mole.

Leading to this moment, with Anthony again insisting that everyone at this table—John, David, Vincent, Charles—take turns saying the word. A little test, for fun.

There was no hesitation. One by one, everyone at the table obliged, saying the word loud and clear.

They finished eating and asked for the bill, prompting Anthony to launch into a rant about tipping. He refused to tip non-white waitresses, he said, like the waitress they had now, the one who had sweetly served them cheeseburgers and fries, and who, if she'd heard them using racial slurs, hadn't done anything about it. When it came time to pay, everyone agreed with Anthony: no tip. Satisfied with their decision and exhausted from their training, the group then walked out of 13 Coins and bid farewell to one another. They got into their cars and drove away, back to their homes across the Evergreen State, where their neighbors and coworkers and family members were none the wiser to what they were a part of.

A short time later, though, one of these white men circled back to 13 Coins, parked, and walked inside. His demeanor was different. Something gentler than before. He looked for the waitress, but she wasn't anywhere to be found, so he found the manager instead.

"Please give this to the waitress," he told the manager, who was Black, pressing $300 into his hand. "Please make sure she gets all of this and tell her I said sorry."

He started to leave but then stopped himself, asking the manager to pass along one more message.

"Please tell her that those guys I was with," he said, "please tell her those guys aren't my friends."

CHAPTER 2
The Making of a Spy

Vincent, and we'll call him Vincent, isn't from Snohomish County, or maybe he is. He won't say where he's actually from. He doesn't think other races are "parasitic," he thinks race is a fiction, one created to justify innumerable atrocities. That part about being from a conservative Christian family but not being that religious anymore? That part's true. He still knows Bible passages by heart.

He's agreed to meet in a West Seattle park, where there are plenty of benches tucked away in the woods overlooking the Puget Sound, as private a public place as he could find to talk about when he went undercover inside Patriot Front, an organization belonging to a horrifying new cadre of white supremacist and neofascist groups that had exploded onto the American political scene over the previous decade. The formation of these groups was part of a greater malaise sweeping the country at the time, with mainstream conservatism growing ever more impatient with democracy and enamored by a politics of outright domination. The rise of President Donald Trump— whose rhetoric about banning Muslims from the country, about stopping the "invasion" of immigrants at the border, about crushing "wokeness," and about eradicating trans people from public life—had emboldened a new generation of white vigilantes to take to the streets of America.

It had also, in turn, inspired a new generation of anti-fascists, Americans who found themselves suddenly engaged in an underground cold war of intelligence and counterintelligence gathering, of sabotage and occasional violence, that often went unseen by the wider public. In the popular imagination—and thanks in part to Hollywood movies like *BlacKkKlansman*, *The Order*, and *Imperium*—it's largely law enforcement that infiltrates white supremacist groups, unmasking their members and documenting their crimes. But from 2015 to 2025, there's an argument to be made that the bulk of such spy work was being done by anti-fascists like Vincent: leftists who did not trust law enforcement to dismantle dangerous groups like Patriot Front. Leftists who felt compelled to take "community self-defense" into their own hands, even if it meant putting themselves in harm's way.

There's a lot Vincent won't share. His real name, his job, his exact age. It'd be too risky. He understands how many fascists, or "fash" in anti-fascist parlance, would love to find him and make him pay. There are cautionary tales out there to prove he's not just paranoid—like the one about the three neo-Nazis arrested in Georgia for conspiring to kidnap and murder an anti-fascist activist and his wife,[1] or the older tales, like the one about the neo-Nazi skinheads who lured a couple of anti-racist punks to the Nevada desert and executed them, leaving their bodies to fester in the sun.[2]

No, he won't be sharing his real name. It's not only fascists who might want to have a word with him—federal law enforcement tends to take a dim, conspiratorial view of people like him, too, labeling him and his friends extremists of a different sort, somehow the moral equivalent, or photo inverse, of the neo-Nazis he's worked so hard to undermine.

What he is willing to share is the story of why he chose to upend his life like this, to be constantly looking over his shoulder, using burner phones, and reading books about countersurveillance to better know when he's being followed.

It's hard to pinpoint a particular moment when he was radicalized into doing militant anti-fascist work, but May 27, 2017, is as good as any. Vincent was on vacation down in Portland, waiting on the platform at the Hollywood/Northeast 42nd Avenue stop for a MAX train, on his way to see some friends. He boarded the train, got off a few stops later, and went on with his evening.

But later he heard the news: That day a white guy named Jeremy Christian had harangued two Black teenage girls, one of whom was wearing a hijab, aboard a MAX train, screaming at them about how all Muslims should die. "Go home, we need Americans here!"[3] he yelled at the girls. Three men had stepped up to intervene, prompting Christian to slice open each of their necks with a knife, killing two of them. So much blood sprayed into the air that one passenger initially mistook the liquid for a sudden, inexplicable rain.[4] In the days that followed, heartbreaking details emerged,[5] including that one of the deceased, a twenty-three-year-old recent college graduate, had uttered the words "Tell everyone on this train I love them," just before perishing.

Vincent realized this had all happened as the MAX train pulled into the Hollywood/Northeast 42nd Avenue stop at 4:32 p.m.—mere minutes after he'd been there.

"If I had taken the later train, I could have easily been one of those people," he says, adding that he hopes and imagines he would've been among those to intervene. "There's like a residual survivor's guilt, where it's like, I wasn't on the train, but I feel I could have easily been in that situation."

The terror visited upon that train felt pervasive in the Pacific Northwest at the time, Vincent remembers, always on the periphery, something that increasingly felt like a threat to people he knew and loved. There was a constant drumbeat of news stories:[6] a Latino family who found their cars' windshields smashed in, one with an explosive device inside, and another with a note warning that Trump would "deport them soon." The Iranian refugee who returned home to find death threats graffitied all over his house: "Terrorist" on the kitchen cabinet; "Fuck you terrorist" on a wall; "Muslim" and "Kill you" in the bedroom; "Die" on a mirror; "Hate" on a door. The Black woman attacked by three men, one hitting her with a brick, and another telling her, "We're going to make America great again by getting rid of n***ers like you." There was the Black DJ at a bar who suddenly found himself surrounded by sieg-heiling white guys, punching him and yelling slurs. And there was the nineteen-year-old Black man run over and killed by a car driven by a member of European Kindred, a white supremacist prison gang.

Even though the Pacific Northwest—and every region in America—has been rife with this kind of racial terror over time, what was happening in 2017 felt like an escalation to Vincent. Like a new kind of darkness had taken hold of so many people's hearts, giving them license to indulge in unthinkable cruelties.

Like many anti-fascists, Vincent considers himself an anarchist and didn't believe in the ability of cops or the government to stop this rising tide of right-wing violence. He wasn't always an anarchist, though. He grew up in a rural, predominantly white area of the country—he won't say where—with a dad who was mostly out of work on disability, and who tended to get in trouble with the law. His mom, meanwhile, suffered severe bouts of poor mental health and was often hospitalized. "Our family income was low five digits or four digits some years. I know that because I helped out with my dad's taxes," he recalls.

As a kid, he never saw the cops or the government as institutions that were there to help his family, but rather as institutions with the power to tear his family apart. "If the cops came over and asked me a question that ended up in my mom being put away for longer, or my dad being put away for longer, that could mean that I was in a foster home," he remembers.

Neither of his parents had high school diplomas, but they wanted one for Vincent. "I loved school, I loved pulling in all the stuff that I could," he says. He loved going to church with his mom, too, and eventually his faith became central to his identity. He loved the community of it, that feeling in his chest on a Sunday morning, the way the Bible sounded when read aloud.

He excelled at school, got that diploma, and went to college, joining a Christian student group, but remembers growing disillusioned with its homophobia, a disillusion he felt at other churches, too, where preachers and congregations seemed more fixated on the culture war issue du jour than, say, just feeding the poor and homeless.

Despite being surrounded by conservatives his whole life, Vincent had always considered himself a little more liberal. Just your basic mainstream Democratic beliefs. "When I grew up, I just had the TV with the channels that you get on basic antenna, no internet, unless I went to school. No computer until I went to college, so I didn't have access to a ton of information," he says.

At college he started meeting students who identified as socialists, communists, and anarchists. "It allowed me to just expand my beliefs," he says, remembering being drawn initially to European-style democratic socialism because it seemed to "actually provide for people." And then over time, he says, his politics became "less and less authoritarian" until he was an anarchist. The word "anarchy" is derived from the Greek *anarchos*, meaning "without authority." Agency, an anarchist media collective that seeks to demystify anarchism for the wider public, once described anarchism as a "struggle against top-down systems and institutions, such as states, capitalism, and racial and gender domination."[7] It strives for a radical direct democracy, for a classless, stateless society without hierarchy.

Derided by some on the left as too idealistic, in everyday practice, anarchism often means providing mutual aid, like giving people food, supporting people incarcerated in prisons and immigrant detention centers, or doing harm reduction for people with addiction. It's about not "relying on the structures" that may be insufficient, "oppressive," or "authoritarian," Vincent says, but instead creating a "second layer of replacement structures" to show solidarity with your neighbors.

And that often means protecting your neighbors from fascists. If anarchists want to abolish hierarchy, fascists are enthralled by it and will enact violence to preserve it. And if cops can't be counted on or trusted to stop fascists, then anarchists feel it's their duty to stop fascists themselves.

Vincent's introduction to anti-fascist work didn't begin with Patriot Front, but with opposing the rise of other violent, far-right gangs in the Pacific Northwest. After narrowly missing that MAX train in 2017, he'd become more politically active, enmeshing himself in anarchist circles. He saw his comrades in these spaces grow more and more concerned about the Proud Boys, a self-described male "drinking club" made up of "Western chauvinists who refuse to apologize for creating the modern world." The group was partnering with white supremacists to terrorize Seattle and Portland, holding "free speech" rallies as thinly veiled pretexts to march through the liberal cities provoking people into brawls.[8] Its members wore Fred Perry black polo shirts[9]—evoking the outfits of both neo-Nazi skinheads from the 1980s and '90s and Benito Mussolini's murderous Camicie Nere, or Blackshirts, in prewar Italy. The Proud Boys were explicitly violent, with group leadership requiring members to "get arrested or get in a serious violent fight for the cause"[10] in order to achieve the highest "fourth" degree of membership.

Yet again and again, Vincent and his fellow anarchists noticed police seeming to allow the Proud Boys to run riot. In fact, Vincent often saw cops attack the counterdemonstrators who turned up to oppose these marauding MAGA mobs. Once, when he joined counterdemonstrators in Portland, police fired a flash-bang grenade, a fire-hot and ear-piercing explosive that temporarily disorients the senses, directly at Vincent, missing his head by mere inches. Again, he felt like he'd narrowly escaped death.

The Proud Boys often didn't hide their identities or mask up in public, but outside scattered local news stories, Vincent noticed that it was leftist activists who were comprehensively documenting the identities of these modern Blackshirts. He stumbled upon Twitter accounts belonging to self-described antifa groups posting detailed dossiers that named and shamed individual Proud Boys. He found himself drawn to this tactic, this grassroots means of identifying and understanding a threat. "Back when I had social media, like you would see people who are unmasking fascists . . . and I was like, yeah, that makes sense," he says. "These people are causing harm to the community, it's good to know who they are."

He wanted to join the fight, too. Taking cues from more veteran activists, Vincent was a quick study. He started to surveil the Proud Boys at their rallies, recording their speeches, covertly snapping photos of their faces and the license plates on their cars. Sometimes Vincent would briefly go undercover as a "chud"—a term used to describe the Proud Boys or other misogynist MAGA types—walking among them, listening to their conversations, introducing himself with a pseudonym and getting their names. He did this in a McDonald's once, where some chuds had retreated from counterprotesters, before he absconded with the Trump flags they left on a table. He returned to the counterprotesters outside, tearing the flags to shreds.

The work was sometimes dangerous, like the time a hulking Proud Boy caught onto Vincent's game and chased him through a parking lot. The guy was on his tail until Vincent dipped into a grocery store, running through the aisles to the back of the store, where he escaped through an employee door into an alley. Yet as dicey as this reconnaissance work could be, it was also fruitful. Vincent started to share the intelligence he gathered with those anti-fascist social media accounts he obtained online, eventually finding himself ushered into a sprawling network of largely anonymous activists who were dedicated to IDing every Proud Boy they could find.

By the fall of 2020, the Proud Boys had turned their attention to overturning the results of the presidential election. Many of the same Proud Boys who had terrorized the Pacific Northwest for years flew to Washington, DC, taking part in violent demonstrations there,[11] demanding officials "stop the steal" and hand Trump a second term. Then, weeks later, on January 6, 2021, these same Proud Boys were among the thousands of Trump supporters who stormed the US Capitol, overturning metal barricades, shattering doors and windows, ransacking congressional offices, stealing the House Speaker's laptop and gavel, and sending legislators into hiding, fearing for their lives—all to stop the certification of the election results that would declare Joe Biden as president.

Over one thousand of these Trump supporters would go on to be arrested in relation to the January 6 insurrection, including multiple Proud Boys leaders, who received some of the most severe charges. Ethan Nordean, the Proud Boy who chased Vincent into that grocery store, was convicted of seditious conspiracy, among other charges, and sentenced to eighteen years in prison.[12]

In the months after January 6, the Proud Boys were in disarray. Many of their leaders had been arrested, leaving rank-and-file members rudderless, fearing prosecution themselves. Vincent saw fewer of them in the streets. It occurred to him that the Proud Boys suffered a strategic weakness—they were too out in the open. Because many didn't hide their faces or identities, this made them liable to prosecution for the violence they inevitably committed, and it also meant they had to withstand a bevy of other social costs: loss of jobs, or families and friends excommunicating them.

Still, there were plenty of other far-right factions operating in the shadows. Vincent and his friends were well aware of these secretive fascist fraternities, the ones more committed to concealing their members' names, requiring aliases and masks, often covertly carrying out their acts of violence and vandalism after the sun had set. These clandestine white supremacists belonged to groups with names like Identity Evropa, Atomwaffen Division, The Base, and Bowl Patrol. They'd developed their own peculiar argot, sometimes assigning gatherings anodyne euphemisms like "book clubs" and "pool parties." They went on "hate hikes" and performed strange fiery rituals in the woods. Unlike their forebears in the Ku Klux Klan—the white-hooded order now nearing the tail end of its long decline into irrelevance—these new fascist formations were profoundly *online*, organizing in private servers and propagandizing on social media from behind avatars. They had emerged seemingly all at once in the mid-2010s, as if working to build a new "invisible empire," like the Klan before them, only this one designed for the digital age.

Among the most secretive of these groups was Patriot Front.

Vincent says he kept seeing the organization's banners and stickers around Seattle, marring parts of the city he knew and loved. It was infuriating, in part, because he knew how deceitful the name "Patriot Front" was, how to the untrained eye or ear it could seem relatively innocuous, like it was some normie conservative organization, a veterans group maybe, that just loved America and wanted to celebrate it.

But Vincent and other anti-fascists knew the origins of the name Patriot Front well: that it was a rebranding meant to obscure the group's connection to one of the most infamous acts of white supremacist terror in the twenty-first century.[13] Years earlier the organization was called Vanguard America. Its members were among the largest contingents of white supremacists who gathered in Charlottesville, Virginia, on August 12, 2017, for the Unite the Right rally. They stood alongside hundreds of other assorted fascists chanting "Fuck you, f*ggots!" at counterdemonstrators, while wearing khaki cargo pants and white polo shirts, carrying shields emblazoned with the group's logo: an eagle carrying a fasces. (The word "fascism" comes from *fascio*, the Italian word for fasces, which is a bundle of sticks wrapped around an axe.)

Among those carrying the Vanguard America shield was James Alex Fields Jr., a twenty-year-old from Ohio who'd spent his high school years scrawling swastikas in his notebook during class.[14] At the conclusion of the rally, Fields got into his silver-gray 2010 Dodge Challenger and deliberately drove the muscle car into a crowd of anti-fascists. The impact sent their bodies flying into the air, injuring thirty-five people and killing thirty-two-year-old Heather Heyer.[15]

The images and videos of the attack spread like wildfire across the globe, the bodies of anti-fascists flying in the air quickly becoming representative of an alarming, radical shift in American politics in the Trump era. (Trump infamously said there were "very fine people" on "both sides" of the rally.[16]) Afterward, Vanguard America knew what Fields had done was bad PR for the group, even if its members didn't object to the deadly attack itself. ("Fields did nothing wrong, fam,"[17] one member wrote in a message.) So, Thomas Rousseau—a twenty-year-old Texan who'd recently wrested control of the group from its founder—decided it was time for a rechristening. They would now be called Patriot Front. "The new name was carefully chosen, as it serves several purposes. It can help inspire sympathy among those more inclined to fence-sitting..." he declared, hinting at his hopes of attracting men who were sympathetic to their cause, if not yet fully realized fascists. "The original American patriots were nothing short of revolutionaries. The word patriot itself comes from the same root as paternal and patriarch. It means loyalty to something intrinsically based in blood."[18]

In the ensuing years, Patriot Front's ranks swelled to some three hundred members, all belonging to different regional networks, each with
their own leaders, all of whom reported to Rousseau. They held flash-mob
demonstrations—brief, unannounced rallies that were less likely to be disrupted by counterdemonstrators or cops—with anarchist book fairs among
their first targets. Members stood outside the fairs in masks, lighting red flares
and banging on the windows, chanting "Reclaim America" while taunting
the lefties inside to come out for a fight.[19] They also joined anti-reproductive-
rights rallies, marching alongside plain old "pro-life" Trump supporters. And
they vandalized communities across the country with Patriot Front graffiti,
stickers, and posters, leaving the propaganda at schools and synagogues and
train stations. Once, under the cover of night in Austin, Texas, members
climbed some one hundred feet to reach a giant billboard on the side of the
highway. The billboard had featured a public service announcement from
the FBI, reading: PROTECTING OUR COMMUNITIES TOGETHER.
REPORT HATE CRIMES. The masked white men unfurled a banner over
this message, disappearing it and replacing it with a new message for morning
rush-hour traffic to see. THEY WOULD MAKE OUTLAWS OF PATRIOTS,
CRIMINALS OF CITIZENS, it read.

There was a good reason Patriot Front was irked by the FBI's anti-hate-
crime billboard: The group was on a nationwide hate crime spree—defacing,
destroying, or otherwise disappearing Black Lives Matter murals at least
forty times across the country between August 2020 and August 2021.[20]
Anti-Blackness was at the very core of Patriot Front, which Rousseau spelled
out in a "manifesto" on the group's website:[21]

> An African may have lived, worked, and even been classed as a citizen in
> America for centuries, yet he is not American. He is, as he likely prefers to be
> labeled, an African in America. The same rule applies to others who are not of
> the founding stock of our people, or do not share the common unconscious that
> permeates throughout our greater civilization, and the European diaspora.

Patriot Front also held particular contempt for queer people, as demonstrated by a disturbing video posted by the network in Michigan, showing
fifteen masked members standing around a campfire at night, holding two
stolen "progress" pride flags (an updated version of the traditional LGBTQ

flag that incorporates transgender pride colors). "To those who destroy our nation, we will destroy your symbols and all that you worship," one of the masked men said into the camera. "If you think we will lay down and perish, you are gravely mistaken."

"Burn 'em," he added, prompting his fellow fascists to toss the flags into the flames. The fifteen faceless American men then stood in silence for thirty seconds, watching the rainbow-colored fabric become black ash.[22]

In August 2021, Vincent started chatting with anti-fascists in the Pacific Northwest about coordinating an infiltration. The way Vincent saw it, an infiltration could mean getting ahold of the group's plans for rallies and vandalism. It could mean documenting their crimes in real time. It could mean collecting more evidence of their neo-Nazism, undermining their efforts to disguise their propaganda with the aesthetics of Americana. More than anything, though, an infiltration could mean collecting intelligence that could lead to the identification of Patriot Front's members, stripping them of their most prized, closely guarded possession: their anonymity.

Initially, Vincent expected someone else to volunteer. "And I was getting more and more frustrated that I couldn't convince anybody to do it," he remembers. "And I wasn't trying to badger anybody to do it. I was like, 'This is something that we're interested in, we have a pretty good understanding of how the group operates. Here's how we would do it safely. Here's what the risks would be.' And I'd be sure to say, 'This is not something where there's a guarantee of safety. There's no real guarantee that you're not going to be identified . . .' And nobody was really willing to take that risk."

And so he started to think about doing it himself. One of his most obvious advantages, Vincent realized, was that he could pass as a chud. He'd grown up with chuds, knew how to hang in conservative circles, had been immersed in their social mores. And he knew how to conceal his progressive beliefs, bury them deep down inside where no one could detect them. He also had skills Patriot Front might find attractive. He was a trained medic and skilled photographer, both skills he'd honed—not without some irony—during the anti-racist uprisings of 2020. And finally, Vincent knew how to handle himself, having trained for years in mixed martial arts. The Patriot Front chuds would *love* that, he thought.

Vincent's ability to throw fists also put his mind at ease a bit—if Patriot Front were to discover he was an infiltrator, he'd have a good shot at defending himself. "If it just ends up with me fighting the group of five or ten people at the interview, because they recognize me right away, so be it," he remembers telling himself. "That sounds like fun. So that's eventually how I came to that decision. And I was like, worst-case scenario, I fight a group of five to ten people alone. Best-case scenario, maybe this infiltration goes somewhere and I get some information out of it." (Was there a chance, in that worst case scenario, that a Patriot Front member might pull a gun on Vincent? Open fire? Yeah, he acknowledges, there had been a chance.)

He consulted with his loved ones first. An infiltration like this could put them at risk, too. Vincent won't, of course, say who his loved ones are, or how many of them he talked to, but what he will say is that they approved, that they trusted him, that they thought it was a worthy cause.

He started to contact anti-fascists who'd done infiltrations before, and was eventually connected to a man who'd briefly, and recently, infiltrated Patriot Front. "But he wasn't super involved," Vincent remembers. "He wasn't willing to go to a lot of the events. And I think he was just so angry at the group and having to be around them when they were saying shitty things . . . he ended up getting kicked out for inactivity."

Still, this infiltrator was able to give Vincent some tips. In order to join Patriot Front, Vincent would first need to fill out an application on Patriot Front's website, bloodandsoil.org ("blood and soil" is the English translation of the German Nazi slogan *blut und boden*). Thomas Rousseau would review the application, and if he approved, Vincent would be invited to have an interview with some of Rousseau's lieutenants and other underlings, via a video conference. Then, if he passed that interview, there'd be a second, final interview with the network director in Washington state. That meeting would happen IRL, in person.

"How would you describe your political beliefs?" read the first question on the application on bloodandsoil.org. "Do you have a healthy lifestyle that includes regular exercise? If not, explain below. How would you describe your religious beliefs? Why do you want to join? Have you read the Manifesto and reviewed our Updates page?"

Vincent realized he was going to need to create a character for this. His mind wandered back to Rousseau's argument that the name Patriot Front would attract "fence-sitters" to the group. Maybe his character should be a fence-sitter, someone who was more fascist-curious than a dyed-in-the-wool

Nazi. Someone who grew up conservative, loved traditionalism, but wasn't necessarily up on all the new far-right lingo and buzzwords. Someone who was "80 percent of the way there," Vincent says, who Patriot Front members felt like they could mold in one of their own. Someone they could fix.

Before joining, Vincent would need to brush up on some basics and familiarize himself with the thinkers Patriot Front admired. He read about how Vanguard America, before it became Patriot Front, had emerged from an online message board called Iron March,[23] founded by a prolific Russian neo-Nazi blogger who went by the pen name Alexander Slavros. Slavros and his followers on Iron March advocated acts of terror in Western countries to hasten the collapse of society so that a whites-only ethnostate could be built in its place. (Iron March influenced the "manifesto" an Australian man wrote before he carried out a live-streamed massacre of fifty-one Muslims[24] at two mosques in Christchurch, New Zealand.) This philosophy was called "accelerationism," and although Patriot Front didn't explicitly subscribe to accelerationism, it certainly seemed like it might be a topic of polite debate, something Vincent might need to know.

Perusing other white supremacist message boards, Vincent noticed there'd been an uptick in chatter about "eco-fascism,"[25] the burgeoning belief blaming the degradation of the environment on the overpopulation of the planet by non-white people, especially those immigrating into Western countries. He thought being an eco-fascist might play well with Patriot Front, a group fond of long hikes together in the wilderness, and especially among its members in the Pacific Northwest, where environmentalism isn't always the provenance of the left, where survivalist, outdoors-obsessed fascists had flocked for decades,[26] determined to transform the remote, rugged landscape of "Cascadia," with all its mountains and rainforests, into a white utopia.

Vincent filled out the application on bloodandsoil.org and a short time later received word—via a message to a burner account he'd set up on Proton-Mail, the encrypted email service—that he had been selected for an interview. He was granted access to the "vetting server" on RocketChat, the messaging platform Patriot Front used to communicate with each other privately, and was told to log on to this server that evening.

At 8 p.m., Patriot Front sent him the invitation to join the video conferencing service Jitsi (similar to Zoom) to begin the interview. He accepted the invitation with a click, the little press of his index finger on the keyboard that commenced a period of Method acting and duplicity that would change his life—and the lives of so many others—forever.

The interview was camera-off. He could hear multiple voices on the call, all of whom introduced themselves by their pseudonyms. Jason-NY. Jason-TX. Patrick-NY. (Patriot Front members always attached the initials for their home state to the end of their pseudonyms.) Vincent had read about Patrick-NY before. He was one of the few active Patriot Front members who had already been identified, with anti-fascists in New York revealing his real name to be Kieran Morris,[27] a twenty-seven-year-old from Poughkeepsie, fond of Irish flat caps and rugby, who'd joined the group after failing to join Atomwaffen—a bloodthirsty cadre of accelerationist neo-Nazis tied to five murders across the United States.[28] Kieran had reportedly left New York after being doxed, shacking up with Thomas Rousseau in Texas and becoming a high-ranking underling.

Here and now on this call, Kieran was interested in what media Vincent consumed, demanding he send over a screenshot of his page on Telegram—the social media platform popular among white supremacists. Vincent hadn't anticipated this. If he sent a screenshot of his Telegram, which he used to monitor groups like Patriot Front, there would be messages he'd posted and accounts he followed proving he was actually "antifa." He had to think on his feet. He pulled up Telegram on his phone, deleted a few messages, took a screenshot, and sent it to Kieran via a chat window on Jitsi.

"What are those deleted messages?" Kieran asked.

"They were with my girlfriend," Vincent heard himself say. "We talk on Telegram sometimes. I didn't want you to see her username." The deleted messages, of course, were not with his girlfriend. There was a pause as Kieran seemed to consider this reply. "Okay," he said.

Vincent breathed a sigh of relief. They moved on to other topics, talking for over an hour. He found himself falling into character, surprising himself with the comfort with which he could improvise and the ease with which he could mine his own history to answer their questions.

The interviewers were stern, maybe owing to the instructions set forth for interviews like these. "Never approve of his answers or make him feel like he's saying anything correct," the instructions stated. "Don't spoon-feed him answers. Let him get to answers himself. It's not a conversation, it's an interview."

Jason-TX took notes.[29] What was Vincent's political ideology? *White nationalist with eco-fascist leanings.* Drugs? *No.* Car? *Yes.* Religion? *Agnostic.* Why join? *Values the white race. Disappointed that the media has made people feel guilt. Regarding the Proud Boys: "not interested in a drinking club" and is a "serious person." Reads a lot of "AI" and "Rationality" stuff that approaches "race science." Other races in America can be parasitic . . . Judaism employs slave morality.*

Ethnicity? *Family is primarily German with some English and French. Father's side grandmother came from Russia, was a "Volle-Deutsche." Mother's side is European as well. Describes self as German.*

Has he applied before? Criminal history? Government employment? *No, no, and no.* Ideological journey? *Grew up in a rural area outside Milwaukee. Saw the differences between white suburbia and the inner city . . . Dad used to wear "Nazi rings" in school . . . Dad voted for Obama, then Trump . . . Figured out there are differences in IQ between races. Being on Twitter and Telegram gave people the opportunity to talk about things society deems unfavorable.*

The biggest threat to society? *Global warming and mass migration. We have a fake two-party system. We put more work into Israel and Middle Eastern conflicts than the US itself. Slow creep of cultural Marxism.*

How did he hear about Patriot Front? *First heard about us one or two years ago. Got interested in PF again after seeing us in the news. Doesn't think antifa is super relevant . . . Antifa has lots of skinny, fat trans people that aren't much of a threat. Never had an interaction with antifa in person.*

Availability? *Is flexible, could offer a couple nights on the weekends. Schedule allows for a weekly meeting. Can put up stickers a few times a week.*

Jason-TX stopped taking notes. The interview was over. He and Jason-NY and Kieran told Vincent to stay on the call while they muted themselves to confer in another chat. There was something a little weird about Vincent, they agreed, a little off. But he'd given some good answers. They got back on the call and told Vincent their decision.

Afterward, Jason-TX started compiling his notes into a message to send to John-WA, the network director in Washington, who would be in charge of doing the second, final, in-person interview with Vincent. "Interviewee: 422754," the message said. "Age: 32/State: WA/City: Seattle (perm res)."

"Result: ACCEPTED," Jason-TX wrote, before adding a note of warning: "Use caution."

CHAPTER 3
We Keep Us Safe

"Some fascists . . . openly spew their bile and are happy to associate their real names with their neo-Nazi activities," the anti-fascist research group Anonymous Comrades Collective explained once.[1] "Most, however, realize that their ideology is repellent to the general public and detrimental to maintaining gainful employment and social relations. They hide behind aliases and false identities. The internet makes accomplishing this an almost trivial task. An alternate email address here, a secret Twitter account there—pretending to be someone else on the internet is easy to do.

"But eventually they slip up. Whether it's through carelessness, ignorance, or hubris, sooner or later they always leave a thread hanging. And we will pull that thread."

By the time Vincent decided to go undercover into Patriot Front, there was a sprawling network of American antifa dedicated, like him, to unmasking their local Nazis.

Doxing serves many vital functions in militant anti-fascist work. First, it identifies the threat. After all, how can you fight fascists if you don't know who they are or where they work and live? Secondly, it serves as a kind of community-wide alert system, the digital equivalent of putting up a "Meet Your Local Nazi" poster on a telephone pole to warn folks about the white guy down the block who might be liable to commit a hate crime.

Doxing creates a social cost for being a fascist: When anti-fascists publish a dox, there's a corresponding pressure campaign to get that fascist fired from their job or kicked out of their apartment. It leverages the existing societal taboo against explicit white supremacy and bigotry to ensure, as one anti-fascist is fond of putting it, that "hate has consequences."

In doing so, it also helps prevent recruitment. A young man thinking about joining Patriot Front, for example, might think twice when he sees dozens of its members doxed, rendered unemployable pariahs in their hometowns.

Lastly, doxing exposes to a community the ways in which fascists are not fringe outcasts, curious anachronisms out of step with some fantasy of a post-racial America, but often are men and women in positions of real power—politicians, pastors, professors, police officers—who pose an immediate threat to the people they are meant to serve.

At first blush it might be easy to dismiss a group like Patriot Front as insignificant—a group with three hundred or so members in a country of over 360 million, but for anti-fascists like Vincent, it's precisely these small white supremacist formations that need to be crushed before they're no longer *small*.[2] Anti-fascists will often point to how when Hitler attended his first meeting of the German Workers Party, which he later renamed the National Socialist German Workers' (or Nazi) Party, the group had only fifty-four members. Or that in 1919 Italy, Benito Mussolini's initial fascist nucleus had just one hundred men, but only two years later Mussolini counted some two hundred fifty thousand Italians among his followers. Or that in 1865, it was just six white men in Pulaski, Tennessee, pulling cruel "pranks" on former enslaved people—menacing them with nightly visits outside their homes, pulling up on horseback carrying torches and disguised as ghosts—but only three years later, in 1868, these six white men had built an "invisible empire," with chapters of their organization all over the old Confederacy, killing and torturing Black people, ensuring that everyone in America and across the world would know their group's name for centuries hence: the Ku Klux Klan.[3]

The irony or paradox of anti-fascist work, the historian Mark Bray noted once, "is that when militant anti-fascists are succeeding in their goal of stopping these groups, they never reach the level of importance for anyone to care that they were stopped in the first place."[4] Vincent wanted to ensure that Patriot Front was one of those groups largely forgotten by history.

Although he didn't think much about it at the time, when Vincent started his infiltration of Patriot Front, he was joining a long legacy of Americans who have gone undercover to disrupt white supremacist groups. Edward

Obertean, a Buffalo police officer, infiltrated the city's particularly large Klan chapter in the 1920s, leading to its demise, and eventually to his murder at the hands of an angry Klansman.[5] Leon Lewis, a Jewish lawyer and World War I veteran who was the founding executive secretary of the Anti-Defamation League, operated a spy network to infiltrate the German American Bund throughout the 1920s and '30s, foiling a plot to kidnap and murder Jewish Hollywood executives, and another plot to form a phony fumigation company to covertly massacre Jews in their homes, a horrifying harbinger of the gas chambers at Nazi concentration camps.[6] Stetson Kennedy, a blue-blooded civil rights activist from Florida, and a dear friend of Woody Guthrie's, infiltrated the Klan in Georgia for four years in the 1940s, exposing the group's campaign of racial terror to the public and convincing the state to revoke the Klan's nonprofit charter.[7] And more recently, in the aughts, an Army veteran named Joseph Moore, working for the FBI, went undercover in a Klan chapter in Florida for ten years, helping foil two murder plots and exposing multiple Florida police officers as Klansmen.[8]

The irony of these historical infiltrations is that while they were all conducted in coordination with law enforcement, they all simultaneously exposed how law enforcement was often *teeming* with Klansmen and Nazi sympathizers. (The year before Vincent decided to infiltrate Patriot Front, a report completed by a former FBI agent found police officers linked to militant white supremacist groups in a dozen states—a tally that, by the agent's own admission, was likely a vast undercount.)

Even though American law enforcement has historically done work to undermine and prosecute white supremacist groups, that work will always fall short for militant anti-fascists like Vincent, who see American law enforcement as intrinsically white supremacist. It is an institution, after all, that was born from slave patrols, that enforced the ethnic cleansing of Native Americans, led lynching parties during Jim Crow, turned fire hoses on civil rights protesters, and continues to mass-incarcerate millions of predominantly Black and brown Americans. Anti-fascists like Vincent believe, as the old protest chant goes, that "the cops and the Klan go hand in hand," or as Rage Against the Machine once put it: "Some of those who work forces / are the same who burn crosses." Rose City Antifa, the Portland-based anti-fascist group, puts it this way: "The state upholds white supremacy at every level of government and the police frequently work with far-right aggressors to brutalize people opposing state oppression and violence. We cannot count on state actors to push forward the cause of justice, equity, and community safety. It's up to us to keep us safe."[9]

It's up to us to keep us safe. It's a formulation of an axiom—"We protect us" or "We keep us safe"—that you hear a lot in Black liberation movements, but also in the wider left, particularly in anarchist spaces. And it was an axiom that took on new meaning for Vincent during the anti-racist uprisings of 2020.

He took part in the uprisings but won't go into too much detail about when or where or how. What he will say is that he remembers the far right being a constant, menacing presence. He remembers the armed white militias that patrolled the streets across the Pacific Northwest, and the stories elsewhere of white vigilantes setting up sniper's nests and readying their guns,[10] always itching for a pretext to open fire on the massive multiracial coalition marching through the streets chanting "Black lives matter!"

These armed militias and far-right groups often harassed and attacked people with the tacit—and very often explicit—support of law enforcement.[11] In Georgia a cop was photographed fist-bumping an armed militia member; in Philadelphia a cop posed for a friendly photo with white vigilantes who roamed the streets with baseball bats; in California, a sheriff's deputy was spotted wearing a "III Percenters" militia patch on his uniform; a California national guardsman, sent to Los Angeles to police protests, posed next to a military vehicle emblazoned with a Proud Boys slogan; and a police chief in Iowa posted a Facebook message encouraging people to drive their cars through Black Lives Matter demonstrators, writing: "HIT THE GAS AND HANG ON FOR THE SPEED BUMPS."

It's up to us to keep us safe.

No, Vincent would not be working with law enforcement. This meant, however, that unlike so many of the infiltrators who came before him—the ones who collaborated with cops—he wouldn't have armed agents of the state at his disposal if he ever found himself in trouble.

*   *   *

John, the Network 8 director, told Vincent to meet him in the parking lot of a Walmart in Snohomish County, north of Seattle, for the second and final interview. If Vincent passed it, he'd officially be a member of Patriot

Front. He changed the license plate on his car first—he had a bunch of license plates for situations like this, for when potentially hostile far-right folks might want to snap a pic of his plate—and arrived early at the Walmart Supercenter in Monroe. He didn't know what to expect of John. From what he could tell, Patriot Front members skewed young, but there were sometimes older members, veteran racists who had weaved their way through different neo-Nazi groups and done stints in prison.

Vincent was a little anxious and his mind wandered a bit. He got out of the car and ambled about the parking lot, looking up at the big white letters spelling out WALMART. Incidentally, it was just about the two-year anniversary of the El Paso massacre, when a twenty-one-year-old white supremacist walked into a Walmart in the Texas border city carrying a WASR-10 rifle, opening fire and killing twenty-three people in what amounted to the deadliest anti-Latino attack, and one of the deadliest mass shootings, in US history. The shooter had posted an accelerationist "manifesto" online before the slaughter, declaring himself an "eco-fascist" and lamenting the "cultural and ethnic replacement" happening in the US due to the "Hispanic invasion" at the Southern border. It was a sentiment sadly not too out of step with mainstream conservative opinion at the time, a racist conspiracy theory you were just as liable to read in a mass shooter's manifesto as hear from a talking head on Fox News or from the lips of the president.[12]

Vincent's phone vibrated.

John had changed the location of their meeting to a grocery store a short drive away. It occurred to Vincent that the Walmart location was likely a "decontamination zone" of sorts. John had probably parked nearby to catch a sight of Vincent first, to make sure he didn't look suspicious, that he wasn't antifa or a fed. Vincent hurried back to his car only to find he'd locked his keys inside. Fucking fuck. Where was his mind? He couldn't text John and admit to what he'd done—would be a bad look for what was essentially a job interview—so he pulled up the directions to the QFC grocery store on his phone and started to run.

He made good time, and found John—early twenties, six-foot-one, 145 pounds, blue eyes, light brown hair—standing outside the store, near the ice machine. They would do the interview here, John said, with Vincent noticing that they'd be in earshot of customers entering and exiting the store. It immediately became apparent that this interview was different from the first. John was doing most of the talking, veering from grievance to grievance, conspiracy theory to conspiracy theory, including some Holocaust denial, the far-right belief that the most well-documented genocide in history—the Nazi mass murder of six million Jews during World War II—didn't actually happen, or that if it did, it didn't happen at the scale "the Jews" said it did. It felt to Vincent like John was probing him for reactions, seeing if he'd freak out at different provocations. Vincent kept calm and kept to his character.[13]

"Well, here's my point of view," he remembers telling John. "I care less about the Holocaust than I care about just making my own people stronger. Let other races have their own lands. And if they really are self-sufficient and strong, then they'll succeed on their own, but give people their own lands, don't mix these people together. . . . I don't agree with Hitler. I would never want to be in a situation where I would be advocating for murder. Just give them their own land."

Vincent heard himself making an argument for ethnically cleansing America of Black people and Latinos and Jews—but peacefully (however the hell that would work). Vincent's character seemed to think the Holocaust did happen and was a little uneasy about it. He just *wasn't sure* about doing genocide. Seemed a bridge too far, though he conceded to John he hadn't read all the books, that he still had a lot to learn. It was all part of Vincent's character being a "fence-sitter," someone who was "80 percent of the way there."

Then John asked Victor to explain his belief in eco-fascism, so Vincent gestured at all the cars parked nearby, suggesting that society should rip up a lot of these parking lots and replace them with trees, that it was time to return to nature, to preserve the beauty of America, that wide expanse of land the white man had conquered, and save it from the overdevelopment and industrialization wrought by immigration. John nodded along, and they moved on to other subjects, with Vincent at every turn attempting to turn the interview into a friendly debate, providing John with the opportunity to preach and proselytize and feel important. To feel heard.

It became clear to Vincent that this was going well. John seemed to enjoy the opportunity to talk, to say slurs without fear of reproach, to speak grandiosely about Patriot Front and all it was going to accomplish. It became clear to Vincent that he was *in*. He'd done it. When it came time to say goodbye, John told Vincent that Network 8 would be meeting soon for a day of activities, and that he should come. Vincent thanked him and strolled back toward his car at the Walmart, simultaneously thrilled and anxious about what lay ahead. He remembered now that he'd locked the keys inside, but no matter: There was a friend already there to give him a ride home, where he had an extra set of keys. There'd been a friend there all along, keeping an eye on Vincent. A fellow anti-fascist we'll call Will, who was in on the infiltration, who'd been covertly snapping photos of Vincent and John talking outside the grocery store, who was ready to jump out of his car at any second if it seemed like Vincent was in trouble.

Five days later Vincent arrived at Pat Ryan Field, that park out by the airport, to take part in his first activity as an official Patriot Front member— a fitness session. His friend Will was there again, this time disguised as a crunchy hippie, picking blackberries up on a nearby hill, plopping them into a basket while covertly snapping photos of Vincent and the four Patriot Front members on the rugby field below, doing sit-ups and push-ups and burpees. Will zoomed in on each of their white, unmasked faces. John. David. Anthony. Charles.

Later, at 13 Coins, the diner across from the airport where John had decided they would eat, Vincent started to get a feel for doing spy work himself. He took mental note of the neo-Nazis' cars in the parking lot, their makes and models. He quickly memorized the license plate numbers, too. (Vincent says he's good with numbers and was that kid in high school who tried to memorize the most numbers of pi, ultimately being able to recite over three hundred.)

Inside the restaurant, John asked for a table for five. The hostess asked for his phone number—she would text him when a table was ready—and John gave it, prompting Vincent to start memorizing those digits, too, so that later he could search public databases for those digits, to see if they might reveal John's *real name*.

Vincent was also starting to get a feel for how challenging this infiltration could be, the moral quandaries it could pose, like when they were seated at their table and he found himself shaping his lips to say the n-word—that abhorrent, altogether American aspersion.

Vincent believes a white man like him shouldn't say that slur in just about any context, except maybe the very specific one he was in: a white man posing as a white supremacist in hopes of destroying a white supremacist group. He feared that if he didn't say the word, it might draw attention and suspicion. Not saying it could have put him in danger.

He's pretty sure the waitress didn't hear them say the word. He went back to 13 Coins and dropped off the $300 tip after dinner, he says, because all the Patriot Front guys were such rude assholes, and because not leaving a tip is such a fundamentally shitty thing to do. He never got the waitress's name or found out if the manager ever gave her that $300. Wherever she is, he just hopes she's okay.

He also had a slight ulterior motive for going back to the restaurant: When he gave the money to the manager, Vincent asked if maybe he could see the receipt John had signed. He wanted to check the price of something, he said, not revealing of course that he wanted to scan the little white piece of paper—to see if there was anything next to the words: CREDIT CARDHOLDER'S NAME.

CHAPTER 4

The Volcano

On a cool August evening in 2021, Vincent found himself with a dozen members of Patriot Front in the lower regions of Mount Rainier, the 14,400-foot volcano that looms over Seattle from sixty miles to the southeast. They were preparing to make a six-hour hike up to Camp Muir in the morning—the glacial ridge, at an altitude of ten thousand feet—named for John Muir, the famed naturalist known as the "father of America's national parks." After setting up tents and cooking dinner on a small portable grill, they gathered in a circle to take turns giving speeches as crickets chirped in the surrounding, darkening woods.

"Our founding fathers came to this savage land and they made it their home, our home . . ." John, the Network 8 director, told his companions.[1] "One notable man who fought to protect our lands was John Muir . . . He founded the Sierra Club in 1892. One of the biggest conservationist groups in the world, it was originally anti-immigration, as immigration is harmful to our land that we cherish. This weekend, we have come together to enjoy one of John Muir's favorite national parks . . . We will be following in his footsteps."

Vincent had set up battery-powered lights on a tripod to illuminate John, who was delivering his homily in front of a large Patriot Front flag—a fasces, surrounded by thirteen stars, all in red, white, and blue—hanging between two poles hammered into the ground. He filmed John with his Fujifilm XT3, which he'd fastened to a camera stabilizer that was strapped to his body, making the footage look extra professional and smooth as he slowly circled the campsite, capturing the eleven other white men, most standing, arms crossed, all in their uniforms—khaki cargo pants, navy-blue shirts, white gaiter masks, beige baseball hats, and sunglasses (even though it was twilight)—listening to their fellow fascist wax poetic about a nineteenth-century naturalist.

A week prior, John had made Vincent Network 8's official photographer and videographer. His first assignment was this trip, a two-night camping excursion meant to build brotherhood among the Patriot Front members, to have them struggle through something together. It was also an opportunity to produce more propaganda—photos and videos of the strong, young, white Americans conquering the wilderness and giving rousing speeches, like the one John was giving now.

Vincent was unsurprised that someone like John would invoke Muir, long considered a progressive or liberal hero for his environmentalism. The summer prior, there'd been a big public reckoning in the press with Muir's legacy,[2] examining how the creation of America's national parks was dependent upon the violent ethnic cleansing of indigenous people from their lands; and how Muir himself often held the "dirty Indians" in contempt, once declaring that they "seemed to have no right place in the landscape." Among the earliest leaders of Muir's Sierra Club were eugenicists who advocated the forced sterilization of non-white women. And one of his close friends was a man who founded the American Eugenics Society, which argued that all non-whites, including Jews, were immutably, irreparably inferior.

This reckoning, of course, had the effect of making Muir a newfound hero to Patriot Front members like John, whose speech veered now into blaming Jews, "those hook-nosed bankers," for the destruction of "our culture and our land." Such fiery proclamations then gave way to more tempered, personal reflections, with John regaling his companions with the story of how Patriot Front saved his life.

"Before I joined this organization, I was living a life of degeneracy, sin, and insanity," he confessed. "I spent most of my time indulging and debating people online . . . I wanted one of them to understand that this international cabal of elites are replacing us. If I was not doing this, I was indulging in substances and depression, clouding and suppressing my mind. However, one day, I hit an all-time low. And I had enough. I put the pipe, the bottle, the pornography, and the nefarious *girls* down. I deleted all my social media . . . and I messaged one of my best friends about this group he was in. 'I'm ready to take the plunge,' I said to him. He knew exactly what I meant."

Vincent immediately recognized this type of speech from his church days. It was a classic "how I got into Christianity" speech, a story of "Amazing Grace," of being lost but now found, of being into drugs and sex and all manner of sins until Christ turned it all around, bringing everything into sudden and miraculous clarity. Only in this case, John had found Thomas Rousseau, the Patriot Front leader, instead of Jesus Christ.

Vincent continued to film, taking note of all these new white guys in his camera's frame. Some wore masks, some didn't. (Any visible faces in the photos he took would be blurred out later before being used in Patriot Front propaganda.) Sparks from the fire danced in the air around the men, who were all standing silently at attention.

Earlier that day, Vincent had tipped off his anti-fascist friend Will about where they would be camping out for the night, a campground at an elevation of about 2,500 feet. Will made the two-hour drive from Seattle to take photos of all the license plates in the parking lot and had then gone home. Will couldn't keep an eye on Vincent this time, couldn't intervene if Vincent was in trouble. Vincent would have to go on this journey alone—a secret anti-fascist hiking up an active volcano with a bunch of Nazis.

After a few other speeches, Vincent retired and tucked himself into his sleeping bag, where he played around with his camera. He would have to give the memory card back to John immediately after the hike, per direct orders from Thomas. "Because you're still a new member," John had explained to Vincent, so it'd be bad operational security to have Vincent "running around with photos of everyone."[3]

"Oh, of course, totally understandable," Vincent had replied, not revealing to John that his camera had two memory cards, and that it was easy to copy a photo or a video from one card to another, and that he planned to give John only one memory card after the hike and to leave the volcano with the other. The goal was to give the other card to anti-fascist researchers he knew, who'd begin the process of matching faces captured in the footage to faces found in social media profiles and yearbook photos and maybe mug shots. They wanted to put thirteen names to these thirteen neo-Nazi faces, to identify the men now sleeping in tents surrounding Vincent's.

Once he finished fidgeting with the camera, feeling ready for his secret mission in the morning, Vincent fell asleep, too.

*   *   *

They arrived at Paradise at 9 a.m., an area on the south slope of the volcano, at an altitude of 5,400 feet, named for the wildflower meadows that explode with color in late summer—yellow buttercups and magenta fireweed and white avalanche lilies. Few other hikers were there, and those who were didn't seem to take notice of the masked white men assembling themselves on the Muir Steps, a stone staircase at the Skyline Trail trailhead, for a group photo.

This was one photo Vincent wouldn't be taking. He took his place on the steps among the other masked Patriot Front members and watched as a woman they all called Rachel lifted up Vincent's camera. "One, two, three," she counted off. To Vincent's surprise, John had allowed a woman on this hike. Rachel was the girlfriend of a Network 8 member called Tyler. Vincent was learning that although there are no women in Patriot Front, on occasion girlfriends were assigned pseudonyms and invited along to events, sometimes to cook for the men.

Rachel was dressed head to toe in hiking attire—a wide-brimmed sun hat over her long brown hair, retro '80s-style Pit Viper sunglasses, a white long-sleeved shirt, brown pants, and brown hiking boots.[4] She pressed the shutter button, capturing Vincent and the thirteen other Patriot Front members, before handing the camera back to Vincent. A short time later, she and Vincent found themselves walking a considerable distance ahead of the group.

"He has shown me things I can't unsee," Rachel said, explaining how Tyler had radicalized her. Rachel, who Vincent put at about thirty years old, had been a Bernie Sanders supporter before all this, left of liberal, an outspoken feminist. Even had transgender friends. But through Tyler, she said, she'd seen the error of her ways.

Vincent listened intently, occasionally turning around to take photographs of the others climbing up behind them. He spotted Tyler, Rachel's boyfriend, unmasked. A little heavier and older than the rest of the members. Mid-thirties, probably. Struggling a bit to keep up. Brown boots and cargo pants, a green T-shirt underneath a brown fisherman's vest, sunglasses beneath a beige hat, dark brown hair connected to a scraggly brown beard.

Rachel had suspected he was in Patriot Front before he admitted it, especially after some of the group's propaganda had popped up in his neighborhood in Seattle.

Tyler had bragged to Patriot Front that he'd been slowly indoctrinating Rachel, explaining that women will do anything, even altogether abandon feminism, to be with a strong, self-sufficient man. "She ditched her liberal friends at my behest," he wrote in a message on RocketChat to his fellow Network 8 members. Later, he'd given Rachel an ultimatum.

"As far as women go, my relationship has gotten serious enough that I'm going to tell my girlfriend I'm a member," he told the group, adding: "If she is not one hundred percent supportive and behind the cause, we're done."[5]

But Rachel had been supportive. "For all you guys that feel like it's impossible to find a woman, two years ago my girlfriend went from being a Bernie supporter and sympathetic to trannies . . ." he wrote, proudly sending a screenshot of a text message Rachel had sent bashing trans people. "More and more are waking up. Focus on becoming the best version of yourself you can be. She'll show up when the time is right."

As they walked and talked, Vincent couldn't help but feel a brief pang of something approximating sympathy. Rachel struck him as a girl under the spell of a manipulative, controlling boy, a tale as old as time, he thought. Did she really know what she'd gotten herself into? He found himself subtly asking Rachel if maybe she was in over her head, letting her know, in so many words, that there was still time to get out. *This is a pretty big, dangerous thing to be doing*, he told her. *Are you sure it's what you want to do?* Vincent was careful, of course, not to denigrate Patriot Front, lest he make himself suspect. He simply wanted Rachel to know the *stakes*. There could very well come a day when he would be the one to dox her, to let the world know her real name and what she'd become a part of.

But Rachel didn't seem to pick up on the warning. She was devoted to Tyler, and thus to Patriot Front. She knew the risks, she said. They stopped to rest, waiting for everyone else to catch up. Once reunited, Rachel and Tyler walked to the edge of a ridge, for a little stolen moment together, to take in the view: the White River down below, snaking away into the horizon, disappearing beneath distant peaks, all under a clear, sunny sky. Vincent studied the couple, then lifted his camera and snapped a photo.

*　　　　　*　　　　　*

They didn't wear masks as they climbed, so Vincent took photo after photo, with everyone understanding their faces would be blurred out in Patriot Front's public propaganda. He snapped a photo of Jack, a twentysomething from Washington, who insisted on being a flag bearer, carrying the Betsy Ross flag all the way up the mountain, mimicking the way a soldier might carry a flag in a parade—a terribly inconvenient posture to maintain now, as the hike steepened and the ground beneath them transformed into loose rocks and then into slippery snowpack. Jack wore bright, orange-tinted sunglasses, with the lightning-bolt logo of the Nazi paramilitary Schutzstaffel force ("SS") emblazoned on the lens, and the word "HAMMERWAFFEN" on the arms. He'd bought them online from an accelerationist neo-Nazi influencer called Hammer, who ran a popular Telegram channel in which he made declarations like "race traitors will get no human rights."[6] Jack seemed to be more of an accelerationist than the rest of the group, which concerned some Patriot Front members, not because they disagreed with accelerationism per se, but because if Jack popped off and did something extreme—he talked once, for example, about attacking power grids to plunge an entire region into darkness, sowing chaos[7]—it might invite scrutiny from law enforcement.

Hiking up behind Jack was Ethan, also from Washington, standing tall at six-foot-four, about two hundred pounds. Like Vincent, he had joined Network 8 only a couple weeks prior, the culmination of a rightward drift in his politics that began back in 2016. He'd been a liberal then, he confessed during the Patriot Front vetting process,[8] but realized he liked Trump during the presidential debates against Hillary Clinton, a revelation that prompted him to start listening to popular right-wing influencers like Ben Shapiro and Steven Crowder. Then he found Owen Benjamin, the popular YouTube comedian and Holocaust denier, and eventually Nick Fuentes, the youthful leader of the white nationalist group America First, before finally finding Hammer, the Nazi who made Jack's "SS" sunglasses. Ethan liked to play Hammer's podcast at home so his wife could hear. Before long, his wife was baking him cookies with little swastikas drawn in chocolate chips.

They marched in a single-file line up the volcano, sometimes in silence, nothing but the sound of wind and their boots crunching imprints into a few inches of wet snow. When they did talk, Brandon was one of the chattiest. Brandon was the leader of a fledgling network in southern California, and the group liked to make fun of him for his voice, which bore an uncanny, and ironic, resemblance to President Barack Obama's, that "basketball American," as they often called Black people. Mid-twenties, with thick prescription glasses and a backward Patriot Front baseball hat, Brandon clearly fashioned himself the intellectual of the group.[9] He got to talking to Vincent about "Third Positionism," a strain of fascist thinking that often appropriates language from the left,[10] espousing the need to protect the "white working class" and advance "white civil rights."

Vincent nodded along, letting Brandon feel heard. They were well past the tree line on the volcano now, an altitude where the pines could no longer grow, with the summit of Mount Rainier looming over them, as Muir once described, "awful in bulk and majesty."[11] It really was a beautiful, breathtaking sight, and a stark contrast to the unpleasantness of the company Vincent was keeping, these white guys who felt even more liberated at these heights to speak in hateful slurs, freed from the masses of scolding, politically correct "normies" below.

As detestable as these Patriot Front chuds were, Vincent couldn't help but notice how young some were, in their early twenties, with so much growing up still to do. Vincent, of course, wasn't that much older, in his thirties, but it felt like a big age gap now. From his perspective, these young Patriot Front recruits had somehow missed out on learning about empathy, and were allowed to carry all these harmful, oppressive beliefs into young adulthood. It wasn't exactly sympathy Vincent felt for them, but he did wonder whether some younger members might grow out of this fascist phase they were having, the way other kids eventually give up shoplifting or smoking. Would doxing them—identifying them to the world as Nazis—have the effect of trapping them in this life forever? What if they felt like there was no path to forgiveness, leaving them no other option but to double down on Patriot Front or whatever other fascist formations were bound to form in the future?

But Vincent knew without reminding himself that what mattered was these white men—and they were men, not kids—currently posed a threat to their communities back down at the base of the volcano. Their neighbors, coworkers, classmates, friends, and families deserved to know what these men were a part of. He lifted up his camera.

It had been six hours of hiking, and they were finally nearing their destination. The expansive Muir Snowfield stretched out ahead of them, the glacial ridge that formed Camp Muir appearing like a mirage in the distance.

They collapsed in heaps on the rocks sticking out of the snow, lying against their backpacks, stripping down to their T-shirts, soaking up the sun while napping and snacking, looking up occasionally at the Cowlitz Glacier and Gibraltar Ledges. There was idle chat. Someone started to talk about race science as it pertains to *The Elder Scrolls V: Skyrim*, a fantasy action role-playing video game, in which players pick a "race" ahead of their journey. John always selected the Nords, a human race that sees Skyrim—a cold, mountainous region—as their rightful homeland, even if other races live there, too.

Then someone started talking about the legend of the Sky King, which might sound like a video game but wasn't. It was a real story about a real white guy, involving the summit of Mount Rainier.[12] About three years earlier, a twenty-eight-year-old airport mechanic named Richard "Beebo" Russell suffered a mental break and stole an empty seventy-six-seat Bombardier Q400 from the runway at SeaTac Airport, fired up its propellers, and ascended into the pink evening sky above Seattle, flying first to Mount Rainier, circling the peak of the volcano—"it's beautiful," he told air traffic control—before heading back over the city to the Puget Sound. He had no flight experience, which made what he did next a miracle: He executed a perfect barrel roll, spinning the aircraft upside down, then right side up again just ten feet from the water, all to the astonishment of the two Air Force F16 pilots who were tailing him. At one point Russell asked air traffic control whether Alaska Airlines might hire him as a pilot if he landed the plane. Yes, air traffic control told him, desperate to get him on the ground. But Russell didn't buy it. People like him didn't get the high-paying jobs anymore. "Yeah, right!" he shot back. "I'm a white guy!" A short time later Russell took the plane into a nosedive, crashing into the southern tip of Ketron Island, ending his life and transforming two wooded acres into an inferno that burned through the night.

Afterward, white supremacists online seized on Russell's comment—that brief assertion of white grievance uttered in the throes of delusion—and claimed him as a hero and a martyr. Hiding behind usernames and avatars, these white guys attached Russell's likeness, against his family's wishes, to viral videos and memes, crowning him the "Sky King." White guys like the ones sitting in heaps now at Camp Muir, staring up at the same summit their Sky King had circled in that stolen jet.

It was time to descend the volcano, but first there were photos to be taken. Everyone put on their navy-blue jackets and beige hats again, lifting the gaiter masks over their faces. They climbed a rocky outcrop and unfurled a giant banner, with the words STRONG FAMILIES MAKE STRONG NATIONS emblazoned in red, white, and blue. Two members held Betsy Ross flags, and two others waved Patriot Front flags. Vincent snapped photo after photo.

The descent was a race against the setting sun. Only a few of them had headlamps or flashlights, meaning it'd be treacherous to hike after nightfall. Vincent rushed ahead, just wanting to get back to camp. All the talk of "basketball Americans" and *Skyrim* and the Sky King was testing his nerves. He feared for the first time he might lose his composure, let his mask slip. The entire day had reminded him of high school, in his overwhelmingly white hometown, where his classmates sometimes cultivated a cruel camaraderie by telling cheap, shitty jokes about Mexicans and Black people and the one gay couple in town. He wondered where those classmates were now, and if they still told jokes like that.

The group made it back to camp four hours later, having barely beat the setting sun. Vincent was desperate to sleep but needed to copy all the photos to the second memory card.

He rose early in the morning and decided to play the good soldier, handing off the original memory card over before John could ask for it. He said goodbye and started his drive out of Mount Rainier National Park, back to his home, where a few days later he'd join all his hiking companions on a conference call with Thomas, who wanted a post-action report.

Thomas had reviewed the photos and was furious at Jack for wearing the HAMMERWAFFEN sunglasses. *That wasn't correct Patriot Front branding*, he told Jack. He also reprimanded a member from Idaho named Marcus for holding the American flag right side up. *It has to be upside down. To represent the moral distress America was in.* And Thomas lightly reprimanded John, too, for not getting an earlier start up the mountain.

But Thomas heaped praise on Vincent for his photos and videos.[13] "You did a really great job," Thomas told him. "And you know, just really happy to have you. And you should look into doing some voice-over work for something because you have a very, very announcer-y voice by the way, and I'm sure you get that all the time."

"Thank you," Vincent replied, screaming with laughter inside.

Thomas got off the call a short time later, but members of Network 8 remained, with John wanting to make an announcement. There was a big march coming up in three months, John told the group. Mandatory attendance.

"December 4," he said. "Thomas says that unless it is your own wedding, or your own funeral, you need to be there. It is going to be bigger than the last one that we had. And he expects a one hundred twenty percent attendance rate, if this is going to be successful. That was the reason why Philadelphia was successful, and why we didn't have guys end up going to jail, why we didn't get beat up by that mob that was following us, was because we had the numbers, right?"

John was referring to a Patriot Front march in Philadelphia a couple months prior, over July Fourth weekend, that had made national headlines.[14] Some two hundred members from different networks had convened in the city's suburbs, where they filed into the back of Penske rental box trucks, crouching in the dark until the hatch doors flew open, revealing the City of Brotherly Love. They had hurried into military formation, flag bearers in front, the "Shield Guard" on the perimeter, commencing a surprise, flash-mob march, parading past the Philadelphia Museum of Art, that den of degeneracy, and then the Horwitz-Wasserman Holocaust Memorial, memorializing something that never happened and even if it did . . . They chanted "Reclaim America!" all the way to City Hall. Philadelphians had then chased them out of town, but not before Patriot Front surrounded one Black Philadelphian, using a smoke grenade to obscure the beating they gave him with fists and metal shields, leaving that "n***er," as one participant later remarked, "fucked up and bloodied."[15] They then retreated into the box trucks, hightailing it back to the suburbs. Police detained them briefly on the highway but released them without charges, allowing the young fascists to retrieve their rental cars and drive to the planes that took them back to their hometowns scattered across their wretched, depraved America. Hometowns where their neighbors, coworkers, and family members were none the wiser to what they'd done.

Now Thomas wanted to do it all over again. The location would be announced soon, John said, so everyone could buy plane tickets. Vincent was familiar with this type of Patriot Front action: essentially, unpermitted political rallies, designed to catch cops and antifa off guard. These rallies were the form of Patriot Front activism that always garnered the most headlines, that made the group seem bigger than it was. They were also the type of actions that attracted the most recruits.

Vincent had never expected his infiltration to last this long. He'd always imagined he would be found out within a month or two, that Patriot Front would somehow detect he was a spy. He had anticipated maybe IDing just a dozen or so neo-Nazis here in the Pacific Northwest, gathering other actionable intelligence, and then going back to his normal life. But now here he was, having earned the respect and trust not only of his network director, John, but of Thomas Rousseau himself. He found himself suddenly privy to Patriot Front's plans for its next big action. A tantalizing thought rushed into his head: If he could keep this infiltration going for just a few more months, he could ruin Patriot Front's big day. He would have time to hatch a plan with other anti-fascists. Whatever he had to do to stay in the group would be worth it if he could sabotage this December 4 march.

Vincent wanted this infiltration to have as big an impact as possible. He still wanted to ID as many Patriot Front members as he could, but now he had an opportunity to *embarrass* Patriot Front. To make them look like the fascist fools they were. To end his infiltration with a big, climactic "fuck you." He did not feel scared. If anything, he had to hide his excitement.

Of course he'd be there, he told John.

*   *   *

The next three months were a blur of activity. Vincent said yes to everything—every banner drop, every propaganda mission, every gathering—so that he could earn everyone's absolute trust, so that they'd be more liable to slip up and reveal clues to their identities, and so that he'd be wise to every detail of the December 4 march. Which is how he found himself one day in an apartment in the Interbay neighborhood of Seattle, watching Tyler show off his recently manufactured "ghost gun."

"This is a P80 frame," Tyler explained, sitting beneath a Nazi battle flag hanging from the wall, cocking his new black pistol.[16] "It's been good . . . I like the P80 frames more than a Glock, the way they feel in your hand, more of a 1911 angle . . . Plus, it's not on paper."

Vincent knew enough about guns to know what "not on paper" meant: Tyler's pistol didn't have a serial number, meaning it couldn't be traced to a record of sale. If there came a day when cops were trying to find the owner of this gun in Tyler's hand, they'd have a hard time doing so. These "ghost guns," like Tyler's P80, were sometimes made from kits bought online, with gun components that could be assembled at home into a workable firearm. It was, to gun control advocates' dismay, largely legal to do this. (It has since been outlawed in Washington state.[17]) Other ghost guns are made with 3D printers, like the 3D printer in Tyler's apartment, which Vincent suspected he was using to manufacture other guns. Just the month before, the US Joint Counterterrorism Assessment Team had issued a six-page report warning about the rise in "violent extremists" seeking "ways to acquire firearms through the production of privately made firearms."[18] The report pointed to a series of alarming incidents. In July 2021, a twenty-one-year-old national guardsman was indicted in North Carolina for allegedly supplying ghost guns to an Idaho-based cell of neo-Nazis made up of other US servicemen.[19] In 2020, the FBI found an AR-15 ghost gun in the Delaware apartment belonging to three members of The Base, an accelerationist neo-Nazi group, who had allegedly plotted to open fire at a gun rights rally in Virginia as a way of kicking off the "boogaloo,"[20] white supremacist parlance at the time for "race war." In 2019, authorities revealed that a South Carolina white man, while attempting to hire a hit man to lynch his Black neighbor and erect a burning cross in his yard, had also tried to obtain a ghost gun.[21] That same year, Seattle police seized ghost gun parts from the home of a leader in the Atomwaffen Division, the murderous neo-Nazi group.[22] And in 2018, a nineteen-year-old college student in Chicago—known around campus for wearing a Patriot Front T-shirt—was sentenced to probation after cops found a small arsenal of illegal ghost guns in his home.

Tyler cocked his pistol again and placed it on his workstation, next to the 3D printer. He also used the printer to create Patriot Front stencils. He was one of only a few members in the whole organization responsible for manufacturing the stencils, the thin sheets of metal with slogans cut into them—NOT STOLEN, CONQUERED, and DEFEND AMERICAN LABOR and RECLAIM AMERICA—that were used to spray-paint messages on top of "opposition" or "adversarial" murals, which was Patriot Front lingo for public art featuring Black and queer people. Taken altogether, one could say Tyler was running a little hate crime factory out of his apartment.

Tyler had invited Vincent, Charles, and Clark over to work on the stencils. Charles was the quarter-Filipino kid Vincent had met at the diner, the one who was maybe too young and not white enough to be in Patriot Front. Clark had been at the hike up Mount Rainier, but Vincent hadn't talked to him much. Tall and skinny with a buzz cut, he looked to be in his mid-twenties and seemed well-to-do, like he'd grown up comfortably.

Tyler and Vincent started to talk about how many stencils they had, taking a quick inventory. As Tyler listed all the different stencils, Vincent took out his phone, pretending to write down everything Tyler was saying in his Notes app, but instead flicked over to his camera and snapped a photo: Tyler, leaning back in an office chair, next to the ghost gun on the workstation, and beneath his flag, which had an Odal rune in the corner,[23] a symbol used in the divisional insignia of Waffen SS divisions during World War II, and a sonnenrad symbol in the center, the "black sun" also used by the Nazis, most infamously on the tiled floor of the remodeled German castle that belonged to Heinrich Himmler,[24] the architect of the Holocaust.

Tyler seemed to trust Vincent enough to let him mosey around the apartment unaccompanied, allowing Vincent to poke around for clues about Tyler's real name and his place of employment. He searched his bathroom cabinets, studied the magnets on the fridge, and snapped a photo of Tyler's key chain, which included a membership card for LA Fitness. It was clearly a bachelor pad. Tyler's girlfriend, Rachel, who Vincent had talked to on the climb up the volcano, lived in another neighborhood. Eventually, Vincent found himself looking at the books on Tyler's shelf. Charles started to do the same, removing a large book and flipping through the pages. He read the title aloud: "*Unintended Consequences.*"[25]

"Have you read that?" Tyler asked him.

"Not a lot of it," Charles replied.

"I've only met one other person who's read that whole book."

"It's huge."

"If you want a book that's total war on the ATF, it's a good one," Tyler explained, referring to the Bureau of Alcohol, Tobacco, and Firearms (the federal agency that had reported recovering ghost guns like Tyler's at the scenes of nearly seven hundred homicides and attempted homicides in the previous five years).[26] "If you like guns and want a fantasy of waging war on the ATF, borrow it."

Written in 1996 by a Second Amendment enthusiast named John Ross, *Unintended Consequences* is a blood-soaked fantasy imagining a white southern man who rebels against gun control laws he views as oppressive, killing ten ATF agents, then butchering their bodies and feeding them to hogs.[27] The act inspires a mass armed revolt, organized by "leaderless resistance," in which a decentralized network of militias carry out attacks, eventually leading to the downfall of the US government. Ross claimed the book was a smash hit, selling over sixty thousand copies, largely from purchases at gun shows.[28] By 2013, *The New York Times* noted *Unintended Consequences* was among the "100 most sought-after titles currently out of print."[29]

"*Unintended Consequences*," Charles said. "I imagine it's a more flushed-out version of *The Turner Diaries*."

Charles wasn't the first person to note the similarities between the two books. *The Turner Diaries* is a 1978 novel written by William Pierce, leader of the neo-Nazi group National Alliance.[30] His book also imagines a bloody revolution, albeit with much more explicit white supremacist themes, including the "day of the rope," in which "race traitors"—namely certain journalists, professors, lawyers, clergy, and other leftists—are lynched en masse. *The Turner Diaries* has inspired multiple acts of white supremacist terrorism, including the 1993 bombing of the Alfred P. Murrah Federal Building in Oklahoma City, which killed 163 people. "If people say *The Turner Diaries* was my bible, *Unintended Consequences* would be my New Testament," Timothy McVeigh, the Oklahoma City bomber, said after reading *Unintended Consequences* while in jail awaiting trial. "I think *Unintended Consequences* is a better book. It might have changed my whole plan of operation if I'd read that one first."[31]

Charles put the book back on the shelf.

The four of them started to add the finishing touches to Tyler's 3D-printed stencils, cutting out the letters and then practicing spray-painting over them on pieces of cardboard. Tyler realized he needed a tool he'd left in his work van outside, he said. He'd be right back. Vincent walked over to the window, looking down onto the street below, and observed Tyler approach a white van with two ladders tied to the top, and with black lettering on the side. KEY MECHANICAL, it said. Tyler opened the back doors of the van and started rummaging inside. Vincent looked around to make sure Charles and Clark weren't looking. He held his phone up to the window and snapped a photo.

*   *   *

Ethan—the tall white guy who'd climbed up the volcano with Vincent, the one whose girlfriend baked him swastika cookies—was pissed. He, Vincent, and Clark were driving around Snohomish County hanging massive Patriot Front banners from highway overpasses, but *someone kept taking them down*. The latest banner they'd put up, hanging above I-5 near the Alderwood Mall, had been removed within just five minutes. How the hell was this happening? They didn't even get a chance to drive back down to I-5 so they could get a video of the banner from below. "Dude, was that antifa walking over there?" Ethan asked from the driver's seat, referring to a small group of people they'd seen walking across the overpass.[32] He took the next exit.

"Let's fucking jump these guys," Ethan said. "Mask-on moment. This is a mask-on moment. We don't need to tell Thomas but somebody needs to get their ass beat. We're gonna catch them. At least get the banner back, right? Dude, actually, Vincent, this is a camera-on moment. Me and Clark getting in a fight. This will be the sickest action report."

Ethan wasn't exactly wrong to blame antifa. Vincent had been discreetly texting Will, his anti-fascist friend, screenshots from Google Maps, tipping him off to the location of the banners. Will would then speed to the scene, removing the large pieces of canvas from the zip ties connecting them to the overpasses, before stuffing them into the trunk of his car. If anti-fascists and fascists agree on one thing, it's that propaganda matters. For Vincent and Will, it was important that these banners be in public for as little time as possible. But if they were honest, it was also fun as hell to fuck with Patriot Front like this. Making them fret about the antifa menace ruining their little propaganda videos.

Ethan pulled into the parking lot at Alderwood Mall, suspecting that's where antifa had gone. He, Clark, and Vincent walked through the rows of cars, looking for suspects. Vincent braced himself. This could be it: the end of the infiltration. If they did find Will, and if they tried to attack him, then the jig was up. Vincent would defend his friend, relishing the opportunity to pummel Ethan and Clark. He imagined the shocked looks of betrayal on their faces.

Vincent's eyes widened. He spotted Will stuffing the purloined Patriot Front banner into his car's trunk, placing it on top of the other two banners he'd stolen that evening. But Will closed the trunk just in time, before Ethan or Clark noticed him. He and Vincent exchanged quick, knowing glances.

Ethan and Clark walked on, hunting antifa outside a La-Z-Boy Furniture Gallery. Ethan spotted two idling cars he deemed suspicious. He lifted his mask over his face. Vincent, who was filming, braced himself again. Ethan approached the first car, rapping his knuckles against the driver's-side window. Likely alarmed at the trio of masked white men approaching them, the driver put the vehicle into reverse and started to pull out of the parking lot. Ethan walked up to the other car, which also quickly pulled away.

"They looked like little antifa fucks," Clark said.

"Yeah," Ethan replied, breaking into a sprint, attempting to catch up to the cars. But they were gone, disappearing into the night. Ethan caught his breath, then asked Vincent if he'd gotten the license plates on film.

No, Vincent replied, lying. The license plates weren't in focus.

In the past few months, Vincent often found himself with Ethan on missions like this. One night, the two of them snuck around White Center, just outside Seattle's city limits, spray-painting graffiti and putting up posters. CHILDREN MUST BE SEEN AS THE PROMISE OF A PROSPEROUS AND BRIGHT FUTURE, NOT AS A SOCIAL LIABILITY, read one of the posters. AMERICA BELONGS TO ITS FATHERS AND IS OWED TO ITS SONS, read another. Vincent studied Ethan as he used a brush to wheat-paste the poster to a telephone pole. It occurred to him that maybe Ethan was a father himself.

As Vincent stood guard while Ethan got to work wheat-pasting another poster, he noticed a police cruiser speeding toward them. "Ethan, we gotta go," he said.

As they sprinted around a street corner, Vincent looked behind them, noticing the cop car's flashing red-and-blue lights turn into an alley, in what seemed to Vincent like a maneuver to cut them off once they reached the adjacent block. He grabbed Ethan. "Wait, wait," he said. They changed direction and sprinted back toward Vincent's car, slamming the doors shut and catching their breath.

Vincent's mind was racing: If he got arrested, Patriot Front would be able to look up his real name in the arrest report after his infiltration was over. Also, what if the news media picked up on the story? "Two Men Busted for White Supremacist Graffiti." How would he let the world know he was an anti-fascist infiltrator and not a neo-Nazi?

He turned the key on the ignition and drove away. *This all better be worth it.* It was a thought he had a lot, like when he was on yet another mission with Ethan, watching him paste a giant Patriot Front poster on top of a West Seattle mural depicting Angela Davis, the famous Black radical activist. BETTER DEAD THAN RED, the poster screamed, making plain Patriot Front's hatred of Marxists and communists. Davis, a lifelong communist, was born in Birmingham, Alabama, in a neighborhood nicknamed "Dynamite Hill" for the frequency with which the KKK bombed Black residents' homes.[33] Later, in 1963, when she was a student in France—where she studied the philosopher Herbert Marcuse, whose theories about fascism being a "preventative counterrevolution" to defend "against a feared revolution"[34] would become central to her life and work—Davis picked up a newspaper one day to read that the KKK had bombed a Black church back in Birmingham, killing four little Black girls, all of whom she knew. "I closed my eyes, squeezing my lids into wrinkles as if I could squeeze what I had just read out of my head," she later wrote of learning the news. "When I opened my eyes again, the words were still there, the names traced out in stark black print."[35]

Ethan finished pasting the poster over the mural, disappearing Davis's determined brown eyes. Vincent tried to assure himself that the destruction he'd bring to Patriot Front one day would be worth this piece of hate vandalism he'd been a party to. He was relieved later in the week when he read an article on the *West Seattle Blog* noting that the Patriot Front poster was no longer there.[36] "It's been cleaned off," a local resident said. "Thankfully the poster was still wet, and my neighbor was able to remove it with soapy water without damaging the art."

And Vincent was further relieved, during another mission, to stumble upon a big clue to Ethan's identity. The two had been driving in Vincent's car—he'd changed the license plate again—when Ethan asked if he could connect his phone to the Bluetooth, to play some music. "Yeah, go ahead," Vincent told him.

A few seconds later Ethan was scrolling through songs on his phone, playing DJ.

Vincent looked at the stereo display on his car's console. "BLUE-TOOTH," it said. "CONNECTED TO JUSTIN'S iPhone."

Ethan—or rather, Justin—didn't seem to notice.

*   *   *

There was something about being in the car that seemed to make Patriot Front members let their guard down. More casual banter, less stringent about protocols. In September 2021 a member named Leo, from down in Oregon, picked up Vincent for a mission. When he got into the car he noticed a piece of mail on the car floor. Something that looked unimportant, like an advertisement. While they drove and chatted, Vincent reached his right hand behind the passenger seat and grabbed the envelope, slowly bringing it to his right jeans pocket, where he gingerly, quietly stuffed it inside. Leo didn't seem to notice.

That same month Vincent went down to California for another two-night Patriot Front hiking excursion, this one at White Mountain Peak in the desert. For part of the long drive from the Los Angeles International Airport, Vincent hitched a ride with Brandon-CA, that member he'd met on Mount Rainier, the self-styled intellectual with a voice like Barack Obama's.

"When I went to Washington that was the first time I flew Alaskan Airlines, which was definitely a nice change of pace considering what I usually have to fly, which is Spirit Airlines, which is basically the N***er Airlines," Brandon told Vincent as they drove through the desert[37] in Brandon's black Ford F-150 truck with tinted black windows. Brandon liked to talk. A lot. So Vincent, sitting in the passenger seat, had pressed record on his phone.

"A lot of guys get in and are like, 'Things aren't happening fast enough' or 'we need to be more radical,'" Brandon said at another point, talking about new Patriot Front recruits. "So I usually point out to them—because almost everybody in our circles has a very large respect for the NSDAP [National

Socialist German Workers' Party] back in the Third Reich days—and I point out to them: you know the NSDAP started off with just doing speeches and putting up posters, right? Baby steps. Baby steps."

The road leading to the White Mountain trailhead is known for having small, sharp rocks that love to give cars flat tires, so the caravan of Patriot Front cars stopped occasionally so that Brandon could inspect everyone's wheels. On one such stop, Brandon went to get out of the truck but first handed Vincent his phone so that Vincent could keep track of any urgent messages he might be getting from members driving in another caravan.

The pin number for the phone, Brandon told Vincent with a smile, was 1492: the year Jews were expelled from Spain.

The driver's-side door shut. Suddenly Vincent had access to a Patriot Front member's phone, alone in a truck with tinted windows so no one could see him. He hurriedly entered in "1492" and got to work going through Brandon's phone, using his own phone to take pictures. There was Brandon's Telegram account with his username. There was his Gmail account. His text messages. His contacts. His Threema account.

Vincent was almost giggling. *Brandon really must trust me,* he thought. But then as Brandon was walking back toward the truck Vincent realized he needed to leave the phone as he found it. He rushed to close all the apps he'd opened and to make sure the apps overview section was in the same order as it had been before.

Brandon climbed back into the driver's seat. Vincent handed him back his phone. No new messages, he said.

* * *

Around 3 a.m. on the morning of October 16, 2021—almost seven weeks before the December 4 march he was planning to sabotage—Vincent lifted up his camera and filmed eight members of Patriot Front, dressed in all black, wearing masks and baseball hats.[38] He captured them as they squeezed through a hole they'd cut in a chain-link fence in downtown Olympia, carrying spray cans and stencils. They'd been preparing for this moment for weeks. On planning calls, they discussed how two of the biggest dudes in the group—Tyler and Frederick, both from Oregon—would be lookouts, dealing with any curious passersby. "If there's a cell phone filming us and that cell phone somehow goes fucking flying and blows up in a million pieces, I'm not gonna cry," John had told them. "Understood?"[39]

Although John was ostensibly in charge as network director, this seemed to be Clark's show. His idea. This was the most engaged Vincent had ever seen Clark. He'd planned everything meticulously: where to park the cars, the escape routes. And of course, he'd chosen the target: a massive Pride mural with the words RESPECT AND LOVE OLYMPIA over a rainbow and a blue sky, taking up the entire side of a large, city-owned building.

The mural had been commissioned by locals in 2014 in response to a series of anti-LGBTQ hate crimes in Olympia, including at Jake's, a nearby gay bar. Still, a month after its completion, an unknown vandal wrote "fags" on the mural,[40] and in the ensuing years other hate crimes had occurred nearby, including in 2016 when a man yelled slurs at a group of lesbian and transgender women before pummeling them, leaving a local drag king without a row of teeth.[41]

"Obviously the objective is to mess up as much of it as possible,"[42] Thomas said of the mural in one of the planning calls. He'd taken particular interest in this mission. "I would start out by having a few guys just going up and down the length of it with turbo cans . . . so that if they are going to repair it, they're essentially going to have to start from scratch."

Vincent filmed as the Patriot Front members did just that, disappearing the whole mural with white spray paint, before flattening the stencils against the wall and quickly spray painting RECLAIM AMERICA in red and blue, and then grabbing the smaller stencils to cover the rest of the wall with the URL for Patriot Front's website.

Vincent felt awful. Should he have stopped this? How could he have stopped this? He didn't want to put his friends in danger—showing up at 3 a.m. in the dark to confront eight neo-Nazis. And he didn't believe in tipping off the police. This was the trade-off he'd decided to make: take part in this so that he could cause *real* damage to Patriot Front further down the line. A bit of ugly pragmatism, he knew. He needed to dox every single one of these fascist fucks in his camera's frame. Let the world know what they were a part of. And then he needed to ruin their big rally on December 4.

This better be worth it.

In the following days, to Clark and John's delight, there were multiple local news articles and TV segments about the vandalism, which they shared in their "trophies" chat. Vincent had hoped the community would make a stand, that it would quickly restore the mural, but instead they elected to paint over the Patriot Front stencils in blue—a temporary solution until they could repaint it. But then the city decided to remove the mural altogether, promising to rehabilitate and relocate it later.[43]

"That thing had been there since 2014," John wrote in a message to the group, gloating that a few minutes of "activism made them feel unsafe enough to remove it forever."[44]

Clark was thrilled, too. "Our recent actions have shown we can . . . deface the largest most well protected mural in shitlib olympia without so much as being accosted once,"[45] he wrote.

They were feeling emboldened. And they were coming together as a group, too, just as John had hoped. Five of them even got together for a Thanksgiving meal, eating and laughing together before stepping outside for a group photo: the five posing next to the couple dozen Black Lives Matter signs they'd stolen from people's yards and repurposed as canvases for Patriot Front stencils. Clark joked that the signs were "ethnically sourced."[46]

In the days leading up to December 4, members of Network 8 and their counterparts across the country—California and Texas and Pennsylvania and Michigan—took part in drilling sessions. Practicing marching in formation and defending themselves from protesters. They had all learned where they were going: Washington, DC. They were going to march in the capital.

Vincent had told everyone he was going, but at 2:19 a.m. on December 3, hours before they were supposed to head to the airport together, he logged into RocketChat for the last time and sent a final message. "I think there are cops knocking on my door," he wrote. "I'm gonna try to get video."

Then he went silent.

"I don't know what's going on, but you need to try to reach out to Thomas immediately," John wrote to Vincent, who never replied. "And if you need a lawyer, here's the best one you can get: https://www.treyzlaw.com."

John was in a panic. He messaged Lawrence, the network director in Florida, and told him what was going on.

"Should his account be locked until further notice?" Lawrence asked, worried that law enforcement might get access to Vincent's phone.

No, John replied, Vincent needed to be able to contact them when he was out of jail. Plus, if cops did get access to his phone, John said, Vincent didn't "have access to a ton of info."[47]

Vincent, of course, had not gotten a door knock from the cops in the middle of the night. That was just an excuse for why he wasn't going to be at the DC march. He thought it might be a fun way to stress Network 8 out. Make them paranoid.

And John was wrong: Vincent did "have access to a ton of info." Info he'd shared with anti-fascists in DC. Detailed info about Patriot Front's big march in the capital.

Vincent's infiltration of Patriot Front was over. Now it was time to watch what his comrades in DC would do.

CHAPTER 5
A Brief History of Punching Nazis

In the years leading up to the Patriot Front march in Washington, DC, which Vincent's anti-fascist friends were now preparing to disrupt, perhaps violently, mainstream American op-ed columnists and TV pundits were also deeply concerned about neo-Nazis—that is, they were concerned that so many neo-Nazis were getting punched.

To these conservative, centrist, and progressive liberal commentators, the proliferation of viral videos showing anti-fascists delivering right and left hooks to Nazi craniums laid bare the "extremism" of the far left. Antifa, the argument went, was "just as bad" and intolerant as Nazis themselves. Violence could never be the answer. It's best, these pundits asserted, to simultaneously ignore Nazis, starving them of oxygen, and to defeat their ideas with robust and open debate—to use facts and reason instead of fists, putting faith in the "marketplace of ideas" to do its magic.

The surge in Nazi-punching deeply offended these pundits' stated belief in free speech—an almost religious conviction best articulated by a frequently shared quote, falsely attributed to Voltaire, that goes: "I disapprove of what you say, but I will defend to the death your right to say it." Resorting to punching Nazis, the pundits warned, was counterproductive, a slippery slope and a breakdown in civility that would lead to widespread social disorder and chaos.

According to a 2017 tally from Fairness & Accuracy in Reporting,[1] in the four weeks after the deadly Unite the Right rally in Charlottesville, where anti-fascists and neo-Nazis had come to blows for hours, six of America's largest newspapers published twenty-eight op-eds devoted to condemning the Nazi-punchers known as antifa, while publishing just twenty-seven op-eds focused on condemning the actual Nazis in Charlottesville—one of whom had just *killed an anti-fascist*.

The Washington Post was perhaps the most forceful in its denunciations. "Yes, antifa is the moral equivalent of neo-Nazis," read the headline of one op-ed.[2] The paper's editorial board issued its own warning, too, headlined: "Antifa groups only help the hateful forces they claim to oppose."[3] The article argued that antifa posed a "danger" to "free speech" and threatened to "discredit, through association, the far broader peaceful movement against racism and hate."

"Antifa activists' deeds hardly promote the moral clarity necessary to isolate right-wing hate groups," the editorial board wrote, adding: "In terms of objective political impact, the group is badly misnamed: 'Profa' would be more accurate."

It was a perplexing, and frankly infuriating, genre of punditry for militant anti-fascists like Vincent to read, one that betrayed an ignorance of antifa's history, and which seemed at odds with wider America's conception of itself, especially in pop culture. Superman, after all, punched Nazis. So did Captain America and Indiana Jones. Why did we as a country seem to celebrate and valorize the fictional Nazi-punchers of yore but condemn the real-life Nazi-punchers of today?[4]

The anti-fascist writer Natasha Lennard calls it "historical NIMBYism,"[5] a line of thinking taken up by both liberals and conservatives, "in which it is only in the past, or in other countries, that violent militancy against white supremacy constitutes legitimate resistance." The logic, Lennard argues, is "premised on the belief (even the tacit one) that while dissent, militancy and violence is fine *there* and was fine *then*, our current context is not so bad." The pundits denouncing antifa, Lennard writes, were part of the "great liberal tradition" of "standing on the wrong side of history until that history is comfortably in the past."

Anti-fascists like Vincent do not see the militant fight against fascism as belonging to a bygone era, one that ended with the bullet Hitler shot through his own skull, or the rope used to string up Mussolini. They frequently invoke the memory of John Brown, the abolitionist whose militant fight against American slavery is often understood for its moral righteousness today. They point to a famous Malcolm X quote, too. "We need allies who are going to help us achieve victory, not allies who are going to tell us to be nonviolent," he said. "If a white man wants to be your ally, what does he think about John Brown? You know what John Brown did? He went to war."[6] For Vincent and his cohorts, the fight against fascism requires a constant, militant vigilance. In their worldview, fascism never went away—it's just very good at designing new uniforms.

Is antifa, like so many pundits claimed, against "free speech"? Maybe if you understand "free speech" to mean "speech without consequences." Many Americans, and perhaps even the anti-antifa pundits themselves, would likely agree that if a man drinking at a bar started yelling racial slurs at people, that man would deserve to be asked to leave, and if he refused, to be *physically removed*. There is an intuitive understanding that a man yelling racial slurs is a threat; that he is liable and likely to commit violence. Removing that man from the bar—maybe, if need be, by punching him—is ultimately an act of self-defense.

Why would that dynamic suddenly change, as *The Washington Post* editorial board and so many pundits seemed to suggest, when an explicitly genocidal Nazi group decides to hold a rally in your city? To shout racial slurs through a megaphone in a park instead of over beers at a bar? From the militant anti-fascist perspective, there is no difference. Such Nazi groups are *inherently* violent, even if they get a permit to hold a rally. They always pose an urgent, immediate threat that needs confronting.

For Vincent and his fellow anti-fascists, perhaps the most galling aspect of the anti-punching-Nazis punditry was the argument, so flatly stated by *The Washington Post* editorial board—as if it was a settled debate—that punching Nazis "only benefits the very forces antifa purports to oppose." There are historical examples directly contradicting this assertion. The editorial board needn't have reached too far back in history for case studies in the effectiveness of anti-fascist militancy. The Nazi-punching history the editorial board, and so many other pundits, were either unaware of, or deliberately ignored, occurred much more recently, within their lifetimes, and here on America's shores.

*   \` *   *

It's hard to overstate the significance of the Anti-Racist Action (ARA) in destabilizing American fascist groups throughout the late 1980s, 1990s, and early aughts, and in laying the groundwork for what we know as antifa in America today. ARA started in Minneapolis in 1987, with a multiracial crew of punks calling themselves the "Baldies."[7] They were "skinheads," but not in the way most Americans know the term. As Mark Bray explains in *Antifa: The Anti-Fascist Handbook*:[8]

> *Although today most people associate skinheads with racism, ironically the movement emerged when elements of British working class "mods" encountered Jamaican music and culture in the late 1960s. Originally derived from the figure of the Jamaican "rude boy," the popular and stylish working-class outlaw celebrated in early ska and rocksteady, British skinhead culture was initially a multiracial site of cultural exchange when it emerged in London around 1969.*

Anti-racist skinhead culture spread far and wide, and wherever it went in the 1980s, a resurgent movement of neo-Nazis appropriated that culture—shaving their own heads, wearing bomber jackets and Fred Perry polos, and lacing up Doc Martens on their feet. These neo-Nazi skinheads stormed punk shows, sieg-heiling and starting fights. And they attacked Black people and immigrants and queer people in the streets. The Baldies in Minneapolis, before they became ARA, fought back. If they spotted a Nazi they hadn't seen before, they'd make them a promise: The next time we see you, if you haven't left this white power bullshit behind, we will treat you to some "righteous violence."[9]

Kieran, a member of the Baldies, explained their tactics to the punk zine *Maximum Rocknroll*: "We made it clear to the Nazi skinheads that they will not organize at shows, they will not organize at hangouts, and we will not be friends with these people. From our experience, the tactic that has worked in Minneapolis includes physical confrontation, which is fighting them and kicking the shit out of them."[10]

These tactics, of course, always risked escalation and retaliation. "One particular time [the neo-Nazis skins] came through and they spray-painted

*Anti-fascists confronting "Gay Bash 93," an anti-queer rally
organized by white supremacist groups, in New Hope, Pennsylvania,
on November 6, 1993. Anti-fascists at the rally belonged to
May Day Skins, ACT UP, Grassroots Queers, and Anti-Racist Action.*

'death to race mixers' on my mom's house," one veteran white Baldie remembers. "My stepdad, who's Black, opens the door. I'm coming down the steps
when somebody fires two shots. The bullets lodged in the ceiling, and they ran
off. And so that was pretty close to home, man, that's when it really escalated.
At that time, I was probably seventeen. I started carrying a gun every day."[11]

There was safety in numbers, so the Baldies started to recruit more and
more members. "Some people get this fear that racist skinheads are these
supermen that can't be beat, but the fact is that any two people should be
able to beat any one person if it comes down to that," Kieran told *Maximum
Rocknroll*. "One of the reasons why the Baldies won so much isn't because
we're on some macho trip, or that we're all huge people, but because we've
been able to get the numbers to support us."

Eventually the Baldies, many of whom were still teenagers, expanded
their tactics beyond punching Nazis. They pressured record shops not to
sell white power music; pressured venues not to host white power bands;
published zines warning their communities about newly identified white
power activists; and were diligent about removing white power propaganda
from the streets.

The young punks started to grow more politically sophisticated, identifying as anarchists or socialists or communists. After reading about Anti-Fascist Action in the UK—a group of leftists battling the British National Front—the Baldies were inspired to form a new group: Anti-Racist Action (ARA).[12] Anti-racist skinheads across the US, all dealing with and punching Nazis in their own cities, heard about the Minneapolis ARA and began to form chapters of their own.

Flyers printed by Anti-Racist Action in Toronto, instructing locals how to identify neo-Nazis and other white supremacists, with space for other chapters to add their contact info.

By 1994, when the ARA organized its first national conference in Columbus, the organization's work had moved beyond the punk subculture and beyond battles between "bald head kids." ARA was determined to fight any group they deemed fascist, by any means necessary, wherever those groups went. Mic Crenshaw, one of the founding Baldies, remembers that first conference in Columbus, looking around at the assembled ARA chapters and marveling at what he and his young, working-class punk friends had helped start. "It felt like we were part of a political movement that was created by us, for us, in our time, and it was an electric moment," he told the authors of *We Go Where They Go: The Story of Anti-Racist Action*, a remarkable oral history of the group. "I remember standing up and looking around, and I actually shed a tear, because it was the first time that I was doing something empowering that had nothing to do with what adults thought I should be doing ... You knew that you had family. Like, these people believed in the same things you did. That was a powerful feeling and a powerful understanding to have."

The ARA chapters used the 1994 conference to discuss and develop "points of unity," a concise articulation of militant American anti-fascism— collectively edited and fine-tuned over the years—that still serves as a guide to modern antifa groups to this day:[13]

1. **We go where they go.** Whenever fascists are organizing or active in public, we're there. We don't believe in ignoring them or staying away from them. Never let the Nazis have the street!

2. **We don't rely on the cops or courts to do our work for us.** This doesn't mean we never go to court, but the cops uphold white supremacy and the status quo. They attack us and everyone who resists oppression. We must rely on ourselves to protect ourselves and stop the fascists.

3. **Nonsectarian defense of other anti-fascists.** In ARA, we have a lot of different groups and individuals. We don't agree about everything and we have a right to differ openly. But in this movement an attack on one is an attack on us all. We stand behind each other.

4. **We support abortion rights and reproductive freedom.** ARA intends to do the hard work necessary to build a broad, strong movement

against racism, sexism, anti-Semitism, Islamophobia, homophobia, transphobia, discrimination against the disabled, the oldest, the youngest, and the most oppressed people. We want a classless, free society. We intend to win!

More ARA chapters formed. As noted in *We Go Where They Go*:

> *Agreeing to the points of unity was the only formal and explicit "require-ment" to join the Anti-Racist Action Network. Otherwise, ARA was always very decentralized and horizontal. Few decisions were ever made on a network-wide level; those that were were sometimes made by majority vote for simple things, while in some cases participants agreed that a two-thirds majority vote was required.... This decentralized structure was a defining and crucial feature of the network, because it allowed individual chapters to respond to local conditions with a certain amount of experimentation and local initiative and prevented anyone from being "in charge" of activists in another area.*

By 1998, the ARA had over one hundred chapters and two thousand members in North America. And in turn, the neo-Nazi skinheads who had inspired so many anti-racist skins to get mobilized largely disappeared from city streets. The Baldies had successfully chased them out of Minneapolis. The Portland, Oregon, chapter of ARA, in alliance with a group called Skinheads Against Racial Prejudice (SHARP), pushed multiple neo-Nazi groups, including East Side White Pride—whose members had murdered an Ethiopian immigrant named Mulagata Seraw—out of town.[14] And in Atlanta, the ARA made militant anti-fascism so commonplace, neo-Nazis from groups like American Front and Old Glory started to disband. ARA expanded the scope of its work and, unlike modern antifa, often operated publicly, out in the open, unmasked, coordinating campaigns to educate communities about their local fascist groups, or setting up tables at "Rock Against Racism" shows, handing out zines and flyers.

Its targets changed, too. ARA activists became active in abortion defense work, escorting doctors and patients into clinics, protecting them from the seething Christian fundamentalists protesting outside, part of an increasingly agitated "pro-life" movement that throughout the 1990s targeted and killed abortion providers.[15] "We decided that they fit the definition of fascism to us," Katrina, a member of Minneapolis ARA, remembered. "They were really trying to limit the rights of women and queer people, so we decided to take them on with the same kind of energy and strategies that we were using against white supremacists."[16]

Still, they continued to monitor and punch white supremacists, even if they were often dogged by the mainstream media over the punching, with liberal and conservative critics alike turning up their noses at ARA. To ARA members, such critiques always smacked of classism.

"It is a privilege to not have to engage in a physical altercation with a Nazi or a racist or a cop," Judith, a member of Toronto's ARA chapter, told the authors of *We Go Where They Go*.[17] "I think there is a class dimension to the organizing and the analysis. Punks and working-class people are just more familiar with physicality as part of their politics. There's just not a big distinction to be made with 'do you raise your fists or not?' It's just more part of people's sense of being in the world and being politically engaged—that it's part of the risk."

Gerry Bello, a member of Columbus ARA, justified punching Nazis this way: "Hitler himself said the only way you could have beaten us is if you'd smashed us off the street from the very first day and with the utmost brutality."[18]

When you ask ARA veterans now about their war stories, or about their greatest victories, many will point to what they call the Battle of York. Althouh the bloody confrontation in the town of York, Pennsylvania, is well remembered in anti-fascist circles, it remains largely unknown to the wider public.

On January 12, 2002, over one hundred white supremacists converged on York, a diverse blue-collar town of forty thousand people about an hour's drive north across the Mason-Dixon Line from Baltimore.

A flyer for an anti-Klan rally in Cicero, Illinois, near Chicago, in 1998.

They were led by Matthew Hale, leader of the World Church of the Creator, a group devoted to the teachings of a book called *The White Man's Bible*, authored two decades earlier by a former Florida state legislator. The book encouraged white people to commit acts of violence to start a prophesied "racial holy war," often abbreviated to "RaHoWa," that would finally rid the earth of Jews and other racial minorities, who the book described as "mud races."[19]

Members of the World Church of the Creator had been tied to multiple acts of violence in the years leading up to the York rally,[20] including the murder of Harold Mansfield Jr., a Black Gulf War veteran; the bombing of a National Association for the Advancement of Colored People (NAACP) lunch hall; and the pipe bombing of a Seattle gay bar.

But perhaps its most notorious act of violence came in 1999, when a college student named Benjamin Smith, who'd risen to prominence in the World Church, went on a three-day shooting spree in Indiana and Illinois.[21] He killed former Northwestern University basketball coach Ricky Byrdsong, who was Black, as Byrdsong and his three kids walked outside their home. He shot and wounded a Black minister in Decatur, Illinois, and then in a series of drive-by shootings shot and wounded nine other people, all Black, Jewish, or Asian. Finally, Smith drove to Bloomington, Indiana, where he shot and killed a Korean graduate student who was on his way to church.

A short time later Smith, an admirer of Adolf Hitler, "followed his leader," as the old anti-fascist expression goes, shooting himself in the head as he drove away from police, crashing into a telephone pole, where he shot himself again in the chest and leg, dying a short time later.

In the following years Hale, the World Church leader, had managed to still grow the organization from forty-one chapters to seventy-six chapters.[22] To keep up the momentum, he announced a series of speeches and rallies he'd be holding, including in York.

Hale had chosen the town for a very specific reason: York's white mayor, Charlie Robertson, was under investigation for inciting violence decades prior, during the city's 1969 race riots, when white mobs had chased and attacked Black people. A recent deathbed confession from one participant implicated the mayor in the violence, prompting Robertson to eventually fess up: while patrolling the riots *as a police officer* in 1969, he had led a white mob in a chant of "white power." He also allegedly handed out ammunition to a white rioter, instructing him to "Kill as many n***ers as you can."[23] The man obliged, killing Lillie Belle Allen, a Black woman in town from Mississippi, hitting her with a "shotgun blast in the chest so powerful," *The New York Times* reported, "that it blew her out of her sneakers."[24]

Although Robertson had recently been arrested and charged, he had thus far refused to step down as mayor. Hale and the World Church, along with other neo-Nazi groups, were going to rally in York to support him.

Some sixty anti-fascists—including from ARA chapters in Columbus, Philadelphia, Baltimore, and Washington, DC—arrived in York to confront them.[25] They were dressed in all black, with ski masks and scarves and sunglasses covering their faces. The tactic, called "black bloc," developed by German anarchists in the 1980s,[26] was meant to conceal their identities both from law enforcement and the fascists they wanted to fight.

As the anti-fascist black bloc marched toward York's library, where Hale was set to give a speech, they were joined by dozens of Black and Latino locals who'd heard about the racists invading their town. "That's the good crowd," a local resident, watching the anti-fascist procession go by, told a reporter from *The York Daily Record*.[27] "They're going to stand up to those people. I appreciate that."

Riot cops were guarding the library, protecting Hale and his followers inside, but when groups of neo-Nazis started to filter out into the surrounding streets, the chase was on. Locals led the charge, ushering the out-of-town anti-fascists through side streets where they could intercept and isolate small groups of Nazis before police could intervene. The rest of the day was a blur of boots and fists, flagpoles and hammers, with scattered street fights breaking out across York. Locals showed ARA members how to turn the metal lids of trash cans into weapons: skipping the lids off the concrete in such a way that they'd bounce upward to knock Nazis in their teeth.[28]

Eventually one Nazi turned his white pickup truck into a weapon,[29] driving through a crowd of anti-fascists, dragging one ARA member for twenty feet, dislocating his shoulder. The Nazi's truck then sideswiped a local twelve-year-old Black girl, who had to be rushed away in an ambulance. Furious locals and anti-fascists chased down the Nazi, shattering his truck's windows before he crashed and was apprehended by police.

Eventually, cops had to give the Nazis an armed escort out of York. They weren't safe here.

*   *   *

Although few Americans know of the Battle of York today, it garnered national press coverage at the time, detailing how twenty-five people had been arrested, all but two of them anti-fascists. Eight people were treated and released for injuries at local hospitals—including, mercifully, that little twelve-year-old girl. Police officers suffered some minor injuries, and two weapons were confiscated. Hale, the World Church leader, had left the library under police protection.

The New York Times was dismissive of the ARA members who'd shown up, describing the group as a "traveling circus of publicity hunters."[30] Established civil rights organizations were similarly disparaging. The Southern Poverty Law Center lamented that militant anti-fascist tactics, typically seen overseas, were now becoming commonplace in America[31] (overlooking the militant ARA activism in America over the previous decade).

"Now, European-style public confrontation—street battles, public marches by formerly secretive groups, in-your-face racist activism—is here," the SPLC wrote. "That is good news for American white supremacists, who live off the attention that they get in the press and who increasingly sense things going their way. For them, the more battles and the more violence— especially of the sort sparked by so-called anti-racists who insist that Nazis have no free speech rights—the better. And it is bad news for York and the rest of us."

For the ARA members who fought that day, this familiar liberal critique elided the participation of local York residents in the violence, who understood the threat posed by the Nazis invading their city.

"The exceptional thing about the Battle of York was not the successful physical confrontation of nazis (we've done that before), it was the active participation of large numbers of local Black, Puerto Rican and white youth (and some older folks as well)," read an editorial in the Winter–Spring 2002 issue of the *ARA Research Bulletin*, an Anti-Racist Action zine. "This is what transformed the action from a clash of politicos into an insurgent community defense."[32]

The *ARA Research Bulletin* also published internal emails obtained from the Nazis who'd invaded York showing that they—despite publicly declaring York a victory—understood in private that they had been defeated. One unnamed Nazi suggested they needed to take more "self-defense classes," buy "knife proof" gloves and mace, and learn how to properly "use a flag staff" during melees. He also suggested it was time to infiltrate the ARA. "The friggin' ARA has files on most of us," he wrote. "What do WE have? Time to start playing the game too!"

Another email showed Pastor August B. Kreis II, the Aryan Nations minister of Information & Propaganda, absolutely seething. "This is a suggestion I am making to all that attended this fiasco!" Kreis II wrote. "We can NOT allow ANYTHING like this to ever transpire again without leaving DEAD bodies of the enemy scattered EVERYWHERE! I left York a changed man no longer caring for ANYTHING non-white, they are nothing but SCUM! If our race does not wake up and fight back as a whole there will be no future for the White Race in this country or anywhere!"

In the ensuing months and years, the main Nazi groups who organized the York event fell into disarray and disbanded. Hale was arrested and sentenced to forty years in prison for soliciting the murder of a judge.[33] William Pierce, *The Turner Diaries* author and founder of the National Alliance, died of cancer.[34] Although the ARA and other anti-fascist groups weren't responsible for these developments, they felt they could take credit for destabilizing these groups to the point that they never recovered from the loss of their leaders.

And so it was that the ARA also entered a period of decline. Beyond the collapse of the fascist groups that they'd fought in the streets across America, the broader left had grown demoralized for its inability, through mass protest, to forestall the US invasions of Iraq and Afghanistan. ARA had trouble recruiting new members and getting the numbers needed to mobilize big direct actions. The authors of *We Go Where They Go*, former ARA members themselves, described other factors:[35]

> The attacks of September 11 led to a rise in Islamophobic and xenophobic racism, as well as to the normalization of a massively escalated level of government surveillance and repression, and ARA struggled to keep up. Finally, the street-level fascist organizing that ARA was best at opposing declined, shifting in part to new arenas like the internet, and the prior century's far-right movement was partially undercut and co-opted by the ultraconservative presidency of George W. Bush. ARA had notable successes even during these transformations, but it was unmistakably in decline.

Tomas, and we'll call him Tomas, was at the Battle of York. These days he lives in Argentina, where he's writing a series of memoirs about his life as an anti-fascist, which saw him punch Nazis across multiple decades, on multiple continents.[36] His family—the descendants of Jews who fled Germany "just in time" in the late 1930s—moved around a lot when he was a kid. He became a young anarchist punk in Greece, part of an anti-fascist scene at battle with the Golden Dawn, a neo-Nazi political party with roaming "attack squads" targeting foreigners. Then his family moved to Paris, where he fell in with the Red Warriors, a multiracial anti-fascist street gang fighting Nazi skinheads who were terrorizing queer people and immigrants, sometimes going *la chasse aux Beurs*, or Arab hunting. The Red Warriors trained in martial arts and "pioneered this idea of 'we're gonna go Nazi hunting,'" Tomas remembers. "Like we're not just gonna defend ourselves from them. We're gonna get in the car and we're going to go look for them whenever we can." Within five years, Tomas says, the Nazi skinheads had been pushed off the streets of Paris.

And in the early aughts Tomas moved to America, to Boston, where he joined the Northeastern Federation of Anarcho-Communists, and its offshoot, the Northeastern Antifascists—a group that frequently collaborated with ARA, as it did in York. His memories of the battle there are still vivid, including when he saw the assembled Nazis waving a German Nazi flag. Despite his years of militant anti-fascist work up to that point, Tomas had never seen fascists waving that flag, with its giant black swastika—such displays were largely banned in Europe.

He remembers standing on the street in York being flooded with memories of the stories his Jewish grandfather told him about life in 1930s Germany, about not being allowed to take the train because he wasn't "Aryan" enough; about the yellow star he and his family were forced to wear; about the time a gang of Hitler Youth brutally beat him, prompting his family to flee the place they'd called home for generations. How could Tomas not want to punch someone waving that flag now?

Although he remembers driving away from the Battle of York with his friends "feeling powerful, happy, and emboldened," Tomas has found it difficult now to write enthusiastically in his memoirs about such victories "when a lot of those same fascists and their ideas have now entered the mainstream."

In the first two decades of the twenty-first century, in all the places Tomas had battled with fascists in the streets, far-right political parties were on the rise: the Golden Dawn in Greece, the National Rally in France, and the Alternative für Deutschland (AfD) in Germany. But nothing concerned him more than what was happening in the US.

"In the decade and a half between the fascist rallies in York and Charlottesville," he wrote in his memoir, "fascists successfully regrouped and rebranded, emboldened beyond their wildest dreams by the political developments of those years—including a president who acted as their cheerleader-in-chief."

As an anarchist, Tomas believes these developments are caused by the ongoing crisis that is capitalism. Over the previous two decades the rich have gotten obscenely richer, while the poor have gotten poorer, often subjugated to lives of intense "drudgery and misery," he says. In times of such worsening economic conditions, Tomas argues, fascism can work as "a defense mechanism of capitalism," channeling anger and resentment toward immigrants, or Black people, or Muslims, or trans people, or any other marginalized group, as long as it's not the people hoarding all the wealth.

"I think the reason we as anti-fascists couldn't stop, or haven't been able to stop, this fascist wave, is that the fascist wave rides on capitalist resentment, and as capitalism today grows more unequal, more virulent, it is the breeding ground for right-wing extremism," he says.

In the Trump era, fascist groups like Patriot Front serve as the "shock troops" or "vanguard" of the capitalist classes, he says. It's what makes him so angry about liberal condemnations of punching Nazis. Working-class people are already subjected to the systemic violence of capitalism—the violence of mass incarceration, the violence of being evicted, the violence of working two jobs and still not being able to pay your bills, the violence of not being able to afford healthcare—and now you expect them to let a bunch of genocidal Nazis come into their towns and not fight them? To take it lying down?

Baked into liberal denunciations of punching Nazis was often the assumption that anti-fascist violence is anarchic, in the false and pejorative sense of the term; that the violence risks wrongly convicting its targets, without judge or jury, of being fascists. That maybe the Americans getting punched weren't *that* bad. But this missed the very real deliberations among anti-fascists about when punches should be thrown; the often-tedious discussions about who constitutes a worthy target. Tomas and ARA activists showed up to York because members of the World Church had already murdered

Black people, murdered an Asian man, shot Jews, and detonated a bomb at a gay bar. The World Church, despite proclamations to the contrary, didn't give a fuck about "free speech"—they wanted to silence non-white people *permanently*. The type of violence ARA visited upon the World Church in York was "a counterviolence," notes Natasha Lennard, the anti-fascist writer, "not an instigation of violence onto a terrain of preexisting peace."[37]

The pearl-clutching pundits denouncing Nazi-punching, in the years leading up to Vincent's infiltration of Patriot Front, always seemed blithely unaware of the constant, simmering, underground cold war between the radical left and radical right in America. They did not appreciate that a variety of tactics were typically deployed—intelligence gathering, infiltrations, pressure campaigns, doxing—before that cold war turned hot, spilling aboveground into the streets.

CHAPTER 6

I'm Gonna Be Famous, Boys

There are many ways to disable a car tire. Some like to use a knife to cut the valve stem, causing the air to hiss out of the tire until it crumples to the concrete. Others prefer to use a crowbar to separate the rubber from the rim. "The good thing about doing it that way—they think their tires are okay, and then when they start driving, it just pops," an anonymous anti-fascist we'll call Chris explained, chuckling. But on the evening of December 4, 2021, as Chris crouched down beneath a U-Haul box truck parked just by the Arlington Memorial Bridge in Arlington, Virginia, he opted for his go-to, tried-and-true technique. "My traditional thing is just to use a very sharp knife and you just drive it right into the side of the tire," he said. "With a car, it happens immediately, it's instantaneous. It cuts it like butter. But these U-Haul tires were a little tougher."

He and maybe a half dozen other anti-fascists had pretended to be taking a sunset jog near the bridge. As soon as they alighted upon the U-Hauls, they quickly got to work assaulting the three trucks. The vehicles had just carried one hundred or so Patriot Front members from a meeting point in Maryland to here, just across the Potomac from the Lincoln Memorial, in the heart of the American capital. The Patriot Front chuds had marched over the bridge into DC, but a few had stayed back to guard the U-Hauls, lurking around on the sidewalk nearby, not immediately noticing the crouching anti-fascists, who'd put masks over their faces. It was only when the anti-fascists got to work on the windshields, "redecorating" them with hammers, that the chuds took notice of the sound of shattering glass. They lunged after the anti-fascists.

But one of the anti-fascists was a big dude, and he looked ready to fight. Maybe bigger even than Frederick-OR, a two-hundred-fifty-plus-pound Patriot Front member from Oregon. He'd been among those who Vincent filmed defacing the Pride mural in Olympia. Vincent had snapped photos of him climbing up Mount Rainier, too: a flannel shirt over his husky frame and a man bun popping out the back of his baseball cap. He'd been unable to make it up to Camp Muir, growing too tired and opting to retreat down the volcano early. And now here he was in Arlington, retreating again. He didn't try to fight antifa, instead warning them that he was taking their photos and that he was going to call the cops. But antifa was already leaving.

Meanwhile, the rest of the Patriot Front members were across the bridge by now, parading through the capital. They were unaware that the U-Hauls they needed to get back to Maryland—where they could retrieve their cars, to drive to the planes that took them back to their hometowns scattered across America, where their neighbors, coworkers, and family members were none the wiser to what they were a part of—had just been attacked.

They were led by Thomas, the Patriot Front leader, who donned his signature cowboy hat and was the only one unmasked.[1] "Left! Left!" he called out like a military instructor, their boots pounding the pavement with the beat of a snare drum. Two members carried a massive banner reading VICTORY OR DEATH. And two others held red-and-blue smoke grenades, the smoke engulfing them as they moved forward. The perimeter of the procession was manned by the "Shield Guard," members carrying large shields, all wearing black shin guards over their khaki cargo pants, with white gaiter masks, sunglasses, and baseball caps obscuring their identities. Thomas had assured arriving police officers that they were unarmed, even if they looked like they were ready to go to war.

More and more police had started to follow them. Only eleven months earlier, after all, a MAGA mob had gathered near here to storm the Capitol. The Patriot Front members waved mockingly at the police helicopter circling overhead, and at the many bemused tourists looking onward, snapping photos of these masked men chanting "Reclaim America!," very few seeming to register what Patriot Front *actually was*.

Thomas led Patriot Front up the steps of the Lincoln Memorial, marching near the giant statue of the Great Emancipator. Then they marched onward until they finally reached the Capitol Reflecting Pool, not far from where, in 1925, some thirty thousand white-robed Klansmen paraded up Pennsylvania

Avenue[2] in protest of the waves of immigrants arriving from overseas, and where Thomas now launched into an anti-immigrant tirade, lamenting the "teeming refuse crowded into our cities."[3]

"Kill yourself like Adolf Hitler!" someone screamed, part of a small crowd of locals who had clearly clocked onto the nature of this group invading their city. "Follow your leader!"

Thomas tried to continue his speech but kept being drowned out by a new chant: "Shut the fuck up!" The Shield Guard started to pound their shields against the pavement. "For the life of our nation!" Thomas screamed.

"Life!" the chuds screamed in response.

"For the liberty of our people!"

"Liberty!"

"For the victory of the American spirit!"

"Victory!"

*   *   *

Meanwhile online, a video of the Patriot Front march was going viral. It had been posted by a Twitter account belonging to "Sheryl Llewellyn"—a smiling, conventionally attractive blond woman who described herself as a "digital/print journalist," a "new dog owner," and an "avocado lover," who believed in "#DCStatehood." Up until this evening "Sheryl" had tweeted only innocuous messages, like one about a bald eagle she'd spotted in her neighborhood, and another about a Thanksgiving charity event. Now she was posting a video of Patriot Front marching down the steps of the Lincoln Memorial. "HAPPENING NOW," Sheryl wrote. "About 500 men with riot shields are marching in #WashingtonDC."

The video quickly garnered over six hundred thousand views, but a coterie of disinformation experts online, academics, and other observers unaffiliated with antifa immediately noticed something fishy about Sheryl.[4] For starters, her profile photo had the hallmarks of being AI-generated. Moreover, the account had been created only a month prior—a telltale sign that it might be inauthentic. Lastly, established journalists reporting from the Patriot Front march put the group's numbers at one hundred to one hundred fifty, not five hundred. The disinformation experts were right to be suspicious: The person behind the account wasn't an attractive blond woman who loved dogs and avocados, but a burly, bearded, bespectacled six-foot-four member of Patriot Front, sitting in a pickup truck in a Maryland parking lot, a laptop propped up against the steering wheel. It was Jason-NY, one of the Patriot Front members who'd done the initial interview with Vincent. The one who thought something was *off* about Vincent, and who'd warned John, the Network 8 leader, that although Vincent had been accepted, he should "use caution."

Jason was the propagandist for this Patriot Front action. "If all goes to plan the first media reports will say that there are five hundred of us, lol,"[5] he'd told a fellow member in the lead-up to the march. Sitting here now, he was planning to also post the viral video of the march—which one of his fellow Patriot Front members had sent him from the scene—to Reddit and 4chan. A poor man's Goebbels, sitting in a pickup with a portable Wi-Fi hotspot.

He had parked his dad's gray 2013 Dodge R15 in a parking lot next to the Riverview Community Center in Fort Washington, Maryland, home to the Coalition for African Americans in the Performing Arts. Aside from executing the social media strategy for the evening, Jason was also tasked with guarding the Patriot Front vehicles parked here, including a "hate bus" that one member had purchased and remodeled to transport a dozen members from the Midwest.

Jason was scrolling with glee on Twitter, watching all the attention the Patriot Front video was receiving, when suddenly the interior of the truck went darker than before. Looking up, he noticed the windshield had been sprayed with purple paint. Then, looking out the driver's-side window, he saw a man dressed in all black attempting to open the door. There was a black object in the man's hand, which Jason suspected was a gun. He quickly put the car into drive and peeled out of the parking lot, driving with his head out the window to see the road in front of him. But a couple minutes later, Jason could hear a loud noise coming from the right-hand side of the truck: the sound of the wheels' metal rims scraping the concrete. His tires had been slashed.

He pulled over on a residential street, called 911, and waited. "I was just attacked," he wrote on RocketChat to a group of Patriot Front members. "Antifa just tried to kill me. I'm waiting for the police. I am dead serious. They destroyed my vehicle and they tried to pull my doors open. They had a firearm . . . Do you think you can swing by and just hang here? I am alone and scared . . ."[6]

*   *   *

After Jason peeled away in his busted-up pickup, black-clad anti-fascists silently scurried around the parking lot with their hammers and knives and cans of spray paint. They shattered windshields and rear windows and side windows. They spray-painted the cars and trucks purple and white. They drove knives into the sides of tire after tire.

And then they went to town on the gray Ford Econoline E450 passenger bus that was the pride and joy of Carter, the Missouri-based leader of Network 12. Carter had bought the vehicle—used previously to transport old, disabled retirees—for $2,200 at a government auction.[7] He'd spent months, and another $1,500, removing the wheelchair lift, ripping out rows of superfluous seats, fixing the interior lighting, and repainting the exterior a dark gray—ultimately transforming it into a "hate bus" that would transport thirteen young fascists from Missouri, Indiana, and Illinois to DC for the big march.

The anti-fascists shattered and painted all eight of the bus's large side windows.[8] They slashed the two front tires and broke the side door. They dumped paint on top of the bus and then finally graffitied a giant message on the side: PATRIOT FAIL. Then they drew the three-arrows symbol of the Iron Front, the Weimar, Germany, paramilitary organization formed to fight the Nazis in the 1930s, a symbol later adapted by a new generation of anti-fascists across the world.

When Patriot Front got back to the parking lot, there'd be no mistaking who had committed this act of sabotage against them.

Footage taken by an officer with the Maryland Park Police shows a Patriot Front "hate bus" severely vandalized by anti-fascists in a Maryland parking lot, on December 4, 2021.

*   *   *

Back in DC, Thomas was leading Patriot Front on a march back across the National Mall. They had an even larger police escort now, many of the officers riding silently beside them on bikes, past the World War II memorial, honoring the four hundred thousand Americans killed fighting fascist armies, and then back over the Arlington Memorial Bridge, where they found their banged-up U-Hauls.

Only one of the trucks was usable, its tires not successfully slashed, and with not enough damage to the windshield to make it undrivable. A couple dozen members squeezed into the cargo hold and began the journey back to Maryland. An irritated Thomas announced that this truck would make multiple trips to and from the "vehicle exchange." For now, the rest of Patriot Front would have to wait, stranded in the cold, surrounded by police.

But when that first contingent of Patriot Front members piled into the U-Haul, for the moment at least, they didn't seem too discouraged. As they crouched in the darkness, cruising on the beltway back to their cars, they removed their gaiter masks, and a few started to sing a verse from "By God We'll Have Our Home Again," a racist ballad set to the tune of an old English folk song[9] popularized by an online white supremacist movement called Männerbund, which is German for "alliance of men."

There's a temptation to imagine fascists as miserable, that their ideology precludes them from feelings of joy and beauty that flow from love, compassion, and solidarity—and there might be some truth to that fantasy. But there is also a joy, however fleeting or ultimately self-destructive, to collective cruelty. A camaraderie born from bloodlust. An intoxication that flows from hate. The philosopher Erich Fromm once described fascism as offering an "escape from freedom"[10]—a mythology that radically simplifies a scary, complex world into a place of absolute, unshakable certainties: one true leader, a defined set of enemies, and shared rituals in which you, *as a member of the only pure folk*, get to take part. All the Patriot Front members in the truck were singing in the dark now, a dim light from a digital camera occasionally illuminating the grins crawling across their white faces. They bellowed out the chorus—"By God we'll have our home again!"—stomping their feet on the floor of the cargo bed.

*   *   *

"Oh man, who did you piss off?"[11] Prince George's County Police Corporal Yordy Diaz asked Jason, surveying the damage to his pickup truck.

"I don't know—maybe they wanted to steal from me," Jason said, stepping out of the truck. "I don't know, dude."

"So what happened?"

Jason stammered his way through an explanation: He was doing some "work" on his computer when someone spray-painted his windshield. One of his assailants may have had a gun . . .

Diaz walked around the truck to inspect the flat tires. "You sure this wasn't your girlfriend, man?" he said, laughing.

"Hell no!" Jason replied. "Absolutely not. I don't live here. I live in New York. It wasn't my girlfriend at all."

Ten minutes earlier Jason had written in a message to Patriot Front that "antifa" was responsible for what happened to him, but talking to Corporal Diaz now, he seemed desperate to obscure the nature of the attack. His friends were simply "hiking" in Washington, DC, Jason explained, and he was just waiting for them to get back. "I don't know what they wanted," he said of his attackers.

With a little more prodding, though, a clearly flustered Jason admitted that his friends were actually "marching in DC" at a "right-wing . . . patriot protest," adding: "I didn't want to go, I'm not interested in what they're doing, really." Jason, of course, was very interested in what Patriot Front was doing. He was one of the group's most active members, responsible for interviewing new recruits, editing propaganda videos, organizing logistics for the DC march, and executing the social media strategy.

He was initially polite and cordial with Diaz, responding to questions with "yes, sir" and "no, sir" and "thank you." But in the middle of their conversation, Jason noticed that Diaz was wearing a body camera—a new requirement for Prince George's County officers implemented after a white cop fatally shot a handcuffed Black man six times. "Is this body cam running?" Jason asked.

"Yes," Diaz responded.

"Is it gonna be public?"

"This is always public information."

"Can I choose not to—" Jason pleaded.

"No, this is public information."

"Oh fuck," Jason said, putting his hands on his head in distress. "Now the people that did this are probably gonna get that footage."

"Why would they target you specifically?"

"Politics. Politics."

Diaz was confused, not understanding why this man from New York, working on a laptop in a parking lot at night, was so worried about being identified. He tried to reassure Jason. "I don't think they're smart enough to do an investigation into who you are," he said.

"You're right, well, they might be," Jason stammered. "I don't know."

"Just relax, man, calm down, man," Diaz said. "You're here. Some people disagree and they don't know how to react or express themselves, so they do this, this kinda stuff."

"Yeah," Jason said, sounding unconvinced. "Thank you, sir."

*   *   *

While Diaz talked to Jason, Prince George's County Police Officer Ryan McClain drove over to the parking lot Jason had fled. He was shocked to find about ten vehicles, all with out-of-state plates, vandalized. A white Chevy Sonic and a Jeep Grand Cherokee had all their windows smashed. A white Ford F150 had its windows smashed, too, and was covered in paint. A white Ram 1500 had flat tires. And then he saw the obliterated "hate bus."

"They spray-painted 'Patriots fan' on it,"[12] McClain told dispatch as he drove around the parking lot, misreading the PATRIOT FAIL graffiti and surmising that all this vandalism might be related to rival football fans. "The Patriots play the Buffalo Bills? Why y'all here? They're not playing in DC!"

"There's not even a game today!" dispatch responded.

"Hold on," McClain said. "There's a truck trying to pull out of here. I'm about to stop it."

McClain put on his sirens to signal for the truck to pull over. He shone his flashlight into the truck's windows, finding four squinting white men inside, all wearing khaki cargo pants and navy-blue jackets.

The men's Patriot Front names were Roger-VA, Kenneth-VA, John-VA, and Vincent-VA (not to be confused with Vincent-WA in Washington). They were all part of a network from Virginia who'd wanted to join the march in DC but through a seeming series of mishaps had missed linking up with their friends at the vehicle exchange. Roger—who had once told his fellow Patriot Front members to "never let the 'minorities' take our history or culture,"[13] and who had a fondness for stealing Black Lives Matter signs from people's yards—handed over his driver's license to McClain, who was Black. Of the four men, Roger was the only one who had his ID on him. The other three had followed instructions from Patriot Front leadership to leave "any ID behind" during missions "so the only way you get doxed is if you tell someone yourself."

Five other police officers arrived, including Diaz. Only one of them was white and the rest Black or Latino. Their body cameras were rolling as they circled the truck, asking each white man to step out and put their hands on the vehicle so that they could be patted down for weapons. Then the officers asked each of them to give their name, age, address, and date of birth. They all obliged.

Vincent-VA identified himself as being from Newport and said he was twenty-one years old. When one of the officers quipped that he "looked like he was fourteen," Vincent replied that he was "very Irish" and had "good genes."

Kenneth—who'd recently been accused of vandalizing and destroying a mural in Richmond, Virginia, honoring Black tennis legend Arthur Ashe[14]— identified himself as being twenty-four years old, and from a town called Wake. When one of the officers asked if he had ever been to the DC area before, Kenneth replied that his family had season tickets to Washington games. "What sport?" the officer asked. "Football, the Washington football team," Kenneth responded, adding: "You can't say Redskins no more."

And John—who a couple weeks prior had glued a giant Patriot Front poster to a utility box featuring an outline of the continental US with the words "Not Stolen Conquered"—identified himself as being twenty-one years old, from Newport News.

All four of them sat in the bed of the pickup truck now, with Roger doing most of the talking, giving vague and evasive and trollish answers to the cops' questions about what they had been doing in the parking lot. "Just hanging out," he said. What was up with the riot shield in the back seat? "Just extra stuff for my buddy." Why were they all wearing the same outfits? "We all got different pants on." (They were all wearing slightly different khaki cargo pants.) By now the officers had heard about the Patriot Front march in DC. Were they part of that protest? "I don't even know what protest you're talking about."

When officers Douglas McMillan and Antonio Frias briefly walked back to the squad car to retrieve something, McMillan quipped that he needed to "make sure they're not the Antichrist or something . . . or a Grand Wizard." Frias pulled out his phone and googled Patriot Front. "They're a 'hate nationalist' group," he informed the other officers.

Still, Diaz tried to lighten the mood, complimenting the men's navy-blue jackets. "That's the same jacket we have, basically," Diaz said, laughing, fist-bumping Roger. At another point he and Roger talked about motorcycles.

But Roger was still indignant at the treatment he and his friends were receiving. Why had they been pulled over? Patted down?

The cops had pulled them over because, ironically, they thought they might have been responsible for the vandalism. They were coming to the realization now that this wasn't the case. Before letting these white men go, however, they put in a call to the US Department of Homeland Security to see if they had any reason to further detain these members of a "hate nationalist" group. No, Homeland Security said, let them go.

But before that, Diaz wanted to let these white guys know something. "For your information," he said, pointing at his body camera, "everything is being recorded, visually and audio, everything you're seeing, it's all recorded, just to let y'all know."

A shit-eating grin crawled across Roger's face, just beneath his mustache, as he quickly realized, and then accepted, that his life was about to irrevocably change.

"Oh, yeah!" he said. "I'm gonna be famous, boys!"

*   *   *

As the last contingent of Patriot Front members returned to the Maryland parking lot, surveying the damage to their cars and figuring out how they were going to get home, their anti-fascist saboteurs gathered at a restaurant in DC to celebrate.

"We were happy as fuck," Chris recalls. "They were all people I'd never met but have chatted with for years." The best part of it all was watching the reaction online, seeing Patriot Front get "clowned on," Chris said, adding:

"A lot of what we try to do is make it not look so cool to join a Nazi crew, you know—embarrassing them and making things difficult. So in that sense, it was quite a success."

A *Daily Beast* article was representative of the mocking coverage the rally received. "White Supremacists Hold Bizarro Rally in D.C., Find Themselves Stranded," read the headline of an article describing the group as the "Khaki-Clad Klan." It noted: "Though they intended to 'reclaim America,' members of Patriot Front had enough trouble reclaiming their own ride." (The articles were largely unaware that it was anti-fascists who disabled the U-Hauls.)

As Chris and his anti-fascist friends ate and drank in DC, their comrades on the West Coast were preparing to publish a series of doxes. In the previous weeks, Vincent had started to share the intelligence he'd gathered—during his *five months* inside Patriot Front—with various anti-fascist researchers. These activists had pored over the intel for clues, reading screenshots of RocketChat messages, examining photos and videos, and listening to secretly recorded audio. When they were certain they'd uncovered a Patriot Front member's real identity, they drafted detailed articles laying out the evidence. The doxes would name and shame each neo-Nazi, sometimes listing their address and place of work.

This initial round of unmasking would not include the Patriot Front members captured on police body camera footage in the Maryland parking lot—those doxes would come later. These doxes would include the identities of Patriot Front members Vincent had met in Network 8, along with doxes of men from other West Coast networks he met on missions or excursions, like the hikes up Mount Rainier and White Mountain.

The anti-fascist network started to publish these doxes in the days and weeks after the march in DC. Article after article started to appear online, authored by anonymous members of Rose City Antifa, Northern California Anti-Racist Action, Corvallis Against Fascism, Pacific Antifascist Research Collective . . .

Tyler, the Network 8 member, was among the first to be doxed. Vincent published Tyler's real name on a website he created called Washington Nazi Watch. The dox included the photo Vincent had covertly taken of Tyler sitting beneath the Nazi flag in his apartment, showing off his "ghost gun." Seattle anti-fascists started posting flyers all over Tyler's apartment building, and throughout his neighborhood, warning his neighbors that they had an armed neo-Nazi as a neighbor. Tyler decided to flee Seattle. He didn't feel safe in the city. John, the Network 8 director, went over to help him pack.

John was despondent. "Avis rang my card for $1975.54," he wrote in a message to Thomas, referring to the rental car he'd used for the DC march, which had been badly vandalized. "I currently have $200 to my name." (He wasn't alone. Multiple members had incurred thousands of dollars in damages.)

But what really ate at John was the creeping realization that Vincent—whom he had trusted with so much—had been an anti-fascist spy all along. Vincent had been incommunicado since bailing on the trip to DC. And the doxes being published across the country proved he was the infiltrator. That photo of Tyler with the ghost gun? Only Vincent could've taken that.

"I just had the worst infiltrator the org has ever seen,"[15] John wrote in another message to Thomas.

"I am aware that you did," Thomas wrote back. "Your personal conduct and degree of culpability, if any, will be reviewed once other matters are out of the way."

John started coordinating with other members to figure out who the hell Vincent was. To get revenge. But for the time being, Vincent was a ghost. Patriot Front members, as pissed off as they were, couldn't help but respect him. "I have to say, I'm impressed," one member wrote. "This guy was very good at his job," another commented.

John braced himself. He knew he was going to be doxed, and he suspected just about every member of Network 8 was going to be unmasked, too. Anti-fascists in Washington had posted a tweet teasing a forthcoming dox of Clark—the member who'd orchestrated destroying the Pride mural in Olympia. "Antifa's tweet about him scared him into quitting,"[16] John wrote in a message to David, his most loyal subordinate. "He told his parents of his involvement in the org. They scared him into quitting. Convinced him they're all going to lose their livelihood if he gets doxed."

"I am going to get doxed I know it," David wrote.

"You're fine," John told David.

"NO I AM NOT," he wrote back.

At another point David asked John whether Patriot Front's RocketChat server had been hacked.

"There wasn't any way he hacked the server," John said. "That was confirmed with the tech team. Which . . . is a relief."

"You can say that again."

"They were up all night digging through coding and stuff . . . I think if he had access to private DMs we'd see wayyyyyy more doxxes."

*   *   *

Vincent no longer had access to RocketChat—Patriot Front leadership had made sure of that after DC—but on December 10, 2021, Vincent wondered whether they'd also revoked his access to the group's server on Mumble, the voice chat app they used for meetings. Vincent was delighted to find he could still log in, and that he'd be able to join a national conference call happening that day: Thomas was going to have one of his debriefs about the march in DC.

There were 135 members on the call, and no one seemed to noticed Vincent was among them. He listened as Thomas proclaimed the march in DC a triumph, no matter the bad coverage in the press, news articles he called "coded in the bile of slander."[17] Thomas talked only obliquely of the group's anti-fascist saboteurs. "Our opposition decided to find further overt, nefarious, slithering, slimy means to impair us," he said. "And we have discovered their methods and countered them!" The group would be taking increased security measures from here on out, Thomas declared, including a more thorough vetting process for new members. He also seemed to address concerns that Vincent may have hacked the RocketChat server. "There were some recent information risks that we saw, and they have all been quashed fully and absolutely," Thomas assured everyone.

During a brief pause in the conference call, when Thomas and his lieutenants were sorting out some technical issues with Mumble, a few members unmuted themselves to yell "N***er!," eliciting chuckles from the rank and file. "This is not the time for your jokes!" Thomas barked.

Vincent kept himself on mute, listening to Thomas while searching YouTube for a song he liked, queuing it up on his computer for when the time felt right. Eventually Thomas left the call, allowing members to chat more informally. But after an hour of eavesdropping, Vincent decided he'd had enough. He didn't want to hear these guys *talk* anymore. He felt the same exasperation and unpleasantness he'd experienced climbing up the volcano, when he had to pretend to like these guys, to be their friend. Now he didn't have to pretend anymore—he could make his real self known. He wanted to say a little hello, for fun.

Vincent unmuted himself, immediately breaking into a fit of laughter. "You guys really forgot to remove the antifa spy's access to Mumble?" There was a stunned silence on the call that was music to Vincent's ears. Then Samuel-VA, the network director in Virginia, tried to take charge, ordering everyone to log off. Vincent immediately called Samuel-VA by his *real name*, a not-so-subtle way of telling him: *Your dox is coming soon*. Other members tried to talk shit with Vincent before he interrupted. "I think I'm just gonna play some music," he said, pressing play on the YouTube video—a song that felt fitting for the occasion.

"Bella Ciao," meaning "goodbye, beautiful," was adapted as an anti-fascist song in Italy in the 1940s,[18] its lyrics telling the story of a young man leaving his girlfriend to fight in the Italian resistance against Mussolini's Blackshirts. "If I die as a partisan," the man sings, "you must bury me / up in the mountain / under the shade of a beautiful flower / and all those who will pass by / will say 'What a beautiful flower / This is the flower of the partisan / who died for freedom.'"

In the ensuing decades, the song became an international anti-fascist anthem, sung by leftists in Brazil, Colombia, Spain, and Turkey. Now Vincent was playing it here, on this Mumble call, to taunt a new generation of fascists in America.

"Everyone log off right now!" Samuel yelled. There had been some fraught moments during Vincent's time in Patriot Front, when he feared his double life would all be for naught. That the hate incidents he found himself party to, the ugly conversations he endured, the very real danger he put himself in, might ultimately have little impact. But when he heard the panic and desperation in Samuel's voice now, any lingering anxiety Vincent had evaporated. He felt the relief of accomplishment. "Everyone log off right now!" Samuel screamed again. ·

In the following, waning weeks of 2021, Vincent had some time to relax and to take a breath. He'd essentially been working an unpaid second job for months. And he had the ephemera to prove it. His closet was stuffed with all the Patriot Front materials he'd pilfered: multiple, giant RECLAIM AMERICA banners, riot shields, posters, pamphlets, stencils . . .

He had an idea. That New Year's Eve, Vincent drove to a house party outside Seattle. His friends helped him unload, carrying everything to the woods out back. Finding a small clearing beneath tall pine trees, they built a pyre out of the Patriot Front plunder on top of a light dusting of snow.

Vincent got a little carried away with the lighter fluid. The fire burned fast and tall—taller even than Vincent. He circled the towering flames with his Fujifilm XT3, fastened to a camera stabilizer strapped to his body, just like he'd done at that Patriot Front bonfire on the volcano, to make the footage look extra professional and smooth. Eventually, after the fire had nothing left to burn, Vincent celebrated the New Year with his friends.

In the first few days of 2022, Vincent started editing the footage into a two-minute clip, which he then posted to Twitter from his *Washington Nazi Watch* account, knowing that Patriot Front would see it. The video was set to a beautiful, old, melancholic version of "Auld Lang Syne."

Should old acquaintance be forgot
And never brought to mind?

The Patriot Front banners—which had hung from so many highway overpasses—now blackened and scorched. One of Tyler's 3D-printed stencils, like the one they used to scrawl "Reclaim America" across the Pride mural in Olympia, melted and wilted into pieces, the heat from the fire creating little puddles in the surrounding snow.

Flames singed the corners of a Patriot Front pamphlet called ACTIVISM CHANGES PERCEPTION OF POPULAR BELIEF, in which Thomas had written, "The acceptance of our propaganda in the visible landscape . . . is the first stepping stone toward the eventual acceptance that our ideals are a legitimate facet of political thought . . ." The way the fire burned had the strange effect of turning the pamphlet from page to page, as if the fire itself wanted to read each word before devouring it.

There had been a couple of items Vincent had wanted for this bonfire but failed to get. His prized target had been Thomas's signature cowboy hat, the one he wore at all the demonstrations. The opportunity to steal the hat never came—Vincent never had the displeasure of meeting Thomas in person. Watching the video now, though, seeing it shared widely online and boosted by anti-fascists accounts across America, it was reward enough to imagine Thomas watching it, too, from behind his computer down in Texas. He imagined Thomas seething by the end of the video, watching as the flames burned low to the ground now, the pyre of his proud Patriot Front propaganda reduced to a tiny black mound of debris.

Should old acquaintance be forgot
For the sake of auld lang syne?

When Thomas and Patriot Front saw this bonfire online, they likely thought this was the end of it. Vincent's big, final "fuck you." But their anti-fascist tormentor had one more surprise. Despite Thomas's assurances to the group that Vincent hadn't compromised the RocketChat server, some of Vincent's anti-fascist friends had, in fact, successfully hacked it, quietly downloading 440 gigabytes worth of Patriot Front's posts, direct messages, photos, and videos.

That quantity—440 gigabytes—was the equivalent amount of data that would be contained in over twenty-one thousand e-books, or thirty-eight hours of video, or fifty-five thousand high-resolution images. And in just a few days, it all would be posted in a giant public database online. Open-source material for hundreds of American anti-fascists to mine, to unmask the secret neo-Nazis in their hometowns.

The hunt had just begun.

PART II
THE DOX

CHAPTER 7
A Brief History of Unmasking

The history of white supremacy in America is marked, in part, by periods when its most ardent practitioners wore masks, and periods when they didn't need to.

The Ku Klux Klan was born in 1866,[1] about a year after the end of the Civil War, when six ex-Confederate soldiers met in a law office in Pulaski, Tennessee, to form a new secret society. It was a fraught moment. Although slavery had been abolished by Abraham Lincoln's Emancipation Proclamation, Southern state legislatures had enacted a series of "Black codes"[2] after the war that threatened to keep Black people so disenfranchised as to render them slaves by another name. This infuriated Northerners who had just won a decisive and costly victory against the Confederacy and its chattel slave economy. In response, when Congress reconvened in December, Northern US senators and representatives refused to seat their counterparts from the South. This set the stage for Reconstruction, when the US military dissolved Southern state legislatures and carved up the South into military districts where handpicked governors were tasked with registering Black voters, protecting them from vigilante violence, and forcing states to hold new constitutional conventions that would guarantee equal governance.

As distraught as the six ex-Confederate soldiers in Pulaski were about these nascent developments, they were also young men looking for camaraderie and a good time—a good time, that is, that often manifested in ghoulish "pranks" targeting freed Black people. As the Southern Poverty Law Center describes in its history of the group:[3]

> *Much of the Klan's early reputation may have been based on almost frivolous mischief and tomfoolery. At first, a favorite Klan tactic had been for a white-sheeted Klansman wearing a ghoulish mask to ride up to a black family's home at night and demand water. When the well bucket was offered, the Klansman would gulp it down and demand more, having actually poured the water through a rubber tube that flowed into a leather bottle concealed beneath his robe. After draining several buckets, the rider would exclaim that he had not had a drink since he died on the battlefield at Shiloh. He then galloped into the night, leaving the impression that ghosts of confederate dead were riding the countryside.*

Before long, armed white men across the South had heard of this new secret society from Pulaski and decided to form their own chapters of the Ku Klux Klan. But the group's "pranks" quickly turned into rampant mutilations, floggings, lynchings, and shootings targeting freed Black people, a campaign of terror to cement white supremacy as the law of the land. Their costumes typically weren't the white sheets we associate with the group today, with Klan victims later recalling their torturers donning animal horns, fake facial hair, women's gowns, or the type of Venetian masks that might be worn at a fancy masquerade or Mardi Gras. Sometimes the Klansmen even wore blackface.

These costumes, beyond a means of inflicting horror on the Klan's victims, also served to protect Klansmen's identity, which became a paramount concern as Congress and the Reconstructionist government sought to crush the group—a task only achievable if it could figure out who the Klansmen were. These efforts to unmask the secret society were sometimes met with extreme violence. From the SPLC:[4]

> *When Tennessee Governor William G. Brownlow attempted to plant spies within the Klan, he found the organization knew as much about his efforts as he did. One Brownlow spy who tried to join the Klan was found strung up in a tree, his feet just barely touching the ground. Later another spy was stripped and mutilated, and a third was stuffed in a barrel in Nashville and rolled down a wharf and into the Cumberland River, where he drowned.*

In 1871, Congress passed the Ku Klux Klan Act,[5] which President Ulysses S. Grant signed into law, giving the Justice Department sweeping powers to target and prosecute the group. Hundreds of Klansmen were eventually unmasked and arrested, which contributed to the Klan entering a period of decline, but in the ensuing years white vigilante violence continued apace, committed by new groups—like the White League and the Red Shirts[6]—who didn't feel the need to hide behind masks, their own campaigns of terror enjoying more widespread support among white Southerners. By the contested presidential election of 1876, when Southern Democrats, in exchange for giving the White House to Republican Rutherford B. Hayes, secured the withdrawal of all federal troops from the former Confederacy, Reconstruction was overthrown and abandoned,[7] ushering in an official government of segregation and apartheid in the South, commonly called Jim Crow. The Klansmen of a few years prior no longer needed their grotesque costumes, exchanging the anonymity of the mask for the anonymity of the lynch mob.

We know of the horror of the ensuing decades in large part through the work of Black investigative journalists like Ida B. Wells, who dedicated herself to documenting, in pamphlets like *Southern Horrors: Lynch Law in All Its Phases*[8] and *The Red Record*,[9] the lynchings of some ten thousand Black Americans from 1864 to 1894 (work that led *The New York Times* to label her "a slanderous and nasty-minded mulattress"[10]). Through painstaking reporting and analysis, Wells determined that the common pretexts for the murders—the "thread-bare lie" of Black men systematically raping white women, among other imagined crimes[11]—were a ruse to violently enforce a system of racial capitalism, forestalling any Black economic progress. (Wells was inspired to do this work after her friend, a Black man who opened a grocery store in Memphis, was murdered by a mob led by a white grocer, who was angry over the competition.)

Whereas the Klan often carried out their lynchings behind masks, under the cover of night, the lynchings of this period occurred in the daylight, and were often spectator events. Though the term "lynching" is commonly associated today with hanging, lynchings often involved even more elaborate forms of torture and cruelty. "Starting in the 1880s, spectacle lynchings attracted crowds of up to 15,000 white participant-witnesses, who booked special excursion trains to reach lynching sites," the writer Alison Kinney notes in her essay "How the Klan Got Its Hood."[12] "They snatched victims' clothing, bone fragments, and organs as souvenirs; they photographed themselves, smiling, posing with their kids beside the broken, burned bodies of their victims; they scrapbooked the photos and mailed them as postcards, confident that they'd never be held accountable for their terrorism. They didn't wear hoods, because they didn't need to."

Lynchings continued through the first two decades of the twentieth century, often with support from prominent politicians—"If it is necessary every Negro in the state will be lynched; it will be done to maintain white supremacy,"[13] Mississippi governor James K. Vardaman said in 1907—as Black journalists took on the task of stripping the lynch mobs of their anonymity, not only identifying individual executioners but documenting the white community's collective cruelty and impunity, in hopes of galvanizing support for anti-lynching laws.

In 1918 Walter White, then an assistant secretary for the National Association for the Advancement of Colored People (NAACP), went to Valdosta, Georgia, to investigate the murder of Mary Turner, a pregnant Black woman who had dared protest the lynching of her husband. As punishment, Turner and her unborn child were lynched themselves. White was light-skinned and could "pass" as white,[14] allowing him to pry local white witnesses for details of the grisly execution. He later recounted one such conversation, with a local merchant, in *The American Mercury*:[15]

> *Little by little he revealed the whole story. When he told of the manner in which the pregnant woman had been killed he chuckled and slapped his thigh and declared it to be "the best show, Mister, I ever did see. You ought to have heard the wench howl when we strung her up." Covering the nausea the story caused me as best I could, I slowly gained the whole story, with the names of the other participants. Among them were prosperous farmers, business men, bankers, newspaper reporters and editors, and several law-enforcement officers.*

Fearing for his own life after white locals became suspicious of the questions he was asking around town, White left Valdosta and filed a blood-curdling dispatch about Turner's murder for *The Crisis*, the NAACP's magazine dedicated to documenting the horrors of race hatred in the South.

A particular passage—fair warning—is arguably one of the most disturbing pieces of writing in American history:[16]

> *At the time she was lynched, Mary Turner was in her eighth month of pregnancy. The delicate state of her health, one month or less previous to delivery, may be imagined, but this fact had no effect on the tender feelings of the mob. Her ankles were tied together and she was hung to the tree, head downward. Gasoline and oil from the automobiles were thrown on her clothing and while she writhed in agony and the mob howled in glee, a match was applied and her clothes burned from her person. When this had been done and while she was yet alive, a knife, evidently one such as is used in splitting hogs, was taken and the woman's abdomen was cut open, the unborn babe falling from her womb to the ground. The infant, prematurely born, gave two feeble cries and then its head was crushed by a member of the mob with his heel. Hundreds of bullets were then fired into the body of the woman, now mercifully dead, and the work was over.*

Though a local jury ruled Turner and her child had "died at the hands of parties unknown"—a cruel refrain of Southern injustice at the time—White had managed to identify some of the executioners, handing over a list of names to the governor of Georgia. Still, no member of the mob was ever arrested or prosecuted. (In 2010, a historical marker memorializing Turner and her child was installed near the site of the lynching by a group called the Mary Turner Project. In the following ten years, the marker was riddled with twenty-seven bullet holes, put there by unknown shooters, and was struck on multiple occasions by an "off-road vehicle,"[17] prompting the Mary Turner Project, in 2020, to announce the marker's removal. According to press reports, it was "unclear" if authorities were investigating the vandalism.)

As White and the NAACP agitated for anti-lynching laws, their pleas and demands often ignored, a new hooded order was forming across the land. In 1921, a factory opened in Atlanta's industrial district. A photo shows a group of garment workers surrounded by white fabric piled around sewing machines, which they were using to transform the cloth into flowing robes with long sleeves, as well as conical hoods with slits through which a man's eyes could peer. The Gate City Manufacturing Company, boasting dozens of employees, had opened.[18] Its task: mass-producing anonymity for a new Ku Klux Klan.

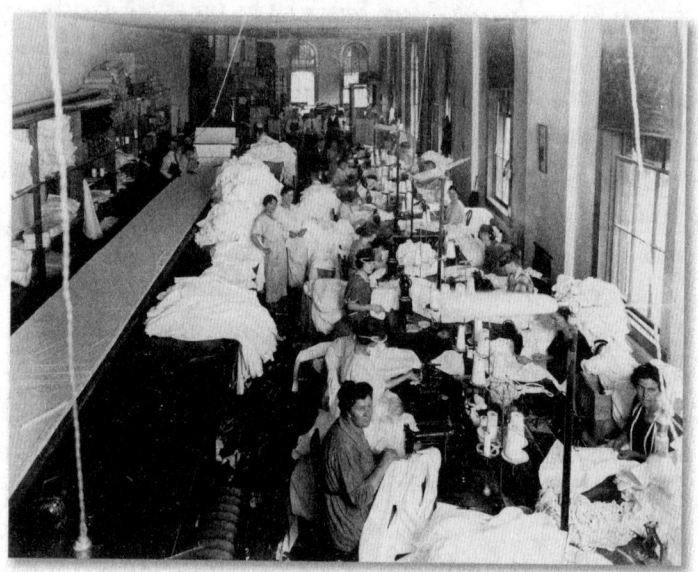

Textile workers making robes and hoods for the Ku Klux Klan at the Gate City Manufacturing Company in Atlanta, Georgia, circa 1921.

Six years prior, the filmmaker D. W. Griffith had released *The Birth of a Nation*, based on a popular historical fiction novel titled *The Clansman*. Like its source text, *The Birth of a Nation* valorized the post–Civil War and Reconstruction-era Klan as saviors of the South.[19] The sheer scale of the film's production enhanced the wildly racist "Lost Cause" mythology at the heart of its narrative: that the Confederacy had been a noble endeavor, and that the hooded nightriders who terrorized Black people after the war were the South's protectors, especially from Black men preying on and raping white women. (The film took other historical licenses, showing Griffith's white-hooded heroes lynching a Black man beneath a burning cross—even though the fiery crucifix, in the late nineteenth century, was not yet a feature of Klan terror.[20])

The film was a blockbuster, earning the modern equivalent of $1.8 billion at the box office.[21] President Woodrow Wilson, a fan of the Klan, screened *The Birth of a Nation* at the White House, with the president reportedly—and perhaps apocryphally—offering this review: "It is like writing history with lightning. And my only regret is that it is all so terribly true."

While the film shows the Klan in various outfits, many of the Klansmen depicted wore white robes and white hoods. So, when William Simmons, a Georgia Protestant minister and a serial joiner of secretive fraternal groups, resurrected the Klan on the coattails of *The Birth of a Nation*'s success, he selected the outfit as the group's official uniform. The group had only a few thousand members in its first few years, but its ranks swelled in 1920 when Simmons hired two publicity agents, Edward Young Clarke and Elizabeth Tyler, who saw an opportunity in exploiting the grievances of white protestants, especially those who were upset over the millions of immigrants flocking to America's shores at the time. They sent Klan field organizers to travel the nation "with instructions to play upon whatever prejudices—anti-Catholicism, anti-Semitism, racism, or moral zealotry—were most acute," the historian Charles Alexander notes.[22]

In just over a year, the Second Ku Klux Klan had upward of one hundred thousand members, with its membership not limited to the South, but spreading across the Northeast and Midwest and West, with Klan cross-burnings, Klan parades, and Klan carnivals becoming a feature of Americana. While the robes and hoods of these new Klansmen were still used during vigilante violence, the costumes also provided something else: status. "Hiding identity through this costume expressed, physically and metaphorically, the secrecy that furthered the Klan's magnetism and prestige," the historian Linda Gordon writes.[23] "To be entrusted with a secret is to receive a gift of high value, and the secret then represents that trust and requires that it not be violated . . ."

Simmons, Clarke, and Tyler were raking in a fortune through initiation fees and the sale of robes, prompting them to open the Atlanta factory and to publish a mail-order *Catalog of Official Robes and Banners*,[24] which featured costumes for various ranks of Klansmen: a green robe with a silk cord and tassels for an Imperial Representative, a yellow robe for a Grand Dragon, and a white robe with red tassels for the Special Terror.

The Klan, for all its noxious ideas, was also in many ways a grift, or what we might recognize today as a multilevel marketing scheme, albeit one finding a home in America's major political parties. As its ranks continued to swell into the millions, Gordon writes, "sixteen senators, scores of congressmen (the Klan claimed 75) and eleven governors"[25] were Klansmen. In some parts of the country, like in Oregon, the Klan mounted complete takeovers of state and local governments. In Houston, the Klan's membership "represented literally a glossary" of the city's "who's who," a local journalist observed, including "silk-stocking men from banks, business houses, and professions."[26] In these positions of power, the men of the Second Klan were poised to make a raft of ethnonationalist proposals a reality, crafting eugenics-based laws that would require forced sterilization and drafting immigration restrictions that would close off America to much of the world.

But despite the Klan's climb to power, the hooded order was also often met with fierce militant resistance—especially in places with large Black, Jewish, immigrant, and Catholic populations. The resistance effort manifested itself in campaigns to literally and figuratively rip off Klansmen's hoods. And perhaps no saga better demonstrates the effectiveness of this unmasking than the story of the Ku Klux Klan in Buffalo, New York.

*   *   *

On the evening of March 5, 1922, a caravan of automobiles arrived at a field a few miles north of Buffalo. "The cars, 297 in all, eventually formed a huge circle that was brilliantly illuminated by the vehicles' headlights," historian Shawn Lay writes in *Hooded Knights on the Niagara*.[27] "The occupants of the automobiles, forty masked Klansmen in full regalia and approximately eight hundred candidates in civilian attire, stepped out and gathered around a large pulpit in the center of the circle. Suddenly, a forty-foot-high cross burst into flame just beyond the ceremonial ring, its light eerily playing off the gaunt trees that surrounded the assemblage."

The cross continued to burn as eight hundred candidates took their oaths and pledged their undying loyalty to the Invisible Empire. At the ceremony's conclusion, the Klansmen got back into their cars as the burning cross collapsed, smoldering on the ground. They drove under the cover of darkness back to their homes, where their neighbors were none the wiser to what they were a part of.

"The majority of the city's residents had no realization that the Klan had been so completely organized," the *Buffalo Courier* reported. "The secrecy shrouding every movement and meeting of the KKK was complete.... An appeal to the common sense of men ought to be all that is necessary to break up the order, but this appeal has been made time and again, in many parts of the country... and yet this Klan that works at night still grows!"

The cross burnings—a distinct feature of the Second Ku Klux Klan, a ritual borrowed from the lynching scene in *The Birth of a Nation*—continued in Buffalo, often as a means of intimidating Black residents, as well as recent immigrants from Poland, Ireland, and Italy. The Klan grew its membership from Buffalo's white Protestant community, which at the time harbored extreme bigotry toward this wave of largely Catholic immigrants. They accused Catholics of a dual loyalty, charging that they were more loyal to the pope than to America. They also smeared their new Catholic neighbors as malcontents, belonging to "alien" cultures steeped in all manners of sin, crime, and vice, indulging in alcohol in defiance of Prohibition. As ever, this bigotry often belied a material fear: that these new Catholic arrivals would steal jobs or start businesses that would compete with Protestant-run enterprises.

As the Klan began to operate from a secret headquarters downtown, a coalition was forming to destroy the group.[28] A small group of Buffalonians formed the Knights of the Invisible Jungle of the Tiger's Eye, a secret club promising to "drag the Klan from its hidden realm." Another group called the Liberty League organized lectures about the horrid history of the white supremacist group, depicting its modern incarnation as a cynical money-making scheme. Black churches in Buffalo were getting organized, too, with one reverend pledging to "resist the invasion of these lawless individuals who preserve a mask of what they term righteousness while committing lawless acts." A local Black newspaperman warned: "With the Northern Negro, it will be 'an eye for an eye, and a tooth for a tooth' with this Klan.'"

This budding coalition found an ally in Buffalo mayor Frank X. Schwab, a brewery owner and the son of German Catholic immigrants. Schwab detested the Klan and, before long, got to work developing informants and spies within the group.

In the spring of 1924, tensions in the city culminated with a bombing.[29] The home of Reverend Littleton E. H. Smith, a suspected Klansman, was blown to bits. Neither Smith nor his family were home at the time, and the culprits were never identified, but the attack signified the lengths to which the Klan's opponents were now willing to go. Then, on July 3, 1924, the Klan's secret headquarters downtown was ransacked, the list of its 18,500 members stolen. That list ended up in the hands of Mayor Schwab. After some deft denials of any involvement in the burglary, or knowledge of who committed the crime, Schwab announced that the full Ku Klux Klan membership list would be on display at the police department headquarters. The public, Lay recounts in *Hooded Knights on the Niagara*, turned out in droves:[30]

> *On August 6, seventy-five residents came to police headquarters to view the document, taking turns carefully reading through the names as armed guards stood nearby. "I always suspected that bird," commented one visitor. "See that fellow there—well, he lives next door to me, can you beat it," another exclaimed. Two days later, the number of visitors had increased to three hundred; viewing was now done by groups, and an additional copy of the list was put on display. Police soon had to extend visiting hours and make a third copy available, a spokesman acknowledging that the department was not prepared for such an influx. On August 13, when the ranks of the curious swelled to more than three thousand, officers transferred the copies of the roster to a more spacious location. . . . As those in the crowd read through the lists, there were numerous "outbursts of anger, displays of bitterness and exclamations of astonishment"; many residents jotted down names from the document, particularly those of tradespeople and neighbors.*

Among those on the list were doctors, ministers, police officers, lawyers, engineers, accountants, bank tellers, and a state assemblyman—a "remarkably high-status" group, Lay observes, which made sense considering that the Klan limited its membership to white Protestants, a distinctly advantaged and privileged demographic. The most overrepresented occupation among Klan members was of small business owners, throwing into relief how the organization was, in many ways, a paramilitary arm of the white petite bourgeoisie, formed to protect its class interests from what it perceived as foreign interlopers.

The fallout from the mass unmasking in Buffalo, as Lay documents, was swift and severe.[31] Only three days after the membership list was posted in public, a Klansman named Henry Lyons, who worked as an engineer at Buffalo General Electric, was so humiliated that he took a revolver and killed his family, before turning the gun on himself. These deaths did not inspire hesitation among the Klan's opponents, who started a shaming campaign, vandalizing Klan-owned businesses with messages instructing "Catholics, Jews, and Negroes" to take their money elsewhere. A slew of Klansmen's homes were graffitied with the letters "K.K.K." There were reports of a

Klansman milkman losing over one hundred customers and Klan insurance agents and stockbrokers losing a large share of their incomes. And there were other reports of Klansmen turning up to their places of employment only to learn they'd been let go.

For all the Buffalo Klan's Protestant-inflected talk of moral virtue and righteousness, its sermonizing against drinking and houses of ill repute, and its demands for "law and order," the group's unmasking quickly revealed many Klansmen to be hypocrites of the highest order.[32] One Klansman was found to be illegally selling rubber condoms. Another was charged with failing to provide financial support to his estranged wife. Another was convicted of statutory rape for sleeping with a seventeen-year-old girl. And one night, a police officer found Reverend Charles Penfold—a prominent Protestant minister who'd been among at least eleven men of the cloth exposed as Klansmen—in a compromising position with a woman in the back seat of his car. Charged with "outraging public decency," Penfold insisted before a judge that the woman was his wife, but it quickly became clear that she was his mistress, moreover a member of his church's choir. He ended up serving time in jail for perjury. Upon his release, Lay writes, Penfold's reputation had been destroyed and he seemed a "broken man."

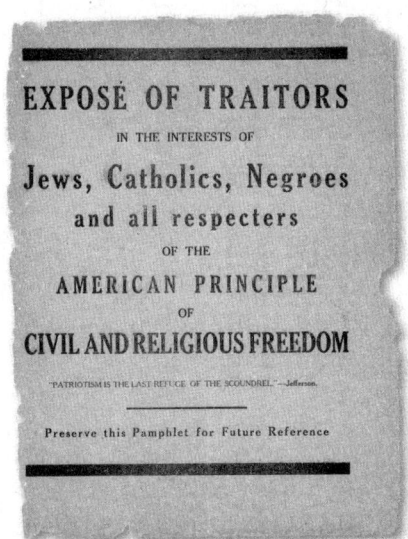
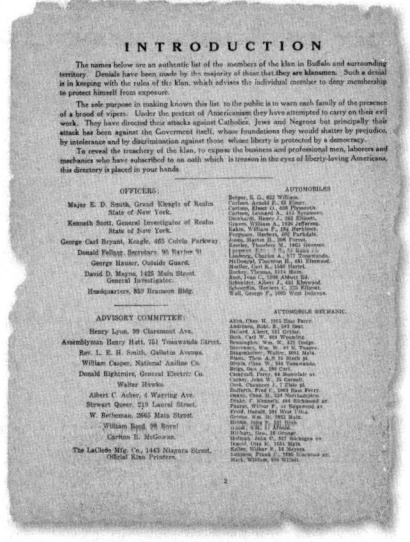

The cover of a pamphlet listing Ku Klux Klan members in Buffalo and the surrounding areas, compiled and published by local opponents to the Klan in 1924–25.

Meanwhile at the Klan's Imperial headquarters in Atlanta, concern was growing over the unmasking of the Buffalo chapter, prompting leadership to dispatch a special investigator to the city. Thomas Austin arrived in Buffalo and quickly ascertained the identity of one of the men who had infiltrated the Klan: Edward Obertean, a former police officer who presented himself as a good Baptist. Obertean was, in fact, a Catholic. And he wasn't a former police officer, but very much an active-duty one, working as an undercover officer for Mayor Schwab. One day Austin and a group of other Klansmen trailed Obertean in his car. A confrontation ensued, with Obertean opening fire first, striking two Klansmen with nonfatal shots. Austin then opened fire, hitting Obertean four times.

Obertean, as he lay bleeding, still managed to get off two more rounds, both hitting Austin directly in the heart. The Klansman and the pretend-Klansman both perished. (The Buffalo History Museum has written that Obertean "is long overdue for recognition as Buffalo's sole martyr in the battle against the Klan."[33])

In the ensuing months, the Buffalo Klan fell into disarray, with pressure growing for the state to prosecute the group over violating the Walker Law, a statute developed to target the Klan by requiring registered nonprofits to publicly disclose their memberships—something the group had refused to do. "From September 1924 on, the order greatly reduced its activities within the city limits; there were no more cross-burnings, anonymous messages were no longer promulgated, and the campaign for improved moral conditions gradually faded away," Lay writes. "The klavern continued to hold secret lodge meetings but increasingly these were exclusively social occasions. By late 1924, the Buffalo Klan had been largely neutralized, permanently removed as a serious factor in the community's political life."

By 1925, Lay adds, the "Buffalo Klan had quietly died."[34]

Throughout the mid- and late 1920s, the national Klan also entered a period of decline. A mix of infighting and bitter court fights had unmasked many Klan members and aired the group's dirty laundry, including that Klan leaders were embezzling funds and gouging the rank-and-file for money. Moreover, horrifying news stories emerged of crimes committed by Klansmen.[35] An Oregon member who worked as a dentist was convicted of raping his secretary, then killing her while trying to perform an abortion. The Grand Dragon of Indiana was also convicted for kidnapping, raping, torturing, and ultimately murdering his secretary. The editor of the Klan's newspaper was sentenced to life for killing a man. Indiana governor Ed Jackson, a Klan member, was indicted for bribery. And in Louisiana, the anti-Klan governor learned that Klansmen had murdered two of his close allies.

But for all this criminality, the historian Linda Gordon argues, the Klan was also in decline because it had, in many ways, triumphed, its ideology everywhere being codified into law:[36]

> *State eugenics laws, providing for forcible sterilization of those of "defective stock," spread to thirty states, and those labeled defective were typically the poor and people of color. The biggest Klan victory was immigration restriction, and Imperial Wizard Hiram Evans repeatedly claimed credit for its passage. The Johnson-Reed Act of 1924, named for Washington Klansman Albert Johnson in the House of Representatives and Pennsylvania's David Reed in the Senate, ensconced into law the Klan's hierarchy of desirable and undesirable "races" by assigning quotas for immigrants in proportion to the ethnicity of those already in the United States in 1890.*

Gordon also argues that perhaps the Klan's biggest victory was shifting what we often refer to today as the "Overton Window"—the spectrum of ideas considered acceptable among the general public:

> *The biggest Klan victory was equally consequential but less tangible. It influenced public conversation, the universe of tolerable discourse. It increased the intensity and spread of bigoted speech and occasionally, action. True, the Klan did not invent bigotry. Sometimes ebbing, sometimes flowing, white racism had appeared as soon as Europeans arrived on this continent. But the Klan spread, strengthened and radicalized preexisting nativist and racist sentiments among the white population.*

The terror of masked Klannishness was in many ways obvious: It was a method of anonymizing violence, protecting those hiding behind hoods from facing justice for their crimes. The cruel costumes created a fear that the white cloth could conceal *anyone*—that the eyes peering through those little slits could belong to your neighbor, your local police officer, your doctor, maybe even a friend. The white hoods imbued those who wore them with an almost supernatural ability to be everywhere at once, haunting every street corner or park or checkout line, rendering every white man a possible Klansman.

Ripping off the hoods of Buffalo Klansmen then, revealing the white faces behind them, had an obvious utility: The mass unmasking was an urgent and successful form of community self-defense. A social cost was created for being in the Klan. People knew which of their neighbors had taken an oath to the Invisible Empire, and so they knew which of their neighbors might want to hurt them. They knew who not to trust. The unmasking created a new social arrangement from which the Klan in Buffalo never recovered.

But the stories of the wider First and Second Klans introduce another, maybe more complicated history of ripping off white hoods. That sometimes, by the time the hoods were removed, they had already served their purpose. It's a history that lays bare the awful efficacy of masks in fascist politics. Those who wear them, after all, do so in hopes of creating a new world, one where they won't need to hide their faces at all.

CHAPTER 8
Patriot Fail

In the summer of 2023, Vincent took a seat again in a high-backed leather booth at 13 Coins, the upscale diner across the street from SeaTac Airport. It had been almost two years since his last meal here, when he said the n-word to burnish his credentials as a white supremacist, beginning his infiltration of Patriot Front.

He took out his laptop, opening it up to retrieve a file. Spinning the computer around, he pointed to a photo on the screen: him with thirteen members of Patriot Front at the start of their hike up Mount Rainier, their faces all hidden behind gaiter masks and sunglasses. The image showed the neo-Nazis, unaware of the spy in their midst, all standing at attention on the Muir Steps. Wildflower meadows sloped upward behind them toward tall pines that gave way to the volcano's towering summit.

"So I think at this point, every single one of these people has been identified," Vincent said.

Vincent ate bacon and eggs as he began to point at each masked white man in the photo, revealing their real names. Each had been exposed because of his work as an on-the-ground spy, their doxes mostly appearing on Washington Nazi Watch, the site Vincent ran. The doxes detailed each Patriot Front member's name, address, and place of employment, alongside evidence of their extremism. There were screenshots of the slurs they posted in Rocket-Chat; audio recordings of their racist diatribes; photos and videos of them committing possible hate crimes.

Vincent pointed at John-WA in the photo. He was the Network 8 leader who'd interviewed Vincent outside the grocery store, who had gotten a door knock from the FBI after defacing that George Floyd and Breonna Taylor mural down in Oregon, and who helped deface the Pride mural in Olympia. John-WA's real name was Colton Michael Brown.[1] He was a twenty-four-year-old electrician making $50,000 a year while training to be an airplane pilot, living with his father and stepmother, who was Vietnamese, in a house in Ravensdale.

When he was doxed, things were already tense at home between Brown and his dad. "I got into a huge argument with him, at like 4 a.m., going up the mountain in the dark, on the second day hunting, about racial politics, and I just snapped," Brown said during a Network 8 call recorded by Vincent, recounting a recent hunting trip with his father.[2] "I was like, 'I don't give a fuck about these non-whites. Fuck these n***ers, fuck these c*inks. I'm tired of them coming here and using our goddamn system. They can go to hell.' That just kind of started off this huge debate. My dad's like, 'Well, this has been a nation of all nations. You need to lose that mindset.'"

Brown's dox, which included the home address he shared with his father and stepmother, seemed to be the final straw.[3] His dad kicked him out. The rest of Brown's life started to fall apart, too. He was fired from the construction company where he worked after his boss started receiving calls. *Why are you employing a Nazi?* The flight school where he was learning to be a pilot started to receive calls, too. *Is it a good idea to train a Nazi to fly?* Brown found himself suddenly grounded and jobless and without a home. He fled Washington, leaving Network 8 behind him. Rumor had it he was shacking up with other Patriot Front members down in Utah.

Brown's most loyal lackey in Network 8, David-WA, was also unmasked on Washington Nazi Watch. David-WA's real name was Spencer Thomas Simpson.[4] He was a twenty-one-year-old history student at Central Washington University in Ellensburg, where both his parents worked. His mom was a professor of health and science. His dad, an Air Force veteran, worked as a career counselor. The dox mocked Simpson for "his extreme social awkwardness" and "incel-like behaviors," and noted his subservience to Brown. It also documented Simpson's intensifying Nazism, including a recording of the time he compared Jews to "Lucifer."[5] A photo showed Simpson wearing a skull mask above a black sweatshirt emblazoned with the Nazi sonnenrad, or "black sun," standing menacingly next to a car with a liberal "Coexist" bumper sticker.

Rumor had it Simpson quit school after the dox, and that he'd also fled Washington, leaving his childhood home to live in a Patriot Front compound in the Tennessee woods.

Tyler-WA fled Seattle after his dox. He was the Patriot Front member who ran that little hate crime factory out of his apartment, using a 3D printer to make Patriot Front stencils. His real name was James Julius Johnson.[6] He was thirty-seven years old and was making $80,000 a year working as a union HVAC (heating, ventilation, and air conditioning) technician.[7] "Johnson drives a Key Mechanical company van and says he works in a position that often requires him to provide on-call services for businesses, including Amazon," his dox stated on Washington Nazi Watch. "As a member of a Nazi organization, Johnson should not be allowed access to other peoples' spaces as a part of his job."

When Johnson skipped town, his girlfriend decided to go with him. She was the former liberal Bernie Sanders supporter, who once had trans friends, before Johnson showed her things she couldn't "unsee." She had talked to Vincent during the hike up Mount Rainier, when he tried to subtly persuade her to leave this all behind. But she never did, and now the world would know what she was a part of. Rachel-WA's real name was Amelia Watts. "Seattle's Patriot Front couple," anti-fascists labeled her and Johnson. Watts was thirty years old and worked as a geographic information system analyst at Critigen, a location intelligence and mapping company, making $60,000 a year. She was fired,[8] suddenly finding herself jobless and fleeing Seattle with her Nazi boyfriend.

Before they left Seattle, though, Johnson had to get rid of his ghost guns. After reading Johnson's dox, Thomas had ordered the weapons be "trashed or destroyed." Johnson reportedly did just that, with another member relaying to Thomas that the guns were lost in a "boating accident"[9]—a popular expression among gun enthusiasts for disappearing firearms you didn't want the government to ever know you had.

Not long after "Seattle's Patriot Front couple" disposed of the guns and fled the city, public records show Amelia Watts decided to become Amelia Johnson.

Ethan-WA was the tallest man in the Mount Rainier photo. Standing at six-foot-four and weighing 195 pounds, he was the Patriot Front member who'd gone on so many missions with Vincent. He'd defaced the Angela Davis mural in West Seattle and sprayed white paint over the Pride mural in Olympia. He'd chased after a car full of alleged antifa outside a La-Z-Boy Furniture Gallery and later attended the march in Washington, DC, where the two cars he rented for Network 8 members got badly damaged by anti-fascists in the parking lot.

The first big clue to Ethan-WA's identity had come during that drive in Vincent's car, when he'd connected to the Bluetooth, causing the words "JUSTIN'S iPhone" to be displayed on the stereo console. Vincent took a little pride in the way he unraveled Ethan-WA's—or rather, Justin's—full name. Looking closely at a photo Ethan-WA posted on RocketChat, showing Patriot Front banners he was making in his backyard, Vincent noticed the image contained an enticing piece of metadata: the geotagged coordinates of precisely where Ethan-WA's backyard was located. Once Vincent tracked down the address, he looked up who the house belonged to in public records, and boom: "Ethan-WA" was twenty-seven-year-old Justin O'Leary.[10] He lived with his wife and their one-year-old child in Des Moines, Washington.

Because O'Leary had joined Patriot Front around the same time as Vincent, he'd immediately fallen under suspicion as a possible second infiltrator. On December 6, 2021, one of Thomas's underlings had ordered Brown (aka John-WA) to "re-vet" O'Leary to make sure he wasn't an accomplice, suggesting he go through the contents of O'Leary's phone. But Brown objected, insisting that O'Leary couldn't possibly be a spy. Brown had visited O'Leary's home recently, playing with his one-year-old kid while O'Leary's wife hung swastika ornaments on the family Christmas tree. She "was crying because she was scared they'd get doxed," Brown said.

And she was right to be scared. O'Leary's wife was identified as twenty-eight-year-old Kendra Cass. Her dox included a photo of the cookies she'd once baked for O'Leary, the ones in which she'd carefully placed chocolate chips in the shape of swastikas. It also detailed how she and Amelia Johnson once cooked Thanksgiving dinner for the boys in Network 8, before they went out back, posing for a photo with stolen Black Lives Matter signs.

Some of the other men identified in the Mount Rainier photo did not live in Washington, so Vincent had passed along the intelligence he'd gathered about them to out-of-state anti-fascist groups. The Pacific Antifascist Research Collective in southern California published the dox for Brandon-CA. He was the Patriot Front member who fancied himself an intellectual, who climbed not only Mount Rainier, but White Mountain in California, where he'd left his phone with Vincent in the car—passcode "1492," the year Jews were expelled from Spain—while he stepped out to check for flat tires, allowing Vincent to photograph his email address and a slew of other identifying material. Brandon's real name was Alexi Guthrie.[11] He was twenty-seven years old and lived in Simi Valley, California, where he worked for a shipping and logistics company. His dox included audio of the conversations he and Vincent had in the car, including when he expressed his support for both Hitler and the American Nazi Party founder George Lincoln Rockwell. "Given Alexi Guthrie's deep involvement with neo-Nazi group Patriot Front, his racist attitudes towards Jews, Mexicans, and Black people, and his goal of achieving a Nazi Third Reich in America, he is a danger to coworkers and customers alike," the Pacific Antifascist Research Collective wrote.

The collective also provided a printable flyer for folks in Simi Valley, replete with a QR code that linked to his dox. COMMUNITY ALERT: WHITE SUPREMACIST, screamed the text above a photo of Guthrie on White Mountain. The flyers quickly appeared all over Guthrie's neighborhood.

"We do not forgive," the Pacific Antifascist Research Collective tweeted. "We do not forget."

Corvallis Antifa down in Oregon published the dox for Frederick-OR, one of the bigger dudes in the Mount Rainier photo. Frederick-OR was the one who retreated down the volcano early. He'd also taken part in defacing the Olympia mural, and later retreated from anti-fascists attacking the U-Hauls in DC. His real name was Lawrence Alexander Norman.[12] But other than locating his residence in Prospect, Oregon, Corvallis Antifa couldn't find much else about him. Still, the group's dox included a warning: "For members of Patriot Front reading this, we assure you, the worst consequences of these infiltrations have yet to come. There is still time to leave this dumbass MLM [multilevel marketing scheme] and make something worthwhile of your life. You will find no satisfaction or glory following the leadership of an insecure loser like Tommy Rousseau. Leave organized fascism NOW before it is your life that's ruined."

Vincent pointed to one more man in the Mount Rainier photo: Clark-WA. His real name was Jacob Stephen Sundt.[13] The dox on *Washington Nazi Watch* described him as being twenty-five years old and from

Olympia, the city where he'd organized the destruction of the Pride mural. It detailed RocketChat messages in which Sundt bragged to other members about plastering Patriot Front propaganda across the college campuses where he worked overnight shifts as a security guard. Evergreen State College was "irreparably and thoroughly stickered," he wrote once. Other messages showed him to be a raging misogynist, arguing that women shouldn't be allowed to work and calling domestic violence "based," a term the far-right used to mean true and good. "Always attack women," he added.

Sundt, however, wasn't so boastful or aggressive in the days leading up to his dox. In the week after Vincent was revealed as the infiltrator, Sundt was scared. "If I am thoroughly doxxed I'm probably gonna be out of home pretty fast," he wrote to another member on December 8, 2021. "Might even get disowned."

After his dox dropped on Washington Nazi Watch, Sundt sent an urgent message to Thomas.[14] "Due to my father's work I can no longer associate with the organization from this point on or else he will lose his job and his medical benefits that pay for his ongoing medical treatment," he wrote. "I must withdraw formally from the organization. I am sorry, Thomas."

Sundt's father, it turned out, was a public official: a judge for the Washington State Office of Administrative Hearings.

Vincent finished his eggs and bacon, asked for the check, and closed his laptop, squeezing it into his backpack. After finishing his infiltration of Patriot Front, he remembered eagerly waiting to see what his spy work would set in motion across the country, to see how the network of American anti-fascists would use the data from RocketChat to unmask dozens and dozens of neo-Nazis in their hometowns.

By then, this anti-fascist network had years of practice in doxing, its members developing sophisticated investigative techniques, style guides, and codes of ethics. Like the fascists they exposed, they often led double lives, keeping "the work" a secret, even from friends and family. They returned home from day jobs and logged online for hours, using pseudonyms and usernames of their own, not only to communicate with each other but to remain undetected while combing the internet for clues. This anonymity, which they maintained out of a fear of retribution, made it hard for the wider public to grasp the contours of American antifa itself, to formulate a mental image of those involved.

It may come as a surprise to the public, then, that antifa was largely a reflection of America itself. It was a network composed of everyday people from different walks of life, with perhaps a couple demographics over-represented, who had all found themselves radicalized by current events, suddenly mistrustful of the country's institutions in which they'd once invested their faith. These people had struggled to find a way to fight back, alighting upon blueprints, symbols, and strategies left behind by previous generations of people who called themselves anti-fascists.

As much as the Trump era was a story of the radicalization of many Americans into organized fascism, there was also a story of a countervailing radicalization occurring, a story that often went unnoticed—an awakening that rarely mustered headlines.

CHAPTER 9

American Antifa

odern antifa—which in the early months of 2022 was sorting through hundreds of thousands of Patriot Front messages on RocketChat—grew largely out of old ARA networks that were revived in the early years of the Trump era, a response to a wave of new American fascists organizing online. The ARA slogan "we go where they go" now meant following fascists not only to the streets but to newer digital battlefields.

On November 11, 2016, just a few days after Trump was elected president, American anti-fascists held a conference in Denver. The assembled groups were all part of the TORCH Network, born a few years prior as a relaunch of the relatively dormant ARA Network. Although still ascribing to a version of ARA's "points of unity," the rebrand was meant to breathe new life into the movement—a new name for the digital age that would appeal to a younger generation of anti-fascists.

"We acknowledge that many of our comrades have lost so much, some their lives, under the banner of ARA," the newfound TORCH members noted in a statement[1] that was published in the long-running ARA zine, *Turning the Tide*. "Their sacrifices will not be forgotten, and their fight is still our fight . . . We are still on the prowl. We will still continue to expose, confront, and act. Fascists beware—we are TORCH."

The gathering in Denver, hosted by Rocky Mountain Antifa, had familiar anarchist programming, including a panel discussion about "confronting machismo" within their own ranks, a workshop on support for anti-fascist prisoners, and an opportunity to talk with participants in the Dakota Access Pipeline, or Standing Rock, protests earlier that year.

But the prevailing topic of conversation was Trump's election. They had gathered, in large part, to answer the question: What does this mean for antifa? In an issue of *Turning the Tide* a month after the conference, members of Rocky Mountain Antifa gave an urgent summary of TORCH's answer:[2]

> *It means our role has increased drastically. We are more than local crews combating local fascists. We are essentially tasked with building resistance to a fascist regime. For those of us who saw this coming as well as those who are just waking up, we need to recognize our significance at this moment. All social movement organizing is now antifascist organizing. We are at a pivotal point in the outcome of this overwhelming shit show.*

Meanwhile, other anti-fascist groups were forming organically across the country. Although not part of TORCH, they often looked to TORCH for guidance, or as a blueprint, ascribing to the ARA points of unity while adapting antifa symbols, creating logos with the two flags of the Antifaschistische Aktion, or the three arrows of the Iron Front.

"I think it was just kind of a supply-and-demand thing, you know?" says Heidi Beedle, a founding member of one such group, Colorado Springs Anti-Fascists. The more fascist groups there were, she explains, the more antifa groups there were bound to be.

Colorado Springs is a conservative city of nearly half a million people that has been called the "Vatican of evangelical Christianity." A slew of megachurches call the town home, as do fundamentalist organizations like Focus on the Family, the $90 million juggernaut known for its rabidly anti-abortion and anti-queer policy positions, with its leaders calling homosexuality "a particularly evil lie of Satan" and trans people "mentally ill."[3]

The area felt like it could be fertile recruiting ground for the new array of "alt-right" groups forming at the beginning of the Trump era. In 2016, when a leftist organization called the Colorado Springs Socialists held one of their monthly meetings at a local brewery, they were met by a bizarre contingent of far-right activists—many of whom would go on to join the Proud Boys— yelling at them and harassing them. Meanwhile, Identity Evropa, a relatively new white nationalist group, was posting its propaganda at the University of Colorado campus in town.

"There was a recognition that things were getting weird and, you know, we needed to maybe do something a little bit more than talking about Trotsky and Lenin once a month at the brewery," Beedle remembers.

Beedle is transgender, an identity she says led her to anti-fascist work in the first place. Originally from Virginia, she joined the Army after high school, rising to the rank of sergeant and deploying to Iraq three times. She left the military after eight years and eventually landed in Colorado Springs, taking a job at Sand Creek High School teaching English when, in 2014, she had a revelation.

"I come out as trans after being a high school teacher for two years and sort of have this kind of upheaval in my personal life, and being a trans person in a lot of ways—it's kind of a stereotype that trans people, they come out, and then they join some kind of far-left 'domestic terrorist organization' or anarchist collective," she says, laughing. "And you know, it is kind of true. A lot of trans people, especially trans women, they come out and then, if you're white, for like the first time in your life you experience sexism and discrimination, all of these things that you knew about intellectually, but never like personally experienced, the unfairness of it, and it's kind of radicalizing in a lot of respects . . . My political evolution was always kind of tied to just pushing back against anti-LGBT stuff, that was the main driver for me. It was a kind of self-defense."

The year after Beedle came out as trans, 2015, would be named the deadliest year for trans women on record,[4] with twenty-two murdered, many of them misgendered or "deadnamed" in the subsequent news reports about their deaths. The hard-won rise in trans visibility and rights in the early aughts was being met by a vicious, reactionary backlash, with state legislatures across the country introducing a wave of anti-trans laws, and with the MAGA movement and the GOP embracing alarming, eliminationist anti-trans rhetoric.

The right's caricature of antifa was frequently transphobic. Conservative figures, including members of Congress, would refer to antifa as "trantifa" as a way of painting the movement as a haven for deranged, confused degenerates.

But it is true that queer and trans people are overrepresented among the ranks of modern antifa in America. "They're in the crosshairs, you know? And they understand the risk better than normies do," a Chicago-based anti-fascist we'll call Hank explains. "All of our existences are on the line with the rising tide of fascism, but they'll be first."

Another anti-fascist, who goes by Stitch and lives in Washington, DC, puts it this way: "There's this super widespread attack on trans/queer spaces and people—it's not a choice for a lot of people to do this work. *You need to know what's going on because they're coming for you.*"

Beedle and the Colorado Springs Anti-Fascists organized one of their first direct actions in January 2017, joining a protest against Milo Yiannopoulos,[5] who was speaking at the University of Colorado campus in town. Yiannopoulos, an editor at Breitbart News and a prominent propagandist for the alt right,[6] was on a campus speaking tour, threatening at each stop to publicly out undocumented and transgender students, making them targets.

There were about a dozen members of Colorado Springs Anti-Fascists at the demonstration, standing in the falling snow among a hundred other protesters. Beedle remembers it as a kind of "kickoff event" for their group, just as it was the kickoff for "the Proud Boys and a bunch of other right-wing dudes" there to support Yiannopoulos.

"We were all at this same protest on opposite sides, and then spent the next four years messing with each other," she recalls.

Beedle and the Colorado Springs Anti-Fascists started a website to publish doxes in the spring of 2017, looking at past doxes published by their neighbors in Rocky Mountain Antifa, the older TORCH group, as a model. Around the same time, It's Going Down, a prominent anarchist website that often operates as a clearinghouse for republished anti-fascist doxes, also published a guide called "Forming an Antifa Group: A Manual,"[7] that included instructions for unmasking your local Nazi:

> *After doing your research, present information about racist organizing in your community. The information you release should present enough information to convince an average reader that the target is clearly a racist. Information should include, if possible: a picture, home address, phone number, social media profiles, and employment information. Be sure to include organizational affiliations and screenshots showing concrete evidence of racist and fascist views. Follow up the doxx with a pressure campaign: call their work and try to get them fired, and inform their neighbors through flyering or door-to-door campaigns . . .*

Also be aware that you will enrage your target by naming them: you might have been ignored as a public group for a year doing antifa stuff, but once you refer to a local racist by name, they will fixate on you.

Make sure your intel is correct. You will lose credibility and create unnecessary enemies if you list a home address or work place that the fascist is no longer associated with. The majority of research can be done online, but some things can only be verified in the real world.

Heidi and her cohorts weren't particularly tech savvy, but learned what's called "open-source intelligence," or OSINT, as they went along.

Some of the fascists made it easy at first. "One of the early ones was on the Proud Boys chapter that was forming here, and they had a Facebook group that was public, and you could see the membership list," Heidi says. "And then you could go to their individual profiles and see all the stuff that they said, all the crazy and controversial stuff." But in the ensuing years, fascists were practicing tighter "operational security," or OPSEC, organizing in more private spaces online. Still, they left plenty of threads for anti-fascists like Heidi to pull.

Michael Hayden, a former reporter at the Southern Poverty Law Center who has published some of the most significant work unmasking the far right, noted once that "every time we go online, we give up part of our identity."

"Sometimes, it comes in the form of an email used to make a Twitter account," Hayden wrote in an article for the *Columbia Journalism Review*.[8] "Other times, it's a phone number for two-factor authentication, or days' and weeks' worth of timestamps suggesting when a user is awake and asleep."

Molly Conger, a Charlottesville-based anti-fascist writer and podcast host, described finding such online clues this way: "I like to tell people if you've ever stayed up all night scouring Instagram for pictures of your ex's wedding, you can do this. It's the same skills."[9]

As best as fascists might try to stay anonymous, hiding behind pseudonyms or avatars online, OSINT—the study of social media, archived websites, web forums, property records, obituaries, wedding announcements, birth announcements, LinkedIn pages, Venmo transactions, and a host of other publicly available information—almost always offers a way to unspool their real identities.

Oftentimes fascists will leave behind a small, innocuous biographical detail that will spell their undoing. An analysis of anti-fascists doxes from

2015 to 2024, for example, shows that at least seven neo-Nazis were exposed, in part, because they posted photos of their dogs online.

Atlanta Antifascists exposed the Georgia state leader of Vanguard America as a local high school football star after he posted a photo of his dog in Discord chats (obtained by an anti-fascist spy). After extensive sleuthing, anti-fascists found the same yellow Lab in a picture posted to Facebook—by the Vanguard America leader's dad. From there, the anti-fascists compiled a mountain of other corroborating evidence tying the high school student to a username on the Vanguard America server on Discord.

This particular Vanguard America leader was only eighteen years old, making him eligible to be publicly unmasked. Anti-fascist groups typically won't dox minors, and will often instead contact their parents, warning them that their child is mixed up in something bad—an example of the informal code of ethics most anti-fascists follow. When antifa publishes a photo of a fascist with their family, for example, they'll often blur out the family members' faces to not make them subject to harassment or other ramifications they might not deserve. (Antifa will also, as a running joke, often blur out a dog's face.)

Mostly, though, what's important to anti-fascists is that the dox is *correct*. It's an incredibly high-stakes line of work: Misidentifying someone as a neo-Nazi or a white supremacist is not only a genuinely shitty thing to do to a person but threatens undermining the whole enterprise.

It's already hard enough to get a community to pay attention to an obscure blog published by a bunch of anonymous anti-fascists and anarchists, so if an antifa group misidentifies an innocent person as a fascist, it all but guarantees that the community will ignore their local antifa the next time they claim to unmask someone. For antifa, maintaining their credibility is crucial in ensuring they're not perceived as hysterical radicals constantly crying wolf.

There are also severe legal ramifications for a misidentification, or a "fail-dox," as it's called colloquially in anti-fascist circles. Most major news outlets would have a lawyer pore over an exposé, for example, of a teacher who's leading a secret double life as a neo-Nazi—triple-checking the research and highlighting every word or bit of phrasing that might make the newspaper liable to be sued for defamation or libel.

Anti-fascist groups, however, are usually made up of working-class and middle-class people. They typically don't have a good First Amendment lawyer in their contacts, or the disposable income to pay for one if they did.

This creates an environment of exacting editorial standards. *Everything has to be right*. If anti-fascists do get even a minor detail wrong, a correction and an apology are quickly appended to the top of the article.

This has had the effect of making a bunch of anonymous anti-fascists, almost all working other jobs, into really good journalists, even if they are almost never recognized as such by the mainstream media. This lack of recognition is due in large part to traditional notions of journalism that prioritize "objectivity," rendering the reporter a neutral observer, a blank slate, presenting all sides of a story equally, reporting from a "place from nowhere." A reporter, the thinking goes, can never be an *activist*.

But for anti-fascists there's no being neutral in the face of fascism, an inherently destructive and genocidal ideology. The "place from nowhere" is a fantasy—journalists arrive at every article with their own biases and interests and limited view of reality, with every headline and word selection and quote placement an *intrinsically political decision*. Every journalist, if their stated goal is to fight for the public interest, is a *de facto activist*. Those who pretend otherwise are inevitably doing fascists' jobs for them.

Abner Hague is the editor in chief of Left Coast Right Watch, a California-based independent news outlet that does deep dives on the far right, sometimes based on antifa research. In an essay called "Make Journalism Antifa Again,"[11] Hague writes about the pitfalls of the traditional journalistic model when covering the far right:

> *To responsibly cover fascists requires you to recognize that they have two primary obsessions: normalizing their genocidal and authoritarian ideas and committing acts of violence against all perceived enemies. Fascists care first and foremost about controlling the narrative about what they do. Back in the day it might have been, "Oh no, we're not white nationalists, we're identitarians! Oh no, we're not identitarians, we're alt-right! Oh no, we're not alt-right, we're dissident Right!" Every time you let them change their label, you allow them to weasel further into a broader milieu of the political right. Every time you let them change their label, you enable them to recruit from larger audiences who may have previously only flirted with the milder forms of these hateful ideas. . . . Every time you fail to clearly say that fascists showed up to an event with the intention to hurt people, and subsequently tried to hurt people, you give them cover to enact even worse violence in the future.*

From the anti-fascist perspective, the mainstream media at the beginning of the Trump era was failing these tasks repeatedly—publishing humanizing profiles of the likes of Richard Spencer, for example, in glossy magazines. Antifa then often viewed the mainstream media as an institution of American white supremacy and would sometimes treat its journalists with a degree of hostility.

Articles published by antifa make no pretense of objectivity, and in some cases can assume a taunting tone, including insults that can be both vulgar and, quite frankly, juvenile. A relatively extreme example of this is a 2014 article, published by Rocky Mountain Antifa, with the headline "Nate Marshall Is a Dumb Ass."[12] The article was about how Marshall—who Rocky Mountain Antifa alleged had founded a neo-fascist group that discussed violence against Muslims—was running for the Colorado State House of Representatives (and had received an endorsement by a sitting Republican state senator).

"Nate's campaign filing affidavit can be viewed right here in .PDF form," Rocky Mountain Antifa wrote, linking to the affidavit. "Nate, in his infinite wisdom, put his address and phone number on the form. You can reach Nate, a fucking moron, at ***-***-**** or send him a package full of gorilla shit at: [his address]."

The phrase "package full of gorilla shit" included a hyperlink to a website called Poop Senders, a company that purported to ship different types of animal feces anonymously to an address of the customer's choosing. It's unclear if Marshall ever received a package full of gorilla shit in the mail. (He pulled out of the campaign, and the neo-fascist group appears to have dissipated.)

The vast majority of anti-fascist doxes, though, especially in the Trump era, were much more measured, even if they might include an occasional phrase like "let's make this motherfucker famous." In fact, some of the writing in the doxes could often be poignant or betray a deep knowledge of different fascist currents that wouldn't be completely out of place in a political science PhD dissertation.

Anti-fascists' grasp of the history of fascism, and their fluency in the jargon modern fascists use to talk to each other, is often earned through the sheer tedium of anti-fascist research. Individual anti-fascists will often devote over forty hours a week (again, on top of their day jobs) reading through far-right posts online or listening to neo-Nazi podcasts, often having to decipher the latest lingo. Paul, a Southern anti-fascist who exposed multiple members of a white supremacist group called Identity Dixie, remembers once reading through a staggering seventy thousand tweets to complete a single dox.

Such obsessive, tedious work can attract a certain type of personality, and many anti-fascists say they are neurodivergent. Just as trans and queer people are overrepresented among the ranks of modern antifa, people with autism and ADHD may be overrepresented, too.

Eric Michael Garcia, author of *We're Not Broken: Changing the Autism Conversation*, says neurodivergent people frequently talk about having a "justice sensitivity" born from "being constantly isolated, bullied and ostracized." Moreover, despite prevailing myths that autistic people have "no empathy," he says, studies have shown they can often be "hyper-empathetic," which, combined with a tendency to find a "focused" or "special" interest, can lead to them being "singular-minded about finding neo-Nazis and extremists."

Eddy, a pseudonymous anti-fascist writer at Left Coast Right Watch, says he was bullied a lot growing up for being autistic, something he feels made him attuned to the threat of fascists. "Bullies have a radar for people that are potential victims," he says. "Those experiences feed inevitably into your perspective." (George Orwell, in his 1944 essay "What Is Fascism?," argued that "'bully' as a synonym for 'fascist'" was "about as near to a definition as this much-abused word has come."[13])

Like trans anti-fascists, neurodivergent anti-fascists often see their work as a form of community self-defense against an insurgent "alt-right" that frequently used online spaces to target young people on the spectrum, either for harassment or recruitment.

Anonymous Comrades Collective, a formidable anti-fascist research outfit that has published some of the most remarkable investigations into the American far right, once described this type of recruitment while doxing "Paul Town," an online celebrity among white supremacists, for, among other troll campaigns, helping appropriate the "Pepe the Frog" cartoon character into the widely recognized racist mascot for the alt-right.[14]

"Paul Town" was outed as a twentysomething man of Coxsackie, New York,[15] who had tweeted that he was autistic and who Anonymous Comrades Collective argued was part of a broader effort to recruit more neurodiverse people into the ranks of explicit white supremacy:

The subject of correlation versus causation of racism and other forms of bigotry with mental health is complicated and disputed. Neurodiversity and mental illness are not the same thing, and both are commonplace in the broader society, and should not be stigmatized. The weird and wonderful human brain governs us all. Many are neurodiverse. Many have grappled with some form of mental illness. Neither of these are excuses for racism, antisemitism, and bigotry. One clear delineation between the alt right and preceding white nationalist and neo-Nazi movements was the very effective technology-driven recruitment efforts. Rather than leaving flyers on car windows and grocery stores or stuffed in random mailboxes, the alt right weaponized group pop culture strategically targeting children and young adults through memes, Disney song parodies, and cartoon characters like Pepe the Frog and the Groyper.

One cruel aspect of this was the specific targeting of vulnerable people in various social media and gaming platforms. The alt right aggressively targeted the socially isolated, the neurodiverse, and the mentally ill. Celebratory terms like "weaponized autism" and variations on "autiste" and "sperg" were used to radicalize and encourage neurodiverse people into increasingly reckless and hateful online behavior. The sole reward being plaudits from other anonymous participants. The anonymity behind the cartoon avatars divorced the online actions from real life, accountability, and encouraged accelerated outrageous rhetoric and behavior.

Beyond the demographics of queer and neurodivergent people being possibly overrepresented in American antifa, most anti-fascist groups report the racial makeup of their membership reflecting the racial makeup of the regions where they live. Right-wing and even liberal caricatures of antifa often depict the groups as predominantly or even exclusively white, and not without reason.

Shane Burley, the author of *Fascism Today: What It Is and How to End It*, notes that in its later days ARA was a predominantly white organization, as was the John Brown Anti-Klan Committee (JBAKC) before it, in the 1980s. The whiteness of these militant anti-fascist groups reflected the segregated nature of American society writ large, but in the case of the JBAKC was partially by design: The group saw itself as a white ally organization to the Black radical movement.

But Burley says predominantly white groups doing anti-racist work tend to "create problems" and "don't really grow politically." Ultimately, he says, "people have to learn from each other, that's better, and I think anti-fascist groups do the intentional work more now of doing that outreach, and they are much more diverse than they used to be."

American anti-fascists are from an array of backgrounds, describing themselves variously as punks, soccer moms, and rednecks. They work as EMTs and teachers, in fashion and tech, at universities and elementary schools. They sling drinks from behind bars and sort packages at Amazon warehouses. Some scrape by paycheck to paycheck in the city, while others have savings and nice houses in the suburbs. Almost none are millionaires. A few are about to graduate high school, and some are already collecting social security. There are military veterans with the scars and tattoos to prove it, and Anti-Racist Action veterans with the scars and tattoos to prove it. Many started doing this work because of personal brushes with fascists in their communities, or because of seminal news events that radically reshaped how they saw their country, namely Trump's election in 2016 and the Unite the Right rally in Charlottesville in 2017.

As radical, militant, and bellicose as they can sound, many American anti-fascists describe experiencing brief pangs of sympathy for the fascists they are fighting or are about to unmask. Not because they sympathize with their views in the slightest, but because they recognize the slippery slope of dehumanizing even those whose politics they detest. They see spiraling inequality spawned by capitalism as a poison that can infect even the otherwise smart and kind; and, specifically for straight white cis anti-fascists, these fleeting feelings of empathy grow out of a certain fatalism, an understanding that through various twists and turns of fate, on a different timeline, through so many sliding doors, they could've been pulled inexorably toward fascism, too.

They all describe the severe emotional toll anti-fascist research can take, how the noxious slurs and memes swim in your head; the recurring nightmares of a neo-Nazi turning up to your door with a gun; and the occasional deep despair that America is on the most inevitable, unstoppable, and darkest of trajectories.

But they also describe moments of empowerment. They describe the camaraderie and community that come from being part of a movement without leaders. And they describe the thrill—or even idle pleasure—of the chase.

Megan Squire is a computer data scientist and professor at Elon University. She is also a former fellow at the Southern Poverty Law Center, where she conducted some of the most in-depth OSINT investigations into fascist groups. In 2017, she narrowly missed being hit when a neo-Nazi drove his Dodge Challenger into a crowd of anti-fascists in Charlottesville.

Although Squire does not consider herself part of antifa per se, she's collaborated with anti-fascist researchers and has also refused to condemn antifa when they punch Nazis. She is among a small group of people, mostly in journalism and academia and the nonprofit sector, who essentially do anti-fascist research for a living.

"I think a lot of people find this work incredibly relaxing. I know I do," she says of the research. "It sounds really, really dorky and dumb to say but at the end of a really hard week, I love to work on finding somebody's identity. It's like a puzzle. It's like I might do a jigsaw puzzle . . . I just really want to crack this nut. Like, how does this website work? What's going on here? What data can I get from this thing? Let me just poke around. It's sort of idle—just poking, poking, prodding, and then every once in a while, you're rewarded with this dopamine rush when you actually make a connection or get to the next level in your video game, right? Like, 'Oh, now I know the street address.'

"I'm good at it, and it's fun, and it needs to be done," she adds. "So like, that's the perfect job, right?"

*   *   *

As this new iteration of American antifa emerged in 2016, fascists organizing online understood the need to retreat into closed-off spaces to communicate with each other, developing private chat rooms on different tech platforms that required permissions and passwords to enter—safe spaces away from the prying eyes of their adversaries. For anti-fascists then, it became of paramount importance to access those spaces, leading them to embrace a specific, sometimes dangerous strategy: espionage.

Years before Vincent began his infiltration of Patriot Front, other anti-fascist spies were pretending to be white supremacists, gaining entry to message servers where they could collect invaluable intelligence, stealing away plans for upcoming rallies, or uncovering evidence of hate crimes. Mostly, though, there was intelligence that could lead to doxes.

These spies were prolific in 2016 and 2017, infiltrating nearly every new far-right group—the Proud Boys, Identity Evropa, Vanguard America, the Oath Keepers—and downloading thousands upon thousands of messages radical right activists were sending to each other. Such a bounty of intelligence, however, needed a place to live. A place where anti-fascist researchers could access it easily.

Enter Unicorn Riot. The nonprofit media outlet formed in 2015, funded through grants and donations, promising to operate "non-hierarchically, independent of corporate or government control."[16] Its original staff was composed of tech-savvy journalists and activists in their thirties who had cut their teeth covering large leftist mobilizations, documenting the brutal police response to protests in the Twin Cities outside the 2008 Republican National Convention, and the NYPD's destruction of the Occupy Wall Street encampment in lower Manhattan in 2011.

Unicorn Riot didn't necessarily set out to cover the far right, much less become a vital hub of fascist groups' internal messages. The outlet initially made a name for itself by conducting marathon live streams from Black Lives Matter demonstrations, interviewing activists on the ground, offering an alternative to mainstream media coverage of the protests, which Unicorn Riot felt was too dependent on government sources and police-friendly narratives. Then, in late 2015, Unicorn Riot's cameras captured masked white supremacists skulking around a Black Lives Matter protest in Minneapolis.[17]

Demonstrations had swept the city in response to the police murder of an unarmed Black man named Jamar Clark. Unicorn Riot live-streamed the uprisings for eighteen straight days until one night they filmed two white men in masks, wearing armbands emblazoned with "/K/." It was a reference to a firearms forum on 4chan, the online message board that had become a far-right fever swamp. These white men belonged to a group called the Kommandos,[18] and four of the group's members returned to the demonstration a few nights later, accosting Black Lives Matter demonstrators with racial slurs. One of the Kommandos, a twenty-four-year-old West Point dropout named Allen Scarcella, had brought a .45-caliber handgun, which he'd bragged to his buddies was "proven to kill Black guys in a single shot."[19] After some Black Lives Matter demonstrators, all of whom were Black, attempted to escort the Kommandos away from the demonstration, Scarcella opened fire, severely wounding five people, including Jamar Clark's cousin. ("I don't believe for a second you wore a mask that night because it was cold," the judge told Scarcella when he was later sentenced to fifteen years in prison. "The only saving grace is that your shots didn't kill their targets.")

The journalists at Unicorn Riot saw new far-right groups like the Kommandos mobilizing everywhere they looked, harassing anti-racist protesters and attacking people of color online with escalating vitriol. The outlet started to cover the far right more aggressively than the mainstream press. No soft-focused profiles or well-lit portraits of right-wing "provocateurs," as *The New York Times* often euphemized prominent racists like Milo Yiannopoulos. No "both sides" coverage drawing moral equivalencies between the right and left. Sometimes Unicorn Riot used anti-fascist research to unmask fascists.

By 2017, the outlet had earned the trust and respect of many on the left. So, when an anti-fascist managed to infiltrate a Discord chat server for white supremacists planning a massive, upcoming rally in Charlottesville, Virginia, he didn't hand over the login information to a big newspaper like the *Times* or the *Washington Post*. He gave it to the upstarts at Unicorn Riot, its journalists working quickly to scrape all the messages therein. They started to build an online database, an open and public repository for thousands and thousands of messages and photos and videos, allowing users to do keyword searches or sort through posts written by individual white supremacists. If it worked, it would be a remarkable feat of data journalism, and a crucial new piece of anti-fascist infrastructure, bringing sunlight and public scrutiny to the inner workings of groups that organized in the dark. Most urgently, the messages in this fledgling database would expose the bloodlust of the fascists set to invade Charlottesville.

The 2017 Unite the Right rally is now most often remembered for the shocking footage of torch-wielding neo-Nazis marching on a university campus, or the video of a neo-Nazi driving his sports car through a crowd of counterprotesters, or the press conference in which the president of the United States said some of these neo-Nazis were "very fine people." But what often escapes the public memory of that day is how anti-fascists warned the public about just *how bad* the rally was going to be, loudly insisting that *people were going to die*, only for their warnings to brushed aside by authorities.

The singular, horrifying event that was Unite the Right set so much of Vincent's story in motion: both the fracturing and rebranding of Vanguard

America into Patriot Front, and the creation of the Unicorn Riot database where his 440 gigabytes of Patriot Front data would find a home.

Moreover, the anti-fascist response to Unite the Right would amount to one of the first mass-doxing events of the Trump era, with anti-fascists determined to name and shame the fascists who invaded the college town, nestled in the foothills of the Blue Ridge Mountains. The response would be a test, or a case study, for whether unmasking fascist groups in the digital era could have an impact—whether doxing might relegate some of these groups to the dustbin of history.

And none of it would have been possible without the work of that one anti-fascist spy in the Unite the Right planning server. That spy, incidentally, was Vincent's friend Will.

CHAPTER 10

Very Fine People

Years before Will helped Vincent with his infiltration—surreptitiously snapping photos of Patriot Front members while picking blackberries, ripping down the group's banners from highway overpasses, or remaining at the ready to throw fists in case Vincent got in trouble—he did an infiltration of his own.

In 2017 Will had some personal reasons for wanting to fuck with fascists. In January of that year his friend, who goes by Hex, was protesting a speech by Milo Yiannopoulos at the University of Washington. When Hex saw a pair of Milo supporters pepper-spraying some of his fellow anti-fascists, he went to intervene, prompting one of them to pull out a gun and open fire. The bullet tore through Hex's abdomen[1] and exited his back, leading to a three-week stint in the ICU. He survived but was left with a long surgical scar, and for the rest of his life would be short one gallbladder and half a colon.

Which is all to say the threat posed by fascists felt visceral, personal, and close to home for Will in the spring of 2017, when he started seeing posters around Seattle for Anti-Communist Action, or Anticom, featuring the web address of a Discord chat for new members. He signed up, creating a suitably horrifying username, "Einsatz"—a shortening of Einsatzgruppen, the German Nazi death squads who murdered over a million people[2]—and with almost no vetting was accepted. He lurked in the chat for months, taking screenshots of the approximately one thousand members of Anticom, an anti-antifa group ostensibly devoted to fighting "leftist terrorists,"[3] as they shared bomb-making recipes and violent fantasies about murdering anti-fascists. One of the group's frequently used logos included an image of a leftist being tossed from a helicopter into the ocean, invoking a meme about Chilean dictator Augusto Pinochet's preferred method of execution.

One day, Will saw a link for members to sign up for the upcoming Unite the Right rally in Charlottesville. Its organizers had advertised it as a defense of a statue of Confederate General Robert E. Lee in a local park—erected in 1924 to great fanfare from the local Klan, whose members celebrated by holding a parade and burning crosses.[4] The statue was one of many such "Lost Cause" monuments slated to be toppled during a reckoning with their racist histories. But defending a statue was just a pretext for Unite the Right. Its organizers communicated to their followers that the rally would be an opening salvo in taking back America for the white man, a coming-out party for the alt-right, an opportunity to step out from behind their online avatars and do real-world violence. To go mask off. "August 12, 2017 is going to be a shot heard 'round the world,'" Andrew Anglin, founder of the Daily Stormer, wrote ahead of the rally.[5] "Thanks to the magnitude of this event, I truly believe, more than I ever did before, that we will eventually win this struggle and secure the existence of our people and a future for white children. It is our destiny. Next stop: Charlottesville, VA. Final stop: Auschwitz. See ya there, faggots."

Will clicked the link and found himself in a sprawling network of Discord chats for organizing Unite the Right. Over the next two months, he spent eighty to one hundred hours a week taking screenshots of Discord posts and recording organizing calls hosted on the platform. Eventually he was connected to a data scientist and anti-fascist activist in Charlottesville named Emily Gorcenski. Will started sending Gorcenski the screenshots so that residents of the city could prepare for what was coming.

The messages were horrifying. A seemingly unending scroll of unadulterated bloodlust and explicit plans for violence. Thomas Rousseau, then in a leadership role at Vanguard America, was eager to see "jackboots on commie skulls, blood on the pavement."[6] Organizer Robert "Azzmador" Ray, a prominent Daily Stormer writer, declared,[7] "I want to invest in race-specific bioweapons and n***er killing robots," and called for "GLOBAL N***ERDEATH NOW!"

An anonymous user going by "Tyrone" posted a picture of a farm machine known as a combine harvester, which cuts and threshes crops, labeling it a "multi-lane protester digestor." He wrote that it "sure would be nice" to use the machine in Charlottesville against leftist counterdemonstrators, adding: "Is it legal to run over protesters blocking roadways? I'm NOT just shitposting. I would like clarification." Elsewhere Tyrone suggested using flagpoles to "bludgeon our enemies" and said he was going to bring a World War II–era rifle that could "shoot through a crowd at least four deep."[8]

A Maryland-based Vanguard America member using the pseudonym "Americana-MD" was among many in the Discord who referred to Dylann Roof, the white supremacist who murdered nine Black parishioners at a Charleston, South Carolina, church, as a "saint." In anticipation of traveling to Charlottesville, Americana-MD wrote that he was "hooking up" a "n***er mulcher" to his truck.[9]

Having become a vocal opponent of the rally, Gorcenski found herself a target of the threats on Discord. "I hope she stands in the street," a user named WV1987 wrote about Gorcenski, who is transgender, posting a photo of his truck bumper, which he said was "hungry" and "eats trannies."

Gorcenski and other local activists campaigned to get the Charlottesville City Council to revoke the permit for the rally, "not because we're anti-free speech," she said, but because it was clear these white guys from out of town were planning to "terrorize our local communities."[10] They showed their elected officials the threats on Discord, providing them a dossier of the posts Will had collected. But it was to no avail. The mayor and city council, citing the First Amendment, wouldn't revoke the permit. Unite the Right was a go.

Charlottesville braced itself. Congregation Beth Israel, learning of direct threats to the city's Jews, thought it wise to remove its sacred Torah scrolls from the synagogue.[11] One congregant volunteered to take a particular Torah—salvaged from an Eastern European Jewish community exterminated by the Nazis—home for safekeeping. The synagogue hired an armed security guard ahead of the rally.

When businessowners downtown announced their opposition to the rally—affixing signs to their shop doors stating IF EQUALITY AND DIVERSITY AREN'T FOR YOU, NEITHER ARE WE—they were met with a wave of threats. A local hair salon received a letter in the mail from a Klansman calling for "the death to all black devils" and "all homo, perverted queer transgender freaks," before exclaiming: "Go Donald Trump! Make America White Again!"[12]

A group of local progressive clergy calling itself Congregate C'Ville scheduled an interfaith church service on the eve of Unite the Right to show residents' opposition. They also made plans to nonviolently confront the invading fascists face-to-face at the rally itself. They issued a nationwide call for "1000 clergy" to travel to Charlottesville. "We need your help and prayerful presence," they wrote in a letter. "We don't have the numbers to stand up to this on our own."[13]

A coalition of anti-fascists from Charlottesville and elsewhere was also making plans. If the city government didn't recognize what was about to happen, they did. This was about community self-defense. "We was prepared because we had intel,"[14] a local activist named Rosia Parker later recounted, referring to the Discord chats Will had collected. "We already knew they was coming here to kill. They wanted to kill us."

*   *   *

Will started to see chatter about a surprise torch march the night before the rally.[15] Eli Mosley, then a lieutenant in Identity Evropa, instructed attendees to buy tiki torches at stores outside Charlottesville so as not to "tip our enemy off." The Daily Stormer told its readers: "Make sure and get some tiki torch fuel/oil too. Otherwise they won't burn."

The march was a deliberate evocation of historical fascist rituals.[16] Fire is a fundamental symbol in fascism, representing purification and renewal, and wielded as a weapon to inflict terror. The 1920s Klan is often associated with its burning crosses, but it also marched in torchlight parades. On January 30, 1933, torchlight parades in Germany also celebrated the ascension of Hitler to chancellor. Months later, Goebbels and the National Socialist German Students' Association orchestrated a nationwide book burning, building towering pyres of "un-German" literature authored by Jews and socialists. Among the texts reduced to ash by the Nazis was a play by nineteenth-century German Jewish poet Heinrich Heine, which included the line "*Dort, wo man Bücher verbrennt, verbrennt man am Ende auch Menschen*": "Where they burn books, they will also ultimately burn people." Then, in 1934, Leni Riefenstahl's Nazi propaganda film *Triumph of the Will* featured dramatic footage of a Nuremberg rally where torch-wielding Nazis marched in formation, eventually aligning themselves to form a giant burning swastika.

The neo-Nazis arriving in Charlottesville were set to meet at Nameless Field on the University of Virginia campus just as night fell, where they'd begin a march to a statue of Thomas Jefferson. Gorcenski and some thirty anti-fascist demonstrators, many of them students, headed to the Jefferson statue to make a stand, linking arms as they heard chants of "Blood and soil!" and "Jews will not replace us!" get closer and closer. The fascists came into view: about three hundred of them carrying tiki torches and marching in rows of two. Suddenly Gorcenski and her comrades found themselves surrounded and vastly outnumbered.

A few blocks away, some one thousand people packed into St. Paul's Memorial Church for the interfaith service, where they sang a new rendition of the old Black spiritual called "Wade in the Water," a song Harriet Tubman used on the Underground Railroad[17] to warn escaping enslaved people to travel by creek or river so that slave patrols' dogs couldn't sniff out their trail. They sang with lyrics crafted to fit the occasion:

> *Wade in the water, wade in the water, children*
> *Wade in the water, God's gonna trouble the water*
> *In 1863 freedom was proclaimed*
> *In Charlottesville 14,000 were still enslaved*
> *In 1865 the freed people sang*
> *Started to build new lives, were thrown back again*
> *Jim Crow and the Klan came with laws and statues*
> *Terrorized the people in sheets and costumes*
> *The people fought, the Black struggle is strong*
> *It's beautiful and good and still moving along*
> *In 2017 new hate arose*
> *Immigrants and Muslims were some of the foes*
> *Jewish people too relived the hate*
> *LGBTQ got more of the same*
> *A call was sent for the faithful to come*
> *Stand against the alt right and the evil it does*
> *The people gathered in Charlottesville*
> *Then came to take a stand and share God's will.*

At the Jefferson statue the neo-Nazis started to attack the counterdemonstrators, punching them and spitting on them and beating them into the ground with their tiki torches. One man—who in the weeks leading up to this night had fantasized on Discord about sodomizing a leftist with a knife, writing that he was prepared to kill "if shit goes down"[18]—burst through the crowd and delivered a flying kick into Gorcenski's chest.

A Black UVA student named Devin Willis, surveying the crowd of neo-Nazis making monkey noises at him, realized that his clothes were wet. It was lighter fluid from the tiki torches, which all these screaming white men were wielding as weapons, with sparks flying. He feared that he might go up in flames.[19] Ray, the Daily Stormer writer and one of the main organizers of the weekend's festivities, shouted: "The heat here is nothing compared to what you're going to get in the ovens!"[20]

A neo-Nazi yelled at Natalie Romero, a Colombian American undergrad at UVA, to "go back" where she came from. Then, everything went dark. Someone had sprayed mace into her eyes. The fascists started to climb the Jefferson statue, waving their torches in the air, yelling "Hail victory!"—the English translation of the Nazi cry "Sieg Heil!"—and "Hail Spencer," referring to one of their leaders, Richard Spencer. "We own these streets!" Spencer barked. "We occupy this ground!"

The clergy inside the church started to receive messages about the violent scenes unfolding outside. State police had finally arrived at the Jefferson statue and intervened, making no arrests, allowing the fascist mob to march in packs back to their scattered cars, extinguishing their torches and dumping them into garbage cans along the way. Congregants in the church could hear their renewed chants of "Blood and soil" outside. Clergy made a decision to shelter in place until the chants faded into the distance.

"I think it's a good time for a prayer for our enemies,"[21] St. Paul's rector, Reverend William Peyton, said from the pulpit. "God called us to the hard work of loving our enemies. Lead them and lead us from prejudice to truth. Deliver them and deliver us from hatred, cruelty, and revenge."

Meanwhile, hundreds of their enemies, those who hadn't made it for the torch march, were on their way to Charlottesville for the main event the next day. James Alex Fields Jr., twenty, climbed into his gray 2010 Dodge Challenger in Maumee, Ohio—where he kept a copy of *Mein Kampf* in his bedroom—to begin the eight-hour overnight drive. "Be careful," his mom texted while he was on the road.

Fields replied to his mom by sending a photo of Hitler. "We're not the ones who need to be careful,"[22] he wrote.

*   *   *

"EVERYONE needs to get to the park as early as possible and defend our territory," Jason Kessler, a Charlottesville-based Proud Boy and the main organizer of the Unite the Right rally, wrote on Discord.[23] His compatriots listened, arriving hours before the noon start time on the rally permit. They marched in military formations as they approached the park. A large contingent from League of the South, the National Socialist Movement, and the Traditionalist Worker Party was led by Michael Tubbs—a hulking former demolitions specialist in the Army's Green Berets once convicted of stealing munitions from the military to bomb Black- and Jewish-owned businesses.[24] Tubbs led the group as they paraded with Confederate flags and Nazi flags with swastikas beneath a banner the city of Charlottesville had strung up above the street declaring DIVERSITY MAKES US STRONGER.

They marched past Congregation Beth Israel, too, where worshipers had gathered for an early morning Shabbat service, hoping to avoid a rally they thought was starting at noon. "There's the synagogue!" one of the neo-Nazis exclaimed, before the group broke into chants of "Sieg Heil!" Ray, the Daily Stormer writer, was carrying his own banner. GAS THE KIKES, RACE WAR NOW! it said.[25]

Meanwhile, on a set of steps at the entrance to Emancipation Park, the clergy from Congregate C'ville, joined by prominent faith leaders who'd answered their call to come to Charlottesville, including Reverend Traci Blackmon and Dr. Cornel West, all in their cassocks, vestments, and stoles, linked arms and waited. They were going to form a blockade at the entrance of the park. A nonviolent direct action to stop the neo-Nazis from holding their rally.

They were immediately overwhelmed. "Kill the faggot priests!" a fascist yelled as the clergy's blockade was broken by fists and flagpoles, sending Reverend Seth Wispelwey flying into a bush. "When I stood up and got my bearings again, a large man was just kind of standing over me and yelling 'Fuck you, faggot' over and over in my face," Wispelwey remembers. Some thirty officers in the Virginia state police stood nearby and watched, doing nothing. "And I'm standing next to Dr. West and he's like, 'Oh my god, no one's getting arrested today.'"[26]

The clergy reassembled their blockade. A group of anti-fascists approached, offering to help. "And we're like, 'All right, just so we're clear, we're going to hold space, but we're committed to not hitting back if hit,'" Wispelwey recalls telling them. "And they're like, 'We're down with that. We'll protect you.'"[27]

The next contingent of fascists was massive, and again the clergy were overwhelmed. The anti-fascists came to their defense, doing what the faith leaders had committed to not doing: fighting violence with violence. The blockade broke again, this time for good. "We would have been crushed like cockroaches if it were not for the anarchists and the anti-fascists who approached," Dr. West said later. "The anti-fascists, and then, crucial, the anarchists, they saved our lives, actually.[28] We would have been completely crushed, and I'll never forget that."

So began three hours of uninterrupted mob violence. The fascists assembled a phalanx of shields on the steps leading into the park, which was now crowded with some seven hundred members of this insurgent alt-right, having traveled there from at least thirty-five states and Canada. Fields, the twenty-year-old who texted his mom the photo of Hitler the previous night, stood next to Thomas Rousseau, the future leader of Patriot Front. Both wore the Vanguard America uniform: khakis, white polos, and plastic shields, while joining in all the chants: "Jews will not replace us!" and "Fuck you, faggots!" A local reporter heard multiple white supremacists encourage each other to "fire the first shot of the race war!"[29]

Charlottesville police chief Al Thomas observed the violence and reportedly told an assistant: "Let them fight, it will make it easier to declare an unlawful assembly."[30] At 11:28 a.m., as videos and images of the pitched battles on the streets of an American city went viral across the country, Virginia governor Terry McCauliffe declared the Unite the Right rally an unlawful assembly. He also declared a state of emergency. The cops finally moved in, attempting to push the fascists out of the park.

The story of the next few hours can be told in four iconic images taken by news photographers.

There was the photo of a snarling Richard Spencer, who put so much of this in motion, with his high-and-tight haircut and black sunglasses, leading a group of his followers in pushing against a line of riot cops, refusing to leave the park. For a while—to the astonishment of some journalists, who'd witnessed police for years use sheer brutality against peaceful Black Lives Matter demonstrators—the riot cops backed up, retreating. Eventually, though, Spencer and his minions fled the park, running through the streets. One of Spencer's supporters was screaming "Black lives splatter!"[31]

There was a photo of a Black counterdemonstrator named Corey Long repurposing a can of spray paint, which a neo-Nazi had thrown at him earlier, into a flamethrower. Slender and shirtless, Long aimed the long flame at a group of fascists swinging a Confederate flag at him. Richard Preston, a Klansman from Maryland, drew a handgun, firing a single round into the ground, just next to Long's leg. Later, Long would explain he'd used the flamethrower to protect an elderly, white counterdemonstrator standing behind him—mostly because the police weren't doing shit. "The cops were protecting the Nazis, instead of the people who live in the city," he said. "The cops basically just stood in their line and looked at the chaos. The cops were not protecting the people of Charlottesville. They were protecting the outsiders."[32]

Then there's the photo of Long's friend DeAndre Harris, a Black twenty-year-old aide to special needs kids at a local elementary school, lying on the concrete floor of a nearby parking garage, his arms wrapped around his head to protect himself from the beating he was receiving from a group of white men who were kicking him and hitting him with a wooden plank, a tire thumper, and a flagpole.[33] One of them said, "Die n***er."[34] Harris managed to get up and retreat into the parking garage's stairwell, where Long and an unknown woman named Karen administered aid and kept him awake. Long held the door to the stairwell shut as a group of neo-Nazis tried to push their way in. Harris had suffered a concussion, a spinal injury, a broken wrist, a chipped tooth, and a head wound that would require ten staples. Less than fifty yards away from the parking garage stood dozens of state police officers, inert.

And finally, there's the photo of the car speeding into a crowd of counter-demonstrators. They had been on the march after the rally ended, chanting "Black Lives Matter!" Despite the horror of the day's events, they had felt victorious. The Unite the Right rally, after all, had been called off before it could begin. None of the neo-Nazis got to give their little hate speeches in the park. "It felt like we had won,"[35] Elizabeth Sines, a law student at UVA, remembered. "We had taken back our town and protected our people." Unbeknownst to them, James Alex Fields Jr., that twenty-year-old from Ohio in the Vanguard America uniform, was idling nearby in his gray 2010 Dodge Challenger, eyeing the diverse, jubilant group of anti-fascists. The Discord chats planning Unite the Right had been rife with memes and fantasies of what Fields decided to do next: accelerate.

"I looked up and just see people in the air, so I did what any person would do: I got my loved one out the way, I pushed Marissa out the way," a local protester, Marcus Martin, remembered of saving his now-wife's life. "And then I got hit."[36] The photo shows Martin as he's thrown into the air. There are two empty pairs of shoes on the street below Martin, and other empty shoes suspended in midair alongside him—the force of the car's impact was such that it *literally knocked people out of their shoes.*

Romero, the UVA student who less than twenty-four hours earlier had been maced during the torch march, was plunged into darkness again. Fields's Dodge Challenger had sent her flying into a parked car, the impact fracturing her skull and rendering her unconscious. When she woke up, she was dripping with blood and wanted desperately to lie down and close her eyes, but feared she wouldn't wake up again.[37]

Nearby, a thirty-two-year-old legal assistant named Heather Heyer lay motionless on the pavement. Heyer had worn all black that day, not to join a black bloc, but because she was scheduled to work a shift at her second job as a waitress that evening. The car hit her directly in the torso, splattering her blood onto the hood and windshield.[38] Arriving EMTs found no pulse, no sign of breathing. Of the thirty-five people injured, many of them critically, Heyer was the only one to never wake up. Later, her grieving mother, receiving a deluge of threats from white supremacists, would elect to bury Heyer's ashes at an unmarked, undisclosed location to protect her final resting place from vandalism.[39]

"It literally looked as though a bomb had been dropped in the middle of that intersection," Don Gathers, the cofounder of Charlottesville Black Lives Matter, said of the aftermath.[40] Fields had put his car in reverse after the attack, driving over people as he attempted to escape. "There is just no describing the carnage that existed there."

Finally, the Charlottesville Police Department Swat Team showed up—in an armored vehicle called a Bearcat. An officer perched atop the vehicle was pointing a gun at all the bloodied counterprotesters below. "Why are you pointing this gun at us?!" a Black man yelled at the cop. "Why are you pointing it at *us*?!"[41]

Meanwhile, two pilots in the Virginia State Police were surveying the scene from a helicopter. "Oh my God, that car just drove through them," one trooper pilot said to the other, witnessing the attack from above. They maneuvered to follow Fields in his Challenger as he made his getaway, helping direct officers below to his location, where they made an arrest. (Fields, for all his bluster, reportedly broke down in tears and apologized.)

Then, a couple hours later, the same helicopter—it's still disputed whether from a malfunction or from pilot error—fell from the sky, crashing into a wooded area outside town, killing both troopers on board.[42] It felt like an apocalyptic closing act to the day.

Three people were now dead, so many others injured. A city was in shock, and much of the nation was reeling from the footage they were seeing. The anti-fascists who warned the city this would happen harbored a profound hatred for just how right they had been.

*　　　*　　　*

Almost a year later, Mayor Mike Signer apologized to Emily Gorcenski,[43] the local anti-fascist who had helped compile a dossier of the Discord posts for local officials ahead of Unite the Right, desperately trying to warn them about what was in store. "I want to credit you with the research you did and the specifics you did find," Signer told Gorcenski at a city council meeting. "It breaks our hearts because we should have been able to foresee and get the facts about what did come. You were right."

Instead, Charlottesville had already entered the pantheon of American locales whose very names—Selma, Kent State, Greensboro—became a sad shorthand for the era-defining political violence that occurred within their borders. People didn't say "Unite the Right" when they talked about the rally, they just said "Charlottesville," and by 2018 the city's name had come to invoke so much, not just the torch march and the beating of DeAndre Harris and the murder of Heather Heyer and the helicopter that fell from the sky, but also how the most powerful person in the country responded to the largest white supremacist demonstration in a generation.

"I think there's blame on both sides, and I have no doubt about it," President Trump said during a press conference at Trump Tower,[44] his gilded skyscraper in Manhattan, a few days after the rally, when asked about the violence that took place.

"The neo-Nazis started this thing," a reporter interjected. "They showed up in Charlottesville."

"Excuse me, they didn't put themselves down as neo-Nazis, and you had some very bad people in that group," Trump said.

"But you also had people that were very fine people on both sides . . . You had people in that group that were there to protest the taking down of, to them, a very, very important statue and the renaming of a park from Robert E. Lee to another name."

Very fine people on both sides.

"You had people—and I'm not talking about the neo-Nazis and the white nationalists, because they should be condemned totally—but you had many people in that group other than neo-Nazis and white nationalists, okay?" Trump added.

"And the press has treated them absolutely unfairly," the president continued. "Now, in the other group also, you had some fine people, but you also had troublemakers and you see them come with the black outfits and with the helmets and with the baseball bats—you had a lot of bad people in the other group, too."

A lot of bad people in the other group, too.

It was, of course, absurd to suggest that anyone who participated in Unite the Right wasn't a racist or a white nationalist or a neo-Nazi. It was also absurd to draw any moral equivalence between the fascists and those protesting them. The rally's organizers picked up on the subtext of Trump's remarks as a show of support for what they'd done. "Thank you President Trump for your honesty & courage to tell the truth," David Duke, the former Klan leader, tweeted. Richard Spencer called Trump's statement "fair and down to earth."[45]

It's often forgotten the degree to which Unite the Right was in essence a Trump rally. Its participants carried Trump signs inscribed with swastikas. They wore MAKE AMERICA GREAT AGAIN hats. They yelled variations of "Trump is going to get rid of you!" to Black and brown counterprotesters.

The so-called alt-right felt it had helped Trump win the presidency, that with their online propaganda they had "memed" him into the White House. Unite the Right was its victory lap. And the white supremacists who gathered there weren't going to let outrage over the violence, and Heyer's murder in particular, spoil their fun.

Will witnessed their glee in Discord messages. "For all it's worth, we fucking killed someone," a user of the Charlottesville planning chat gloated. A member of Vanguard America wrote: "This was the biggest victory for our movement in history. It was glorious. We fucked up many commies . . . We hospitalized dozens . . . We got our guys out, without police help. We won . . ." Another added: "I don't think we should hand out shields anymore . . . We should hand out Dodge Challengers instead."[46]

Two weeks after the rally, Unicorn Riot started to publish these messages online, part of a massive trove of Discord screenshots Will had collected. He'd also given the outlet's journalists his login info. Eventually the entirety of the server was scraped of its content. Unicorn Riot's database was born, containing a staggering 575,000 posts.

The database would go on to serve as the basis for *Sines v. Kessler*, the landmark federal lawsuit against fourteen of Unite the Right's organizers, plus ten organizations that took part, detailing how the violence that day was premeditated. The plaintiffs, all counterprotesters injured during the day's events, filed a 111-page civil complaint that might stand as one of the most horrifying documents in modern American history, showing a bloodthirsty and emboldened fascist movement on the march in the twenty-first century. Eventually, after a jury trial, every single defendant was found guilty, with the plaintiffs winning a $24 million judgment, which was later reduced to $2 million.[47] The lawsuit sent some of the defendants, like the Daily Stormer's Ray, into hiding. It bankrupted others and hastened the demise of multiple groups, including League of the South, the National Socialist Movement, and Vanguard America.

"If those chat leaks hadn't existed, that federal lawsuit wouldn't have happened. It's kind of amazing," Will says. "It's incredible. I'm pretty happy I was able to do that. I never would've done the legal route or anything, but that stuff can work."

Prosecutors also used the Discord leaks to win a conviction against Fields for the car attack—he was ultimately sentenced to two life sentences, plus 419 years, with no possibility of parole.[48]

But beyond these legal outcomes, the leaks served as the basis for a wave of unmaskings, either published by a burgeoning coterie of digital media journalists, suddenly finding themselves on the "extremism" beat, or by a burgeoning new coalition of anti-fascist researchers, all doing their part to name and shame Trump's "very fine people."

The man at the torch march who delivered a flying kick at Gorcenski? He bragged in an online chat afterward that he'd "drop kicked" that "tranny" and that he'd "cracked 3 skulls open with virtually no damage to myself." ProPublica and *Frontline* exposed him as eighteen-year-old Vasillios Pistolis.[49] "At the end of the weekend that shocked much of the country, Pistolis returned to his everyday life: serving in the US Marine Corps," ProPublica wrote in its story.

Gorcenski herself unmasked the user on Discord who went by "Tyrone"— the one who inquired, "Is it legal to run over protesters blocking roadways?" ahead of the rally. He was a Marine, too. It took Gorcenski only ninety minutes to find his real name. She pored over Tyrone's posts to find clues, coming across a recent birth announcement for him and his wife, who were expecting twins. "Reversing White Genocide, 2 at a time," Tyrone had written. Gorcenski found a Facebook post from a thirty-six-year-old named Michael Chesny revealing he'd just welcomed twin baby girls into the world. After finding more evidence connecting Chesny to the "Tyrone" pseudonym, Gorcenski doxed him on Twitter. Al Jazeera picked up on the story,[50] revealing that before Chesny went to Charlottesville, he had a specialty in explosives in the Marines, serving a six-month tour of Afghanistan as part of a light armored reconnaissance unit. Before that Chesny was stationed at Guantanamo Bay, where the US military tortures prisoners, almost all of them brown and Muslim, who have never been charged with a crime.

"Americana-MD" in the Discord chats, who boasted he was bringing a "n***er mulcher" to the rally, was also in the military. Using the messages in the Unicorn Riot database, *The Daily Beast* reported that his real name was Brandon Troy Higgs.[51] A Navy cryptologist, Higgs was later sentenced to twenty-five years in prison[52] for shooting a Black concrete mason in the leg during a dispute outside his home in Reisterstown, Maryland, near Baltimore, after shouting "go back to Africa!" The leaked chats showed Higgs had fantasized about killing Black people in the area,[53] writing, "I decided I'm going to create my own group called Baltimore Animal Control and buy those dog patrol poles with the snare at the end and wrangle n***ers with it." He added: "Also want to leave bear traps in Baltimore city with buckets of KFC chicken."

When a pseudonymous mainstay on the neo-Nazi podcast circuit, "Coach Finstock," revealed during an episode of "The Fatherland" that he'd attended Unite the Right, wearing a "hat and sunglasses" to avoid being identified, the Southern Poverty Law Center started digging. Turned out Coach Finstock's real name was Matthew Gebert,[54] and he was a foreign affairs officer for the US State Department's Bureau of Energy Resources. He lived in a large, $533,000 house in suburban Virginia where he hosted frequent fascist soirees with guests like David Irving, the world-infamous Holocaust denier. While Gebert was making appearances on neo-Nazi podcasts, once advocating for the creation of a nuclear-armed white ethnostate, he was also clocking in to work at Foggy Bottom in DC, reporting to deputy secretaries and political appointees for his job in the State Department and joining important policy meetings about Iran, Russia, and India. In a subsequent report, Unicorn Riot was able to find his pseudonym in Discord chats[55] planning the violence in Charlottesville. The State Department official's posts included a meme expressing admiration for Hitler and Mussolini, a photo of a swastika-shaped cookie, and a photo of a pilfered yard sign, reading NO MATTER WHERE YOU'RE FROM, WE ARE GLAD YOU ARE OUR NEIGHBOR, ridden with bullet holes.

One Unite the Right attendee, returning home after the rally, paid tribute to Fields by buying the same make, model, and color car that Fields used to kill Heather Heyer. "I done did it," a man going by "Rhodes Slovka" wrote on Facebook, posting a photo of himself standing next to his very own gray 2010 Dodge Challenger. An anti-fascist researcher who operated a Twitter account called MakePalsOnline revealed Slovka to be an Army veteran and former staff assistant to US Senator Roy Blunt, a Republican from Missouri. Slovka had gone to Unite the Right as a member of Identity Dixie, a neo-Confederate group, and a photo of him there shows him shaking hands with David Duke, the former Klan leader.

Another Identity Dixie member went by "scNazi" on Discord. The leaked messages showed him coordinating travel and lodging ahead of Unite the Right, renting a "hate van" and booking a series of Airbnbs near Charlottesville where dozens of neo-Nazis would party after the rally. scNazi once wrote on Discord that South Carolina, where he lived, was the "first in secession," referring to how it seceded from the union at the onset of the Civil War, and would be the "first to rehabilitate fake shower rooms." It was a reference to how Nazis at Auschwitz disguised gas chambers as washrooms, emitting Zyklon-B from the showerheads instead of water, a method used to mass-murder over a million Jews. scNazi, according to evidence uncovered by the anti-fascist MakePalsOnline, was actually Tim Manning,[57] a social studies teacher at Pleasant Hill Middle School in Lexington, South Carolina, where he also coached the girls volleyball team.

The story about the middle school teacher went viral, picked up by news outlets across the country. Manning, through a lawyer, denied that he was scNazi but was suspended from his job pending an investigation. He decided to take a job at another South Carolina school soon after, where he was promptly fired amid accusations that he wrote "n***er" on the whiteboard during a class.[58]

The anti-fascist behind the MakePalsOnline Twitter account, who we'll call Paul, doxed many members of Identity Dixie after Unite the Right, but there's one dox that still haunts him. One day Paul posted a photo to Twitter showing a man wearing a light-blue polo shirt and carrying a Confederate flag, marching in Charlottesville on his way to the park. Paul needed help: Did anybody recognize this man?

Identity Dixie members saw Paul's tweet, posting it into a private chat they shared. They recognized the man in the photo, prompting one of them to post his name: James Lee Ginther III. Identity Dixie members started to talk more about Ginther, hoping that he would not be identified by anti-fascists. "A convicted murderer being tied to us would not be a good look," one member wrote. They were unaware that Paul had infiltrated their chat group, lurking and reading their messages. They had just unwittingly identified Ginther for an anti-fascist.

Paul started to read up on James Lee Ginther III and was horrified. Three months after marching in Unite the Right,[60] the Navy veteran had kidnapped his ex-wife, with whom he had two children, and took her to a forest where he'd already dug a hole in the ground. He forced the mother of his children, twenty-seven-year-old Suzette Ginther, to kneel down by the hole before shooting her in the back of the head "execution-style,"[61] hastily burying her in a shallow grave. Hours later a hunter noticed Suzette's foot sticking out of the ground[62] and called the police. Ginther was arrested in Kentucky as he attempted to flee across the country to Wyoming. He was later sentenced to life without parole.

The doxes after Charlottesville were rife with stories of violence against women, prompting Paul to muse why white supremacist groups weren't more frequently described as anti-women. "When these misogynistic hate-group members commit violence against men or groups, we assign their hate group some blame," Paul wrote in his dox of Ginther. "Why don't we do that when they beat or kill the women around them?"

Paul had started to do anti-fascist work after watching the horror of Unite the Right on the news. He felt like something had shifted in American politics, and he needed to do *something*. He'd seen anti-fascists on Twitter unmasking the neo-Nazis who terrorized Charlottesville. "I figured I might be able to do it, too," he says. "And if I can, I should ... And if I can't, if I fall on my face, and I can't do it, then fine. But if I can do it, and I don't, then it feels like I am abdicating my share of responsibility for this world."

As he unmasked Identity Dixie, Paul found himself ushered into a sprawling subculture of anti-fascist researchers, most of whom went by pseudonyms, operating individually, or in small affinity groups, or in older, more formalized antifa organizations. Most of the people, he says, tended to be younger than him and "further to the left." Some were tech savvy, some weren't. What united them, Paul says, is they all just universally seemed to "give a shit."

And many of them, like him, had been radicalized by what they'd seen in Charlottesville. If Unite the Right's legacy is one of horrific violence and what that violence represented, its legacy is also of inspiring a new generation of anti-fascists.

"Charlottesville was pivotal: a true historical inflection point, when, for many, illusions shattered, and it became clear that the fascist threat was viscerally, horrifically real," Shane Burley, the anti-fascist scholar, reflected once.[63] "Yet the events of that day did not represent a final culmination. Their true significance will play out over decades, and whether Charlottesville stands as a symbol of trauma or the beginning of a rebellion against white supremacy will be determined by what comes next."

CHAPTER 11
Good Night White Pride

In the ensuing years, the Unicorn Riot database grew and grew. In 2018, an anti-fascist successfully infiltrated Identity Evropa, a white supremacist group that played a major role at the Unite the Right rally in Charlottesville. This infiltrator, after passing a series of vetting interviews on the phone, was granted access to the Identity Evropa's server on Discord, where he lingered for six months, collecting messages. (Unlike Vincent, this spy only had to pretend to be a fascist *online*, not in real life. Identity Evropa, unlike Patriot Front, didn't require in-person attendance at group events to maintain membership.)

This spy, whom we'll call Dylan, eventually gathered over 770,000 messages authored by hundreds of Identity Evropa members, all hiding behind pseudonyms. Dylan had coordinated this infiltration with a large network of anti-fascists, who in the early months of 2019 started using the stolen messages to prepare a wave of doxes. He remembers his comrades in this coalition having different reasons for doing the work. One guy was a military veteran radicalized after fighting in "this country's dumb wars," Dylan says. Someone else started doing the work after a neighbor called Immigration and Customs Enforcement (ICE) on their mom, who was an undocumented immigrant.

Dylan and his comrades had fun thinking up a name for this mass-doxing project of theirs. It had to be something kind of stupid that belittled Identity Evropa, a group that reveled in its own supposed grandiosity, regarding itself as more educated than other fascist groups, its members often drawn from university campuses and the professional classes. Identity Evropa was fond of high-and-tight haircuts and suits and ties, which its members wore while ingratiating themselves with Republican Party officials. Three Identity Evropa members had managed to become paid employees of Republican Kris Kobach's campaign for Kansas governor.[1] James Allsup, a prominent Identity Evropa member, had become a precinct committee officer for the Whitman County, Washington, Republican Party.[2]

Patrick Casey, the Identity Evropa leader, had encouraged members to enter local politics like this. "Today I decided to get involved in my county's Republican party," he wrote on Discord. "Everyone can do this without fear of getting doxed. The GOP is essentially the White man's party at this point (it gets Whiter every election cycle), so it makes far more sense for us to subvert it than to create our own party."[3]

Eventually Dylan and the other anti-fascists landed on a suitably silly moniker for their project: "Panic! In The Discord Antifa," a play on the name of the pop rock band Panic! At The Disco.

On March 10, 2019, Panic! In The Discord launched a website featuring an old American anti-racist skinhead piece of art: a silhouette of a person in black bloc kicking a neo-Nazi, surrounded by the words "GOOD NIGHT WHITE PRIDE."[4]

"Following a wildly successful deep dive into the Identity Evropa Discord servers," the site's inaugural post announced, "we are proud to bring you the subsequent detailed dossiers on Discord users, compiled by combing through messages finding context clues, the members' own poor executions of #opsec, then comparing it to unearthed social media profiles, publicly available information, and anything else we could find in order to present Panic! In The Discord doxes."

The subsequent doxes linked to and cited some of the 770,000 Discord messages Dylan had collected, which were now accessible to the public in the Unicorn Riot database.[5] Over the next year, Panic! In The Discord, collaborating with other anti-fascist groups, would unmask a jaw-dropping one hundred members of Identity Evropa.

The doxes laid bare how the fascists had made real inroads with the wider conservative movement, enmeshing themselves inside a network of university groups funded, in part, by David and Charles Koch, the far-right billionaire industrialists. One Identity Evropa member was the leader of the Federalist

Society on his campus. Another held a leadership position in the Koch-funded group Young Americans for Liberty. Another delivered a speech at a gathering of the Koch-funded Institute for Humane Studies. And yet another was a regional field coordinator for the Koch-funded Leadership Institute, which trains conservative activists.[8]

Three Identity Evropa members were exposed as high school teachers, including Kevin Pummill—alias: UndercoverAcademic—who taught social studies and ran the Politics Club at Pekin Community High School in Pekin, Illinois. He bragged in Discord chats that he was indoctrinating his students with white nationalism, giving them the "redpill" on immigration, telling them, "We are being invaded" by immigrants.

"We believe that Kevin is entirely unfit to teach children," the anti-fascist author of Pummill's dox wrote.[9] "Not only does he promote white nationalist ideas in the classroom, but he's a virulent bigot. His ignorance and intolerance should in no way be tolerated in the classroom. We demand he be suspended immediately and ultimately fired." (Pummill resigned.[10] The other two teachers were placed on leave and eventually fired.)

This wave of Identity Evropa doxes were often done in conjunction with pressure campaigns. After the group Atlanta Antifascists exposed a member using the alias Why Tea, activists called his employer, a prominent tech company, where he had a plum gig as a managing consultant, letting his bosses know he should probably be fired. They also mailed one hundred flyers to the man's neighbors featuring a photo of his face and the words "ALERT: WHITE POWER AGITATOR IN YOUR NEIGHBOR-HOOD."

The dox, noting Why Tea's white-collar job, also included a bit of anti-fascist class analysis. "We hope to dispel the idea that organized white nationalism is largely or exclusively the product of poor and uneducated white people," the dox stated. "The movement has upper- and middle-class constituencies, who are arguably a greater danger due to their increased access to resources and heavier political clout."

One of the more attention-grabbing doxes was of a sixty-six-year-old Identity Evropa member—alias Singleton Mosby WV—named Howard Fezell,[12] a lawyer who had served on the board of directors of the National Rifle Association (NRA), the powerful gun lobby group. Sometimes Fezell had to ask the younger members to help him understand all the latest lingo.

"I am an old fart who is out of touch with many new things," he'd written once. "What is a chad? And a manlet?"[13]

Anti-fascists would sometimes send doxes to mainstream media outlets, hoping journalists there might write a story of their own, giving the dox wider exposure and credibility. *The Daily Beast* wrote about Daniel Morley,[14] an Identity Evropa member unmasked by anti-fascists as a Virginia police officer. "Doesn't get more real than cruising around, listening to music, and kicking ass," he'd written on a message board once. Morley was fired.[15]

But not every unmasked Identity Evropa member lost their job. A member who went by the alias Nick_Night was exposed as a manager at Boeing, the aerospace company, where he was responsible for overseeing the upgrade of a global satellite communications network. "It is concerning and worrying that Boeing employs a white nationalist in such a role," the group Eugene Antifa noted. Although anti-fascists contacted Boeing about Nick_Night, it's unclear if the company ever fired him. Boeing didn't respond to a request for comment.

Meanwhile, the US military kicked out only six of the eleven service-members exposed as Identity Evropa members. When asked by *HuffPost* about the white supremacists the military was allowing to remain in its ranks, officials largely declined to answer.[17]

Still, as the doxes continued—a pharmacist, a nurse, a realtor, a sheriff's deputy in training—it was clear they were having an impact. Casey, the Identity Evropa leader, attempted a rebrand: The group would now be the American Identity Movement.[18] The change, he explained, was in part to avoid bans on social media platforms for violating their terms of service regarding hate speech. It was also to lose the "baggage" of Identity Evropa's association with the rally in Charlottesville. (Multiple members were named as defendants in a multimillion-dollar lawsuit over the day's violence.)

Meanwhile, Casey's subordinates were reeling from being unmasked. They formed a "Dox Support" group on a new chat platform called Matter-Most (which other anti-fascists later infiltrated).[19] One member wrote that his wife had "lost her job of 6 years" after being exposed as a supporter of Identity Evropa, Unicorn Riot reported. Another member expressed deep anxiety about his family's reaction. "My uncle, whose son is dating a black girl, hasn't made eye contact and he turns his back to me every time we're in the same room . . ." he wrote. "No one really wants to talk to me at all.

This kinda sucks guys." Another member recommended paying an "online reputation management company" to create "positive internet real estate occupying the top results" of search engines. Some discussed changing their legal names so that they'd still be able to get jobs.

Eventually, on November 2, 2020, the eve of the presidential election between Biden and Trump, Casey posted a statement announcing that American Identity Movement, formerly known as Identity Evropa, was disbanding.[20] "The membership organization model is simply not the vehicle that will take us across the finish line," Casey said. "For this reason, the disbanding of AIM is best understood as a strategic reorientation, one that will allow the dissident right to network, host events, create content, and engage in activism in more fruitful ways."

Dylan, the spy who started it all, was thrilled. "It feels like if you're a left-wing person you don't get a lot of wins, you don't come out of too many situations victorious, but we got those guys. We got everything we wanted. That's a rare feeling if you're a left-wing activist. I haven't felt that way since."

＊　　　＊　　　＊

"I can't shout out and credit the Unicorn Riot Identity Evropa leaks enough," Heidi Beedle of Colorado Springs Anti-Fascists says. "That was like Christmas for researchers. So much came out of that."

She's particularly proud of one Identity Evropa dox. The bald, thirty-something man was "brazen," Beedle remembers, turning up to Identity Evropa demonstrations in Colorado Springs unmasked. Then one day an anonymous tipster sent her group a name for the man: Cory Reeves.

The tip came with little other info about Reeves, except a suggestion that he might be in the Air Force. This, of course, wasn't nearly enough information to publish a dox, so Beedle got to work. She searched Google for "Cory Reeves" in the military and found nothing but dead ends for hours until eventually coming across an archived KHON2 News TV segment from 2015 about a home break-in in Kailua, Hawaii.

The local reporters had interviewed a "Cory Reeves" on camera about the break-in, which occurred in the house next to his. The footage showed a bald man with a distinctive tattoo on his left arm. Likely unbeknownst to the KHON2 News team, the man in the footage was wearing a T-shirt with white supremacist imagery, specifically a skull in a Nazi helmet.

Beedle searched the Identity Evropa Discord leaks for the word "Hawaii," to see if any members mentioned having lived in the state. A user going by "Argument of Perigee CO" wrote that he had been "the only IE member in Hawaii for a long time" but had moved recently to Colorado Springs. Argument of Perigee had also posted a photo of himself inside his new Colorado house, where he was hosting a small Christmas party for Identity Evropa members. He wore a black turtleneck and a suit jacket, standing next to his fireplace and holding up a book, its title illegible. His was the only face visible in the photo, prompting a discussion among members on Discord whether it was good OPSEC to appear in IE communications or propaganda unmasked. Argument of Perigee waved away any concerns, writing: "High-resolution photos of my face are all over Antifa websites and they are clueless to my identity."

Beedle searched assessor property records and eventually found an address for a Cory Reeves. She then cross-referenced that address with the same address on Zillow, the real estate site, finding interior photos of the home, including the exact same living room, with the exact same fireplace, where Argument of Perigee had hosted his holiday soiree.

She also found a photo Argument of Perigree had posted showing his arm, with that same distinctive tattoo from the TV news segment in Hawaii. "There were so many levels of verification," Beedle remembers.

The dox went live,[21] with Beedle using her own knowledge of the military to describe Reeves's concerningly high-level position in the Air Force. "Cory Allen Reeves is a Master Sergeant with the US Air Force of the 50th Space Wing at Schriever Air Force Base located in Colorado Springs . . ." the dox stated. "Cory Reeves has one of the most sensitive and technical jobs in the Armed Forces outside of Special Operations Command. He most certainly has a security clearance, at least a Secret, but due to the nature of his work he might have a Top Secret clearance . . ."

HuffPost quickly picked up on the story:[22]

"We are aware of this allegation and Air Force officials are looking into it,"
an Air Force spokesman told HuffPost . . .

After reaching out to Reeves for comment, HuffPost received an email from his lawyer, [. . .] a Florida man who was also recently exposed as a member of Identity Evropa.

"MSgt Cory Reeves is a highly decorated Airman with fifteen years of service to our country," [the lawyer's] email read. "I respectfully submit that creating a news article based on an anonymous social media post generated by nameless and faceless individuals who, by their own admission, are anarchists is extremely careless."

[The] email did not deny that Reeves was part of Identity Evropa.

Reeves, [the lawyer] wrote, is "free to join a responsible and professional organization" without "fear of reprisal by Department of Defense officials."

The military eventually demoted Reeves from master sergeant. Then, months later, an Air Force spokeswoman announced he'd been discharged but, citing the Privacy Act, wouldn't disclose the circumstances of his separation.[23]

Beedle believes she is good at anti-fascist research, in part, because she is neurodivergent. "You have to spend so much time sifting through ridiculous data, pages of Google searches, and all of these chats, and you have to have this kind of obsessive level of attention and this obsessive kind of drive," she says. "The right kind of coined the term 'weaponized autism,' which is awful and problematic, and I don't really like that kind of language, but I mean, there are certain things about different ways of thinking and being that shine in certain areas of research and data collection."

As much as the right wants to paint antifa as violent, she adds, "The vast majority of what being Antifa is, is just like, computer research, internet stuff, and then kind of basic, basic journalism." There was, admittedly, also evidence to suggest that Colorado Springs Anti-Fascists were doing more than just online activism. Neo-Nazis kept getting their cars redecorated around town, NAZI SCUM scrawled in red paint on the exterior, their tires slashed.

Once, when a Patriot Front banner appeared hanging on a highway overpass, it was quickly removed, reappearing again at an anti-fascist fundraiser and benefit show. "We charged people $1 to write snarky messages on it and helped raise over $800 for the Colorado Immigrant Rights Coalition," a Colorado Springs Anti-Fascists member told a local paper.[24]

They were really starting to piss off the far right in Colorado. "Be aware that you will enrage your target by naming them," "Forming an Antifa Group:

A Manual" had warned new anti-fascists years earlier when it circulated in anarchist spaces online. "You might have been ignored as a public group for a year doing antifa stuff, but once you refer to a local racist by name, they will fixate on you."

Colorado Springs Anti-Fascists acknowledged the blowback in an article on its website.[25]

"So in the last 24 hours our Facebook page has been flooded by reactionary trolls . . ." the group wrote. "They insult us for being weak, effeminate, queers (which, yea, is true, we're a bunch of LGBTQ+ people and most of us are sassy bottoms) . . . but the fact is we have been kicking ass in Colorado for over two years now, and we're not fucking going anywhere."

Fake Colorado antifa accounts, clearly created by neo-Nazi trolls, started to appear on Twitter and Facebook, posting extreme and violent messages to smear the area's anti-fascists as dangerous radicals. Posters with similar messages started appearing in the Denver and Colorado Springs area, too. Local media reported stories about how extreme antifa seemed to be getting, without verifying whether this propaganda was *actually being produced* by antifa. A spokesperson from Colorado Springs Anti-Fascists talked to *Westword*, a local alt-weekly, to correct the record:[26]

> *These tactics are classic counterintelligence. They're muddying the waters, obscuring the truth, and covering everything in moral ambiguity . . .*
>
> *The right's narrative is that "antifa" are violent thugs (or delicate snowflakes—we're fucking Schrödinger's leftists over here). These fake sites make outrageous calls for violence in the kind of tone used by caricatures of Stalin from the 1950s: "Capitalist, racist swine that needs to be slaughtered." GTFO with that nonsense. We don't issue calls to violence. We don't make grandiose accusations about who deserves to live or die. We'll confront white supremacists marching and organizing in our streets, we'll dox active racists and white supremacists, and we'll try to keep those people out of public spaces and platforms. We're not Marxist street thugs looking to attack hapless Trump supporters, but the rhetoric of these fake antifa accounts is designed to portray us that way to those who don't know.*

There were also far-right counterintelligence efforts underway to dox members of Colorado Springs Anti-Fascists. In late 2019, when Beedle's involvement with the group was still unknown outside a small circle of leftists, she started to see chatter among Identity Evropa accounts on Twitter about doxing her. And they were getting close.

Beedle had recently been named "Teacher of the Year" at a local high school but had left education to make a go of it as a freelance journalist and columnist for some local newspapers. Online she had been operating multiple Twitter accounts, and by her own admission was sloppy with her OPSEC, making "stupid, basic" mistakes, including using similar usernames across multiple accounts, one of which was only semi-anonymous and frequently linked to articles that she'd written for the *Colorado Times-Recorder*, among other publications, that were bylined with her real name.

Local fascists put the pieces together and her name started to circulate in far-right spaces online, along with her address. She decided to get ahead of the story. "So, I guess it is time to come clean,"[27] she tweeted in October 2019. "They are kinda right. You know what they say about broken clocks. I did start the [Colorado Springs Anti-Fascists] account, and the blog. I did my part to stem the rising tide of fascism, but I have been 'retired' for a while now."

Beedle had, in fact, stepped back from Colorado Springs Anti-Fascists, finding the workload too much to sustain. She remembers bracing herself for blowback after the dox and noticing Identity Evropa and Patriot Front stickers in her neighborhood but not being able to tell if they were targeted at her. Things stayed relatively quiet.

Then on November 13, 2020, a Colorado-based conservative podcaster and activist named Joel Oltmann filed a sworn affidavit, at the behest of Trump campaign attorney Sidney Powell, claiming he had infiltrated an "antifa Zoom call"[28] in Colorado just before the November 3, 2020, presidential election. Oltmann claimed a man on this call named Eric assured everyone not to worry about a Trump victory, saying: "Trump is not going to win. I made fucking sure of that . . . Hahaha."

It's unclear what Zoom call this actually was, or if it ever even took place, but Oltmann baselessly claimed in the affidavit that the "Eric" in question was Eric Coomer, the director of product strategy and security for Dominion Voting Systems, a company responsible for manufacturing and maintaining voting machines across the country. Oltmann's reason for thinking the Zoom call was organized by antifa? He asserted—again, without evidence—that a journalist present on the call was Heidi Beedle, who had been outed as a member of the Colorado Springs Anti-Fascists.

Later that week, Trump's legal team, including Powell and former New York City mayor Rudy Giuliani, held a bizarre press conference during which they repeated the allegations that a Dominion Voting Systems employee was cavorting with antifa.[29] (Trump's legal team, *The New York Times* later reported, parroted Oltmann's antifa accusation even after an internal campaign memo emphatically stated: "There Is No Evidence to the Claim That Dominion's Head of Strategy and Security Has Ties to Antifa.")[30]

Beedle felt like she had somehow Forrest Gumped herself into Trump's historic, anti-democratic effort to deny the results of the 2020 election. A month later, Coomer, from Dominion Voting Systems, would file a lawsuit against Oltmann and Trump for defamation. When Oltmann was deposed, he referenced Beedle a dozen times.[31] "Heidi is a man," he said at one point, misgendering her. "Heidi is a man who dresses up as a woman." He also admitted that he could not be sure if Beedle was on the "antifa Zoom call" at all. (Beedle says she was never on any such call.)

Things again stayed relatively quiet for Beedle until a year later, when the world's richest man decided anti-fascists like her shouldn't be on Twitter. In 2022, far-right activist and journalist Andy Ngo started tagging Twitter's new owner, Elon Musk, in posts about antifa, egging him on to ban the "violent extremists" from the platform.

The Portland-based Ngo, author of *Unmasked: Inside Antifa's Radical Plan to Destroy Democracy*, had risen to prominence in right-wing media as the go-to man for anti-antifa propaganda, frequently doxing or unmasking leftist radicals he claimed were a graver threat than white supremacists or neo-Nazis. (His work earned him a viral bit of reprisal in 2019 when anti-fascists were seen in a video punching him and throwing a milkshake in his face during a rally in Portland, an incident that would become central to a burgeoning anti-antifa panic sweeping the country, with Ngo its cause célèbre.)

When Musk bought Twitter in 2022 for an eventual price of $44 billion, he promised to make it a bastion of "free speech," which in practice meant making the social media platform a fascist free-for-all, a slew of banned neo-Nazi accounts risen from the dead and given license to spew vitriol. Ngo had over a million followers on Twitter, Musk among them, so when he started to tag the Tesla and SpaceX founder, asking him to boot anti-fascist accounts off the platform, the billionaire obliged.

"Breaking: @COSAntiFascists, the Colorado Springs cell of #Antifa, has been suspended on Twitter," Ngo wrote in a tweet that would be viewed one million times. "The account has operated for years instructing comrades to assault people & directing members to get the home addresses, phone numbers of targets. It had 15k followers."

In the next tweet, he pretended that he had personally unmasked Beedle, who he called a "violent extremist," even though she'd admitted to being in antifa two years prior:

"Breaking: The #Antifa member who ran the violent Twitter account of the Colorado Springs cell of Antifa @COSAntiFascists/@COSAntiFa is trans furry activist/Colorado Times reporter @HeidiBeedle, formerly known as [deadname redacted] Beedle. Beedle was or is a teacher."

Right-wing news outlets picked up on Ngo's thread. *The Daily Mail* published an article with a headline that screamed: "REVEALED: Left-wing activist who founded banned Colorado Springs Antifa Twitter account is trans reporter and former teacher accused of 'brainwashing' students and giving them kinky books."[32]

Beedle was like a right-wing fever dream. A tatted and nose-pierced "trantifa" indoctrinating America's youth. She had, in fact, written on a blog about once comparing Trump's rhetoric to Hitler's while teaching a class and later received a warning from the principal after a parent complained. Beedle had also written about giving a student a copy of the novel *Nevada* during Transgender Awareness month, which features a trans protagonist. By her own admission, Beedle realized afterward that it maybe wasn't the "best judgment call" as the book opens with a "kinky sex scene."

Ngo and *The Daily Mail* cited a tweet from the Colorado Springs Anti-Fascist account as evidence of Beedle's "violent extremism." "A nationwide recall has been issued on all transphobe's teeth," the tweet read. "It's up to each and every one of us to help out where we can."

Beedle denied writing the tweet but didn't denounce it, calling it a "banger." She had decided to strike a defiant tone in her response to this round of doxing, mounting a concise defense of militant anti-fascism. "Do I support violence?" she tweeted. "Yes. F*ck 'em. Remember Unite the Right? This year's Idaho Pride? Club Q? Countless examples show these people can and will harm marginalized people, and the cops and the system aren't going to stop them."

Only a few weeks prior, a few miles from where Beedle lived in Colorado Springs, a twenty-two-year-old man had entered a queer bar called Club Q, on the eve of Transgender Remembrance Day, and opened fire. He killed five people and wounded another twenty. Police would later testify that they found rainbow-colored shooting targets in his home.[33]

"I am [very] proud of how miserable I made all those asshole's lives," Beedle tweeted about her time researching the far right. "If I could go back in time, not only would I do it all again, but knowing what I know about Jan. 6, I would do it with a renewed vigor and ferocity. You can do it too! Form an affinity group, dox some chuds."

Finally, she added: "If they want me to shut up they will have to kill me. Support your local antifa, your local alt-news source, and your local LGBTQ youth center. All you fascists are bound to lose."

Despite the defiant tone she struck publicly, the whole experience left Beedle rattled. Mostly she had never wanted any of her antifa activism to be *about her.* Beyond anti-fascist anonymity providing a defense from recriminations, it's also a way to forestall any individual anti-fascist from becoming a figurehead. A public face. It's a mostly anarchist enterprise after all—there are no leaders.

Looking back, she has a confusing mix of feelings about her time in antifa. She remembers all the research she did into groups like Identity Evropa being a total "mind-fuck," experiencing a baffling mix of horror and sympathy. "Like I read the frickin' *Turner Diaries,* you know? . . . You consume all this media and you just sit with it, and it definitely takes a toll, right? Like, when you gaze into the abyss, the abyss also gazes into you.

"It's just listening to people talk about how disgusting and awful they think you and your friends are, and how they want to, like, kill you," she adds. "And that sort of thing is rough." Still, she says, "You spend so much time combing through these guys' digital footprints and their social media and the things that they post and say, and trying to piece together these things about these people—and it's kind of bizarre . . . I don't know, like, maybe I've turned into like this soft liberal since I've left the radical spaces or whatever, but it's hard not to have empathy for some of these guys, because like, these groups do systematically prey on these kind of disaffected young men."

She also feels a little ambivalent about her statements ardently supporting punching Nazis. "I don't feel as self-righteous these days," she says, adding: "I have this very kind of Christian approach now to non-violence.

"I wish there was some way we could turn the temperature down and get people to stop being Nazis, you know? But antifa, in a lot of ways, it's *all you have at hand.* And when you're, like, a scared queer person, it's very—it's something empowering to do. You hear these new stories about all these regressive trans laws that are being passed now, and you hear stories about hate crimes and drag clubs getting like firebombed, and like the Club Q shooting here in Colorado Springs, and you see all these things, and you feel so powerless, and like for me, doing that antifa work, it was doing *something,* you know? To have some kind of target that you could punch back against, like these deplorable Nazis that are kind of free game."

Heidi had been part of an anti-fascist network that helped destroy the alt-right groups that had invaded and terrorized Charlottesville. Almost all the fascist organizations in attendance that day were in shambles, scared from rallying in the streets, rocked by doxes and lawsuits. Many, including Identity Evropa, had disbanded.

Even though Beedle had left Colorado Springs Anti-Fascists, by 2022 the group was still very active, its members excited to hear that a comrade out in Washington had gone undercover into Patriot Front, a fascist group that was still very much alive. This comrade, the anti-fascists heard, had acquired a treasure trove of messages from Patriot Front's RocketChat server.

They couldn't help but hope these leaks might help the group meet the same fate as Identity Evropa. They waited for the leaks to drop on Unicorn Riot. They were eager to get to work.

CHAPTER 12
A Little Army

The loot from Vincent's infiltration of Patriot Front—55,249 RocketChat messages, seventeen hours of audio recordings, plus a slew of videos and photos—went live in the Unicorn Riot database[1] on January 21, 2022, just as Thomas Rousseau was leading his masked minions back to Washington, DC, only six weeks after anti-fascists sabotaged their previous foray into the capital. This time, they were there to join the massive anti-abortion March for Life, parading in their masks and uniforms while passing out Patriot Front flyers to the many pro-Trump evangelical Christians in attendance. These MAGA faithful thanked the masked white men for "supporting the right to life" and implored them to "be safe out there." When a photojournalist explained to one attendee that Patriot Front was a white supremacist group, she replied: "Well, as long as they're pro-life."[2]

Patriot Front was having a good day, it seemed, successfully building bridges between itself and the MAGA movement, unaware that years of its private messages had just been made public. The timing was no accident— Unicorn Riot had learned of Patriot Front's plans for March for Life ahead of time. When Rousseau led his subordinates out of DC, surely buzzing from the march, they would discover that many of them were about to be doxed.

"Ostensibly private, unedited videos and direct messages reveal a campaign to organize acts of racial hatred while indoctrinating teenagers into national socialism (Nazism)," Unicorn Riot wrote in an article announcing the leaks. "The information stands as a chilling reminder that fascist organizing thrives in secrecy and obscurity."

A week later, on January 28, 2022, Thomas himself acknowledged the authenticity of the RocketChat leaks during an interview on a podcast hosted by neo-Nazi "Eric Striker" (whose real identity, Joseph Jordan, had been exposed by anti-fascists five years prior).[3] "They do these things to inspire paranoia and hysteria," Rousseau said, attempting to downplay the significance of the leaks. "They want you to be afraid."[4]

Vincent watched as all the spy work he'd done in relative isolation—the vetting interview, the workouts, the hikes, the tedious meetings, the group dinners, the vandalism missions, the banner drops—started to send shock waves across the country.

Suddenly the RocketChat leaks were a major news story. "Inside Patriot Front: The Masked White Supremacists on a Nationwide Hate Crime Spree," read a *HuffPost* headline.[5] "A White Supremacist Group Got Hacked, Airing Its Dirty Laundry," wrote Ars Technica.[6] "Leaked Chats Reveal Fascist Group Patriot Front Shames Members About Their Porn, Junk Food Habits," wrote *Vice*,[7] describing the iron fist with which Thomas Rousseau ran the group. *Vice* also noted that these leaks were bound to lead to more stories. "Since the Unicorn Riot published the data, anti-fascists . . . have been trawling through it, aiming to identify some key members in the once secretive, shadowy group."

In the ensuing months, anti-fascists would use the RocketChat leaks Vincent obtained to help dox dozens and dozens of members of Patriot Front. "Anti-fascists are stacking up the count of Patriot Front membership identified," a group called Sunny South Dallas AFA boasted.[8] "We personally didn't know you could stack shit that high."

In Aurora, Colorado, an eighteen-year-old was just a few days away from walking at his high school graduation when a group called Sunlight Anti-Fascist Action posted an article identifying him as "Kevin-CO" in the RocketChat leaks. The anti-fascists, a small coalition of seasoned researchers from across the US, had hesitated to expose Kevin, a star lacrosse player, because he was still so young. Ultimately, though, they decided "the escalating violent and threatening content of his tweets" posed an imminent risk to the community. The RocketChat messages showed Kevin-CO frequently admitting to running a series of pseudonymous Twitter accounts in which he advocated killing immigrants and Black people. "They got what was coming," he posted once, above a photo of the wreckage from the Oklahoma City bombing.

After the dox published, high school administrators disinvited Kevin from walking at his own graduation and increased security at the ceremony. His classmates also contacted Colorado University at Boulder to warn administrators there of the young white supremacist planning to matriculate at the school that fall.

But that fall Kevin was at the university, enrolled as a freshman. When Colorado Springs Anti-Fascists got wind of this, the group decided to act. Using the research compiled by Sunlight Anti-Fascist Action, the group designed flyers to warn students at CU Boulder about the "Nazi Activist on Campus." Students from the school's chapter of the Democratic Socialists of America printed out the flyers and posted them across the school's buildings. "On social media [Kevin] has expressed a desire to shoot up an immigration center, lynch Black people, alongside support for the Ku Klux Klan, the Oklahoma City bombing, and Adolf Hitler," the flyers said.

The student newspaper, the *CU Independent*, reached out to Kevin for comment, asking him about his murderous posts on Twitter. "I'm not going to try and excuse or play away what I did, obviously," he said. "I'm not going to apologize for it either. It's just something that's in the past for me."[10]

Kevin claimed he was no longer in Patriot Front. He said CU Boulder administrators had pressed him about his social media posts the previous summer but nevertheless allowed him to enroll at the school. "They kind of understood that I wasn't going to go out and harm people or menace the student population," he said.

When the *CU Independent* published its story about Kevin, however, there was a twist:

> *Early Thursday morning, Jan. 26, several hours after [Kevin] spoke with reporters for this story, the University of Colorado Police Department (CUPD) responded to reports of suspicious activity in [Kevin's] residence hall.*
>
> *According to police records, officers found [Kevin] with two people that police described as "older friends from Longmont," just before 2 a.m. [Kevin] failed to clarify to law enforcement how he knew the two individuals in his room, and witnesses told police they felt uncomfortable with the presence of [Kevin] and the other adults.*

One of the witnesses told police the pair of older adults were part of the white nationalist group [Kevin] has been affiliated with. The two individuals were "told to leave the building" and did, according to police records.

According to the police report, witnesses also saw Patriot Front messages and propaganda on [Kevin's] laptop. Witnesses told police [Kevin] was communicating with members of the hate group through the messaging app Telegram.

The next day, the newspaper reported, Kevin moved out of his dorm. School administrators wouldn't clarify whether Kevin had dropped out of the school or been kicked out.

Students expressed outrage that Kevin had been allowed to enroll at all. "The school can't continue to promote itself as an inclusive and diverse school and continue to do that for just a PR stunt when they have students that are obviously going completely against what the school stands for," Crisol Corral-Guzman, a first-generation immigrant student, told the *CU Independent*.

"I don't feel safe on my own campus—on a campus that I worked so hard to get to," she said.

Reached a year later for comment about the school's handling of the situation, a CU Boulder spokesperson noted university policies "prevent the university from considering certain prior disciplinary records when admitting students." All students, the spokesperson added, are still subject to "sanctions ranging from a warning up to suspension or expulsion" for violating the school's code of conduct. Citing student privacy laws, the spokesperson didn't comment on whether Kevin committed such a violation but confirmed he was no longer enrolled.

*   *   *

When journalists at the Southern Poverty Law Center—the civil rights institution that since Trump's election in 2016 had built a formidable investigative news team for its Hatewatch website—dove into the RocketChat leaks, they found a concerning pattern.[11] "Roughly one in five applicants to the white supremacist group Patriot Front claimed to hold current or former military status, according to leaked documents reviewed by Hatewatch," the organization wrote, referring to the eighty-seven Patriot Front membership applications contained in the leaks. These eighteen applicants, according to the SPLC, offered to bring Patriot Front the skills they'd attained in the military, including with firearms, medical training, and intelligence gathering. "One of the applicants, who claimed to be a former Marine, also stated in his application that he currently works for the Department of Homeland Security (DHS)," the article stated.

Anti-fascists in San Diego took note of this purported DHS employee, Applicant 441215, who said in the leaks that he lived in San Diego and became radicalized during his time in the Marines, where he "found out about the Jews." This applicant also claimed to have been doxed once already by antifa. To the anti-fascists in San Diego, Applicant 441215 sounded a lot like Victor Krvaric,[12] who first came on their radar in 2020, when he harassed a Black Lives Matter demonstration in the city, driving his black sports car—with a novelty license plate that read PLOTTING—through a crowd of protesters in the Scripps Ranch neighborhood. Applicant 441215 noted that his parents were from Sweden, that his family was Catholic, that his "like-minded" brother first introduced him to "right-wing literature," and that he worked at his "father's financial practice."

All this info lined up with Krvaric. His LinkedIn profile stated he worked for his dad's company, Krvaric Capital and Risk Management, and that he was a former Marine who did contract work for DHS. Victor's older brother, Oliver Krvaric, was indeed "like-minded," becoming the leader of the San Diego State University College Republicans in 2020, where he rejected "lukewarm" conservatism,[13] according to an article in the student newspaper, transforming the chapter into a den of edge-lordy, far-right trolls. He'd even been interviewed once by Tucker Carlson on Fox News.[14]

Victor's dad, Tony Krvaric, was a powerful player in local politics, having served as the chairman of the Republican Party of San Diego County from 2007 until 2020. Tony was indeed a Catholic and a Swedish immigrant, whose tenure as leader of the local GOP included a bizarre scandal involving an old animated video produced in Sweden in the early 1990s that resurfaced in 2020, showing pictures of him surrounded by images of Hitler and Nazi symbols.[15] "Kill a commie coz here's Strider!" read text in the video, referring to Tony's nickname in a Swedish hacker collective he admitted to being part of at the time. Tony had initially refused to condemn the video but eventually claimed that he "didn't create" the animation and found its Nazi imagery "disgusting."

The Patriot Front leaks showed that when Applicant 441215 was accepted as a member of the group, he decided to choose a unique pseudonym: Strider, the same nom de plume Tony Krvaric had used as a young hacker in Sweden. Victor, it seemed, had decided to pay tribute to his dad.

Anti-fascists published Viktor Krvaric's dox on Twitter, identifying him as a member of Patriot Front, with local press picking up on the story a short time later. Krvaric, it turned out, was still in the Marine reserves, but a month later was kicked out of the military during the subsequent investigation into his ties to the white supremacist group.[16] The DHS had declined to comment on his employment.

So began a trying few years for the Krvaric family. In 2023, *USA Today* published a story, based on the research of anonymous anti-fascists, identifying Victor's older brother Oliver, who'd started a promising career in Republican politics, as a pseudonymous poster on the Iron March neo-Nazi forum.[17] That wasn't all, though: Sleuths investigating the January 6 attack on the Capitol had used facial recognition software to identify Oliver's face among those in the violent MAGA mob. "A *USA Today* review of arrests concluded Krvaric would be the first full-time employee of the Trump administration identified entering the Capitol in the insurrection," the newspaper reported. "On Jan. 6, 2021, Krvaric was working for the Office of Personnel Management on a short-lived Trump executive order that sought to rid federal agencies of certain diversity and inclusion training." (Oliver was never arrested for his participation in the attack.)

Less than a year after the *USA Today* report, local prosecutors filed a gun violence restraining order against Victor, the brother in Patriot Front, after he made "threats of violence through social media towards LGBTQ + other races." When police raided his dad's business, where he was working, they found Victor to be in possession of "illegal firearms," including an assault rifle, as well as explosives. Later in court, prosecutors would allege Viktor made social media posts in which he suggested firebombing local homeless encampments.[18]

"Our family is going through a difficult time and ask that our privacy be respected," Tony Krvaric said in a statement.[19] "As a father, I wish that the children of former public figures could experience life privately, like everyone else."

＊　　　　　＊　　　　　＊

The doxes of Patriot Front members frequently revealed them to be the progeny of well-to-do or otherwise established, respectable Americans.

Amy Freeze is a famous meteorologist.[20] According to her Wikipedia page, she is "a five-time National Academy of Television Arts and Sciences Emmy Award winner" who had a "cameo appearance" in the hit NBC comedy series *Scrubs* and was "featured in the American quiz show *Jeopardy!* in two different categories."

She grew up Mormon in Utah and attended Brigham Young University, where she was a cheerleader for the football team. She eventually fell in love with a student named Gary Arbuckle,[21] who dressed as the school's mascot, Cosmo the Cougar, on the sidelines during games. They married after college, with Freeze pursuing meteorology while Arbuckle became a chiropractor. In 2011, the pair appeared on ABC's *The Dr. Oz Show* to sell a miracle weight-loss product they claimed helped them each shed thirty pounds in forty days: "body drops," a tincture made from a natural hormone produced by the placenta during pregnancy. The FDA sent them a stern letter after their appearance on *Dr. Oz*, warning them to cease selling the "body drops" as they were "illegal" and did not cause weight loss.[22]

Freeze later got a job in New York working for Fox Weather. In late June 2023, she recorded a promotional ad for the network celebrating the upcoming Fourth of July.[23] "Here's what I love about America," she said over aerial footage of the Statue of Liberty at sunset. "Friends, family, freedom, and the tradition of the Fourth of July. Ever since I was a little girl, we celebrated big time. It all starts in the morning with a parade, waving the flag, the red, white, and blue, the marching bands, the whole nine yards. And one year after the fireworks, it really got spectacular. My son was born! He went on to serve in the Air Force, and in the tradition of our family we celebrate on the Fourth of July every single year. And that's what I love about America." The commercial ended with footage of a waving American flag and the screech of a bald eagle.

It also featured a photo of Freeze and her smiling son, Tyler Arbuckle, in his Air Force blues after graduating from basic training at Lackland Air Force Base in Texas. What Freeze did not mention in the Fox Weather promo was that a year prior, on February 22, 2022, the group Texas Against Fascism identified Tyler Arbuckle, twenty-three, as a member of Patriot Front who went by the alias "Anthony-UT" in the RocketChat leaks.[24] Public records showed he was born on July 4, 1998.

He was doxed, in part, because of posts his mom made on Instagram, where she has over 115,000 followers. "Hey man, I'm coming to NYC for the 24th to the 30th," Arbuckle wrote to "Jason-NY" in a November 16, 2021, RocketChat message.[25] "Is there anyone in the NYC area who can meet up?" On November 26, 2021, Freeze posted an image of her son, having arrived in New York, standing on a Manhattan street. A little over a week later, Arbuckle traveled to Washington, DC, to join Patriot Front's march on the National Mall.

And still other messages showed Arbuckle stating that he was working as an EMT in Utah—a secret white supremacist tasked with treating and saving the lives of Black, Latino, and Jewish patients. Texas Against Fascism confirmed that his place of employment was Gold Cross Ambulance Company 7 in Salt Lake City. The ambulance company didn't respond to a request for comment about Arbuckle. The US Air Force, reached for comment, said Arbuckle left active service in 2021 but was on "individual ready reserve," meaning he could still be called into action during a time of war.

Neither Arbuckle nor his parents have publicly acknowledged his secret double life as a neo-Nazi. On July 4, 2023, according to an Instagram post, Freeze took her kids to Lake Powell to celebrate Tyler's birthday aboard a boat, eating cake off a red-white-and-blue tablecloth. "Happy Birthday Son!" she wrote. Arbuckle didn't respond to a request for comment about whether he is still a member of Patriot Front.

*   *   *

Doxing "Clarke-IL" was easy. On December 17, 2021, he sent a copy of his résumé to a fellow Patriot Front member on RocketChat, asking him for advice on getting a new job. The résumé showed that Clarke had graduated high school earlier that year and was working as a roofer and concrete laborer. His real name was spelled out in big, bold letters: Logan Plank.

An antifa group called Chicago Anti-Fascists published the dox of eighteen-year-old Plank on January 22, 2022.[26] It noted that Plank's mom was a high school math teacher, his stepdad was a former cop, and his father was a city councilman in Wood River, Illinois, a 98 percent white "sundown town,"[27] where up until the mid-1990s there reportedly still stood two street signs that, citing old ordinances, prohibited Black people from being in town after nightfall.

In the months after the eighteen-year-old Plank's dox, journalists studying the RocketChat leaks connected him to two acts of vandalism. The SPLC's Hatewatch published an article about Plank's participation in a Patriot Front mission to destroy a mural honoring famous Black Americans on the campus of Washington University at St. Louis.[28] Plank and his accomplices covered the mural—titled *Never Ending Story*, featuring images of late Senator John Lewis and the late *Black Panther* star Chadwick Boseman—in white paint and Patriot Front stencils.

Unicorn Riot also identified Plank among a gang of Patriot Front vandals who filmed themselves defacing a rainbow mural on the Phoenix Center in Springfield, Illinois.[29] "Those fags are gonna lose their mind," one of Plank's accomplices, a Patriot Front member identified by anti-fascists as Mitchell Wagner, said after they vandalized the center, which provides housing and education for at-risk LGBTQ+ youth in central Illinois.

But despite the SPLC and Unicorn Riot's reporting on Plank's involvement in both crimes, he was never arrested. Only Wagner—whose stepmother, incidentally, was a city council candidate in Chesterfield, Missouri—was charged with felony first-degree property damage in connection with the destruction of the mural in St. Louis.[30] Plank's dad, city councilman Jeremy Plank, never publicly commented on his son's involvement with Patriot Front.

*   *   *

Police seemed to be prosecuting Patriot Front's hate crime spree in an uneven fashion, only sometimes willing to use the extensive cache of documents in the Unicorn Riot database for their investigations.

On February 9, 2022, Detective Jacob Theis with the Olympia, Washington, Police Department was assigned the investigation into the destruction of the RESPECT AND LOVE OLYMPIA rainbow mural. His superiors handed him a thick packet of purported evidence related to the case, a packet given to them by a city council member, who received it from an "acquaintance" who wouldn't identify themselves or talk to law enforcement. Inside the packet, Detective Theis found photographs of Patriot Front members in Washington state, snapshots of messages written by members to each other, and hyperlinks to different websites. Theis later wrote in a supplemental case report that information in the packet suggested all this intelligence had been gathered by "an anti-fascist activist" who "infiltrated the Patriot Front's local chapter."[31]

Theis started perusing the RocketChat database online and reading articles on Unicorn Riot and Washington Nazi Watch, which claimed to identify the eight men who had participated in destroying the mural. The articles identified Jacob Sundt (Clarke-WA) as the ringleader. He was apparently the son of a local judge.

But in reviewing all the video footage that the anti-fascist infiltrator had filmed, Theis couldn't find a clear shot of Sundt's face. One video showed a man anti-fascists claimed was Sundt leaning against a tree during the mission. "I noticed that the top of the suspect's head was even with the point at which the tree splits into several branches," Theis wrote in his report. "In the early morning hours of February 14, 2022, I went down to the specific tree and used measuring tape to measure from the ground to the point where the suspect's head reached and measured it at 6'4". Of note, although the video does not show the suspect's face, I find it compelling that Jacob Sundt is listed as 6'4" tall on his [driver's license]."

That same week Theis met with two FBI agents in Washington who confirmed that they were investigating Sundt as a member of Patriot Front. Still, Theis's investigation dragged on for months. Then, on June 11, 2022, he read a breaking news story out of Idaho.

Police in Coeur d'Alene, a scenic and fast-growing city nestled in the mountains of the state's northern panhandle, had received a tip about a "little army" of dozens of masked men in matching uniforms, many carrying shields, squeezing into the back of a U-Haul. When cops pulled the truck over, they found Thomas Rousseau inside carrying a document that detailed a plan to establish a "confrontational dynamic" at a Pride event that day by a lakeside park in Coeur d'Alene, where queer people and their straight allies, many with their children in tow, were set to enjoy a warm sunny day. Police arrested all thirty-one men on charges of conspiring to riot.[32]

It was one of Patriot Front's most brazen gambits yet. Had they succeeded, they would've arrived at the park and escalated an already tense situation: A ghoulish coalition of far right activists was protesting the Pride event, including men carrying AR-15s, other men wearing neo-Nazi skull masks, and still other men carrying signs reading CITING THE LEVITICUS VERSE THAT RECOMMENDS HOMOSEXUALS BE PUT TO DEATH. This coalition had gathered here after a hysterical nationwide moral panic, with buy-in from prominent Republican politicians and mainstream conservative media, smearing this particular Pride gathering as a haven for "groomers" and "pedophiles."[33]

But mercifully, at least this time, police had intervened before things could get worse. Journalists on the scene snapped photos of the Patriot Front members as cops unmasked them, zip-tying their hands behind their backs. News of the arrests went viral, with many people sharing a photo collage of the thirty-one white men's mug shots, their names spelled out in the caption. Anti-fascists immediately recognized the arrests for what they were: a mass-doxing event.

Anti-fascists quickly connected one of the men, Jared Boyce of Utah, to the "Logan-UT" username on Rocket Chat, where they found he posted a photo of himself standing atop a stolen transgender Pride flag.[34] They also connected him to alarming social media posts in which he threatened violence against queer people, often falsely equating them with pedophiles. *The Daily Beast* reported that after his arrest, Boyce returned home to Utah and received an ultimatum from his mother.[35] "I told him 'You can choose between the Patriot Front and your family,'" his mom, Karen Amsden, recounted. "And he's like, 'Well, I can't quit Patriot Front.' I'm like, 'Well, then you've just chosen. So pack your stuff and get out of my house.'" Boyce left. (The following year he pleaded guilty to nine counts of possessing child pornography and confessed to exchanging sexually explicit pictures of himself with a sixteen-year-old girl.[36] He was sentenced to a year in prison.)

A group called Utah Antifascists had been trying unsuccessfully for months to identify RocketChat user "James-UT." They knew from James's posts that he lived in a town called Kaysville, that he was older than most Patriot Front members, that he and his wife were expecting a child, and that he was currently in flight school. The arrests in Coeur d'Alene solved the mystery for them: James-UT was thirty-five-year-old Brendan Haney, a Kaysville resident studying at FLT Academy, "Utah's Top Aviation School."[37] Haney called Adolf Hitler "Uncle A" in chats and talked about trying to turn his friends and family into neo-Nazis. "You have to keep pressing on people's opinions," he said. "Talk to your friends and family and try to make Nationalism grow. It is an uphill battle against the lies people have been convinced of all their lives." In the article Utah Antifascists published about

Haney, they included a recent family photo he'd used on a baby registry website—the group, however, took care to blur out the faces of his wife, young child, and newborn infant.

Vincent, meanwhile, recognized one of the faces in the Idaho mugshots from the climb up Mount Rainier: Winston Durham, who he'd known on the hike as "Marcus-ID." Turned out, per a report in the *Spokesman Review*, Durham was a "cadet in the Idaho National Guard and a Washington State University ROTC student who had been awarded a scholarship for room, board, books and a monthly stipend."[38] The military told the paper Durham was suspended pending an investigation into his extremist ties.

Vincent recognized a few more faces among the Idaho mug shots—faces that Detective Theis back in Olympia had just recognized too: Colton Brown, Spencer Simpson, Justin O'Leary, and Lawrence Norman. All part of the eight-man crew anti-fascists had doxed and documented destroying the LGBTQ+ mural in Olympia.

On July 1, 2022, prosecutors in Olympia issued arrest warrants for only two of the men: Brown and Simpson.[39] They were charged with aiding and abetting, or complicity with, graffiti. Theis noted in his report that he was able to match the pair's mug shots in Idaho with their briefly unmasked faces captured in footage by the anti-fascist infiltrator. The other men's faces, he wrote, were obscured in the footage, but added that there was still "probable cause to arrest Justin O'Leary and Lawrence Norman." They never were.

And although Theis stated that "the vandalism was an act of discrimination and an offense against the LGBTQ+ community in Olympia," neither Brown nor Simpson was ever charged with committing a hate crime.

Sundt, who was central to the vandalism, was never arrested, even though secretly recorded audio available to Theis captured him bragging that their successful mission proved they could "deface the largest most well protected mural in shitlib Olympia without so much as being accosted once."

The city of Olympia prosecutor's office didn't respond to a request for comment on why these other Patriot Front members implicated in the vandalism were never charged.

Citing this kind of uneven prosecution, on July 18, 2022, a coalition of America's most prominent civil rights organizations, including the Southern Poverty Law Center, the Anti-Defamation League, and Western States Center, along with smaller groups like North Idaho Pride Alliance, sent a letter to

Attorney General Merrick Garland begging him to have the Justice Department investigate Patriot Front for violating federal hate crime statutes.[40]

The letter noted that despite the mountain of evidence provided in the RocketChat leaks documenting the group's hate crime campaign across America, "very few jurisdictions have sought to hold members of Patriot Front accountable" for the acts of vandalism and intimidation. "This has created an atmosphere of impunity in which Patriot Front has continued to escalate its activities, allegedly leading to a coordinated plot to riot against Coeur d'Alene Pride in the Park," it stated.

The letter continued: "The need for federal intervention is both clear and urgent. After all, Patriot Front's coordinated plan to disrupt Pride in the Park was only thwarted because a concerned community member alerted local law enforcement about a 'little army' of masked men. In no small way, Coeur d'Alene was very lucky. But, as Patriot Front continues to organize and agitate, the next city targeted by their menace and vandalism might not be."

*   *   *

Over the next year, Vincent noticed that the RocketChat leaks were being used to file federal lawsuits in civil court. Civil rights groups were attempting to destabilize or bankrupt Patriot Front by bringing the group to court for violating the Ku Klux Klan Act, the 1871 statute passed during Reconstruction prohibiting conspiracies to intimidate people or deprive them of their civil rights based on their race.

Human Rights First sued Patriot Front on behalf of Charles Murrell III, a Black musician in Boston who the white supremacists assaulted during a July 2022 march through the city, shouting a racial slur while pushing him up against a street pole and beating him with shields, feet, and fists. The lawsuit noted that Murrell, who had to be treated at a hospital for his injuries, had since been "plagued by severe anxiety, mental anguish," and "nightmares." Whenever he "goes to open his music composition book, which was on his person on July 2, 2022," the lawsuit stated, "he sees residue of his own blood spattered on the cover—a gruesome reminder of the attack."[41]

In Richmond, the Lawyers' Committee for Civil Rights Under Law filed a lawsuit against Patriot Front for destroying a mural honoring hometown hero Arthur Ashe, the Black tennis legend.[42] Suing on behalf of residents of the majority-Black neighborhood where the mural was located, the lawsuit named twenty-seven defendants, nineteen of them listed as unidentified John Does. The eight named defendants included Thomas Rousseau and a twenty-eight-year-old Pennsylvania man named William Ring. Ring was served notice of the lawsuit in prison, having recently pleaded guilty to a charge of ethnic intimidation for punching a seventeen-year-old Puerto Rican girl in the jaw at a Starbucks after calling her skin color "ugly" and telling her to "go back to where you came from, you Mexican."[43]

The six other named Patriot Front defendants had previously been unmasked because of Vincent's infiltration. Four of them were part of the crew who had been pulled over by Maryland police responding to the anti-fascist assault on Patriot Front cars parked at the "vehicle exchange" for the disastrous DC march. Unicorn Riot had filed a public records request for the police body camera footage, publishing an article identifying John-VA as Jacob Brown, Vincent-VA as Aedan Tredinnick, Kenneth-VA as Thomas Dail, and Roger-VA as Nathaniel Noyce.[44]

Noyce was the one who laughingly said "I'm gonna be famous, boys!" after one of the cops informed them that his body camera was filming. Noyce's statement proved a little prophetic when he made national news: The FBI arrested him for taking part in the January 6, 2021, attack on the Capitol.[45] According to court documents, Noyce was among the last rioters to be forced out of the Rotunda that day before he allegedly assaulted a police officer, striking the cop "in his face with his right hand."

Another defendant in the Richmond lawsuit may have taken part in the insurrection. Daniel Turetchi was fired from his job as a real estate agent in Maryland after Antifa Seven Hills identified him as "Grant-MD" in the RocketChat leaks.[46] Sedition Hunters, a group of online sleuths unaffiliated with antifa, devoted to investigating the January 6 attack, listed Turetchi as a "person of interest" in the insurrection, publishing photos of a man on the steps of the Capitol building who bears a strong resemblance to the Patriot Front member.[47]

The final named defendant in the Richmond lawsuit, Paul Gancarz, had also been fired from his job because of the RocketChat leaks. Antifa Seven Hills, based out of Richmond, teamed up with NYC Antifa to identify Gancarz as "Samuel-VA," Patriot Front's network director in Virginia.[48] He was a prominent Patriot Front member, the one who desperately begged everyone to "log off!" the group call Vincent had disrupted by blaring "Bella Ciao." Gancarz had been making $107,000 a year as a civil engineer working on the $3.9 billion Hampton Roads Bridge-Tunnel Expansion project, "the largest highway construction project in Virginia's history,"[49] before his dox led to his firing. He was also kicked out of the American Society of Engineers.

Although Gancarz didn't participate in the January 6 attack on the Capitol, anti-fascists found evidence he did participate in the 2017 Unite the Right rally in Charlottesville. Photos appear to show Gancarz in attendance wearing a black MAKE AMERICA GREAT AGAIN baseball cap, red goggles, leather fighting gloves, and a black-and-yellow Fred Perry polo shirt—the uniform of the Proud Boys. Gancarz, anti-fascists surmised, had gone to Unite the Right as a member of the Fraternal Order of Alt-Knights, the militant branch of the already punch-happy Proud Boys. (Anti-fascists believed Gancarz joined Patriot Front two years later, in 2019.)

As the lawsuits against Patriot Front wound their way through the court system, the doxes continued—a Google software engineer, a Subway sandwich artist, a librarian, a PhD student, a bouncer, a roofer, multiple national guardsmen—until the RocketChat leaks Vincent obtained had helped unmask a staggering eighty members of Patriot Front.

The group wasn't too pleased with Vincent. Patriot Front members were starting to fixate on him. In the weeks after his infiltration ended, when he was booted out of RocketChat, his tech-savvy comrades had found a way to briefly maintain access to the message server so they could monitor how various Patriot Front members were reacting. There was one message, on December 8, 2021, that piqued Vincent's interest.

"If it makes you feel better, our cyber security team has made large steps in figuring out who Vincent actually is and who he associates with," wrote Jacob Sundt, the member who spearheaded the Olympia mural vandalism, attempting to assuage a fellow member's worries about being unmasked.[50]

Patriot Front leadership had, in fact, almost immediately figured out Vincent's real name. "Dude's the leader of John Brown gun club," Colton Michael Brown (aka John-WA) wrote in a message to Thomas, referring to the militant, armed leftist group with chapters across the country. "I got his real name and identity."[51]

Brown sent Thomas links to articles about the Puget Sound John Brown Club, which had a noticeable presence during the anti-racist uprisings of 2020 in Seattle. The articles included interviews of the man they knew as Vincent, alongside photos of him carrying a large gun. The articles also included Vincent's real name—or what Patriot Front members thought was his real name. They didn't know yet that Vincent had legally changed his name multiple times over the years.

One day, Brown drove to a Seattle-area house where he thought Vincent might live. He parked outside and waited. And waited.[52]

"Been sitting on this guy's street all day now," he told Thomas. "Still no sign of him."

Vincent was a ghost. He was confident in his ability to remain a ghost, to elude these chuds who might want to hurt him, or worse. These fascists who wanted to punish him for his treachery. He had known there was a chance this would happen when he decided to go undercover into Patriot Front—that the group would stumble onto these articles with pictures of his face, seeing one of his old names in a photo caption. It had been a risk he was willing to take.

What he hadn't anticipated was Patriot Front maybe enlisting the help of the feds.

One day in the spring of 2023, Vincent heard from a friend: An FBI agent had called, wanting to know where Vincent was. The agent had received a tip that Vincent was manufacturing ghost guns. The agent asked his friend: Was Vincent a dangerous anarchist? A left-wing "extremist"?

Suddenly, ironically, Vincent *really* knew what it was like to be in Patriot Front: nervously waiting to be doxed himself, and wondering whether he might get a knock on the door from armed agents of the United States government.

PART III
OUTSIDE AGITATORS

CHAPTER 13

Antifa Supersoldiers

B y the time Patriot Front and the feds were searching for Vincent, America had been in the grips of anti-antifa hysteria for about six years.

That it was a prefabricated or manufactured moral panic was clear from the jump. Microchip spelled it all out. The well-known, pseudonymous alt-right troll, in the weeks after the Unite the Right rally in Charlottesville, had launched a viral petition to the Trump White House to designate antifa a "domestic terror group," earning coverage across right-wing media. By Microchip's own admission, he knew the petition, which garnered over three hundred thousand signatures, wouldn't affect policy—there is, after all, no domestic terror statute with which to make such a designation—but that wasn't the point. He explained his motives in a remarkably frank interview with Politico published on August 24, 2017:[1]

> *Microchip told Politico he wrote it with the explicit intent of stoking conservative rage and forcing the GOP establishment to take a stand or risk becoming targets themselves.*
>
> *"It was to bring our broken right side together" after Charlottesville, he said, "and prop up antifa as a punching bag.*
>
> *"So the narrative changed from 'I hate myself because we have neo-Nazis on our side' to 'I really hate antifa, let's get along and tackle the terrorists,'" he explained . . .*

His petition was promoted by heavy hitters on conservative and "alt-right"
Twitter, including Breitbart editors, YouTube stars and lesser-known players
from the Twitter "rooms."

… "This was a test," Microchip said, to see whether an even more massive
social media campaign could drive media attention and deflect criticism of
the alt-right toward liberal hooligans. "You can call it an extreme form of
'whataboutism,'" he explained.

Although he sees this as a successful test, Microchip questioned whether his
strategy can work absent "controversial public gatherings" like Charlottesville
and last week's protests in Boston and other cities.

"Our biggest problem is being able to replicate what we did over the last
5 days," he tweeted on Wednesday. "I wish we could turn this into a well oiled
machine."

Microchip's wish would come true. Taking his lead, a group of far-right
influencers developed a well-oiled machine for producing anti-antifa propaganda. They churned out stories grossly exaggerating antifa's use of violence
and baselessly implicating antifa in nearly every American mass shooting or
natural disaster during the first Trump presidency, cynically crafting conspiracies from devastating tragedies that they could then wield as political cudgels.

On October 1, 2017, a sixty-four-year-old white man named Stephen
Paddock unpacked a small arsenal in his thirty-second-floor room at the
Mandalay Bay hotel in Las Vegas.[2] There were twenty-four legally purchased
firearms in total, fourteen of them .223-caliber AR-15-type semi-automatic
rifles, some fitted with bump stocks, enabling them to shoot upward of ninety
rounds in ten seconds. Paddock used hammers to shatter the windows of his
hotel room so he could take aim at his target: the Route 91 Harvest outdoor
music festival on the Las Vegas Strip. He rained hellfire down upon the
festivalgoers, who were enjoying a performance by country musician Jason
Aldean. Paddock's fusillade of 1,049 bullets killed 61 people and wounded
another 413. He fired his final 1,050th round,[3] from a Smith & Wesson
revolver, into his own head.

It was the deadliest mass shooting in American history, but Paddock's
motives weren't immediately clear—an information vacuum that various
far-right actors rushed to fill with baseless accusations and outright lies.
"They found antifa information in the room and photos of the women in the

Middle East," infamous conspiracy theorist Alex Jones said on his InfoWars show.[4] "There was antifa crap everywhere. That is directly from the hostage rescue team by the way . . ."

Many conspiracists also pointed to a purported antifa Facebook account in Australia. "One of our comrades from our Las Vegas branch has made these fascist Trump supporting dogs pay," the account wrote after the shooting, which the *Daily Mail* in the UK reported as news, failing to verify whether the account belonged to antifa.[5] The account did not belong to an antifa group—but it was well-known in Australia as an anti-antifa troll account.

These lies, as the adage goes, had traveled the world before the truth could put its shoes on, the American right absolving itself of any guilt for the shooting and the left finding itself on the defensive, stuck debunking unfounded accusations. Seven months later, the same far-right influencers who pushed the Paddock antifa conspiracy were largely silent when a law enforcement investigation revealed Paddock had expressed familiar far-right sentiments ahead of the mass shooting, conveying a paranoia about the federal government disarming citizens and putting them into FEMA concentration camps.[6] He reportedly, during a conversation with an unnamed man, also invoked the memory of Ruby Ridge, the deadly 1992 FBI standoff with a white supremacist in the Idaho woods that became a rallying cry among far-right militants, including for Oklahoma City bomber Timothy McVeigh.

"Somebody has to wake up the American public and get them to arm themselves," Paddock said in the weeks before unpacking his arsenal in a Las Vegas hotel room. "Sometimes sacrifices have to be made."

*   *   *

In the weeks after Paddock's shooting, right-wing media was in a frenzy about upcoming anti-Trump demonstrations scheduled for November 4, 2017. The demonstrations were being planned by Refuse Fascism, an offshoot of the Revolutionary Communist Party, or RevCom. (The left-wing group, although ostensibly anti-fascist, often faces criticism or denunciations from antifa and the wider left for the cult of personality surrounding RevCom leader Bob Avakian, with accusations that the organization is a pyramid scheme, more interested in profits than social justice—allegations Avakian and RevCom deny.)[7]

There was no indication that the Refuse Fascism demonstrations, scheduled for dozens of cities across the country, would be anything but peaceful. But far-right actors online were working overtime to hype up the rallies as the beginning of the next American civil war.[8] Paul Joseph Watson, an InfoWars conspiracist with a massive online following, wrote an article headlined "Antifa Plans 'Civil War' to Overthrow Government."

The anti-communist conspiracists of the John Birch Society, the Oath Keepers militia group, and various disinformation artists jumped into the fray, too. A YouTuber published a viral video in which he stated that antifa would start off "by attacking police officers, first responders, anybody that's in uniform. They will then go after the citizens and the people and the government and all of that. So if you're white, you're a Trump supporter, you're a Nazi then, to them. And it will be open game on you."

A leftist Twitter account decided to parody this anti-antifa hysteria, writing: "can't wait for Nov. 4th when millions of antifa supersoldiers will behead all white parents and small business owners in the town square." As if to prove the satirical point at the heart of the tweet, the Gateway Pundit, a widely read far-right site, published an article holding up the post as *actual evidence* of antifa's murderous plans.[9]

When November 4 arrived, the Refuse Fascism demonstrations were peaceful and sparsely attended affairs. No white parents or small business owners were beheaded. No first shots of a new civil war were fired. The next day, however, America did have another mass shooting. A twenty-six-year-old man walked into First Baptist Church in Sutherland Springs, Texas, and opened fire, killing twenty-six people.

"Photos of Texas shooter is consistent with profile of Antifa member," wrote Mike Cernovich, a far-right influencer and date rape apologist with over a million followers on Twitter.[10] "This is looking more and more like Antifa terror."

There was no basis for Cernovich's assertion, aside from a clearly doctored image, spread by far-right forums and junk conspiracy sites, of the suspected shooter holding up an "Anti-Fascist Action" flag.[11] Viral articles spread showcasing a laughably fake text message from a purported witness to the shooting, who described how the shooter draped an "ANTIFA flag over pulpit," "said 'this was a communist revolution,'" and "pulled out a copy of *Das Kapital* and demanded people quote specific sections."[12]

The shooter, Devin Kelley, was not part of antifa, but a disturbed white guy with a history of domestic and sexual abuse, who had received a bad conduct discharge from the Air Force years earlier. First Baptist Church was where his estranged wife and her mother worshipped. His wife was not at the service when Kelley opened fire, but her grandmother was.[13] Kelley killed her, and a short time later, while driving away from police, killed himself, too.

None of the far-right influencers fearmongering about antifa faced consequences when their wild assertions proved to be false. (If anything, they just gained more followers.) That's because the truth was never the point. What mattered, as Microchip said from the beginning, was to distract and deflect, to always exculpate the right of any wrongdoing, for anything.

But baselessly blaming antifa for mass shootings, and for a coming civil war, was also doing something perhaps more sinister: creating a justification for attacking the left in the streets.

*   *   *

The story of the anti-antifa panic in the ensuing years can't be told without Andy Ngo. The right-wing pseudo-journalist's coverage of clashing protests in his hometown of Portland, Oregon, would become a pretext for a wave of far-right incursions in the city. His videos would shape Fox News's growing fixation on antifa. And a picture of his bruised face would help lead to the president of the United States calling for antifa to be designated a domestic terrorist group.

Ngo got his start in the national media spotlight in 2017 while a master's student at Portland State University, where he was fired as an editor for the college newspaper for a "dangerous oversimplification that violated very clear ethics outlined by the Society of Professional Journalists" after he tweeted a selectively edited video of a Muslim student purportedly condoning the killing of "apostates" in Muslim-majority countries.[14] The video was picked up by Breitbart, among other right-wing outlets, in furtherance of familiar Islamophobic narratives, and earned Ngo a byline in *National Review*, where he published an op-ed titled "Fired for Reporting the Truth."

The brief saga would become a sort of playbook for Ngo: promote an out-of-context video portraying members of marginalized groups or leftists as "extremist" or "violent" and then play victim when those in the marginalized groups and the left inevitably cried foul. The schtick had a particular purchase coming from Ngo, who did not present as your typical American far-right activist. He is gay, the son of immigrants from Vietnam, and speaks in a transatlantic British accent—which his detractors claim is a put-on affect to make himself sound more intelligent, and which Ngo has said is due to a few years he lived in London while in high school.

He often used his identities as queer and as a second-generation Asian American to deflect criticism that he was running interference for white supremacists and other fascists. That, of course, was exactly what he was doing, producing propaganda that obscured and distracted from the far right's violence, always creating a false equivalency between their extremism and the supposed extremism of antifa.

In October 2018, Ngo appeared on Tucker Carlson's primetime program on Fox News to discuss a video he'd boosted online purportedly showing anti-racist demonstrators in Portland harassing an elderly white man driving his car—evidence, according to Ngo and Carlson, of a city overtaken by dangerous leftists. But the video left out crucial context: *that the man had just plowed his car through the protesters*, carrying one protester on the car's hood for over thirty feet. When the driver eventually stopped down the block, there was indeed a brief confrontation that involved a protester shoving the driver once and others banging his vehicle with their hands. "Get out of here!" the protesters screamed at the man, who eventually did just that.

Ngo omitted all this context again when he published an article titled "A Leftist Mob Polices Portland" in the *Wall Street Journal*, inveighing against the "angry, agitated ingrates and criminals" in his hometown.[15]

The incident caught the attention of Patriot Prayer—the far-right group based in nearby Vancouver, Washington, with a well-documented history of associating with white supremacists—who saw it as an opportunity to throw a retaliatory rally. A week later, Patriot Prayer held a "flash march for law and order," which predictably descended into fights in the streets.[16] The group, often in partnership with the Proud Boys, was routinely invading the city like this for "free speech" rallies that were always thinly veiled pretexts for committing violence—and Ngo had become a trusted ally.

On May 1, 2019, Ngo tagged along with Patriot Prayer as they prepared to brawl with leftists celebrating May Day, the annual holiday celebrating the labor movement, at a Portland bar called Cider Riot.

Unbeknownst to Ngo, a progressive Navy veteran named "Ben" had gone undercover in Patriot Prayer and was filming the group as it geared up for a confrontation. The *Portland Mercury* later reported on Ben's footage of Patriot Prayer:[17]

> As the group waits, they discuss their weaponry. A few men try to guess which way the wind's blowing to avoid getting "spray" in their eyes, presumably when they use it against members of antifa. Another man holds a thick wooden dowel, and practices swinging it like a baseball bat. A woman carries a red brick in her hand. Some don goggles, helmets, and tactical gloves . . .
>
> Ben captures someone telling a person on speakerphone, "There's going to be a huge fight," and gives them directions to Cider Riot.
>
> Ngo doesn't film any of the conversations, and smiles when the group cracks jokes.
>
> "He overheard everything," Ben recalls, "and said nothing."

Ngo only started filming amid the ensuing violence, posting videos to Twitter that made it seem like antifa were the instigators, even though three Patriot Prayer members later pleaded guilty[18] to felony riot and assault charges, one for knocking a woman unconscious with a baton, reportedly fracturing her vertebrae[19] in the process. After claiming he'd personally been sprayed with bear mace during the melee, Ngo received another invite to go on *Tucker Carlson*, where he called May Day a "celebration of Marxism, Communism, and political violence."[20]

Which is all to say that by June 29, 2019, when Ngo attended a Proud Boys demonstration in Portland, filming a contingent of anti-fascist counter-demonstrators in black bloc, he was a known entity.

The anti-fascists were less than enthused by Ngo's presence, suspecting he was filming anti-fascists to publicly identify them later. A viral video shot by a bystander showed activists in black bloc making their feelings known: one punched Ngo, another kicked him, while others pelted him with eggs and silly string and doused him with milkshakes. Yet another anti-fascist, however, perhaps disagreeing with this attack, appeared to shield Ngo from any further violence, briefly escorting him as he walked away. A short time later, Ngo live-streamed himself recounting what had just happened, his face covered in milk and bruises and cuts.

The assault, depending on which anti-fascist you talk to, was either a well-deserved piece of comeuppance and self-defense or a tactical blunder, helping Ngo further catapult himself to conservative fame and cementing antifa as the American right's go-to bogeyman.

Ngo later claimed to have suffered a traumatic brain injury, with right-wingers crowdfunding nearly $200,000 for his medical expenses.[21] "To federal law enforcement: investigate & bring legal action against a Mayor who has, for political reasons, ordered his police officers to let citizens be attacked by domestic terrorists," Senator Ted Cruz tweeted after the video of Ngo's assault went viral, blaming Portland's Democratic mayor Ted Wheeler for permitting chaos in the city.[22] (Wheeler also condemned the assault.)

On July 18, 2019, Cruz and a fellow Republican senator, Louisiana's Bill Cassidy, introduced a resolution that would designate antifa as a domestic terrorist organization.[23] It read in part:

> *Whereas members of Antifa, because they believe that free speech is equivalent to violence, have used threats of violence in the pursuit of suppressing opposing political ideologies . . .*
>
> *Whereas, on June 29, 2019, while covering demonstrations in Portland, Oregon, journalist Andy Ngo was physically attacked by protestors affiliated with Antifa . . .*
>
> *Whereas the [Immigration and Customs Enforcement] office in southwest Portland, Oregon, was shut down for days due to threats and occupation by Antifa members . . .*
>
> *Whereas Rose City Antifa rejects the civil treatment of individuals the group labels as fascists, stating: "We can't just argue against them; we have to prevent them from organizing by any means necessary . . ."*

Ngo went on *Fox & Friends*, the network's morning program, and a favorite of Trump's, to advocate for the resolution.[24] "This will provide a framework for local authorities and, especially, federal authorities to start investigating this criminal cartel for the street thugs that they are," he said. "But in addition to the street hooliganism that we see over and over on the streets of America, this movement also has a political ideology that is agitating for a violent political revolution."

Ultimately, Ngo was finding success in exploiting the general public's confusion about what antifa, a sometimes hard-to-define leftist subculture, *actually was*. This confusion created the perfect conditions for Ngo to manufacture a bogeyman. A new Red Scare. With his help, the wider conservative movement started to adapt an expansive definition of antifa—suddenly the word was being used as a label for anything vaguely left-wing, collapsing any difference between radical anarchists and moderate, centrist Democratic Party officials. In this formulation, any American opposed to the MAGA agenda could be designated an "extremist."

Back in Portland, the Proud Boys were gearing up for another demonstration. Citing the assault of Ngo earlier that summer, and the Senate resolution to designate antifa a domestic terror group, the Proud Boys would hold the "End Domestic Terror," or "Better Dead Than Red," rally on August 17, 2019.

The morning of the rally, as the Proud Boys gathered along the riverfront in Portland, the violent fascist street gang received a big endorsement for its cause.[25]

"Major consideration is being given to naming ANTIFA an 'ORGANIZATION OF TERROR,'" President Trump tweeted. "Portland is being watched very closely. Hopefully the Mayor will be able to properly do his job!"

* * *

In the viral video, you can hear Martin Gugino's skull crack.[26]

On the evening of June 4, 2020, the seventy-five-year-old was among just three protesters remaining on the steps of City Hall in Buffalo. The rest of their fellow demonstrators—part of a nationwide anti-racist uprising that began a week earlier after the police murders of George Floyd and Breonna Taylor—had dispersed ahead of an 8 p.m. emergency curfew issued by the city's mayor.

Gugino, a lifelong Catholic peace activist in the midst of a battle with cancer,[27] had initially come to the demonstration to see if police officers would say the Rosary with him.[28] He'd been moved by images from a day earlier showing several Buffalo cops kneeling in unison with activists marching under the banner of BLACK LIVES MATTER, a sign of "solidarity," one of the officers said. But here and now, as the clock approached curfew, the officers seemed uninterested in reciting the set of Rosary prayers with Gugino.

He believed the curfew to be unconstitutional, a violation of the First Amendment, so he'd also planned to do what he'd done most of his adult life: engage in a little act of nonviolent protest. Gugino was a man of deep faith, steeped in the tradition of the Catholic Worker movement, believing in housing for all, immigrants' rights, and the redistribution of wealth, in the abolition of prisons and the abolition of nuclear weapons, and in "the sacred power of nonviolent resistance to injustice." He'd been particularly active in a group called Witness Against Torture, which performed acts of civil disobedience against the indefinite detention and torture of people, predominantly Muslim men, held at the US prison camp in Guantanamo Bay. The burgeoning Black Lives Matter movement had brought into focus for Gugino and his cohorts an "uncomfortable truth: that many of the abuses in War on Terror prisons, like solitary confinement, are routine in America's domestic prisons, holding predominantly people of color," one of his friends in Witness Against Torture reflected.[29] "Access to the law, moreover, is no guarantee of justice. Sometimes the law is the problem."

His challenge to the curfew in Buffalo would be courteous and polite: He'd wait until the police moved in and then he'd approach them and ask why the curfew seemed to apply only to protesters, and not people shopping and running errands in other parts of the city.

Gugino sat on the steps of City Hall with the two other men, looking out over an empty Niagara Square. There was little to no unrest, the curfew seeming to have its desired effect. Nevertheless, fifty-seven members of the Buffalo Police Department's heavily militarized Emergency Response Team, all dressed in riot gear and wielding batons, got into formation a few minutes after 8 p.m.

"Move Forward March!" some of them yelled, beginning to walk in Gugino's direction. He made his move, approaching them and attempting to talk. "Push him, push him," the cops chanted.

A reporter from WBFO, the local public radio station, filmed what happened next:[30] One officer held up his baton and pressed it against Gugino's chest, while a second officer shoved Gugino with his arm, while a third pushed the other two cops from behind, giving their shoves extra force and sending the seventy-five-year-old Catholic peace activist, wearing jeans and a blue sweatshirt and an N95 COVID mask, stumbling backward and falling, his head hitting the concrete, blood quickly pouring out his ear and forming a small pool, as his right hand lost grip of the cell phone he'd been holding. The rows of officers continued to march past him as he lay bleeding and unconscious.

Less than an hour later, the Buffalo Police Department released a statement announcing that, during a "skirmish involving protesters, one person was injured when he tripped and fell." Twenty minutes later WBFO published the video that laid bare the police department's lie: It wasn't a "skirmish" and Gugino hadn't "tripped"; he'd been pushed.

The video instantly went viral, eventually accruing seventy million views and becoming representative of the often heartless, heavy-handed police response to the uprisings across America, which from the protesters' perspective proved the grievance at the heart of their cause: Police don't protect us. (One of the officers who'd shoved Gugino was among those who'd knelt in "solidarity" with protesters the day before.[31])

In the days that followed, right-wing media worked to manufacture a new narrative about Gugino, to make him out as anything but a peaceful old man with cancer. One America News Network (OANN), a far-right cable channel competing with Fox News for Trump's affections, aired a segment on June 9, 2020, that claimed Gugino was using "common antifa tactics"[32] and that the incident in Buffalo was a "false flag provocation by far-left group antifa." Citing an unhinged MAGA conspiracist site called The Conservative Treehouse, OANN also claimed Gugino was using a device on his phone that could scan the police officers' communications, allowing him to track their locations and also disrupt the frequencies they used to talk to each other. There was, of course, no basis for any of these claims, but at 8:34 a.m. the president nevertheless gave them a big boost.

"Buffalo protester shoved by Police could be an ANTIFA provocateur," Trump tweeted. "75 year old Martin Gugino was pushed away after appearing to scan police communications in order to black out the equipment. @OANN I watched, he fell harder than was pushed. Was aiming scanner. Could be a set up?"

Thrilled by Trump's attention, OANN would publish story after story about Gugino over the next week, spinning yarns about his apparent links to antifa[33] and "anarchist messaging boards," and sowing doubt about the seriousness of his injuries, citing unnamed medical sources who said it was "unlikely" Gugino hit the ground hard enough to fracture his skull.

But Gugino had fractured his skull. He suffered a concussion, too, and was in the intensive care unit before spending a whole month recovering in the hospital. This was who Trump and American conservatives wanted to label as "antifa" now: a seventy-five-year-old Catholic man with cancer, who'd devoted his life to nonviolent actions, who'd wanted to *pray with cops*, but ended up getting pushed by them instead, now laid up in a hospital bed during a deadly pandemic.

*   *   *

By July 2020, *The New York Times* announced in a headline that "The Black Lives Matter Demonstrations May Be the Largest Movement in U.S. History." The statistics were breathtaking, especially considering that the protests sweeping America wouldn't ebb until later that fall.[34] "Four recent polls . . ." the *Times* reported, "suggest that about 15 million to 26 million people in the United States have participated in demonstrations over the death of George Floyd and others in recent weeks."

There was an average of 140 protests per day, according to a *Times* analysis, since the first demonstrations on May 26, 2020, in Minneapolis—where a video captured Officer Derek Chauvin putting his knee to George Floyd's neck until he stole Floyd's last breath—with turnout ranging "from dozens to tens of thousands in 2,500 small towns and large cities."

Later, the Armed Conflict Location & Event Data (ACLED) project would give its final tally for 2020: "more than 10,330 demonstrations associated with the BLM movement across more than 2,730 locations in all 50 states and Washington, DC . . . The vast majority of these events—94%—involved no violent or destructive activity . . ."[35]

When the mainstream and liberal media invoked that last statistic, it was often to state that the uprisings were "largely" or "mostly" peaceful, sending right-wing pundits and politicians into fits about the 6 percent of demonstrations that *weren't*. Protesters, after all, had *seized the Third Police Precinct in Minneapolis, sending officers fleeing, before burning the building down.* They kicked the cops out of certain parts of American cities, like in Seattle and Atlanta, creating self-governing autonomous zones. Whole commercial districts, like in Manhattan's SoHo, were shut down, shops boarding up their windows, for fear of fires and looting and property destruction. Some of the most enduring images of that spring and summer were of cop cars set on fire, like in Brooklyn, where the flames curled out of police cruiser windows, just above the decals declaring the NYPD's "Courtesy, Professionalism, and Respect." This was very real violence, the right screamed. These were riots.

There were many leftists who similarly resisted the moderate, pacifying narrative of "largely peaceful demonstrations." Some of the uprisings, especially in late May and early June 2020, *were riots*, they insisted, just not in the pejorative way right-wingers wielded the word.

From their perspective, descriptions of the demonstrations as "largely peaceful" were an effort at defanging them, eliding the very real revolutionary rupture taking place across America. It was an effort at painting the scattered violence that did take place as the condemnable work of "bad protesters" or "a few bad apples," insinuating that the fires and looting and property destruction were born out of an apolitical abandon or opportunism, instead of recognizing them for what they were: a righteous, popular, Black-led mass uprising against racial capitalism.[36]

This wasn't just about the murders of George Floyd and Breonna Taylor— or attaining guilty verdicts against their murderers, but about the oppression that their murders represented. It was a revolt against the incessant, daily violence that always disproportionately impacted Black people: the violence of mass incarceration, of being evicted, of working two jobs and not being able to pay your bills—the violence of not being able to afford healthcare, of being left to suffer pain and illness for which there was a cure only richer people could afford.

It was the initial riots after Floyd's murder, after all, that sparked all the mass peaceful demonstrations across America in the first place, helping radicalize a whole new generation into understanding how systemic violence was rarely ever described as such, into understanding the ways we've been made and conditioned to accept the unacceptable.

The writer Tobi Haslett, in a remarkable *N+1* essay reflecting on the 2020 uprisings called "Magic Actions," wrote:[37]

> *But the riots worked. The beast groaned. Despite the many criticisms streaming through the media, the destruction of property struck many as a defensible answer to state violence:* Newsweek—*not known for its anarchist*

sympathies—reported that a full 54 percent of Americans saw the siege on the police precinct as "justified." The riots were too large and widespread, and expressed too popular a discontent, to be explained away by belting out the familiar anthems of condemnation. One old lament—that looters were destroying their own neighborhoods—seemed especially flimsy this time as, post-Minneapolis, crowds waged war on the (well-insured) commercial districts of the nation's downtowns . . .

To the scattered victories of abolitionists toward the tail end of [2020]—the weakening of police unions, the severance of several law enforcement contracts with universities and public schools, the (token) shrinking of police budgets in a handful of major cities—we might add an ideological one: Black radicalism has hacked a path back to the mainstream political scene.

American history has shown, of course, that such moments of Black radicalism, revolution, and advancement are met with the swiftest and most brutal of responses not only from the state, but from its white vigilante collaborators—and 2020 proved no exception.

*   *   *

The specter of the "outside agitator" has haunted every period of rebellion and Black advancement in the US. The phrase was invoked by white Southerners during Reconstruction to dismiss the rapid gains of freed Black people as the work of nefarious Northerners and "scalawags."[38] In 1921, after the Tulsa race massacre in Oklahoma, when white mobs mass murdered Black residents and burned down the thriving commercial district known as "Black Wall Street," white Tulsans blamed outside agitators like W. E. B. Dubois—who a local reverend called the "most vicious Negro in America"—for stirring Black locals into seeking equality in the first place.[39]

In the 1930s, the Ku Klux Klan in Alabama posted flyers that read NEGROES BEWARE: DO NOT ATTEND COMMUNIST MEETINGS, explaining that "paid organizers for the communists are only trying to get Negroes in trouble."[40] The flyer continued: ALABAMA IS A GOOD PLACE FOR GOOD NEGROES, BUT IT IS A BAD PLACE FOR NEGROES WHO BELIEVE IN SOCIAL EQUALITY. THE KU KLUX KLAN IS WATCHING YOU. TAKE HEED.

Dr. Martin Luther King Jr., during the civil rights era, was constantly labeled a "communist" and an "outside agitator," which he addressed in his famous "Letter from Birmingham Jail":

> *I am cognizant of the interrelatedness of all communities and states. I cannot sit idly by in Atlanta and not be concerned about what happens in Birmingham. Injustice anywhere is a threat to justice everywhere. We are caught in an inescapable network of mutuality, tied in a single garment of destiny. Whatever affects one directly, affects all indirectly. Never again can we afford to live with the narrow, provincial outside agitator idea. Anyone who lives inside the United States can never be considered an outsider anywhere within its bounds.*

The "outside agitator" trope has always been a white counterrevolutionary project to both distract from the grievances at the heart of movements for Black liberation, and to paint those movements as artificial, the work of conniving, clandestine provocateurs. From the very beginning of the 2020 uprisings, the anti-antifa panic of the previous few years was repurposed into an "outside agitators" narrative on steroids. "Antifa" became a synonym for the phrase, in the same way "communist" and "Northerner" had signified "outside agitators" in previous generations. Trump, with perhaps the biggest platform in the world, was constantly throwing fuel on the fire, tweeting that "ANTIFA led anarchists" and "Radical Left Anarchists" were responsible for the unrest. His mouthpiece, Fox News, reliably ramped up its coverage of antifa, too.

"Between May 31 and June 6, 2020, Fox News ran a total of forty hit pieces blaming Antifa for the protest violence," the journalist David Neiwert writes in his book *The Age of Insurrection: The Radical Right's Assault on American Democracy*.[41] "Between June 8 and early September came fifty-seven more pieces. The national narrative that emerged from all this coverage, and which became entrenched not just among Fox-watching conservatives but in rural and suburban America generally: Antifa and BLM had burned down American cities in the summer of 2020. None of it was true."

Like so many conspiracy theories, the anti-antifa panic contained a kernel of truth: Antifa was participating in the riots and demonstrations and subscribed to the militancy of those taking part, but antifa was not leading or directing these uprisings, nor could they. Antifa in its current incarnation is a small subculture and phenomenon, without the numbers to propel millions of Americans into the streets. "Blaming anarchists and antifa, with absolutely no evidence, is a way to make what's happening seem fringe and marginal when these are popular uprisings," the anarchist scott crow noted in a press release for the Agency,[42] a group that tries to explain anarchism to a wider audience. "This is a time of mass outrage at an unjust system."

Still, a modern folk devil had been born, and tales of this antifa bogeyman were spreading far and wide, the monster growing bigger and bigger, developing new and horrifying dimensions with every tweet and Facebook post and Nextdoor comment and YouTube video. By late June 2020, according to the media intelligence firm Zignal Labs, the unfounded claim that antifa was orchestrating the riots and looting was the most significant piece of social media misinformation swirling around the uprisings.

Of 873,000 pieces of misinformation about the demonstrations studied by Zignal Labs, nearly 600,000 involved antifa. Erin Gallagher, a social media researcher, told *The New York Times* this anti-antifa panic was spreading because "long-established networks of hyperpartisan social media influencers now work together like a well-oiled machine."[43]

To believe right-wing propaganda in the summer of 2020 was to fall into an "outside agitator" fever dream, to believe that literal "busloads of antifa" were roaming the countryside, threatening to come to your town to set fires to businesses and loot homes and kill white people.

"I am not one to spread false information," started a Facebook post spreading false information in a group for residents of Klamath Falls, Oregon. "There are two buses heading this way from Portland, full of ANTIFA members and loaded with bricks. Their intentions are to come to Klamath Falls, destroy it, and murder police officers. There have been rumors of the antifa going into residential areas to 'fuck up the white hoods.'"

What might've been dismissed as an unsubstantiated rumor was lent the imprimatur of legitimacy when a commenter replied with a screenshot of a direct message from Colonel Jeff Edwards, the commander of the Oregon Air National Guard's 173rd Fighter Wing. "Team Kingsley, for your safety I ask you to please avoid the downtown area this evening," Edwards wrote in a message to his subordinates. "We received an alert that there may be 2 busloads of ANTIFA protesters en route to Klamath Falls and arriving in downtown around 2030 tonight."

NBC News later confirmed the authenticity of the message, and that the "alert" the colonel had received had come from local law enforcement.[44]

There was no basis, of course, for the rumor, but that didn't stop hundreds of white men from turning up in Klamath Falls one evening, standing across the street from a small anti-racist demonstration. They carried shotguns, rifles, and pistols, ostensibly to protect businesses downtown. In reality it felt like an excuse for intimidating those screaming "Black Lives Matter!"

"It felt like walking through an enemy war camp," Frederick Brigham, one of the few Black men in town, told NBC News of walking past the armed white men on the way to join the BLM protest.

"A lot of these people came out because they swore that antifa buses were in town," he said. "They couldn't believe that I was from here. They thought I must be a Black man that came from somewhere else."

A pattern was emerging across America, the antifa rumors[45]—all of murky provenance, but many generating from a post by a fake antifa account created by Identity Evropa that was boosted by Donald Trump Jr.—spread far and wide, from Indiana to Idaho to Kentucky to Washington, where they were often lent credence by unskeptical law enforcement officials. This anti-antifa propaganda had the effect of mass-producing pretexts for armed occupations of towns and cities by white vigilantes, where they often harassed, intimidated, and attacked their neighbors taking part in peaceful anti-racist demonstrations.

In Sandpoint, Idaho, when some local high school students staged a small racial justice protest on a bridge over the clear blue mountain waters of Lake Pend Oreille, they were followed by about forty men in camo gear carrying AR-15s[46]—many of them militia members who had been patrolling the town's streets for days, waiting for the antifa buses. One of the students, a seventeen-year-old girl, later recounted that one of the gun-toting men told her she deserved to be raped. Other students reported hearing the armed white guys say, "Go live in Compton." One was called a "n***er-lover."

An hour's drive south in Coeur d'Alene, Idaho, another group of thirty to fifty men armed with semi-automatic weapons and dressed in tactical gear occupied the city's streets for upward of a week, on the lookout for the antifa buses. "If you guys are thinking of coming to Coeur d'Alene, to riot or loot, you'd better think again," one of them said in a video. "Because we ain't having it in our town."

Armed white men in Leitchfield, Kentucky, waited for the antifa buses too.[47] Antifa never came, which they took as evidence that they'd done their job scaring antifa off. One of the white men, Mike Johnson, told the Associated Press he'd heard that a bus had arrived in town, with fifteen antifa inside, but that they'd complied with an order by law enforcement and some of his fellow vigilantes to leave. But Grayson County Sheriff Norman Chaffins—among some law enforcement officials that summer who pushed back against the antifa bus rumors—told the Associated Press that didn't happen.

In rural Oregon, amid rumors that antifa was responsible for devastating wildfires in the state, small, armed militias started setting up checkpoints on roads, demanding drivers hand over their IDs before asking them questions about their political views. In Clackamas County, the sheriff pleaded with the militias to stop.[48] "It is illegal to stop somebody at gunpoint," he said.

But one of the sheriff's deputies was encouraging the white vigilantes, seen in a pair of videos on YouTube expressing his belief in the antifa rumors. "Antifa motherfuckers are out causing hell, and there's a lot of lives at stake and there's a lot of people's property at stake because these guys got some vendetta," he said.[49] He also was filmed coaching the checkpoint militias how to avoid charges for shooting antifa. "Now you throw a fucking knife in their hand after you shoot them, that's on you . . ." he said.

*   *   *

"When you can delegitimize authentic expressions of discontent, then you can mobilize violent force against them," Aldon Morris, professor of sociology and African American history at Northwestern University, said during the uprisings, observing how the myth of "outside agitators" was being used as a pretext to enact violence.[50]

Across the country in the summer of 2020, per data collected by Alexander Reid Ross, a professor at Portland State University, far-right groups showed up to oppose anti-racist protests at least five hundred times.[51] There were sixty-four cases of simple assault committed by these far-right activists, thirty-eight incidents of vigilantes driving cars into demonstrators, and nine times they opened fire. Six anti-racist protesters were hit by vigilante bullets in the summer's violence, three of whom died from their wounds. "There just isn't really anything to compare it to," Ross said at the time. "I've never seen anything like this in my life."

Meanwhile, the Trump administration, the Justice Department, and the GOP were still fixated on antifa. In July, US Attorney General William Barr was summoned by the House Judiciary Committee to testify about law enforcement's often brutal crackdown of the uprisings—some fourteen thousand people would be arrested that year during demonstrations—but ended up talking about antifa instead. "Antifa is heavily represented in the recent riots," Barr told Congress, offering no evidence of his claim.[52]

A week later, Senator Ted Cruz held his own committee hearing, this one focused on "how Antifa and other anarchists are hijacking peaceful protests and engaging in political violence that is not only criminal but antithetical to the First Amendment." The lone member of the media invited to testify at Cruz's hearing was Andy Ngo, who held forth before America's highest elected body, warning them that antifa is a "violent insurrectionary group."

But the American right, meanwhile, had been showing signs of its own burgeoning insurrectionary fervor. Armed right-wingers had stormed the Michigan statehouse in May, the Idaho statehouse in August, and the Oregon statehouse in December, all to protest coronavirus lockdown measures. These events were among some "2,350 right-wing demonstrations that took place across more than 1,070 locations in all 50 states and Washington, DC," in 2020, the ACLED Project, which tracks civil unrest, reported.[53]

The right-wing demonstrations that year had three phases. In the spring demonstrators were focused on ending pandemic-related policies; in the summer they were focused on countering the wave of anti-racist uprisings; and by the fall they were chanting "Stop the steal!" in an attempt to reverse the results of the presidential election, which Trump had lost. Right-wing paramilitary groups, including the Proud Boys, the Three Percenters, and others, were involved in at least 11 percent of the right-wing demonstrations that year.

No one knew it yet, but the storming of statehouses had been dress rehearsals; and the coalition of paramilitary groups on the streets of American cities was a preview of the coalition that would fly to Washington, DC, in early January 2021.

These outside agitators, if you will, stormed the Capitol. In the immediate aftermath—when the death and devastation of the insurrection came into focus—the right reached for its go-to bogeyman, blaming antifa "provoca-teurs" for stirring up the violence, deflecting blame for all the carnage Americans were seeing on their TVs and timelines. Of at least fifty-seven GOP officials identified at the rally leading to the insurrection, twenty blamed antifa for the ensuing mayhem.[54] "Those who stormed the capitol yesterday were not Trump supporters. They have been confirmed to be antifa," Texas Attorney General Ken Paxton said, offering no evidence of this claim. Representative Matt Gaetz of Florida, *The New York Times* reported, "stood on the ransacked House floor and claimed that many rioters 'were members of the violent terrorist group antifa.'"[55] *The Washington Times*, a conservative news outlet, published an article stating facial recognition software had spotted known members of antifa in the mob that stormed the Capitol. It was a false claim, and the paper corrected the story a short time later, but not before its original headline earned over 360,000 likes and shares on Facebook, eventually ending up being cited by Laura Ingraham on Fox News.

Within six weeks of the January 6 attack, a poll showed 58 percent of Trump supporters believed the riot was "mostly an antifa-inspired attack."[56]

But in the ensuing months and years, you heard the American right blaming antifa less and less for the storming of the Capitol. A historical revisionism started to take hold, in which the insurrectionists weren't criminals or extremists, but patriots turned political prisoners.[57] Martyrs for the MAGA cause. As the years wore on, the right wanted to take credit for the insurrection. They wanted to celebrate it.

CHAPTER 14
To Catch an Anti-Fascist

S uddenly Vincent's real name, or *names* as it turned out, were everywhere. In *The Seattle Times*, the Associated Press, and *Rolling Stone*, the latter of which ran an August 10, 2023, article with the headline: "He Infiltrated a Notorious White Nationalist Group. Now, He's Being Sued for Exposing Them." It began:[1]

> To hear Patriot Front members tell it, David Alan Capito II is basically an antifa superspy—a man who is known by myriad aliases, including "Vyacheslav Arkhangelskiy," "Nick Vasiliy," and "Vincent Washington." This last name was the one Capito used to infiltrate Patriot Front and doxx members of the white nationalist group, according to a federal lawsuit brought in late July by five members whose identities were revealed. What emerges from the 20-page court document is a cinematic tale of an epic doublecross. The suit decries how the left-wing activist conned Patriot Front into thinking he was a fellow traveler, "lying about his background and values," only to expose its members through photography, secret recordings, and a massive computer hack. . . . The litigation paints Capito [as] the menacing party—describing him [as] an affiliate [of] "the Puget Sound John Brown Gun Club, a heavily armed anarchist militia." It casts him as a 3-D-printed "ghost gun" enthusiast, a practitioner of the martial art of Krav Maga, a seasoned lock picker, and perhaps even "immune" to pepper spray.

The lawsuit's plaintiffs were Paul Gancarz, aka Samuel-VA, the engineer from Virginia; Daniel Turetchi, aka Grant-MD, the real estate agent from Maryland; James and Amelia Johnson, aka Tyler-WA and Rachel-WA, the couple who fled Seattle after they were doxed; and Colton Michael Brown, aka John-WA, the Network 8 director who, by his own admission, was responsible for "the worst" infiltration Patriot Front had ever seen.

All had kept their involvement with the white supremacist group a closely guarded secret but now were attaching their real names to documents filed in a federal district court admitting their allegiance to Patriot Front. They had suffered "severe harm" from Vincent's espionage, including job losses and fallouts with their families, after being exposed as part of a secret organization whose mission, the lawsuit noted, was simply to "reforge . . . our people, born to this nation of our European race . . . as a new collective capable of asserting our right to cultural independence." Now they wanted damages.

The lawsuit not only amounted to a dox of Vincent but lifted the curtain on how four hundred gigabytes of Patriot Front data had ended up on Unicorn Riot. The plaintiffs had first learned that Vincent was actually David Alan Capito Jr., or whatever his name might be now, after finding a photo of him on a social media account belonging to the Puget Sound John Brown Gun Club. From there, they traced his history as a leftist activist in the Seattle area through various news articles.

"We do our actions proportional to the threat, so when other people are out with rifles, we'll be out with rifles," Vincent told a reporter from *The Guardian* in the summer of 2019, in an article that identified him as a web designer named Nick Vasiliy.[2] He wore a camouflage baseball hat with a patch featuring the outline of an AR-15 over a Trans Pride flag.

He and his cohorts in the Puget Sound John Brown Gun Club had been asked by organizers of Seattle's Trans Pride March to provide armed security after evidence emerged of white supremacist groups plotting to disrupt the celebration. While the club was known to carry rifles for such assignments, Vincent explained why its members were carrying only concealed handguns this time. "In this case, we don't want to appear threatening for the people that we're trying to protect and support," he said. "We want this to be a happy atmosphere, especially for a population that may have faced gun violence on the street just for being who they are."

The Puget Sound John Brown Gun Club was a militant, aboveground anti-fascist organization, whose members didn't wear masks, even if they often used pseudonyms while talking to the press. Per its manifesto, the club worked to "counter the rise of fascist and far-right groups" and would not wait for "the state to do our work for us." As *The Guardian* explained, it was "part of a long American leftist tradition of armed groups, from the Black Panthers to current groups like Redneck Revolt, the Socialist Rifle Association, Trigger Warning Queer & Trans Gun Club, and the Los Angeles Black Coyote Collective"—groups that were increasingly being asked to protect queer gatherings around the country as right-wing rhetoric targeting trans people intensified.

Earlier that summer a friend of Vincent's and a longtime member of the Puget Sound John Brown Club named Willem Von Spronsen had officially cut ties with the group and said his goodbyes. A few weeks later, the sixty-nine-year-old Dutch-born immigrant brought an unregistered AR-15—a "ghost gun"—to the Northwest Detention Center in Tacoma, Washington, a private immigration detention center, where he attempted to set fire to ICE vehicles. Police who arrived on the scene ordered him to drop his weapon, and when Spronsen refused, they opened fire, killing him.

"For me, my friend was killed by the police while trying to destroy buses that were going to be used to round up and deport my neighbors," one of the Puget Sound John Brown Gun Club members reflected.[3] Spronsen, clearly anticipating his own death, had sent his comrades a letter that read, in part:[4]

> *When I was a boy, in post-war Holland, later France, my head was filled with stories of the rise of fascism in the '30s. I promised myself that I would not be one of those who stands by as neighbors are torn from their homes and imprisoned for somehow being perceived as lesser . . .*
>
> *I'm a man who loves you all and this spinning ball so much that I'm going to fulfill my childhood promise to myself to be noble . . .*
>
> *I'm a black and white thinker. Detention camps are an abomination . . .*
>
> *My trans comrades have transformed me, solidifying my conviction that we will be guided to a dreamed-of future by those most marginalized among us today. I have dreamed it so clearly that I have no regret for not seeing how it turns out. Thank you for bringing me so far along.*

I am antifa. I stand with comrades around the world who act from the
love of life in every permutation. Comrades who understand that freedom
means real freedom for all and a life worth living.
Keep the faith!
All power to the people!
Bella ciao.

A year later, in the summer of 2020, Vincent joined his comrades in the
Puget Sound John Brown Gun Club as they held a memorial in honor of
Spronsen on the one-year anniversary of his death. A photographer captured Vincent wearing a necklace with a bullet that had once belonged to
his fallen friend.[5]

Before it was included in Patriot Front's lawsuit, information about Vincent appeared on a short-lived website called Flarelight in May 2022.[6] An
archived "About" section on the website states: "The team at Flarelight, in
collaboration with our partners, uses open source intelligence and on-the-
ground reporting to exact retribution on antifa organizers and their collaborators by exposing their identities and getting them fired from their jobs."
There were indications that Flarelight was a Patriot Front project, including a
photo of the group marching in Washington, DC, and language extolling its
resiliency after so many of its members were unmasked. The website published
only five articles, including one titled "How to Avoid Being Doxed: A Guide
for Activists," which offered advice on how to "be hard to find online" and
"avoid facial recognition software." The last article Flarelight ever published
was about Vincent, labeling him a "violent anarchist in Seattle" and offering
seemingly inside information alleging he'd "exploited administrator privi-
leges" in Patriot Front's RocketChat server in order to "download private
chats and intercept video links." Flarelight disappeared not long afterward.

The lawyers representing the five Patriot Front members in court took a
novel strategy, accusing Vincent of violating the Computer Fraud and Abuse
Act, an anti-hacking statute. *The New Yorker*, writing about the lawsuit, noted
that a victory for Patriot Front in the case "could set a precedent for severely
penalizing vigilante infiltrators, and help end the leaks that have bedevilled
the far right."[7]

One of Patriot Front's lawyers, Glen Allen, knew what it was like to be
unmasked.[8] In 2016 the Southern Poverty Law Center published a report

identifying him as a longtime member of the National Alliance, the neo-Nazi group, and a close associate of the group's late founder, William Pierce, author of *The Turner Diaries*. Allen, the SPLC noted, had recently been "hired as an employee by the Baltimore City Law Department and is now defending the city in a lawsuit alleging that police officers withheld and fabricated evidence to wrongfully arrest and convict an African American man for a murder it appears he did not commit." The city of Baltimore fired him.

Now he seemed to be developing a roster of white supremacist clients, defending Patriot Front members being sued in Virginia for defacing an Arthur Ashe mural in Richmond and secretly providing legal counsel to a Unite the Right organizer who was a defendant in *Sines v. Kessler*, the seminal lawsuit related to the Charlottesville rally.[9]

Allen had a problem with this Patriot Front lawsuit in Washington, however. *No one could find Vincent to serve him notice of the lawsuit.* They had hired a private investigator who declared in a February 2024 court filing that he'd visited multiple addresses associated with Vincent in public records, but to no avail. The investigator also claimed to have visited one such address in Tacoma, speaking to a tenant who claimed to have never heard of Vincent.

But according to Tacoma's *News Tribune*, the property the private investigator claimed to have visited no longer existed.[10] The home had been purchased as part of a hospital expansion and demolished seven months before the private investigator claimed to have paid it a visit. Allen and his cocounsel, Christopher Hogue, did not respond to a request for comment about the discrepancy.

Vincent, it seemed, had vanished.

*   *   *

Vincent had mentioned knowing how to disappear. When he agreed to meet in a West Seattle park, with the city ferries passing by on the blue waters of the Puget Sound below, he explained his interest in making himself the rare exception to a digital age in which most of us, at most any time, are so eminently findable.

"I don't have my name on any property, don't have my name on my vehicle, don't have my name on my utilities. I don't have my name on a phone bill. I buy prepaid phone cards and smartphones every once in a while. I don't use

Google. I don't use Facebook. Don't use Google Maps, even. I put in a lot of work into making it difficult to track where I am using VPNs."

The VPNs came in handy once, right after the infiltration, when Patriot Front members sought revenge. They'd looked up Vincent's old username on the RocketChat server, or maybe it was on the Mumble server, and saw an IP address in Lakewood, Washington. "And John Washington went to that address, and they were waiting for my car," Vincent says. "He was having conversations with Mason-TX about destroying my vehicle. It's in the chat logs. I never lived at that place. But they wanted to get back at me and trash my vehicle. They were looking for me."

Patriot Front couldn't find him, of course. The lawyers for the five Patriot Front members suing Vincent couldn't find him either. Now Vincent had heard through the anti-fascist grapevine that the FBI was making inquiries about him, calling at least one former comrade to ask whether Vincent was dangerous. To ask about his ghost guns. (The Patriot Front lawsuit had cited an article in the publication *GEN* by journalist Kim Kelly that documented certain anti-fascist activists using ghost guns—including Vincent.)[11]

There was a certain irony in law enforcement coming after Vincent, when the 440 gigabytes of RocketChat data he'd procured had been cited by law enforcement in criminal cases and submitted as evidence in civil courts. The same legal apparatus whose prosecutions of the far right were occasionally dependent on the extralegal methods of antifa was now potentially chasing after one of those very anti-fascists.

It was the spring of 2023 when Vincent agreed to meet in that park. Trump was running for president again, and it did not feel paranoid in the slightest to worry about a second Trump administration commencing some kind of anti-antifa crackdown that would target people like Vincent. The 2020 killing of Michael Reinoehl felt like a possible harbinger of how far Trump would be willing to go.

Reinoehl, a forty-eight-year-old Oregon man who called himself "100% antifa,"[12] was attending the ongoing anti-racist uprising in Portland with a companion when he crossed paths with Aaron Danielson, a member of Patriot Prayer, the far-right group that had routinely antagonized the demonstrators. Danielson, thirty-nine, was armed with a metal baton when he charged at Reinoehl and his friend while spraying bear spray at the pair, prompting Reinoehl to pull out a gun and fire two shots, one of them hitting

Danielson in the chest, killing him. Mistrustful of police to believe that it was self-defense, Reinoehl fled the scene and then Portland altogether. He remained on the run for five days before appearing in a video interview with *Vice* to explain why he'd opened fire.[13] "I had no choice," he said. "I mean, I had a choice. I could have sat there and watched them kill a friend of mine of color. But I wasn't going to do that." Eventually US Marshals found Reinoehl at a hideout in Lacy, Washington, and killed him. Authorities initially claimed he had pulled a gun, but eventually a joint investigation by ProPublica and Oregon Public Broadcasting included witnesses recounting how law enforcement arrived and immediately opened fire on Reinoehl, before they ever identified themselves as police.[14] Moreover, according to *The New York Times*, although officers suggested Reinoehl opened fire on them, the gun recovered from his pocket had a full magazine.[15]

Appearing on Fox News, Trump touted the killing as "retribution." At a rally in Greenville, North Carolina, he also gave his version of events: "We sent in the U.S. Marshals. Took fifteen minutes, it was over, fifteen minutes it was over. We got him. They knew who he was. They didn't want to arrest him, and fifteen minutes, that ended."

Tim Dickinson at *Rolling Stone* observed that Trump's characterization of the incident made it sound like an "extrajudicial killing by law-enforcement"[16] that came "uncomfortably close to casting the U.S. Marshal's service as his death squad."

Vincent and the wider anti-fascist community were bracing themselves, going deeper underground, clutching onto their anonymity. It felt like the anti-antifa panic of 2020 was always about manufacturing a pretext for something worse; that Trump and the GOP could foment a wave of selective prosecutions, initiate a raft of anti-doxing legislation, or launch a series of McCarthyite congressional hearings.

Beyond guarding from these attacks from the state, preserving anonymity can also provide something else to anti-fascists like Vincent: It can forestall any individual activist's personal failings or abuses from distracting from the larger collective project of anti-fascism. Neo-Nazis like those in Patriot Front relish pointing out the hypocrisies of anti-fascists, digging up moments when they failed to live up to their ideals. It is a method of sowing division in antifa circles and undercutting anti-fascist claims to the moral high ground.

Patriot Front's lawsuits noted that in the spring of 2019, a woman who Vincent dated obtained a temporary restraining order against him for harassment. In an affidavit filed in court, the woman accused Vincent of sending a "long list of messages" and calling "repeatedly" after she broke up with him—thirty-eight text messages and seven calls over four days. Vincent also allegedly "brought flowers to my doorstep, despite being told not to come to my place of residence, and contacted my friend through social media about us," the woman wrote.

"I am concerned for my safety, as he has several firearms as well," she stated. "He is trained in Krav Maga and has boasted he is immune to pepper spray. He is proud that he can pick locks and has explained several ways he has or would like to hack certain computer systems."

The woman acknowledged in a subsequent affidavit that the judge "correctly points out that perhaps [Vincent] needs more time to let the finality of this relationship sink in." She added: "He has never made a direct threat to my safety, verbal or posturing or physical abuse, apart from the stalking above, I am not requesting his firearms be removed. I am requesting that a line be drawn so he leaves me alone. He has not been able to do this of his own accord, and I'm filing this as further motivation for him to not contact me or visit me."

The temporary restraining order—which forbid Vincent from contacting or surveilling the woman, instructing him to stay away from her residence and workplace—lasted one month, with a judge not seeing it necessary to be extended. (The woman could not be reached for comment.)

There were many questions to still ask Vincent about Patriot Front's lawsuit. What was it like to be doxed himself? To see his name in the news? What was his response to his ex's accusations? Had the FBI found him? What did he think Trump's possible return to the White House would mean for groups like Patriot Front, the group he worked so hard to destroy?

But Vincent seemed to be going underground. Anti-fascists in Seattle reported losing touch with him. He became slow to respond to calls and texts via an encrypted messaging app.

By the fall, in the run-up to the 2024 presidential election, he stopped responding at all.

CHAPTER 15

Ignite the Right

While Vincent seemed to be pulling a disappearing act, there was a long roster of antifa groups across America that were still very active. On the coasts were Long Beach Antifa and Miami Against Fascism. In Appalachia were Kentucky Anti-Fascists, Murfreesboro Anti-Fascist Action, and Pennsylvania Rural Resistance. Out west there was Utah 161 (the alpha-numeric code for "anti-fascist action") and Biggest Little City Antifa in Reno and Redoubt Antifascists in Idaho.

Wherever fascist groups became active, antifa often blossomed, and while these anti-fascist groups were largely location or community-based, new per-mutations had formed that weren't tethered to any single locale but dedicated to fighting specific genres or subcultures of fascists. DezNat Exposed focused on unmasking a burgeoning movement of "Deseret Nationalists," a subset of fundamentalist Mormons who believed in creating a white ethnostate across a wide swath of the American West.[2] Among the fascists DezNat Exposed helped unmask was an assistant attorney general in Alaska—a powerful offi-cial responsible for representing the state in cases where incarcerated people appealed their incarceration.[3] (He eventually resigned or was fired—state officials wouldn't clarify which.)

Iron March Dossiers was a collective of anti-fascist researchers mining a treasure trove of leaked data from the notorious Iron March forum, the neo-Nazi fever swamp online that birthed Vanguard America and eventu-ally Patriot Front.[4] Among the Iron March users the project doxed was an ex-Marine who *Vice* quickly confirmed was a senior official at an Immigration and Customs Enforcement detention center in Pahrump, Nevada.[5] The jail was operated by CoreCivic, the country's second-largest private prison company, raking in billions in annual revenue to keep people behind bars. (The official was fired.)

But perhaps one of the most remarkable anti-fascist undertakings was called Ignite the Right, formed by a coalition of at least a dozen researchers on August 12, 2022, the five-year anniversary of the Unite the Right. The group promised to expose "every single person who participated" in the Charlottesville rally.

"We do not forgive," the group declared.[6] "We do not forget. This project is dedicated to Heather Heyer and all the victims of racism."

It was one of the most ambitious anti-fascist endeavors to date, which would eventually set in motion localized political fights across the country, with communities grappling with the secret neo-Nazis who had been living in their midst—white men in positions of power.

Ignite the Right began with an online database of 277 white faces seen in Charlottesville, 67 of whom were unidentified. "We expect this database to grow to over 500 as we start working on random faces from footage," the group wrote. At their disposal were years of leaks published on Unicorn Riot—from Vincent's infiltration of Patriot Front, from Dylan's infiltration of Identity Evropa, and from Will's infiltration of the Unite the Right planning servers—and a host of newly developed tools, including facial recognition software.

Among the first white faces they investigated belonged to a man seen in a video acting as a bodyguard for Richard Spencer in Charlottesville. He wore a suit in the hot summer sun with aviator sunglasses beneath that fashy high-and-tight haircut ubiquitous among Spencer's apostles at the time. Speaking into the camera of a right-wing live-streamer, he identified himself by a pseudonym: "Johnny O'Malley."

A user by that name could be found in the leaked Identity Evropa Discord server on Unicorn Riot.[7] Johnny O'Malley had posted fond memories of his time in Charlottesville, describing getting a cab to a party after the rally. "And I was redpilling the fuck out of the driver about the JQ," O'Malley recounted, using alt-right lingo to describe awakening someone to the "Jewish Question," the antisemitic belief in a vast Jewish conspiracy to control the world.

O'Malley wrote that the party he'd gone to was at a house rented by Robert "Azzmador" Ray, the Daily Stormer writer. As the neo-Nazis drank and celebrated the day's events, Azzmador led a sing-along, with chilling custom-made lyrics extolling the genocide of Black people and Jews, set to the tune of "Battle Hymn of the Republic."[8] At another point, Spencer—the man O'Malley had been tasked with guarding all day—gave an angry speech, lashing out at the anti-fascists who dared try to spoil their big day.[9] "Little fucking kikes!" he seethed. "They get ruled by people like me! Little fucking octaroons! My ancestors fucking enslaved those little pieces of fucking shit!"

When O'Malley returned home after Unite the Right—to somewhere in Massachusetts it seemed—he wasn't worried about being identified as a neo-Nazi. "[Anti-fascists] can review all the footage they want, but unless there is a massive effort, they're not going to be able to dox every person there," he wrote.

He was brazen about his beliefs back home, writing on Discord about wearing a "Right Wing Death Squad" T-shirt to his local gym. "Got some looks. If you're not wearing offensive clothing to the gym, the kikes win," he wrote. The T-shirt included an illustration of antifa being thrown from a helicopter into the sea. MAKE COMMUNISTS AFRAID OF ROTARY AIRCRAFT AGAIN. PHYSICAL REMOVAL SINCE 1973, it said, a reference to dictator Augusto Pinochet's preferred method of killing political opponents.

The anti-fascists at Ignite the Right sometimes resorted to using facial recognition software when other investigative avenues had been exhausted. They plugged a screenshot of O'Malley's face, which had a distinctive scar above the right eye, into the software and got a hit: an identical-looking man from a profile page on Zillow, the online real estate marketplace. The man's name appeared to be John Donnelly, a Woburn, Massachusetts, Realtor catering to clients in the police and military.

But a corresponding LinkedIn page showed Donnelly worked a few other jobs, too. He was part owner of Precision Point Firearms, a "federally licensed manufacturer and dealer of firearms" in Massachusetts. On social media Donnelly had posted an image of a black pistol next to a Precision Point Firearms–branded sticker. "Black Guns Matter," it said. He was also the president of a nonprofit called Irish Angel, which offered support for cops and military veterans suffering PTSD. Irish Angel's social media accounts were flush with "Thin Blue Line" and "Blue Lives Matter" symbols, common iconography in law enforcement communities developed as a racist response to the Black Lives Matter movement.

And lastly, Donnelly's LinkedIn page listed him as working one other job: "Police Officer, City of Woburn."

Donnelly had been a cop in the Boston suburb since 2015, meaning he'd taken off his police uniform in August 2017, traveled to Charlottesville to protect arguably America's most famous neo-Nazi during a deadly fascist riot, and then returned home to Woburn to rejoin the boys in blue.

Ignite the Right went to great lengths to verify they had the right guy—any anti-fascist researcher will tell you that facial recognition tools aren't 100 percent—and found other biographical details that matched. O'Malley had mentioned on Discord that he worked as a real estate agent in the Boston area. And on August 20, 2017, he wrote: "My sister got married to a huhwhite guy today . . . I'm trashed." A Facebook profile belonging to John Donnelly's sister noted that she was married on the same day.

When Ignite the Right published its dox, they included a photo Donnelly had posted to Instagram: him standing with his German shepherd, beneath a giant billboard advertising his real estate business. "Buying or selling in or around Woburn?" it said. "Call or Text John Donnelly at 857-523-2787." The billboard had a giant picture of Donnelly's smiling face.

In the dox, the anti-fascists made sure to blur out the face of the German shepherd.

HuffPost immediately followed up on the story.[10] The Woburn Police Department told the outlet that Donnelly had been placed on administrative leave pending an investigation, but within a week he'd resigned. Irish Angel, the Blues Lives Matter nonprofit, removed him as president. And Century 21, the real estate agency where Donnelly worked, quickly fired him.

The local district attorney also announced that her office would be reviewing every case in which Officer Donnelly was involved. Every arrest, every bit of court testimony, every traffic ticket.

The New England Innocence Project, a civil rights group dedicated to preventing and correcting wrongful convictions, called on the district attorney to go further. "Every case this officer touched should be dismissed, every conviction vacated," the group said in a statement. "There is no integrity in a system that relies on his credibility, judgment, or fairness. Nothing he has said or done in the job can be sufficient to bring criminal consequences to someone else."

The group's statement also expressed disbelief. *Surely someone in the police department knew about Donnelly's double life?*

"This white supremacist officer had partners, supervisors & trainers," the statement said. "If he made arrests, prosecutors and judges relied on his reports and testimony. Yet, NONE of these people recognized and exposed him; they enabled him to be in a position of power over our community."

Later, the law firm WilmerHale, commissioned by the state to investigate Donnelly's time on the force, issued a report[11] finding that although he "encountered Black and Hispanic individuals at a higher rate than might be expected solely on census data," there was no "discernible pattern of discriminatory policing" during his nearly five hundred interactions with members of the Woburn community. None of the convictions stemming from his arrests would be automatically vacated, nor any of the ongoing prosecutions.

*   *   *

By the following year, in 2023, the Ignite the Right coalition had gathered an entire terabyte, or one thousand gigabytes, of videos and photos from the Charlottesville rally, taken by activists, journalists, and live-streamers, to aid in their research. The group also started receiving anonymous tips from people who recognized the men in the footage as their neighbors, classmates, coworkers, and family members.

The group announced it had expanded its database "from 240 entries to over 600."[12] That included "200 new identities for previously unnamed Unite the Right participants, bringing the total number of identified participants to 320."

The anti-fascist researchers in Ignite the Right were among some of the most formidable in the country, steeped in the techniques of open-source intelligence (OSINT), most of them self-taught. Over the years they had published some of the most significant and impactful doxes: an elementary school teacher who moonlighted as a prominent neo-Nazi writer[13]; a Lutheran pastor preaching sermons on Sunday and podcasting his praise for Hitler on Monday; a family doctor in Tennessee who helped pay for white supremacists to travel to Charlottesville; and an Ohio couple who led a social media channel for parents who wanted to legally homeschool their kids to become "wonderful Nazis."[16]

With all their success, though, many of the anti-fascists in Ignite the Right described having their own white whales—fascists whose identities remained vexing, infuriating mysteries. Many of these white whales were pseudonymous propagandists, neo-Nazis with large followings who published podcasts or blogs imploring their fans to commit mass murder and hate crimes. For years, "Vic Mackey" was a white whale. Mackey was a leader of The Bowl Patrol, a group whose name referenced the "bowl cut" hairstyle of Dylann Roof, the white supremacist who mass-murdered nine Black parishioners in a Charleston, South Carolina, church. Mackey and his Bowl Patrol cohorts maintained a frightening hagiology of shooters like Roof, calling them "saints" and canonizing them with medieval-style church drawings. Mackey also bragged that his Bowl Patrol propaganda may have helped inspire "Saint" Robert Bowers to shoot and kill eleven Jews inside the Tree of Life synagogue in Pittsburgh. Bowers followed Mackey on Gab, and Mackey boasted that the two had interacted on the social media platform.

His identity confounded researchers for years until, in July 2020, the group Anonymous Comrades Collective, which later joined the Ignite the Right coalition, exposed Mackey as Andrew Richard Casarez, a twenty-seven-year-old pizza delivery driver living in Sacramento.[17] *HuffPost* followed up on the story,[18] and a few days later police arrested Casarez on a gun violence restraining order. "Based on my training and experience now that Casarez has been outed as a white supremacist and he has lost his anonymity there is a likelihood that he could become a 'lone wolf' attacker to prove his status to the cause," a sergeant in the sheriff's office wrote in a July 13 statement requesting the restraining order.

The sergeant wrote that he found evidence that Casarez had plans to build his own AR-15, which was illegal in California, and during a search of his home, authorities found Casarez in possession of "a 9 mm gun, a gun case with two empty magazines, and a 'black Teeshirt with skull and crossbones with bowl cut hair piece on top.'"

Later, the Southern Poverty Law Center would report that Casarez had been on a federal no-fly list[19] *before* he was unmasked by Anonymous Comrades Collective, suggesting federal law enforcement may have known about his role encouraging neo-Nazis to commit mass murder, but for whatever reason—likely investigative secrecy—had not made that information available to the public.

The anti-fascists in Ignite the Right had their own white whale: a man they called Red Beard. He'd taken part in an era-defining act of violence at Unite the Right, but afterward became a ghost, disappearing back somewhere across America with no trace, presumably living a life free of consequence for taking part in the beating of DeAndre Harris in a Charlottesville parking garage.

The photo of the beating had gone viral, with *The Washington Post* later describing how "the sight of a white nationalist mob setting upon a Black man evoked images from the Jim Crow era, particularly a 1961 front-page newspaper photo showing Ku Klux Klan members in Birmingham, Ala., pummeling a black bystander."[20]

A video of the assault was viewed millions of times across social media showing six men taking part in pummeling Harris. Red Beard—in black pants, a white Under Armour T-shirt underneath a green button-down, a "Marmot Mountain" baseball cap sitting atop a mane of red hair, and a long red beard—delivered one of the final blows, striking the twenty-year-old aide to special-needs kids with a flagpole as Harris crawled across the floor, trying to escape.

The next day, Harris—who suffered a concussion, a spinal injury, a broken wrist, a chipped tooth, and a head wound that would require ten staples—watched the video of his own beating and told photojournalist Zach Roberts: "I don't know if I'm safe in this town anymore. I could have lost my life yesterday if it wasn't for [my friends]. I could have been beaten to a pulp right there, man. Every time I look at the video, and I just think about it, it just . . . blows me [away], man."[21]

Outrage over the video led to a brief period of a massive, viral, crowd-sourced effort to identify Red Beard, with amateur internet sleuths doing their best attempts at OSINT, but misidentifying—or "fail-doxing"—various men with red beards as the assailant. These public misidentifications, made by people outside anti-fascist circles, were infuriating to the researchers in Ignite the Right, who feared the fail-doxes hurt the credibility of doxes that *were correct*.

By 2019, four other men involved in the assault of DeAndre Harris were arrested and charged.[22] Alexander Ramos, a member of the Fraternal Order of

Alt-Knights (an even more militant branch of the Proud Boys), was convicted of malicious wounding and sentenced to six years in prison. Jacob Goodwin, a member of the Traditionalist Worker Party, got eight years. Daniel Borden, who wore a white helmet inscribed with the words COMMIE KILLER during the beating, got nearly four years. And Tyler Watkins, a member of League of the South, entered an Alford plea—in which a defendant asserts his innocence but accepts a sentence—and got two years.

"In the next six years, all these guys will be right back at it. I thought they'd be going to jail for a longer time," Harris told the *Post*. "If it had been a white guy who was attacked, and it was all *my* friends beating him up, we would never have seen the light of day again."

The hunt for Red Beard had gone cold. The Charlottesville Police Department tweeted out a photo of his face, asking for the public's help. "I've pretty much exhausted everything I can do with this case," said Declan Hickey, the detective in charge of the investigation.

Meanwhile, Harris occasionally received threats. He suffered bouts of PTSD, too, recounting to the *Post* how on the second anniversary of Unite the Right he went for his lunch break at work and he was suddenly flooded with memories of the beating. He told his boss he had to go home.

"He couldn't stop crying," his mom told the paper. "He said, 'I don't know why I am feeling this way.' He cried all day long. I hugged him. I told him I loved him. But he's never seen a therapist. He doesn't want to do it. He keeps saying he's okay."

In the fall of 2022, more than five years after the assault, Ignite the Right published an article on its website with a message directed at Red Beard. "We have not forgotten," it said. The article implored the public to send in tips. It also included identifying details they'd gleaned from the many photos and videos of Red Beard they'd collected.[23]

"Red Beard has a mole or scar on his right hand . . . he appears to suffer 'cauliflower ear'—a condition usually caused by repeat injury to the ear. . . . This is an approximation of what Red Beard might look like without his beard. . . . Red Beard is a smoker—he seems to prefer leaving the cigarette dangling from his mouth, rather than holding it. . . . Red Beard can be seen alongside various League of the South, Traditional Worker Party, and Vanguard America members at various times throughout the day, although it is unknown whether he is a member of one or more of those groups."

Still, few credible tips came in.

Anti-fascists have a fraught relationship with facial recognition software. It is, after all, the apotheosis of a surveillance state or surveillance capitalism, a tool for American law enforcement to identify and further mass-incarcerate people, a tool for authoritarian governments to target dissidents, and a tool for massive, greedy corporations to mine ever more data about individual citizens to better squeeze every last penny out of their pockets.

Moreover, facial recognition in its early incarnations proved remarkably racist, falsely identifying Black and Asian faces ten to one hundred times more than white faces.[24] And some of the technology's biggest progenitors were billionaire authoritarians like Peter Thiel, a main investor in the facial recognition company ClearviewAI, who maintained alarming ties to outright white nationalists.[25]

"I think that people will use the tools while they're there, but that doesn't preclude us from fighting for them to not be available at all," Megan Squire, the computer data scientist and former fellow at the SPLC, says of anti-fascists using facial recognition software. "It's more complex than just simple hypocrisy, like we can be against the surveillance state, but still use the tools while they're available, until hopefully they're not."

Sal, a member of Ignite the Right, says anti-fascists mostly use the technology as a last resort, or as "a confirmation tool after many hours of research have already taken place." He also notes that law enforcement and fascists have started to use facial recognition in attempts to unmask anti-fascists like him. "It doesn't make sense to enter a battle without the same or more superior weapons as an opponent," he says.

Feeling like they'd hit too many dead ends, the researchers with Ignite the Right plugged a photo of Red Beard into a facial recognition tool. The software pulled his biometric facial characteristics and then ran them against its giant database of photos, obtained from the vast expanse of the internet.

There was a match.

The software shot back a photo of a baby-faced, beardless white guy with a shaved head. He was in Army fatigues, standing outside somewhere among a group of other baby-faced soldiers, all standing along a rope line waiting to meet a white guy in a navy suit and red tie, an American flag pin affixed to his suit lapel. The photo showed Red Beard, *if it was Red Beard*, waiting to shake hands with President George W. Bush.

A corresponding link to the photo's origin led to a page on Alamy, a stock and news photo company, that explained in a caption: "President George W. Bush greets Fort Benning soldiers in Fort Benning, Georgia, Thursday, January 11, 2007."[26]

The photo op was part of a PR campaign by Bush to sell his controversial troop surge in Iraq, sending twenty thousand more troops to manage "sectarian violence" in Baghdad. By this point, three thousand American troops had already been killed in Iraq, in an illegal war, launched under false pretenses, that would go on to claim the lives of half a million Iraqi civilians.

Maybe the photo of Red Beard captured him just before he was deployed overseas. The anti-fascists with Ignite the Right zoomed in closer and closer on the photo, trying to bring into focus the name tag on the young soldier's uniform.

*   *   *

As the hunt for Red Beard continued, Ignite the Right continued to unmask more and more Unite the Right attendees.

Each unidentified attendee in their database was given a nickname, most often based on their appearance or an article of clothing they wore. In October 2022, Ignite the Right received an anonymous tip about #PoloHatUTR, a diminutive middle-aged man seen in a baseball cap that he kept low across his face as he marched into the Emancipation Park. The tipster identified him as Christopher A. Healy, a tenured computer science professor at Furman University in Greenville, South Carolina.

Healy had made a name for himself in academia for researching "grade inflation" at universities, collecting data he said showed students these days having it easier than previous generations, graded at an easier curve. Such research—which is disputed by other academics—was catnip for right-wing pundits, eager to scream about "education Marxism" and the "coddling" of the American mind, fodder for a narrative with an often racist subtext: that the influx of students of color in colleges meant students were simply less smart, and professors, out of fear of "political correctness," were giving them better grades than they deserved.

The New York Times quoted Healy in a story[27] about his research, but for such an established academic, pictures of the professor were hard to come by—signaling to the Ignite the Right researchers that he may have attempted to scrub the internet of his likeness. They fired up the facial recognition tool and were treated to a slew of otherwise hard-to-find photos, each of Healy at Furman University events, with the software reporting a 99.7 percent degree of certainty that he was #PoloHatUTR. In one photo, of Healy attending a graduation ceremony at Furman, the anti-fascists noticed that he was wearing the same loafers he'd worn in Charlottesville.[28]

It wasn't immediately clear how Healy ended up in Charlottesville, or with what group, if he belonged to one. He was, however, frequently spotted at Unite the Right with a well-known white supremacist named Kyle Rogers, head of the South Carolina chapter of the white supremacist group the Council of Conservative Citizens (CCC). Photos captured the pair reuniting throughout the day, and a video showed them chatting in the park. Rogers is perhaps best known for writing wildly misleading articles about the supposed epidemic of "black on white crime" for CCC's website, articles that would go on to help radicalize Dylann Roof.[29]

Ignite the Right also found Healy's name, email address, and hometown—Pickens, South Carolina—listed in the leaked membership rolls for a fascist political party overseas: the British National Party, or BNP.

"That's irrelevant," he told *The Greenville News* of his BNP membership after his dox had been picked up by multiple local news outlets.[30] Furman University had immediately put Healy on paid suspension pending an investigation into his involvement at Unite the Right. Healy had decided to kick up a fuss on First Amendment groups, quickly hiring a lawyer who stressed that his client had committed no violence in Charlottesville, but had simply traveled to the city to "demonstrate political opposition to the removal of a statue of General Robert E. Lee, a man nearly universally regarded as one of the finest commanding generals the United States Military Academy at West Point has ever produced." It was Trump's "very fine people" argument in miniature, the absurd assertion that anyone participating in that rally, standing in the park amid Klansmen and flags with swastikas and chants of racist and homophobic slurs, had simply come to defend a statue.

A major civil liberties organization also came to Healy's defense. The Foundation for Individual Rights and Expression (FIRE), funded to the tune of millions by right-wing billionaires, including the Koch brothers, sent a letter to the Furman University president, arguing that the school had "violated" Healy's right to "free expression." It cited Supreme Court rulings about how the "bedrock principle underlying" freedom of expression is that speech may not be limited "simply because society finds the idea itself offensive or disagreeable." FIRE urged the school to "restore Healy to teaching immediately."[31]

About six months later, the school fired him, prompting Healy to sue for wrongful termination. A lawyer for Furman University noted in court that a school investigation found that Healy "gave African-American students and women students full letter grades lower than white males."[32] The school was alleging that Healy, whose own research alleged academia writ large was guilty of grade inflation, had deflated the grades of students who weren't white males like him. His lawyer strongly rejected the results of the investigation, and the lawsuit is ongoing.

It was a success, of course, for Ignite the Right to get someone like Healy fired. This was the whole point—to keep fascists out of positions of power where they could potentially do harm, and to *create a social cost for being a fascist*. To let other would-be fascists know that there are consequences for choosing that path in life. *We do not forgive. We do not forget.* But as the coalition carried on its work, it kept running into examples of communities or institutions that didn't *seem to care* about certain white guys' involvement with Unite the Right, or were more concerned about keeping it as an embarrassing secret, sweeping it under the rug.

Patients arriving at Oklahoma State University's Psychological Services Center in 2021 had no reason to believe that Logan Michael Smith, one of the therapists on offer, was an influential white supremacist propagandist. His contact page on the school's website showcased him smiling in a suit, beneath a giant BLACK LIVES MATTER web banner with the OSU logo.

Smith was a PhD doctoral candidate studying clinical psychology, meaning he'd conduct therapy sessions with patients under supervision from veteran psychologists on staff at the school. The services were offered to the community in Stillwater, Oklahoma, at a bargain rate, on a sliding scale based on income, an attractive offering for working people otherwise unable to afford mental health counseling. After enough training, Smith would conduct sessions on his own.

Unbeknownst to his patients and fellow professors and classmates, Smith went by the pseudonym "Levi Smith" online, which he'd used for years to operate a series of popular "/pol/ News Network" (PNN) accounts across social media platforms. Smith would mine 4chan's /pol/ channel—arguably one of the extreme far-right forums on the internet, where mass shooters were known to deposit their racist "manifestos" before opening fire—for toxic memes he'd then repost on the PNN accounts for wider circulation. By the spring of 2017, Smith had gained such a large following, particularly on Twitter, that he found himself being ushered into the upper echelons of alt-right influencers and celebrities. He did a Q&A on 4chan for his fans.[33]

"Why are you doing this?" an anonymous 4channer asked him.

"It started as just having fun . . . but now I legitimately think I can make a difference, especially since big names follow the account, like Donald Trump Jr.," Smith responded, adding that he hoped to "gradually lead people to think" like people do on 4chan's /pol/.

The next month, Smith traveled to Charlottesville for Unite the Right. Photos showed him at different times standing near Richard Spencer and David Duke. He documented the day's events on Twitter, his PNN account quickly emerging as one of the single most influential of the day, spreading viral disinformation, including that Heather Heyer was killed after "antifa caused a car accident."[34] The following year, in 2018, Smith was accepted into the master's psychology program at Oklahoma State University, where he'd also work as a graduate teaching assistant. That fall, Robert Bowers, one of PNN's followers on Gab, walked into the Tree of Life synagogue in Pittsburgh and opened fire, killing eleven Jews.

By 2021, Smith had graduated from the master's program at Oklahoma State and started the PhD program at the school, where he would start treating patients under supervision. The PNN accounts were still up and running, posting horrifying memes, until April 2023, when Sunlight Anti-Fascist Action—part of the Ignite the Right coalition—published his dox.[35]

The evidence anti-fascists gathered proving Smith was the Levi Smith behind the PNN accounts was extensive. They even found an on-camera interview he'd done with white nationalist influencer Brittany Sellner during his drive home from Unite the Right, when he pulled over at a rest stop to recount the day's events, insisting to Sellner that "the right" had been "very peaceful," while "antifa and Black Lives Matter" had "showed up ready to fight." He also described being moved by seeing different factions of the alt-right find "common ground" throughout the day.

Ignite the Right's dox included an action item: "Please contact Oklahoma State University to warn them about Logan Smith's online campaign of hate." The next day Smith's name and photo were removed from the "Current Clinicians" page of Oklahoma State University's website. It seemed like a promising sign.

But then, crickets.

Ignite the Right's thread on Twitter about Smith had garnered nearly 250,000 views, yet no media outlet nationally or locally in Oklahoma had picked up on the story. The university didn't issue a statement. There were no protests on campus. The anti-fascists pondered whether the school had quietly expelled him, wanting to avoid a PR headache. They got caught up working on other doxes.

Then a year later, in the fall of 2024, they were sent a link to a faculty page on the website of Austin Peay State University in Clarksville, Tennessee, which listed Dr. Logan Smith as a new assistant professor. His bio read:[36]

> *Dr Smith earned his PhD in Clinical Psychology from Oklahoma State University in 2024. He completed his internship at The Ohio State University Wexner Medical Center as part of the suicide and trauma reduction initiative. . . . His research interests largely focus on suicide prevalence prediction and prevention, especially for high risk populations or groups that are underrepresented in research; typically, he has studied military populations, firefighters, and firearm owners. . . . Dr. Smith's clinical interests involve suicide prevention trauma, obsessive compulsive disorder, and mood and anxiety due to disorders more broadly.*

Ignite the Right updated its dox, promoting it on Twitter, and this time word quickly spread at the university. Smith addressed the allegations he was a neo-Nazi with his graduate students, initially denying the accuracy of Ignite the Right's research, but then conceding that years earlier he'd been in some online spaces that "got out of hand."[37] One of the graduate students decided to check out the dox herself. "The first thing I did when I got home was look up these allegations," Jordana McLaughlin told the *Nashville Scene.* "Having spent, on average, six or seven hours a week with him, you get to know somebody's voice and likeness in front of you. I had no doubt it was him."

A statement from the university president, Michael Licari, noted that the administration faced "a challenging balance between respecting individual freedoms protected by the First Amendment and ensuring our community feels welcome and heard."[38] Meanwhile, the details in the dox—the slurs Smith used, his praise for Hitler, the photos of him in Charlottesville—were being shared over and over again via the school's messaging app, Peay Mobile.

"I'm genuinely scared to go to school," one student wrote.[39] "I don't know who is there anymore, if I can be myself, what I should say aloud in case someone bad is watching."

Gracie Foutch, a junior animation major, wondered whether malice lurked behind Smith's desire to be a therapist. "His position gives him access to vulnerable groups that could become targets, so he presents an active threat to the marginalized people on campus, as well as the student body as a whole," Foutch told the student newspaper, *The All State*.

Derrick Tims, a psychology graduate student, argued that a neo-Nazi could not ethically be a therapist. "We don't have a direct ethical guideline that says, 'Don't be a neo-Nazi,'" he told the *Nashville Scene*. "But we do practice in a field that emphasizes multiculturalism, inclusivity and an understanding of client identities and how those identities can impact their experience in the world. For an individual who has expressed such strong negative opinions of individuals with marginalized identities, I believe it would be extremely difficult for that person to completely put those biases aside."

Frustrated by the school president's prevarications about "the challenging balance" between First Amendment concerns and keeping a Hitler-admiring therapist on faculty, doctoral students in the Department of Psychology formed a new group called Freedom Allies to organize a series of protests, including outside the school's board of trustees meeting, to call for Smith's removal.

Eventually the administration relented. On September 23, 2024, two weeks after Ignite the Right updated its dox, President Licari announced that "Austin Peay State University and Dr. Logan Smith mutually agreed to end employment, effective immediately." A public records request filed by *Clarksville Now* later revealed that the school and Smith had agreed to a confidential severance package worth $56,000, contingent on Smith giving up any rights to file legal complaints.[40] He was also not allowed to make disparaging comments about his former students.

Could all this—the fear that Austin Peay State University students felt, the protests, the severance payment—have been avoided had Oklahoma State University acted on Smith's dox over a year earlier? Later, one of Smith's former graduate students at APSU shared an email Smith had sent them, in which he claimed that this was the "second time" he'd been accused of being a neo-Nazi:[41]

> *The first time occurred during my graduate school training at Oklahoma State University, and it was an awful experience. When that happened, I provided evidence disputing the false claims against me. . . . Everything was investigated, and the false allegations were not found to be substantiated. . . . It is true that in 2016–2017 (before graduate school), I, along with two other people, ran a meme page on Twitter, but I walked away from it all once it spiraled into bigotry and evilness. . . . It is also true that I went to Unite The Right event in 2017 (before graduate school), but I went as someone paid to "live tweet" from the event on behalf of a social media client I had at the time. . . . This is not the first time being stalked and harassed with false allegations, and I'm deeply sorry if anyone else feels caught in the crossfire. The last time this happened, it certainly felt like the sky was falling—but it all blew over within a week or so. I think that will happen here too . . ."*

Reached for comment, Oklahoma State University administrators would not explain how it handled Smith's case, or if the university had investigated him, or talked to patients he'd seen at the school's clinic. "All OSU records pertaining to this student are subject to FERPA protections and are not disclosable," the school said in the statement, referring to the Family Educational Rights and Privacy Act, which protects students from public disclosure of their education records.

*   *   *

As the anti-fascists in Ignite the Right watched the saga surrounding Dr. Logan Smith unfold, they were keeping an eye on another developing, concerning story in Oklahoma.

In early 2023, a Unite the Right attendee named Judd Blevins,[42] who'd been unmasked by anti-fascists years earlier as the Oklahoma regional coordinator for Identity Evropa, was running for city council in Enid, a military town of fifty thousand people an hour and a half north of Oklahoma City. Photos clearly showed him marching in Charlottesville, wearing a helmet and carrying the original Oklahoma state flag. When a local newspaper asked the candidate about the research identifying him as a member of the white supremacist group, Blevins didn't deny the allegation, but told the paper "they were smears then and they are smears now.

"The labels applied to me are the same applied to any American who speaks out against the ruling liberal establishment," he said. "I am proud to have served this country honorably and defended our rights in the United States Marine Corps. I am absolutely opposed to the erasure of America's history and heritage."

In February 2023, even after mountains of evidence proving Blevins had joined an infamous neo-Nazi riot were made public, voters in Enid elected him anyway. To the anti-fascists in Ignite the Right, it wasn't immediately clear if Blevins won despite his apparent white supremacist past being exposed—or if he won *because* voters had learned of that very past.

*   *   *

Red Beard's name tag wasn't in focus. As much as the anti-fascists in Ignite the Right zoomed in, the only visible letters were the last three, "M-A-N." The last three letters of so many surnames. It turned out that Red Beard, *if it was Red Beard*, could be found in multiple photos online from that day in 2007, when President Bush visited Fort Benning, but in the one image where his name tag might have been legible, the framing and focus and distance *just right*, it was blocked by Bush's outstretched arm, reaching to shake hands with another young man likely being sent off to fight one of his wars.

When Bush visited Fort Benning, the military under his command was struggling to maintain enlistment numbers to sustain troop levels needed for the "War on Terror" in Iraq and Afghanistan. As a result, military restrictions about neo-Nazis and white supremacists serving in the armed forces were being largely ignored, in what a 2005 Department of Defense report called a "don't ask, don't tell" policy pertaining to extremism.[43] "If individuals can perform satisfactorily, without making their extremist opinions overt ... they are likely to be able to complete their contracts," the report said.

Scott Barfield, a DoD investigator turned whistleblower, told the South-ern Poverty Law Center in 2006 that neo-Nazis "stretch across all branches of service, they are linking up across the branches once they're inside, and they are hard-core. We've got Aryan Nations graffiti in Baghdad."[44]

For decades, scholars of extremism had raised alarm about the risks of allowing white supremacists in the US military, where they pose a threat to their fellow service members, are liable to commit war crimes, can recruit or radicalize other members to their cause, and can receive combat training they can use to inflict violence on civilian targets once they're back home. Tim-othy McVeigh, the Oklahoma City bomber, is the most oft-cited example.

"In my research, basically, white supremacists and neo-Nazi activists see the military as a way to gain military training courtesy of the U.S. taxpayer, and to bring back to the U.S. and start a domestic race war," journalist Mat-thew Kennard, author of *Irregular Army*, observed in 2012.[45] He added: "In terms of future attacks in the United States, it might already be too late because they've spent 10 years training some of the most violent people in the United States. That's the scary thing."

The scholar Kathleen Belew, in her book *Bring the War Home*, posits that defining eras of racial violence in America often followed its wars:[46] the first Ku Klux Klan after the Civil War, the second Klan after World War I, and the violence of a revived Klan after Vietnam. "After each war," she wrote, "veterans not only joined the Klan but also played instrumental roles in leadership, pro-viding military training to other Klansmen and carrying out acts of violence."

The Ignite the Right anti-fascists contemplated whether Red Beard, *if this was Red Beard*, already held the views that would bring him to Charlottesville years later when he shook Bush's hand at Fort Benning. Or maybe it was serving in Bush's wars themselves—which anti-fascists viewed as inherently racist, neocolonial enterprises—that radicalized him, the very nature of the occupations encouraging the enlisted young men and women to see Iraqis and Afghans as something less than human.

The anti-fascists received help from their own friends who served in the military, who got ahold of yearbooks from 2007 at Fort Benning. They flipped through the pages, looking for faces that were beardless and baby-faced. They looked at last names that ended with "M-A-N." But still, no luck.

Eventually someone had the idea to contact the George W. Bush Presi-dential Library in Houston, Texas, which had archives of official photographs from Bush's presidency. Maybe there were photos of this young soldier they hadn't seen yet, or at least higher-resolution versions of the photos they'd seen. The library promptly informed them that their public records request for photos of Bush's visit to Fort Benning in 2007 would take approximately fifty-nine months, or nearly five years, to fulfill.

As skilled journalists as Ignite the Right's members were, there are some tasks, namely official requests to the US government to expedite public record requests, that are more likely to succeed coming from a reporter working at a mainstream media outlet or, say, someone writing a book. The expedition request would require demonstrating to the government that these photos were "a matter of widespread and exceptional media interest in which there exist possible questions that affect public confidence in the Government's integrity."

A letter to the Freedom of Information Act (FOIA) coordinator at the Bush Library made that case: Fifteen major media outlets had written about the ongoing, seemingly futile hunt for Red Beard. Moreover, the assault of DeAndre Harris by white supremacists in Charlottesville, in which Red Beard took part, had generated upward of one thousand articles.

The search for Red Beard also certainly raised questions that could "affect public confidence in the Government's integrity." His possible service in the military "underscored concerns over the armed services remaining a breeding ground for white supremacists, where they could get combat training they'd then use to inflict harm on civilian populations." Moreover, "the failure of law enforcement to find and identify Red Beard was a significant story of public concern."

Within a week the FOIA coordinator responded: "We consider your request for records related to meet the requirements for expedited processing." Five months later, the photos arrived. These were much higher-resolution than the photos online, and this time, zooming in, the letters on the young soldier's name tag were clearer: "HEILMAN."

In the following months, the Ignite the Right anti-fascists scoured the internet for a man with the last name of Heilman who served in the Army, who likely would've been eighteen or nineteen years old in 2007. They searched public records databases and data breaches and news archives, but again and again they were thwarted. A seemingly never-ending exercise in dead ends.

Then one day they saw a Facebook profile belonging to a white guy who occasionally grew a red beard. Who had posted photos of himself while younger and in the military, holding a big gun in a distant land. There were photos of a woman who was maybe his girlfriend, and pro-Trump memes, including an illustration of the president as Rambo, firing two machine guns.

And there was a GIF from the Batman movie *The Dark Knight Rises*, too, showing Bane, the masked supervillain played by actor Tom Hardy, strutting into frame for a fight. "The Fire Rises," read big white letters over the GIF, a reference to a line Hardy delivers at the beginning of the film, signifying all the death and destruction that is about to commence. It was a line that the far right sometimes appropriated as its own, as a sort of half joke, but it was also just a memorable line from a blockbuster film. What stood out about the GIF was not so much its content, but *where and when* Facebook said it had been posted.

"Charlottesville," it said. "Aug. 12, 2017."

CHAPTER 16

The Fire Rises

According to a Pentagon spokesperson, Jay D. Heilman enlisted in the Army in October 2006. He served as an infantryman, deploying to Afghanistan for a year, and came home with some chest candy: "two Army Commendation Medals, an Army Good Conduct Medal, National Defense Service Medal, Afghanistan Campaign Medal with campaign star, Global War on Terrorism Service Medal, Army Service Ribbon, Overseas Service Ribbon, NATO Medal, Combat Infantryman Badge, and the Expert Infantryman Badge."

According to court records in Bell County, Texas, just before Heilman went to Afghanistan, he was charged with "assault that causes bodily injury to a family member," but court hearings were delayed due to his deployment. When he returned stateside a year later, in 2009, the charge was dismissed after he "successfully completed counseling." He left the Army in 2011.

According to photos on his Facebook account, Heilman climbed a tall radio tower on June 14, 2016, maybe for his job.[1] "Found an osprey nest on a microwave dish at about 200ft," he wrote, posting photos of his find. "Momma osprey was not happy with my presence!"

According to his Facebook "check ins," Heilman visited Charlottesville, Virginia, on August 12, 2017.

According to records at the Court of Common Pleas, Domestic Relations Division, in Summit County, Ohio, Heilman and an ex had accepted the terms of a child support agreement on June 14, 2019.

According to a police report in Copley, Ohio, on May 19, 2020, Heilman allegedly "smacked" his stepfather in the face multiple times, "bending his glasses," before pointing a "Stoeger 12 gauge shotgun" at him.

And according to Barberton Municipal Court records, Heilman was charged with assault and aggravated menacing over the incident with his stepdad. He got ninety days in prison, including time served, plus probation and a requirement he undergo treatment at a Veterans Affairs hospital. As part of a plea deal, prosecutors agreed to give Heilman back his shotgun.

He seemed to stop using Facebook in 2021, got a three-year Ohio state fishing license in 2022, and then, well, there wasn't much else to find out about Jay D. Heilman, except that there was a greater likelihood than not, according to facial recognition software, that the blue eyes in his Facebook photos were the same blue eyes as Red Beard's.

As far as writing doxes went, this was scant information to work with. It didn't feel right for Ignite the Right to go public yet, to announce that it had finally found Red Beard, without knowing more. Like what Heilman did for work, whether he was still mixed up with fash, whether he could be connected to a username in the leaked chats on Unicorn Riot, and if there were any clues about how he ended up in Charlottesville, and with whom.

Save for the old, dormant Facebook account—the anti-fascists speculated whether he'd forgotten his password and never bothered to log in again— Heilman seemed exceptionally *offline*, especially for an attendee of Unite the Right, which was attended by an extremely *online* crowd.

"I'm hitting a wall with internet stuff," Murph texted the Ignite the Right group chat on an encrypted messaging app in September 2024. "I've only hit walls like this a couple times with people that were very visible at Unite the Right. Almost always able to find something, so that's why it weirds me out so much."

It was even unclear where exactly Heilman lived, with public record databases listing a few addresses in Ohio and Kentucky. Ignite the Right put out a call for help, and some comrades in Ohio responded, volunteering to see if they could get eyes on Red Beard in a suburb of Akron.

"We're planning on running a couple of shifts of drive-bys/stakeouts (rotating out people and vehicles) this Sunday," an Ohio anti-fascist who went by Iron Side texted. Iron Side put Ignite the Right at ease: He understood that Heilman was a veteran, and maybe a little volatile, and that he'd pulled a shotgun on his stepdad, a shotgun he still apparently owned. Iron Side and his crew wanted to help anyway.

That Sunday, Iron Side and another anti-fascist started their stakeout. "We've been on site for about five hours now. So far no sighting as of yet."

An hour later he texted: "I just want this fucker to run down to the circle k to get a sleeve of winter green skoal so I can see his face walk out the door."

Another hour later: "My comrade pointed out that tis the season for political canvassing which is a perfect excuse to knock on someone's door and most of us have experience with that. So next time we may change up vehicles and bring a clipboard."

And another two hours later: "We called off for today." They hadn't seen Heilman at all. Ignite the Right was apologetic that nothing had happened.

"We went into this eyes wide open to that potentiality," Iron Side said, adding that his crew "knew the importance of this" and were eager to do "whatever we can do to help." The next day Iron Side texted to say that it might be a while before they could stake out Red Beard's place again.

"We're shifting gears to focus on Springfield," Iron Side texted. "Shit has been hot for weeks now and last night Trump just poured gas on the fire."

*　　　　*　　　　*

On September 10, 2024, Trump, the Republican nominee for president, doubled down on a vicious lie, previously promoted by his running mate, Senator J. D. Vance, that Haitian immigrants in Springfield, Ohio, were stealing people's pets and eating them.

"In Springfield, they're eating the dogs," he said during a primetime presidential debate with Vice President Kamala Harris, the Democratic nominee.[2] "The people that came in, they're eating the cats. They're eating—they're eating the pets of the people that live there. And this is what's happening in our country. And it's a shame."

It was an ugly, baseless piece of propaganda, indistinguishable from the kind cooked up on 4chan or Gab. In fact, there was evidence the lie initially gained traction on Gab[3] after it was shared by Blood Tribe, a newer neo-Nazi group making headlines for its masked marches targeting Drag Time Story Hours. The group had held an "anti-Haitian immigration march," carrying flags adorned with swastikas, in downtown Springfield earlier that summer.

The pet-eating rumor made its way from Gab to other platforms via the same far-right influencers who frequently whipped up a panic about antifa. Eventually Vance, the GOP's vice presidential nominee, gave it a big boost on September 9, 2024. "Months ago, I raised the issue of Haitian illegal immigrants draining social services and generally causing chaos all over Springfield, Ohio," Vance posted on X (formerly Twitter). "Reports now show that people have had their pets abducted and eaten by people who shouldn't be in this country." (The majority of Haitian immigrants in Springfield, fact-checkers pointed out, were in the US legally—not that it should matter.)

Vance's embrace of such nakedly fascist propaganda, depicting a marginalized subgroup of people as inherently savage or uncivilized, was in keeping with his history of associating with far-right figures[4]—a history that often went underemphasized in the press. A few years earlier, Vance, then a poorly polling Senate candidate, appeared on a podcast popular in the "manosphere," an online subculture steeped in misogyny, and said that were Trump to ever return to the White House, he'd encourage him to purge DC of everyone but MAGA loyalists. "I think that what Trump should do, if I was giving him one piece of advice: Fire every single mid-level bureaucrat, every civil servant in the administrative state, replace them with our people," he said.

"And when the courts—because you will get taken to court—and then when the courts stop you, stand before the country, like Andrew Jackson did, and say, 'The chief justice has made his ruling, now let him enforce it,'" Vance added, referring to when America's seventh president defied a Supreme Court ruling to stop the ongoing genocide of Native Americans.

"I tend to think that we should seize the institutions of the left," he said at another point. "And turn them against the left. We need like a de-Ba'athification program, a de-woke-ification program." (When Vance, a Marine veteran who served as a public affairs officer in Iraq, said "de-Ba'athification,"[5] he was referring to the US-led process of purging the Iraqi government of Ba'ath Party officials and civil servants during the Iraq War, a project many observers believe entrenched sectarian violence and destabilized the region.)

Vance's vision was of a dictatorial presidency, a vision he shared with one of his benefactors, billionaire Peter Thiel, who funded his Senate campaign with millions of dollars, and who had once written: "I no longer think that freedom and democracy are compatible." It was also a vision Vance shared with Curtis Yarvin, a former Silicon Valley programmer who labored for years behind the pseudonym "Mencius Moldbug" to articulate an authoritarian vision[6] he called "the Dark Enlightenment," which turned him into a kind of court philosopher for a coterie of hyper-libertarian tech billionaires. Yarvin wasn't subtle about his vision, once flatly stating that he advocated a "national CEO, [or] what's called a dictator," in America. He and Vance were friends.

"We are in a late republican period," Vance said on that manosphere podcast, a reference to the Yarvinian framing of the US as a Roman Empire in need of saving by a Julius Caesar–like figure. "If we're going to push back against it, we're going to have to get pretty wild, and pretty far out there, and go in directions that a lot of conservatives right now are uncomfortable with."

Scapegoating subgroups of people like Haitian immigrants, of course, has always been part and parcel of authoritarian propaganda, a way of consolidating support, presenting a strongman leader as the protector of the *one pure folk*, in this case "real," native-born Americans, with Trump the only thing standing between them and the barbarians at the gates.

The Wall Street Journal reported[7] that city officials in Springfield had told Vance's staff that the pet-eating rumors were false, but the vice presidential candidate continued to push them anyway, later admitting that it was in service of a wider anti-immigrant agenda.[8] "The American media totally ignored this stuff until Donald Trump and I started talking about cat memes," he told CNN's Dana Bash. "If I have to create stories so that the American media actually pays attention to the suffering of the American people, then that's what I'm going to do."

When Trump repeated the lie during the debate, Christopher Polhaus, the former Marine who founded Blood Tribe, was thrilled and took credit. His neo-Nazi group, he wrote on Telegram, had successfully "pushed Springfield into the public consciousness."[9]

Trump's continued strength in the polls served as a menacing backdrop for anti-fascist work throughout 2024, the seeming impunity he'd enjoyed after fomenting the January 6, 2021, attack on the Capitol emboldening him to go further and further to the right, embracing more and more toxic figures. A few months after Ignite the Right launched in late 2022, the group that was determined to identify every Unite the Right attendee, Trump had dinner with one at his Mar-a-Lago mansion.

Nick Fuentes went to Charlottesville in 2017 as an eighteen-year-old Boston University student and fledgling far-right influencer. "You can call us racists, white supremacists, Nazis, & bigots . . ." an energized Fuentes wrote[10] after attending Unite the Right. "But you will not replace us. The rootless transnational elite knows that a tidal wave of white identity is coming. And they know that once the word gets out, they will not be able to stop us. The fire rises!" He claimed to receive threats after news of his participation in the deadly rally spread, prompting him to leave Boston University. (The Fox News headline about his departure from the school described Fuentes as a "conservative.")

In the ensuing years, Fuentes would use marathon live streams to deny the Holocaust, state that segregation was "better" for Black people, and argue that rape was "not that big a deal." He emerged as the leader of the America First, or "groyper," movement, an explicitly white supremacist political project determined to radicalize the GOP. "If we can drag the furthest part of the right further to the right, and we can drag the center further to the right, and we can drag the left further to the right . . . then we're winning," he explained once.

Fuentes played a major role in the "stop the steal" movement[11] that culminated in the January 6, 2021, attack on the Capitol, where he was spotted using a megaphone to urge on the rioters. "Keep moving towards the Capitol; it appears we are taking the Capitol back!" he told them through a megaphone. "Break down the barriers and disregard the police. The Capitol belongs to us!"

In February 2022 he stated on a live stream,[12] "All I want is revenge against my enemies and a total Aryan victory." That same month he demonstrated the inroads he was nevertheless making with the Republican Party, hosting the America First Political Action Conference[13] (AFPAC) in Orlando, where speakers included two members of congress, Paul Gosar and Marjorie Taylor Greene, former Congressman Steve King, former Maricopa County Sheriff Joe Arpaio, Idaho Lieutenant Governor Janice McGeachin, and Arizona State Senator Wendy Rogers. (Thomas Homan, who oversaw a brutal anti-immigrant regime as head of ICE in Trump's first term, was slated to speak at the conference. He arrived at the event but claimed he left after googling Fuentes's name, disturbed over his support for Russian President Vladamir Putin. "I'm not saying this is a bad group," he clarified to *HuffPost*, speaking about Fuentes and the groypers. "I'm saying I don't know.")

Speaking from a lectern, Fuentes praised Hitler and led the crowd in a chant of "Putin!" as bombs fell on Ukraine. Another speaker called for Dr. Anthony Fauci, who led the US response to the COVID pandemic, to be executed. And Rogers, the state senator from Arizona, expressed her support for Fuentes before calling for their mutual enemies to be hanged.

"I truly respect Nick because he's the most persecuted man in America," Rogers said, adding: "I've said we need to build more gallows. If we try some of these high-level criminals, convict them and use a newly built set of gallows, it'll make an example of these traitors who have betrayed our country."

Thomas Zimmer, who teaches the history of twentieth-century fascism at Georgetown University, watched the clips from Fuentes's conference with some despair. "I fear that—after four years of Trumpism in power, after January 6, with rightwing fascistic militancy now all around us—we have become so accustomed to outrageous political acts that we might be becoming numb to how bizarre, how extreme, how dangerous these developments are," he wrote.

Fuentes ended up having dinner with Trump at Mar-a-Lago in November 2022. He'd tagged along with Ye, the artist formerly known as Kanye West, the pair having found a common cause in antisemitism. *The New York Times* described the scene inside Mar-a-Lago:[14]

> *During the dinner, according to a person briefed on what took place, Mr. Fuentes described himself as part of Mr. Trump's base of supporters. Mr. Trump remarked that his advisers urge him to read speeches using a teleprompter and don't like when he ad-libs remarks.*
>
> *Mr. Fuentes said Mr. Trump's supporters preferred the ad-libs, at which Mr. Trump turned to the others, the person said, and declared that he liked Mr. Fuentes, adding: "He gets me."*

Afterward Trump claimed he had never heard of Fuentes before the dinner. The president still refused multiple opportunities to rebuke him. By 2024, as Fuentes continued making incendiary comments—like calling for the execution of non-Christians and "perfidious Jews"[15]—Trump's rhetoric on the campaign trail wouldn't have sounded out of place on one of Fuentes's live streams. It felt like an escalation, even for a man who launched his first bid for the White House by calling Mexican immigrants "rapists" and calling for a ban on Muslims entering the US.

Trump said immigrants were "poisoning the blood" of the nation,[16] a phrasing historians noted was familiar. "All great cultures of the past perished only because the originally creative race died out from blood poisoning,"

Hitler wrote in *Mein Kampf*. Trump argued a wide swath of immigrants were "murderers," too, immutably and genetically criminal.[17] "Many of them murdered far more than one person, and they're now happily living in the United States," he said. "I believe this, it's in their genes. And we got a lot of bad genes in our country right now. They left, they had 425,000 people come into our country that shouldn't be here, that are criminals."

His warnings about the nonexistent threat of noncitizens fraudulently casting ballots in the upcoming election—"Our elections are bad, and a lot of these illegal immigrants coming in, they're trying to get them to vote"— invoked the "Great Replacement,"[18] the idea that Jews or Democrats or other nefarious actors were importing non-white immigrants into the US to replace white voters. It was a conspiracy theory that animated many mass shootings in the years prior, and which gave birth to the neo-Nazi chants "You will not replace us!" and "Jews will not replace us!" in Charlottesville.

When Trump promised to start the largest mass deportation of immigrants in US history if elected back to the White House, he paired his pledge with the word "remigration," a term seemingly no other GOP politicians had used up to that point. The term, however, was well-known in Europe as a euphemism for ethnic cleansing, embraced for over a decade by a slew of fascist groups and political parties on the continent. Its arrival on American shores could be seen in the Unicorn Riot database, in the leaked messages of Identity Evropa and Vanguard America in 2017, where it was used dozens of times.[19] "It was bad that Blacks were brought over, the best form of reparations is a one way remigration to Africa," wrote Thomas Rousseau, then a member of Vanguard America. Identity Evropa, before it disbanded, had "remigration" in its list of policy proposals. Now it was on Trump's.

In the week leading up to Trump's September 10, 2024, debate with Kamala Harris, journalists started to spot a thirty-one-year-old conspiracy theorist named Laura Loomer in his entourage, by the candidate's side.[20] Loomer called herself a "proud Islamophobe" and "pro-white nationalism," associating herself with some of the vilest figures in American politics, including Nick Fuentes. A video once captured the pair toasting glass pints of beer. "To the hostile takeover of the Republican Party," Loomer said.[21] "Absolutely," Fuentes responded. "Cheers."

Fuentes had dined with Trump at Mar-a-Lago. Now Loomer was on Trump's plane to Philadelphia for the debate. She was tweeting incessantly to her 1.2 million followers about the nonexistent scourge of Haitian immigrants stealing and eating pets. "Send those savages back to where they came from and tell them 2A was created for the sake of protecting our pets from murderous invaders who don't belong here," she wrote.[22] Another tweet read: "If Kamala Harris wins, she will allow third world invaders to kill your pets. Import the third world. Become the third world."[23]

The next day, sixty-seven million Americans watched Trump debate Harris on live television. "In Springfield, they're eating the dogs . . ." he began.

*   *   *

"It's a bad situation that's turned to shit," Iron Side texted Ignite the Right from Ohio. "We don't have much of a footprint in Springfield so we're attempting to make inroads with the Haitian community to find out what they need. Right now all we can do is be reactionary."

Another Ohio-based anti-fascist chimed in: "I just keep hearing from people with contacts down there that anyone working with immigrants or refugees is getting constant threats right now . . ."

The mayor of Springfield would later report that the city received more than thirty-five threats of violence in the ten days after the presidential debate, including a wave of bomb threats.[24] Hospitals were locked down, local colleges closed campuses and resorted to remote learning, elementary schools and supermarkets were evacuated. Fascist groups started to make their presence known, too, with residents finding Ku Klux Klan flyers[25] calling for the "mass deportation" of "disease-ridden and filthy" immigrants. The Proud Boys arrived, patrolling the streets. Neo-Nazis returned, carrying their swastika banners, protesting outside the mayor's house. An unidentified group protested outside city hall with their own banner that read, HAITIANS HAVE NO HOME HERE[26]—a message the group wrote in English but was considerate enough to write in Haitian Creole as well.

City officials eventually announced that "in light of recent threats and safety concerns" they had decided to cancel Springfield's annual CultureFest, an annual "celebration of unity through diversity."[27]

Pressed about the bomb threats and other disturbances he'd unleashed in the city of fifty thousand people, Trump said: "I don't know what happened with the bomb threats. I know that it's been taken over by illegal migrants, and that's a terrible thing that happened. Springfield was this beautiful town, and now they're going through hell." Then, less than five weeks out from the election, Trump pledged to revoke Temporary Protected Status (TPS) for Haitian immigrants[28] in Springfield, which had allowed them to come to the US legally, fleeing political instability exacerbated by a massive earthquake in the island country. "You have to remove the people, and you have to bring them back to their own country," he said.

There were what felt like real anti-fascist victories during the first Trump presidency. The so-called alt-right—that insurgent fascist coalition—fell to pieces after Unite the Right, with so many of the groups involved disbanding after its members were confronted in the streets, or doxed, or arrested, or sued. "Antifa is winning," Richard Spencer had conceded. But watching Trump now, seeing how he was parroting the language of that noxious movement, watching the havoc and harm he was already wreaking in a place like Springfield, and seeing polls indicating he had a real shot at getting his chance to mass "remigrate" entire communities of people just trying to get by—it felt like a time to reassess.

Maybe it was time to consider the alt-right hadn't failed but did what it was designed to do: supply the shock troops for MAGA, a vanguard sacrificed to tug the Overton Window open wider and wider so ideas once thought unspeakable were suddenly speakable. Maybe these fascist groups had, in a way, won. They had made their beliefs, once condemnable, just commonplace enough that they could now be shed of their cruel costumes, rendering an entire generation of pseudonyms, disguises, and masks obsolete. They could step into the daylight and feel the sun on their faces.

Robert Paxton, author of *The Anatomy of Fascism* and widely considered one of the foremost scholars of fascism, initially declined to call Trump a fascist during his rise to the White House in 2016. That changed after the insurrection. "Trump's incitement of the invasion of the Capitol on January 6, 2021, removes my objection to the fascist label," Paxton wrote at the time.[29] "His open encouragement of civic violence to overturn an election crosses a red line. The label now seems not just acceptable but necessary."

But you can't really dox—in the anti-fascist sense of the term—someone who isn't hiding anything, who uses their real name on TV and on voting ballots, who slaps their name in gold letters on skyscrapers, and whose addresses in Palm Beach and on Pennsylvania Avenue are known the world over. In the lead-up to the 2024 election, an unnerving question started to haunt the work anti-fascists were doing: If doxing is dependent on leveraging an existing societal taboo against explicit white supremacy, bigotry, and fascism to ensure that "hate has consequences," what happens when that taboo starts to disappear?

There had been a steady drip of doxes seeing diminishing returns.

After journalist Taylor Lorenz, then at *The Washington Post*, unmasked Brooklyn real estate agent Chaya Raichik[30] in 2022 as the creator of the anti-trans social media account LibsOfTikTok—which served as a homing beacon for where bigots should target queer people and sometimes send bomb threats—Raichik went on to enjoy celebrity status in the GOP. She appeared frequently on Fox News, amassing over 127,000 followers on Substack and over a million on Twitter. Eventually she was tapped to join the Oklahoma Library Media Advisory Committee by the state's Republican schools superintendent, where she was poised to pull books depicting gay and transgender people from the shelves of public school libraries.[31] When *USA Today* published a front-page story[32] with the headline "When LibsOfTikTok Posts, Threats Increasingly Follow," Raichik had a photo of herself taken holding up the newspaper, smiling.[33] She made the photo her profile picture on X (formerly Twitter).

In 2023 *HuffPost* revealed that Richard Hanania—"a prominent conservative writer, lionized by Silicon Valley billionaires and a US senator"—had hidden behind a pseudonym to write for white supremacist websites years earlier, including Richard Spencer's webzine AlternativeRight.com.[34] Using the name "Richard Hoste," Hanania had advocated the forced sterilization of "low IQ" people, who he suggested were most often Black, among a raft of other horrifying policy proposals. At the time of *HuffPost*'s exposé, which was based on anti-fascist research, Hanania was a visiting scholar at the University of Texas. He was building an impressive résumé:

The 37-year-old has been published by The New York Times *and* The Washington Post. *He delivered a lecture to the Yale Federalist Society and was interviewed by the* Harvard College Economics Review. *He appeared twice on* "Tucker Carlson Tonight," *Fox News' former prime-time juggernaut. He was a recent guest on a podcast hosted by the chief writing officer of Substack, the $650 million publishing platform where Hanania has nearly 20,000 subscribers.*

Hanania has his own podcast, too, interviewing the likes of Steven Pinker, the famous Harvard cognitive psychologist, and Marc Andreessen, the billionaire software engineer. Another billionaire, Elon Musk, reads Hanania's articles and replies approvingly to his tweets. A third billionaire, Peter Thiel, provided a blurb to promote Hanania's book, The Origins of Woke, *which HarperCollins plans to publish this September. In October, Hanania is scheduled to deliver a lecture at Stanford.*

None of those billionaires or prominent institutions responded to *Huff-Post*'s requests for comment about their relationship with Hanania. Nor did then Senator J. D. Vance, who had called Hanania a "friend" and a "really interesting thinker." Hanania himself eventually published a mea culpa on Substack titled "Why I Used to Suck, and (Hopefully) No Longer Do," addressing his white supremacist past, *if it was really his past*. His essay didn't address the many disturbing comments Hanania had been making *under his real name*, for years, that had nevertheless seen him reach minor conservative celebrity status. The writer Parker Molloy summed up some of Hanania's recent work:[35]

> *Hanania claimed just last month that college African American Studies departments had been run by "street hustlers and illiterates." In May, he tweeted that "we need more policing, incarceration, and surveillance of Black people," lamenting that "Blacks won't appreciate it, whites don't have the stomach for it," in defense of a wildly misleading and racist chart about "interracial crime." Also in May, he referred to Black people as "animals, whether they're harassing people in subways or walking around in suits." Also in May, Hanania published a blog post titled, "Why Do I Hate Pronouns More Than Genocide?" about why he treats the mere existence of trans people as worse than genocide . . . because he is "an individual concerned with truth."*

Yet there were no clear signs that all the billionaires and institutions associated with him were going to now denounce him or withdraw their support. Meanwhile, Hanania accused the *HuffPost* reporter of trying to get HarperCollins to cancel the publication of his forthcoming book, *The Origins of Woke*, a 288-page screed against the 1964 Civil Rights Act.

"He's growing increasingly frustrated as he's realizing he's only brought more attention to it. Preorder now," Hanania tweeted. A short time later the owner of X (formerly Twitter), and the world's richest man, Elon Musk, responded: "Interesting, will read."

In 2024, Musk, whose politics were taking the hardest of right turns, would do the bidding of a neo-Nazi exposed by the anti-fascist collective Anonymous Comrades Collective. The group had unmasked "Stonetoss"—a wildly popular white supremacist cartoonist with hundreds of thousands of followers on Twitter—as Hans Kristian Graebener, an IT worker based in Texas.[36] His vile four-paneled illustrations, the group noted, had been included in two mass-shooter manifestos, including the one uploaded online by an eighteen-year-old white man before he live-streamed himself opening fire with a Bushmaster XM-15 rifle at a Buffalo grocery store, murdering ten Black people. Anonymous Comrades Collective had posted its dox of Graebener in a long thread on X. Graebener, upset at being unmasked, essentially asked to speak to the manager. From his Stonetoss account he tweeted:[37]

> One of you has a direct line to @elonmusk – and you need to use it. I'm too obstinate to be intimidated out of anything, but I realize my temperament is something that less than 1% of people have. If Elon's idea of a "free speech" website is one where people can be intimidated into silence, the outcome will be a site where the Stasi will drive out all dissent. This transition to a monoculture is already Underway. I will stay to the end, of course, but I am an outlier, not the mean. If he needs a shortlist of the worst offenders, that can be easily Provided.

Musk had shared Graebener's cartoons before on X. Soon after the cartoonist's plea to him for help, one of the Anonymous Comrades Collectives' accounts was suspended, and another was warned by X to delete a post or risk suspension, even though neither of the accounts had violated X privacy policies. (Neither, for example, had posted Graebener's home address.) There was more fallout, too, as Anonymous Comrades Collective later described:

> But Musk's defense of Stonetoss and his attempt at damage control did not end there. Other X users, even high-profile ones, discussing the topic were

being censored and suspended. Links to our original article were being blocked under the pretense of being a "malicious site" (also not true). Furthermore, even mentions of the name "Hans Graebener" were flagged by X.

Not long after, NBC News reported that Twitter had "changed its privacy policy . . . to ban users from publishing the real names of people behind anonymous accounts after some users appeared to unmask a pseudonymous cartoonist who drew antisemitic images."[38]

Anti-fascists had previously flourished on X, especially when it was called Twitter, making connections with each other, sharing tips, coordinating to share intelligence with communities about fash coming to town, and connecting with journalists to make sure that important doxes got coverage in the press. Now the richest man in the world, and a self-proclaimed "free speech absolutist," had not only resurrected thousands of neo-Nazi accounts on the platform, but was going to bat for them, making sure if they wanted to spew vitriol, they could do so anonymously.

Throughout the rest of 2024, Musk campaigned for Trump, becoming a fixture at his rallies and donating millions to his campaign. He also promoted the Great Replacement Theory[39] and endorsed some of the farthest-right political parties around the world, including Germany's Alternative für Deutschland (AfD).[40] Earlier that year journalists in Germany reported AfD members held a secret meeting with neo-Nazis[41] to discuss plans for the "remigration" of millions of asylum seekers, the "non-assimilated," and the "non-German" out of Germany, maybe to a "model state" in North Africa. The plan bore an unnerving resemblance to Nazis' initial scheme in 1940 to forcibly expel Jews to Madagascar, before they settled on the Final Solution, their campaign of wholesale extermination, instead.

*   *   *

"Doxing is still effective," insists Murph, a member of Ignite the Right. "I stumbled into this work on accident through the internet. There are people who have been doing anti-fascist activism for years starting at the street level, and they are absolutely incredible," she says, adding that "so much of the fight" has moved to "online spaces," though, which are "very efficient at spreading hate and disinfo and no longer geographically confined."

"To me," Murph says, "'we go where they go' also applies to the digital world."

Murph grew up in a conservative part of Texas that didn't have any real anti-fascist or even leftist scene to speak of, but it was a diverse community where she remembers people knowing how to treat each other with kindness. "I didn't even know what 'antifa' was until about five years ago," she says. "Politically, I'd say I started as left-leaning. Now I consider myself to be significantly further left, and that's because I've formed more opinions on things I was neutral about before."

It was the massacre at an El Paso Walmart that put her on that path. She had friends who lost family members in the mass shooting, and she couldn't understand what would drive someone to cause the pain she was seeing in her friends' eyes. Murph went online and started searching for where young people like the El Paso shooter might have been radicalized, where they could be convinced that Latinos were immutably lesser than or an existential threat. "First, I hunted Discord servers that were serving as backups to 8chan, which had finally been dropped by Cloudflare because mass shooter manifestos kept showing up. I would join a server, report it down (which was pretty quick because they were always filled with gore and other awful material), hop over to the next server, and repeat. Once they started to give up on hosting 8chan on Discord, I looked for other places that hateful materials were coming from. It turned out that a lot of the mainstreaming of hate from the image boards into the public sphere was done through Twitter. So I ended up there."

It was still almost a hobby at that point, sitting down every day for a few minutes, reporting abusive, anonymous fash accounts to Twitter. She found a community of people online doing the same thing, and she feels like they made a real dent there for a while. And then Elon Musk bought the platform. "Almost all of the work that we did reporting violent extremism on the site was reversed," she says. "So, I figured, if we can't get it taken down, maybe I can shine some light onto whoever is creating and sharing this awful stuff."

One of her proudest doxes happened to be among her first. "Jinjerzilla" was another popular neo-Nazi cartoonist whose disturbing drawings were also included in the manifesto of the Buffalo mass shooter. After casting a big digital dragnet, Murph gathered enough clues to prove his real name was Joshua Thayer LeGoff of Cranston, Rhode Island, an artistic director at LearningWorks Inc., a school for special needs kids.[42] She handed off all this information to Anonymous Comrades Collective, which did a beautiful job putting the dox together, and in emphasizing why it was concerning that LeGoff was in any way involved with children:

> One of "Jinjerzilla's" most cringe-inducing illustrations is also perhaps one of his most dangerous. In the illustration pictured below, "Jinjerzilla" portrays Adolf Hitler saving a young man from committing suicide by gun. While this is a ridiculous and unintentionally ironic premise since we all know that Hitler himself committed suicide, it is also dangerous because it demonstrates one of the strategies white nationalists use to recruit: exploiting young people who are experiencing emotional distress.

LeGoff was fired.

Yes, Murph still believes in the power of unmasking fascists. Any particular dox can have a long and unpredictable lifespan.

Take the story of Judd Blevins up in Enid, Oklahoma.[43] Admittedly it doesn't sound great at first. Yes, in early 2023, voters in Enid elected Blevins to the city council despite anti-fascists identifying him four years earlier as a leader in Identity Evropa. Yes, it was disheartening that voters in Enid elected Blevins despite clear photos of him at the rally in Charlottesville, and at the infamous torch march the night before. Yes, it was unsettling to see the support Blevins had in town from prominent pastors, businessmen, and politicians, who didn't mind having a neo-Nazi in city hall, or who refused to believe that Unite the Right was all that bad—that "very fine people" *really* were there. Yes, Blevins's election victory felt representative of an alarming far-right strategy of targeting low-turnout elections to get *their guys* elected to low-level positions, a plot to take over the GOP from the bottom up. And finally, yes, it was infuriating the way Blevins, an Iraq War veteran who worked at his father's roofing business, refused again and again not only to apologize, but to even *acknowledge* that he'd taken part in a famous fascist riot.

But what Murph and other anti-fascists across America found heartening about the situation in Enid, which had started to generate national media attention, was how a small, loud group of moderate and progressive locals, not "antifa" by any real measure, were turning up the heat. On November 7, 2023, nearly a dozen members of the newly formed Enid Social Justice Committee took seats inside the Dr. Martin Luther King Jr. Municipal Complex for a city council meeting. They'd all signed up to make public comments. ESJC chairwoman Kristi Balden went first, taking her place at the lectern. "I want the people here and watching at home to have complete clarity about who Judd is by reading his own words from the leak of his Discord chats," Balden said. For the next five minutes, she and other members took thirty-second turns at the microphone, reading Blevins's words back to him, for everyone to hear:[44]

> *"Hitler never would've allowed this shit."*
> *"The burden of rehabilitating the Roman salute will fall on a future gener-*
>   *ation. Our burden is to ensure that generation exists."*
> *"Damn, I'm excited. Is it Aug. 12 yet?"*
> *"I'll be flying the original state flag of Oklahoma . . . such a shame Oklahoma*
>   *lawmakers cucked to the Indians in 1925 and adopted the current flag."*
> *"Jewish hag."*

These vile words had taken a remarkable journey to get to this point. Typed in private by a pseudonymous white supremacist, stolen away by anti-fascist spies, put online for anyone to read them, used by Oklahoma anti-fascists to dox a Unite the Right attendee, and now read into the public record at a taped city council hearing in Enid, the beginning of an effort to recall the elected official who had written them.

"I am eager to see who, if anyone, is willing to attach themselves to the so called 'Enid Social Justice Squad' a small group of antifa-adjacent leftists," Blevins seethed in a statement after the meeting, "who seek to bring 'family friendly' drag shows to our community, promote a gospel contrary to the teachings of Jesus Christ, and whose rhetoric and behavior is actively dividing and destroying our nation. It is unfortunate that Enid is being held hostage by a group of people who harbor so much hate against those with different views that they cannot control themselves in our public meetings.

"The attacks against me are inspired by the same antifa radicals that rioted and burned cities across this country in 2020," he added. "Despite the best efforts of this fringe group, great things are coming to Enid in the years ahead, and I look forward to being a part of that process."

The recall election was still close. Blevins won 40 percent of the vote. *But he lost.*[45] It's not like his opponent was any kind of progressive—she was a Republican in Oklahoma, after all. But the Enid Social Justice Committee, in a conservative part of arguably the most conservative state in America, had successfully preserved the lowest of bars for a person in a position of power: You can't be a Nazi.

"Sometimes things have to get a lot worse before they get better," reflected ESJC member Father James Neal, a priest sipping a beer at an Irish pub in downtown Enid. "The good thing about all of this is that it's bringing all of this latent hatred out into the open. And people are beginning to be forced to have to deal with it."

Father Neal got a taste for anti-fascist research during the whole saga, eventually helping *Huff Post* uncover a significant wrinkle in the whole story: Of Blevins's two campaign donors, one was a local woman who donated ten bucks. The other donation was much more significant, from a Texas man named Joshua Berkau, for $1,944. A look at public records showed Berkau owned a series of LLCs with a man named Robert Whitted, who had been arrested with thirty other Patriot Front members in Idaho when they attempted to storm the Pride gathering in Coeur d'Alene. Later, documents released by police in Charleston, West Virginia, showed Berkau had rented the U-Haul truck the group used for one of its flash-mob marches in the city. Father Neal had discovered that Blevins's sole significant campaign donor was a member of Patriot Front.

"Are you a member of Patriot Front?!" Father Neal asked Blevins over and over, confronting him after an election debate with his opponent. "Are you a member of Patriot Front?!" The councilman refused to answer.

Father Neal is about as far away from the right's hysterical caricature of antifa as you could get. Not only a priest, he's a military veteran who will talk to you about how much he loves his country. He doesn't wear black bloc, he wears a black cassock and a white clerical collar. He doesn't self-identify as antifa, but he'd seen how impactful its work could be, how integral it was to stop a neo-Nazi from holding elected office in his hometown. He'd read about Ignite the Right and decided to reach out, sending the collective a message: Was there a way to get involved?

Murph was so grateful for Father Neal and the Enid Social Justice Committee. "I was just really happy that it's not being ignored anymore," she said of the neo-Nazi councilman.

She and Ignite the Right were still looking for Red Beard, or rather Jay D. Heilman, but were also drowning in other doxes. "I have at least two dozen

Nazi identifications that I'm sitting on that I have not had time to finish writing up, and leads on dozens of others," Murph said.

The group wondered whether law enforcement, with all its money and gadgets and tools, had identified Heilman yet. If this motley crew of anti-fascists sitting at computers could do it, why couldn't the police? Anti-fascists often nurse a profound ambivalence about the fascists they unmask getting arrested. Most of them are prison abolitionists after all. An anti-fascist group in the Midwest called Anne Frank Army once described this ambivalence while considering what to think of the over 1,500 pro-Trump insurrectionists arrested for their part in the attack on the Capitol:[46]

> With regard to abolition, there are two million people incarcerated in this country, all who we care more about than the fate of these MAGA rioters, who in all their privilege have rarely before in their lives experienced the pain caused by these prisons. This said, we do not nor ever will work with cops to bring "justice" to these insurrectionists, as doing so gives legitimacy to the police state apparatus which has never taken the very real threat of these racists and fascists seriously at all. They will use this legitimacy in order to strengthen their ability to prosecute "extremists," which will then be weaponized against the left.

Murph put it this way: "The criminal justice system is messed up in so many different ways, but if a neo-Nazi is in a place where they can't cause harm to others or inspire more mass shooters, that is fine by me. It's unsurprising how many of these people we find with records of violence and domestic abuse, and this just seems like harm reduction."

There were signs that prosecutors back in Charlottesville were still searching for the fascists who invaded the city. In 2023, seven years after Unite the Right, a slew of neo-Nazis were arrested and charged for their role in the violent torch march. Maybe prosecutors were gearing up to arrest Heilman, too.

But Ignite the Right had also read that DeAndre Harris was struggling to move on with his life. That he didn't want to be defined forever by those ten violent seconds in a Charlottesville parking garage, where the photo of him being beaten was a symbol of where American politics had gone. Harris wasn't a symbol. He was a young man trying to make a life for himself. Ignite the Right considered whether he'd care about Heilman's dox, or want it published at all.

Reached for comment, Charlottesville Commonwealth Attorney Joseph Platania seemed to suggest his office had in fact tracked down Jay "Red Beard" Heilman, but after considering Harris's wishes, decided not to pursue prosecution. "When making charging decisions, our office takes a trauma-informed approach to ensure that subsequent criminal proceedings do not inflict further pain and suffering," Platania said. "Sometimes that approach results in a potentially prosecutable case not being filed based upon the input from the victim."

It was the fall of 2024, and Murph was steeling herself for the years to come. Trump had just won the election, promising to mass-deport millions and pardon all the January 6 rioters and purge the government of everyone but his loyalists. The dox of Red Beard, Ignite the Right's white whale, was put on the shelf for now. It would remain among many unpublished drafts, ready when the time was right. Mostly, Ignite the Right just couldn't *find the time*. "If I could get paid to sit and do all this all day, I totally would, but I don't," she says. "It's a lot of hard work."

"Somebody's gotta do it," she adds. "Everyone thinks someone else is going to come and make things right, but nobody is coming. It's just us."

CHAPTER 17

Fire Brigades

George, and we'll call him George, used to be in Patriot Front. He's agreed to meet at a bar somewhere in America, but he'd rather you not know which one—or even whether it's east or west of the Mississippi. You may have already met him in this book, you may have not. He may have been doxed, or he may have gone undetected by American anti-fascists.

There's a lot that George won't share. The pseudonym he used in Patriot Front, the missions he took part in, the exact date he joined, or any detail specific enough to identify him. Patriot Front members might not take too kindly to him talking like this. He's seen the guns they have, and he's heard what they've threatened to do with them.

What he is willing to share are pieces of the story of why he left the group, and the wider white nationalist movement, behind him. He talks eagerly, sometimes breaking down in tears, and occasionally has the wide-eyed look of someone who just woke from a nightmare, anxiously scanning the room to make sure he's awake now, and in a better place.

His path to white nationalism started early, when he was a troubled kid just wanting to feel good about himself. It was fascism's essentialism, its low bar for entry, that he found alluring. "It made me feel better to believe in an ideology where I was superior to others just on the basis of my race," he says. "That was what I wanted to believe in." When he was twelve or thirteen, he was playing an online video game when an older guy with a profile picture of Adolf Hitler joined his chat. This older guy later encouraged George to watch *Europa: The Last Battle*, a profoundly antisemitic film that lauds Hitler as a leader who "ensured racial security for his people." George watched it and was immediately enthralled by Nazism, becoming a precocious student, reading foundational texts like Gottfried Feder's 1932 book, *The Programme of the NSDAP*, and later the writings of Julius Evola.

But it was the propaganda he found on 4chan and the Daily Stormer that got him the most worked up. "It was these videos where they'd show like the refugees coming in, and then they'd cut the footage with attacks on women, and they'd cut the footage of like refugees breaking down barriers or jumping onto trucks, all to make it seem like it's just this wave of people forcing their way into Europe and destroying everything. That's what brought the emotions out."

Looking back, he thinks the wave of fascist groups that emerged during Trump's first rise to the White House was also a phenomenon of a society grappling with a still relatively new invention: the internet. "White national-ism was always a very potent and very easily propagandized ideology, right? But white nationalist propagandists were often forced into the shadows because you're not going to publish them in the newspaper, you're not going to put them on the TV. The internet allowed them to make their videos and get it straight to people, and it's simply a convincing ideology. It's very simple. You don't need to spend a lot of time going over, like, dialectics and stuff. You just say it's the Jews; it's the Blacks."

He eventually found Patriot Front propaganda on Twitter and was desperate to join, later passing the vetting interview with flying colors. He hadn't been too cognizant of antifa before, but he remembers Patriot Front being *very* wary of the leftist radicals—seeing them as a constant menace. "Antifa, if you really knew them well, then you treated them seriously, and you didn't say, 'Oh, they're just a bunch of pussies and losers.' You were actually like, okay, no, we need to take precautions against antifa. Most antifa had more resources than we did, and most antifa had much stronger community connections . . . So, I didn't take them as a joke. Thomas didn't take them as a joke. The leadership did not take antifa as a joke."

He remembers the shock waves from Vincent's infiltration and the begrudging respect Patriot Front members had for the anti-fascist spy after-ward. "It was like a game where you have one side versus the other side, and he, you know, the other side won," George recalls.

Still, despite the ensuing wave of doxes, George says Thomas was able to steady the ship, assuring everyone that they would get through this. Flare-light, the defunct site that doxed Vincent, which seemed to have been a Patriot Front project, had an article explaining why the group survived his infiltration:[1]

> Organizations like Patriot Front in the United States are able to bounce back from attacks so well because of their centralized structure. When a member is doxxed and his livelihood is threatened, the collective will spring into action to get him back on his feet, offering him a job or a place to stay. At the end of the process, the activist is made stronger, having lost his fear of being doxed. This hardens the organization even further . . .
>
> The threat of doxing is our enemy's most valuable tool in this fight. Building resiliency to doxing should be the priority of every activist organization.

George has mixed feelings about anti-fascist doxing. It's impactful in a way that's hard to quantify. "It's been effective because people think of Patriot Front, and then the first thing they think is, 'If I join Patriot front, I will be doxed,'" he says. By his estimation, doxing was integral to preventing Patriot Front from growing too big.

But he also witnessed firsthand how Patriot Front members, once unmasked, sometimes retreated further into organized fascism, feeling that society would never forgive them—that there was no way out. "You feel like if you don't have the white nationalist community, then you'll be destitute," he says. "Most of these guys who've been doxed now are relying on other white nationalists for their employment, for their housing. And they also need a support network, because they need to talk with guys who've been doxed."

It's partly why George has agreed to talk: to tell the men in Patriot Front that there is a way out. That he did it. It's hard to pinpoint the exact moment he started growing disillusioned with white nationalism, but he remembers it happening in large part because of where he worked. He won't, of course, say what this job was, only that it was a sometimes agonizingly boring gig where none of his coworkers were white. "I really had no choice but to find people to talk with in order to make the day go by quicker, and the only people around were non-whites," he remembers. The conversations weren't anything deep or existential or political, just idle chitchat about the weather and workplace drama. Sometimes they watched stupid TikTok videos together and laughed.

"They became more humanized to me, and I found it harder to make generalized statements about non-white people, because I realized that the people I was talking about were people who I considered to be friends," he says. It dawned on him that all the alleged, immutable biological differences between him and his non-white coworkers—which he'd read about with abandon in so many books and message boards until he joined Patriot Front—simply didn't exist. His coworkers, of course, had no idea he was a white supremacist when they talked to him, nor that they'd inspired such a giant revelation in George. He left that job a while ago now. He hopes his old coworkers are doing well.

One of the scariest parts of leaving Patriot Front was the loneliness that loomed ahead. "You go from having three hundred friends, good friends, who let you stay at their house, to having nowhere," he says. He didn't immediately feel relieved or happy when he left the group—just like he was walking into the great unknown. "I was completely confused as to what was going to come next, because I just left that ideology—I didn't join another one. So, I felt like I had nothing."

For all the bravado of anti-fascist slogans like "we do not forgive, we do not forget," anti-fascists will show forgiveness to "formers" like George, people who appear to have genuinely left fascism behind. This kind of empathy is reflected in a common tactic used by anti-fascist groups across the country: an offer of amnesty. On December 14, 2023, the group Atlanta Antifascists posted an article titled "Change Your Life for the Better in 2024: Leave the White Nationalist Movement."[2] It read:

> Some advice for the new year: if you want this year to be better than 2023 was, then you need to make a permanent break with the fascist movement. The fascist movement is not one you want to be associated with, and the consequences are often life-ruining. Even if you make it to the top of a far-Right group, you are not protected from job loss and your career being destroyed. Your organization can also fall apart leaving you alone to face the consequences.
>
> There are, however, options to leave the white power movement. Contrary to the established mythology around "red-pilling", people leave all the time, both publicly and privately. There are even networks in place that can help

you exit the movement—let us know if you need help establishing contact with them. Merely saying you are no longer a racist or fascist while still organizing and associating with your fascist pals is not acceptable. We will know if you are insincere.

Because our priority is countering active white supremacists, Atlanta Antifascists will not go after you for your past. If it's clear that you've left white nationalism behind, we'll leave you alone. Just send us an email with an account of your time in the movement as a token of good faith/sincerity (what you've done, with what organizations, etc.), be ready to answer some follow-up questions, and make clear in your actions going forward that you've left white nationalism behind. We can't speak for anyone else you may have harmed, but we don't get in the way of people trying to do better by themselves and others.

Let 2024 be a year of turning your life around. Reach out for help leaving the fascist movement if you think you need it.

Paul, the anti-fascist who helped unmask so many members of Identity Dixie after Unite the Right, claims to have privately accepted amnesty offers from dozens of white supremacists—even deleting their doxes if they seemed sincerely contrite. The challenge, of course, is determining where a former white supremacist can fall on the political spectrum to deserve amnesty. In 2025, for example, is it enough for a neo-Nazi to just become an average Trump supporter? Each anti-fascist makes their own determination. Mostly, though, "formers" can get amnesty by giving an earnest apology and then staying quiet for a while. By logging off and taking some time to reflect.

George is still sorting out his politics. He has an omnivorous media diet these days. "I look at conservative news. I look at liberal news," he says. "I read *The New York Times*. I look at Democracy Now." He's taken particular interest in Israel's ongoing destruction of Gaza. It's the subject most liable to make him cry. He recognizes the cruelty of it, in part because he recognizes the racial supremacy driving the genocide in Palestine from his days in Patriot Front. "I feel guilty," he says. "I feel like I was trying to establish that type of thing here, and I was basically advocating for Zionism, but under a different here . . . I just feel really like I was, in a way, contributing to what happened to Palestinians, because by normalizing that type of ideology over here, I was making it okay for it to be done over there, right?"

By "that type of ideology" George means ethnonationalism—the idea that certain races were bequeathed pieces of land by their ancestors, and that other races either are not welcome there, or don't deserve the same rights. Patriot Front members, he says, are vile antisemites, so will call out Israel's genocide as a way of attacking Jews, falsely conflating the nation-state with Judaism as a whole. This is not to say, of course, that Patriot Front gives a shit about the well-being of Palestinians either—its members want Muslims and Arabs expelled from the US.

But Patriot Front is also envious of Israel, George says. "They're seeing the Palestinians being killed. They're seeing how Palestinians are forced into certain neighborhoods, but they don't look at that and be like, 'Well, we shouldn't do that, because it's not right.' They look at it and they're like, 'Great. We need to do that over here.'"

George is increasingly worried "that"—genocide—could happen again here, in America. He recognizes Patriot Front's brand of ethnonationalism in the rhetoric of the second Trump administration. In the early months of 2025, the president and other White House officials were frequently using terms like "remigration," while the Republican Party had taken to calling immigrants "invaders." Sometimes when George heard the president give speeches, he thought to himself: *Thomas could have written this.*

Every day brought new, horrifying footage of ICE agents abducting immigrants off the streets, or from their workplaces, sometimes ripping them away from their children. George read a story out of California about how immigration agents, executing a mission they called "Operation Trojan Horse,"[3] had piled into the back of a Penske rental box truck for an immigration raid, jumping out to detain sixteen people outside a Los Angeles Home Depot—*the exact same way Patriot Front arrived at their flash-mob marches.* ICE agents also often wore uniforms that bore an uncanny resemblance to Patriot Front's: gaiter masks, sunglasses, baseball caps, and khaki cargo pants.

It was ICE agents now who closely guarded their anonymity so that they couldn't be doxed, so that their neighbors wouldn't know what they were part of. Right-wing politicians were introducing bills that would make it illegal to name and shame ICE agents[4]—who are taxpayer-funded government employees—legislation that would essentially codify the federal agency as the GOP's secret police.

New immigration detention centers were being built, with stories emerging of horrid conditions at already existing ones, where immigrants were stuffed into cells with limited water. News stories about deaths in these places became routine. The Trump administration was also sending immigrants it falsely labeled gang members to a notorious gulag in El Salvador,[5] with no due process, in defiance of a court order, with no timeline for when they might be freed. Kristi Noem, the homeland security secretary, posted a video of herself to X visiting the El Salvadoran prison, standing in front of a cell packed with shirtless brown inmates, their heads having been forcibly shaved by guards.[6] "I also want everybody to know, if you come to our country illegally, this is one of the consequences you can face," Noem said into the camera. The administration's propaganda felt indistinguishable in tone and message from the crude, cruel videos George used to see on 4chan. The White House posted a video of ICE officials cuffing immigrants' hands and ankles before perp walking them onto a plane. "ASMR: Illegal Alien Deportation Flight," the caption to the video stated, using the initials for autonomous sensory meridian response—a pleasant sensation caused by soft, gentle sounds. In this case, the sound was of human beings being put into chains.

Such footage was widely shared and celebrated on X, which since Musk's takeover had become a playground for fascists. Musk—who Trump put in charge of the Department of Government Efficiency (DOGE), an agency tasked with gutting the federal government of seemingly everyone but MAGA loyalists—appeared to give two Nazi salutes from the stage at a rally celebrating Trump's inauguration.[7] Now he'd transformed X into a powerful propaganda arm of this new regime.

By George's estimation, it was X that was driving a wave of new recruits into Patriot Front in 2025. He was still inside the group's Telegram channels, where he saw comments claiming Patriot Front had about doubled in size. The three lawsuits against the group, which cited Vincent's Rocket-Chat leaks, hadn't yet hobbled the organization. A federal judge awarded Charles Murrell—the Black musician assaulted by Patriot Front members in Boston—$2.75 million in punitive damages,[8] but it was unclear if Murrell would ever collect on that money, and what assets Thomas Rousseau and the other defendants even had.

Meanwhile Patriot Front was collaborating and cross-pollinating more and more with Active Clubs, a decentralized network of neo-Nazi fight clubs, founded by Unite the Right attendee Rob Rundo in 2020.[9] Active Clubs were designed "to connect and cooperate but stay operationally independent," the Counter Extremism Project noted in a study,[10] so that "infiltrations and arrests of leadership figures, or even the shutdown of an Active Club, should have little if any effect" on the wider network.

The clubs fetishized fitness and violence, building camaraderie and "white unity" through mixed martial arts, kickboxing, and weight lifting. "Make fascism fun," went one of their slogans. There were fifty cells across America, each with up to a dozen members, amounting to what the CEP study warned was a "stand-by militia" that could "be activated when the need for coordinated violent action on a larger scale arises."

George felt it was inevitable that Patriot Front, collaborating with Active Clubs, would commit violence in the years to come. "All of what Patriot Front does is training for a future of violence," he says. "The only thing that they don't train with is guns, but they encourage members to train with guns on their own time. But every training meetup includes MMA practice, practicing with shields and things like that. Also, just the nature of their belief is violent. The goal of Patriot Front is to remove non-white people from America. Everyone knows that's the goal. It's written in the manifesto. The goal is to remove non-white people . . . Everyone understands that you have to be violent to accomplish that."

He worries now that Patriot Front, Active Clubs, and other groups are poised to be deputized by the MAGA movement. "If things keep moving in the same direction, there's going to be some form of extrajudicial manpower that is used to enforce whatever the will of Trump is, unless things change."

George is also concerned that anti-fascist doxing may be losing its effectiveness in preventing Patriot Front from attracting new recruits. "If there's no social stigma around being a white nationalist, doxing no longer works, and thanks to Elon Musk and Donald Trump and the people around them, there's almost already no stigma around it," he says. "It's only a matter of years before no one cares about doxing, because you won't lose your job if you get doxed for being a white nationalist."

He quips, darkly, that soon it might be advantageous to put "Patriot Front" on his résumé.

*   *   *

Much of the liberal and centrist punditry in the early days of the Trump era was stuck on the question "Is this fascism?" or "Is it happening here?" The debates over these questions could be tedious, hairsplitting affairs, hyper-focused on creating checklists of characteristics America would need to exhibit to be called a "fascist" state akin to the regimes of Nazi Germany and Mussolini's Italy. In this rendering, the philosopher Alberto Toscano notes, American fascism is discussed as if it's a "dreadful anachronism imported from the Old World," eliding the ways in which America's "liberal democracy" has always created the experience of fascism for wide swaths of its population.[11] The writers Christopher Vials and Bill Mullen, in their book *The U.S. Anti-fascism Reader*, put it this way:[12]

> For people of color at various historical moments, the experience of racialization within a liberal democracy could have the valence of fascism. That is to say, while a fascist state and a white supremacist democracy have very different mechanisms of power, the experience of racialized rightlessness within a liberal democracy can make the distinction between it and fascism murky at the level of lived experience. For those racially cast aside outside of liberal democracy's system of rights, the word "fascism" does not always conjure up a distant and alien social order.

American anti-fascists don't see fascism as something that could happen, but that's been *happening all along*. The second Trump administration was an intensification of these underlying, oppressive social structures—a right-wing insistence that America's hierarchies needed to be reified, strengthened, and made more explicit. Groups like Patriot Front wanted to be the street-level enforcers of this political project.

George is racked with regret for his time in the group, harboring a profound guilt that makes him wary and mistrustful of his own political instincts, hesitant to label himself a supporter of any ideology just yet. Still, George believes only something radical could forestall the nightmare future taking shape for America. "I think the most plausible way is to push more messaging that the actual conflict is rich versus the workers," he says, not among races or ethnicities or religions. This framework, he says, has the benefit of being true, and would make fascism much less palatable not only to the type of young men who join Patriot Front, but to the wider public.

He was beginning to articulate a Marxist worldview that wouldn't sound out of place in anti-fascist circles. Vincent had articulated this, too, once, before he disappeared, while coming to terms with what his infiltration, and antifa more broadly, could and couldn't accomplish. "The mental health stuff I had to navigate was the obsessiveness with wanting to like, dive in and get all this information," he said. "It was learning to let go of it, because it's like, I don't think this is going to be a total-eradication-of-Nazis project, right? It's gonna be just one stepping stone along the way of creating a slightly more equitable world. It's letting go and understanding that I'm not gonna be able to fix everything . . . It's more important to maybe build a community and figure out how to fix it there, with help, than it is to try to fix it as one person . . . It's going to be a lot of projects, all working together from various parts of anti-fascism and anarchism—and even some normies contributing in their own ways. That's going to be what fixes it."

The anarchist writer scott crow once compared antifa to "fire brigades,"[13] a "reactive set of ideas and strategies and tactics that are really good for this very limited thing, which is confrontation and bringing witness . . . to egregious exclusion—neo-Nazis and fascists of all forms . . . There are limits to it because it is a politics of reacting to something that is rising or fear of something that may become bigger."

crow argues that the task of tearing down the system that creates those fascist groups has always been a larger revolutionary project. "I think if we really want to stop this stuff, we need to begin to think about . . . how is it we want to build our power," crow said. "How do we want to build autonomy? How do we want to build resilience, not just for myself or my group or my campaign, but larger than that? In my neighborhood, in my community, in my overlapping communities that I'm in."

Such a revolutionary project can feel impossible and daunting, sometimes engendering despair. But what often gets lost in the right-wing panic about "antifa"—and the liberal denunciations labeling anti-fascists as mere "extremists" on the other end of the political spectrum—is the romanticism at the heart of the people doing anti-fascist work. The abiding faith that another world is possible.

Emily Gorcenski, the Charlottesville activist attacked by neo-Nazis during their tiki-torch march, who later went on to unmask many of the fascists who invaded her town, reflected on this romanticism in an essay called "Antifascism through the Lens of Transgender Identity":[14]

Antifascism is fundamentally a politics of hope. Antifascism is by its nature a struggle against institutional and exclusionary power; there is no antifascism that is not an uphill battle. It is a battle given to frequent despair, a despair that is too familiar for trans people. Studies show that trans people have a high prevalence of suicidality, largely brought on by unfair and discriminatory treatment in society and loss of social support. There are times when the fight for equality seems overwhelmingly impossible.

Gorcenski now lives in Berlin, having moved there, in part, because of the many recriminations she was facing back in America for her anti-fascist work. Sometimes, walking through the city, she passes a memorial where Nazis, in 1933, ransacked the archives of the Institut für Sexualwissenschaft—the Institute for Sexual Science—building a towering, burning pyre of books that sought to understand and humanize trans people like her. She writes:

I look around, knowing that although they may have momentarily lost the struggle then, that my presence there now—a free transgender woman, an anti-fascist activist, a queer woman, a mixed-race woman, an immigrant— breathing free air is proof that we won. And I believe that we will win again.

For all the horrifying footage in 2025 of masked ICE agents abducting immigrants from the streets of America, there was also footage of a mass resistance: of communities chasing ICE agents out of their neighborhoods, demanding that these new secret police take off their masks, show their faces, and take responsibility for the ethnic cleansing project they were a part of. People were putting their bodies on the line to protect their immigrant neighbors, displaying a kind of revolutionary love that risked, and often led to, getting beaten and arrested by police.

"Mutual aid offers us an opportunity to reconnect at the most basic human level with our potential co-strugglers in a fight against fascism," Kelly Hayes, the anti-fascist writer and organizer, said once.[15] "Community care creates new bonds of solidarity and reminds us that we must care for and protect each other.

"We cannot win without caring for one another," she added, "and they cannot win without stripping away our empathy and will to protect and care for one another."

George was rediscovering this empathy while trying to find forgiveness from the world, and ultimately forgiveness for himself, for what he was a part of. He found himself drawn to and inspired by the uprisings against ICE, and the protests against America's support for the genocide in Palestine, but isn't quite ready to join such demonstrations. He wants to start small, to build a new community first.

Until then, he's interested in destroying the group he was once a part of. He has some info about Patriot Front. Intelligence he'd been privy to that hasn't been made public yet. Tantalizing details about some businesses Patriot Front members own. The web forums where they're recruiting white men to Nazism. Maybe even a few members' real names.

He's curious: Do I know anyone who would be interested in this information?

Acknowledgments

Writing this book would have been impossible without the support and guidance of so, so many people. Words kind of fail to express the gratitude I feel for you all, for your generosity, and for the faith you put in me—but here's my best shot.

Thank you to Amanda Annis, my wonderful agent at Trident Media, for believing I could write a book long before I really believed it myself. This never would have happened without you. I still have the bar napkins we used to sketch out the roughest outline for *To Catch a Fascist*—a title that was your idea.

Kate Napolitano, the fearless editor of this book, for taking a chance on me, for believing in this project, for giving me the space and time to find the story I wanted to tell, and for shepherding me through a journey that, at times, felt impossible. It's been a privilege to write a book at all, and to experience the occasional joy that comes from moments of revelation and clarity. I will always treasure those moments, many of which came as the result of your guidance, your edits, and your encouragement.

Hannah Frankel, who provided vital and insightful edits, and who completed the herculean task of dragging this project across the finish line, coordinating so much to ensure this book would come out in 2026 instead of the next century.

Everyone else at Atria and Simon & Schuster for making this book a reality. The designers, proofreaders, copyeditors, lawyers, and everyone in publicity and marketing.

Everyone at Unicorn Riot, namely Chris Schiano and Dan Feidt, whose generosity and commitment to the public good over profit are manifest in the Discord Leaks database, allowing non-paywalled access to vital intelligence about the far right, which allowed me to find and reconstruct a narrative out of this busy, chaotic political moment. I'm a fan and an admirer of you all.

The many academics, historians, reporters, writers, and activists whose own writing and perspectives greatly informed the words on these pages. Nigel Copsey, Stanislav Vyotsky, Mark Bray, Shawn Lay, Shane Burley, Alberto Toscano, Natasha Lennard, Alison Kinney, Daryle Lamont Jenkins, David Neiwert, Spencer Sunshine, Abner Hague, Emily Gorcenski, Molly Conger, Redoubt Antifascists, It's Going Down, Devin Zane Shaw, Jason Wilson, Devin Burghart, Seth Cotlar, Zach Roberts, Nora Neus, the authors of *We Go Where They Go* (Shannon Clay, Kristin Schwartz, Michael Staudenmaier, Lady), and Linda Gordon. In memory of Stetson Kennedy.

Everyone at *HuffPost*, where I worked for fourteen years and was given so much space to grow as a writer and reporter, where I was pushed to take risks and big swings and trusted to travel the country writing about fascists. The reporting I did at *HuffPost* ultimately led to the idea for this book. In particular I'd like to thank George Zornick and Ani Vrabel, the best editors a reporter could ever hope for.

The HuffPost Union and Writers Guild of America East, which ensured I got a good severance when I left *HuffPost*, allowing me to pay the bills while finishing my first drafts.

Nick, one of my best friends, who selflessly read and edited my book proposal, later reading different drafts of the book itself, providing crucial feedback and encouragement.

Jess, who graciously read these pages and offered advice, and who is one of the kindest people I know.

Michael Edison Hayden, who's always been a bit of a North Star for sorting through all this madness, who approaches this beat with humor and grace, and who is the commissioner of our fantasy football league.

Hannah Gais, a reporter and writer I deeply admire, for sharing your perspectives on this work with me, and for all your jokes in the darkest of moments.

Andy Campbell, my forever reporting partner, who inspired me to try to write a book after writing one of his own, the brilliant *We Are Proud Boys*, and who sent me the stupidest memes.

Jason, the most loyal and devoted friend who carried me through a very trying time, and without whom I would not have been able to do this.

Samuel Freedman, the legendary reporter and journalism professor, for getting back in touch with me years after I took his class to encourage me to write a book.

Carolina—it turns out talking honestly and openly about your feelings and fears is good. Really don't think I could've done this without you.

Ali Winston, a tremendous and fearless journalist with whom I published an investigation into Patriot Front in 2022, and who's pretty okay at soccer, too.

Emily, who took me out for drinks years ago—when I was considering giving up on making it as a journalist—to call me a dumbass.

Mari, for so generously letting me crash at your place during a reporting trip, and for introducing me to the miracle of crows.

Brian and Kim, thank you so much for the car (also, I'm so sorry lol).

Spencer, for maybe the nicest text message I've ever received.

Erika and Jo, for generously offering up that beautiful, special space you built so I had a place to write.

Anna M., for the late-night pep talks on the roof.

Rex, for the late-night debates about whether it's fascism.

Everyone who let me crash during a weird summer in my life. Andy, Emily, Grace, Tess, Laura, Jason, Patrick, Sam, Sarah, Tiara, Laura, and Seb.

L.A., who was there at the beginning of this journey. Life is big and strange and hard, and through it all you never stopped believing in me.

N. and H., for the support from overseas, and for making me feel like I'll always be at home in London.

Thank you, Slags, Sanna, Sad Bois, Tottenham chat, Pads Phils Os Nats Mets, and Ball Boys.

My bowling team, for the turkeys.

My bachelors—Andrew, Dusty, Deus, Jonesy, Dirty, Shae, Kevin H., Jack, Nolan, Kevin M., Chris F.M.—where the hell would I be without you?

All the dogs in my life. Harper, Ernesto, Dolly, Pedro, Ziti, Jerry.

Everyone in Gettysburg. The teachers and the coaches and friends and Pastor Fritz Foltz.

In memory of Martin Sipkoff, a writer who taught a bunch of sixth graders how to write—Trust Yourself, Be Brave, Read, Read, Read—and whose debates in the car are still some of the best conversations I've ever been a part of.

Ben and Susan, who believed when I was only like twelve years old that I could do this one day.

M.M. for the Monday texts, and A.L. for the songs you sent *every morning*.

D. and T., I'm hoping this book is good enough for the little library.

K., L., and C., the coolest kids I've ever known.

J.A. for fact-checking it all.

All the libraries. Clinton Hill Library. Brooklyn Library. Jefferson Market Library. Butler Library. Adams County Library.

All the cafes. Joe's, Primrose, Ragged Edge, Denim Coffee, Locals.

All the bars. Hartley's, Peg's Cavalier, The Canuck, Connolly's, Rose Den, Holiday Cocktail Lounge, Central (RIP). Everyone at Clover Club, too, where I found my footing in New York.

Those who trusted me with their stories before, and whose grace I will always be in awe of: Elvis, Renton, and Constance.

Rockaway Beach, maybe my favorite place in the world, which took me in, where I wrote a significant bulk of this book, and where I figured some stuff out.

My mom, who taught me a love for words, and my dad, who showed me how to be kind.

M., a truly talented writer who was the first to read the first draft, making edits by hand in the margins; who saw me still working at the kitchen table when she woke up in the morning; who loved and supported me unconditionally; who made me laugh constantly; and who forced me to keep going.

Finally, to my beloved Buffalo Bills and Tottenham Hotspur Football Club, for teaching me about the importance of keeping the faith, understanding that we will reach glory one day, even if not in this lifetime.

Notes

Introduction

1 Robert Paxton, *The Anatomy of Fascism* (New York: Alfred A. Knopf, 2004), 218.
2 Alberto Toscano, "The Long Shadow of Racial Fascism," *Boston Review*, October 28, 2020, https://www.bostonreview.net/articles/alberto-toscano-long-shadow-racial-fascism/.
3 Devin Zane Shaw, *Philosophy of Antifascism: Punching Nazis and Fighting White Supremacy* (Lanham, MD: Rowman & Littlefield International, 2020), 16.
4 Tariq Khan, "Masking Oppression as 'Free Speech': An Anarchist Take," Agency, October 28, 2015, https://anarchistagency.com/masking-oppression-as-free-speech-an-anarchist-take/.

CHAPTER 1 Those Guys Aren't My Friends

1 Chris Schiano and Dan Feidt, "Patriot Front Fascist Leak Exposes Nationwide Racist Campaigns," Unicorn Riot, January 21, 2022, https://unicornriot.ninja/2022/patriot-front-fascist-leak-exposes-nationwide-racist-campaigns/.
2 Destiny Johnson, "NE Portland Came Together to Repair Defaced Mural Honoring George Floyd, Breonna Taylor and Ahmaud Arbery," Kgw.com, July 26, 2021, https://www.kgw.com/article/news/local/community-coming-together-to-repair-defaced-portland-george-floyd-breonna-taylor-and-ahmaud-arbery-mural/283-621fcc94-28cd-4ae6-a019-53be2c94337b.
3 "Colton Michael Brown, aka 'Network Director John-WA,'" *Washington Nazi Watch* (blog), January 24, 2022, https://wanaziwatch.com/colton-michael-brown/.
4 "Colton Michael Brown, aka 'Network Director John-WA.'"
5 "Spencer Thomas Simpson, aka 'David-WA,'" *Washington Nazi Watch* (blog), June 17, 2022, https://wanaziwatch.com/spencer-thomas-simpson/.

6　"Message from PF-3527," Unicorn Riot Discord Leaks, December 7, 2021, https://discord
leaks.unicornriot.ninja/rocket-chat/message/0e8b66aa-ab83-4253-92f2-5184c1bd2ce8.

7　"Colton Michael Brown, aka 'Network Director John-WA.'"

8　"Colton Michael Brown, aka 'Network Director John-WA.'"

9　"Extremist Files: David Lane," Southern Poverty Law Center, accessed on August 2,
2025, https://www.splcenter.org/resources/extremist-files/david-lane/.

10　A. C. Thompson, "4 Members of Violent White Supremacist Group Face Riot Charges,
Federal Authorities Say," ProPublica, October 24, 2018, https://www.propublica.org/article
/rise-above-movement-white-supremacist-group-face-riot-charges-federal-authorities-say.

11　Carol Schaeffer and Fritz Zimmermann, "They Are Racist; Some of Them Have Guns.
Inside the White Supremacist Group Hiding in Plain Sight," ProPublica, November 18,
2019, https://www.propublica.org/article/they-are-racist-some-of-them-have-guns
-inside-the-white-supremacist-group-hiding-in-plain-sight.

12　Chris Schiano, "'Southern Front' Logs Expose Neo-Nazi Extremist Cell," Unicorn Riot,
November 9, 2017, https://unicornriot.ninja/2017/southern-front-logs-expose-neo
-nazi-extremist-cell/.

13　Chris Schiano, "'We're Americans and We're Fascists': Inside Patriot Front," Unicorn Riot,
March 5, 2018, https://unicornriot.ninja/2018/americans-fascists-inside-patriot-front/.

14　Kelly Weill, "Alt-Right Charlottesville Marcher Brandon Higgs Accused of Trying to
Kill Black Men," *Daily Beast*, February 12, 2019, https://www.thedailybeast.com/alt
-right-charlottesville-marcher-brandon-higgs-accused-of-trying-to-kill-black-men/.

15　Christopher Mathias and Ali Winston, "Inside Patriot Front: The Masked White
Supremacists on a Nationwide Hate Crime Spree," *HuffPost*, February 10, 2022, https://
www.huffpost.com/entry/patriot-front-white-supremacist-group-hate-crime-vandalism
_n_620293abe4b0725faad01783.

CHAPTER 2　The Making of a Spy

1　Ben Makuch and Mack Lamoureux, "Neo-Nazis Who Plotted to Kill Antifa Activist
Sentenced to Prison," *Vice*, November 19, 2021, https://www.vice.com/en/article/neo
-nazis-who-plotted-to-kill-antifa-activist-sentenced-to-prison/.

2　Lynda Edwards, "Death in the Desert," *Orlando Weekly,* June 17, 1999, https://www
.orlandoweekly.com/news/death-in-the-desert-2263332.

3　Nigel Jaquiss, "Portland Double Murder Suspect Allegedly Ranted on Tape About
Stabbing Victim: 'That's What Liberalism Gets You,'" *Willamette Week*, May 30, 2017,
https://www.wweek.com/news/2017/05/30/portland-double-murder-suspect-allegedly
-ranted-on-tape-about-stabbing-victim-thats-what-liberalism-gets-you/.

4　Meerah Powell and Conrad Wilson, "Witnesses Describe Victims Final Moments
During MAX Train Killings," OPB, June 3, 2020, https://www.opb.org/news/article
/portland-prosecutors-max-stabbing-trial-call-eyewitnesses-killings/.

5　Christopher Mathias, "On Portland Hero's Last Day, Two Loving Goodbyes," *Huff-
Post*, June 2, 2017, https://www.huffpost.com/entry/portland-attack-hero-good
byes_n_5931c983e4b0c242ca24124d.

6 Christopher Mathias, "The White Terror Crisis in Portland," *HuffPost*, June 1, 2017, https://www.huffpost.com/entry/portland-oregon-white-terror_n_592ef9cbe4b09ec37c31055b.

7 "What Is Anarchism?," Agency, n.d., https://anarchistagency.com/what-is-anarchism/.

8 Christopher Mathias and Andy Campbell, "Violent Proto-Fascists Came to Portland. The Police Went After the Anti-Fascists," *HuffPost*, August 5, 2018, https://www.huffpost.com/archive/ca/entry/violent-proto-fascists-came-to-portland-the-police-went-after-the-anti-fascists_ca_5cd55ea4e4b07bc7297779a1.

9 Kyle Swenson, "The Alt-right's Proud Boys Love Fred Perry Polo Shirts. The Feeling Is Not Mutual," *Washington Post*, July 10, 2017, https://www.washingtonpost.com/news/morning-mix/wp/2017/07/10/the-alt-rights-proud-boys-love-fred-perry-polo-shirts-the-feeling-is-not-mutual/.

10 Charles R. Davis, "Violence, Chauvinism, and No Masturbation Allowed: 'We Are Proud Boys' Details the 4 Tiers of Membership in the Extremist Group," Business Insider, October 14, 2022, https://www.businessinsider.com/we-are-proud-boys-4-tiers-membership-in-extremist-group-2022-9.

11 Cassie Miller, "Proud Boys Destroy Churches' Black Lives Matter Signs During Protest in Washington, D.C.," Hatewatch, December 16, 2020, https://www.splcenter.org/resources/hatewatch/proud-boys-destroy-churches-black-lives-matter-signs-during-protest-washington-dc/.

12 Lindsay Whitehurst, "Proud Boys Leader Ethan Nordean Gets 18 Years in Prison, Tying for Longest Sentence in Jan. 6 Insurrection," Associated Press, September 1, 2023, https://www.pbs.org/newshour/politics/proud-boys-leader-ethan-nordean-gets-18-years-in-prison-tying-for-longest-sentence-in-jan-6-insurrection.

13 "Extremist Files: Patriot Front," Southern Poverty Law Center, n.d., https://www.splcenter.org/resources/extremist-files/patriot-front/.

14 Steve Almasy, "Teacher, Ex-Classmate Describe Charlottesville Suspect as Nazi Sympathizer," CNN, August 15, 2017, https://www.cnn.com/2017/08/12/us/charlottesville-car-crash-suspect-idd.

15 Sasha Ingber, "Neo-Nazi James Fields Gets 2nd Life Sentence for Charlottesville Attack," NPR, July 15, 2019, https://www.npr.org/2019/07/15/741756615/virginia-court-sentences-neo-nazi-james-fields-jr-to-life-in-prison.

16 Politico staff, "Full text: Trump's Comments on White Supremacists, 'Alt-Left' in Charlottesville," Politico, August 15, 2017, https://www.politico.com/story/2017/08/15/full-text-trump-comments-white-supremacists-alt-left-transcript-241662.

17 Chris Schiano, "'Southern Front' Logs Expose Neo-Nazi Extremist Cell," Unicorn Riot, November 9, 2017, https://unicornriot.ninja/2017/southern-front-logs-expose-neo-nazi-extremist-cell/.

18 "Extremist Files: Thomas Rousseau," Southern Poverty Law Center, n.d., https://www.splcenter.org/resources/extremist-files/thomas-rousseau/.

19 Garrett Gravley, "What the Fuck Is Happening in Denton?," Central Track, July 30, 2019, https://www.centraltrack.com/what-the-fuck-is-happening-in-denton/.

20 Christopher Mathias and Ali Winston, "Inside Patriot Front: The Masked White Supremacists on a Nationwide Hate Crime Spree," *HuffPost*, February 10, 2022, https://

www.huffpost.com/entry/patriot-front-white-supremacist-group-hate-crime-vandalism _n_620293abe4b0725faad01783.

21 "Extremist Files: Thomas Rousseau," Southern Poverty Law Center.

22 Christopher Mathias and Ali Winston, "Inside Patriot Front."

23 Michael Edison Hayden, "Visions of Chaos: Weighing the Violent Legacy of Iron March," Southern Poverty Law Center, February 15, 2019, https://www.splcenter.org/resources /hatewatch/visions-chaos-weighing-violent-legacy-iron-march/.

24 Michael Edison Hayden, "New Zealand Terrorist Manifesto Influenced by Far-Right Online Ecosystem, Hatewatch Finds," Hatewatch, March 15, 2019, https://www.splcenter .org/resources/hatewatch/new-zealand-terrorist-manifesto-influenced-far-right -online-ecosystem-hatewatch-finds/.

25 Adryan Corcione, "Eco-fascism: What It Is, Why It's Wrong, and How to Fight It," *Teen Vogue*, April 30, 2020, https://www.teenvogue.com/story/what-is-ecofascism-explainer.

26 Ryan Lenz, "Harold Covington, Founder of White Separatist Group, Dies at 64," Hatewatch, July 25, 2018, https://www.splcenter.org/resources/hatewatch/harold -covington-founder-white-separatist-group-dies-64/.

27 "Kieran P. Morris," *NYC Antifa* (blog), March 13, 2020, https://nycantifa.wordpress .com/2020/03/13/kieran-p-morris/.

28 Christopher Mathias, "1 Neo-Nazi Group. 5 Murders in 8 Months," *HuffPost*, February 1, 2018, https://www.huffpost.com/archive/in/entry/atomwaffen-nazi-murder-bomb -plot_a_23349719.

29 "Message from PF-3527," Unicorn Riot Discord Leaks, December 7, 2021, https://discord leaks.unicornriot.ninja/rocket-chat/message/0e8b66aa-ab83-4253-92f2-5184c1bd2ce8.

CHAPTER 3 **We Keep Us Safe**

1 "'The Spooky Nationalist': Freelance Writer Benjamin Miller Welton," *Anonymous Comrades Collective* (blog), May 24, 2021, https://accollective.noblogs.org/post/2021 /05/24/the-spooky-nationalist-freelance-writer-benjamin-miller-welton/.

2 Mark Bray, "Antifa: The History and Politics of Anti-Fascism," Dartmouth, January 26, 2018, YouTube video, 1:13:56, https://www.youtube.com/watch?v=fUtMeMU6Cu8.

3 "Extremist Files: Ku Klux Klan," Southern Poverty Law Center, n.d., https://www .splcenter.org/resources/extremist-files/ku-klux-klan/.

4 Mark Bray, "Antifa: The History and Politics of Anti-Fascism."

5 Shawn Lay, *Hooded Knights on the Niagara: The Ku Klux Klan in Buffalo, New York* (New York: New York University Press, 1995), 130–1.

6 Anna Diamond, "The Nazis' Plan to Infiltrate Los Angeles and the Man Who Kept Them at Bay," *Smithsonian Magazine*, October 25, 2017, https://www.smithsonianmag .com/history/stopping-nazi-plots-1930s-los-angeles-180966961/.

7 "Stetson Kennedy Dies at 94; Infiltrated Ku Klux Klan," Associated Press, August 28, 2011, https://www.nytimes.com/2011/08/29/us/29kennedy.html.

8 Jason Dearen, "Inside a KKK Murder Plot: Grab Him Up, Take Him to the River," Associated Press, AP News, July 27, 2021, https://apnews.com/article/government

-and-politics-business-race-and-ethnicity-racial-injustice-only-on-ap-2b4106de3ebcb
fae85948439a7056031.

9   "Frequently Asked Questions," Rose City Antifa, n.d., https://rosecityantifa.org/about/.

10 Eric Griffey, "A Weatherford, Texas Protest Turns Violent," Spectrum News 1, July 29,
    2020, https://spectrumlocalnews.com/tx/south-texas-el-paso/news/2020/07/28
    /a-weatherford-protest-turned-violent-.

11 Christopher Mathias, "White Vigilantes Have Always Had a Friend in Police," *HuffPost*,
    August 30, 2020, https://www.huffpost.com/entry/white-vigilantes-kenosha_n_5f
    4822bcc5b6cf66b2b5103e.

12 Christopher Mathias, "A White Supremacist Killed Her Dad in El Paso. Now, GOP
    Politicians Sound Like the Shooter," *HuffPost*, February 2, 2024, https://www.huffpost
    .com/entry/el-paso-shooting-anti-immigrant-rhetoric_n_65bbe7a2e4b0102bd2d84f24.

13 "Extremist Files: Holocaust Denial," Southern Poverty Law Center, n.d, https://www
    .splcenter.org/resources/extremist-files/holocaust-denial/.

CHAPTER 4 The Volcano

1   "Colton Michael Brown, aka 'Network Director John-WA,'" *Washington Nazi Watch*
    (blog), January 24, 2022, https://wanaziwatch.com/colton-michael-brown/.

2   Alex Fox, "Sierra Club Grapples with Founder John Muir's Racism," *Smithsonian Maga-
    zine*, July 23, 2020, https://www.smithsonianmag.com/smart-news/sierra-club-grapples
    -founder-john-muirs-racism-180975404/.

3   Chris Schiano and Dan Feidt, "Patriot Front Meetings Spell Out Racist Network's Plans
    & Hateful Operations," Unicorn Riot, May 13, 2022, https://unicornriot.ninja/2022
    /patriot-front-meetings-spell-out-racist-networks-plans-hateful-operations/.

4   "Seattle's Patriot Front Couple: James Julius Johnson and Amelia Watts," *Washing-
    ton Nazi Watch* (blog), December 5, 2021, https://wanaziwatch.com/james-julius
    -johnson/.

5   "Seattle's Patriot Front Couple: James Julius Johnson and Amelia Watts."

6   Ben Makuch, "Leaked Chats Show Ex-Marine Wants to Make Maine Safe Space for
    Neo-Nazis," *Vice*, June 14, 2021, https://www.vice.com/en/article/leaked-chats-show
    -ex-marine-wants-to-make-maine-safe-space-for-neo-nazis/.

7   "Transcript: Olympia Mural Planning," Unicorn Riot, October 8, 2021, https://vault
    .unicornriot.ninja/patriotfrontleaks/2021-transcripts/2021-10-08_Olympia_Mural
    _Planning.pdf.

8   "Justin O'Leary, aka 'Ethan-WA,'" *Washington Nazi Watch* (blog), February 28, 2022,
    https://wanaziwatch.com/justin-oleary/.

9   "Alexi Guthrie, 27, of Simi Valley: Neo-Nazi and Patriot Front Director," *Pacific Antifascist
    Research Collective* (blog), March 23, 2022, https://pacantifa.is/people/alexi-michael
    -guthrie-27-simi-valley-neo-nazi-director-patriot-front-socal/.

10 Shane Burley, "As the 'Alt-Right' Strays from Its Roots, Will It Turn to Open Fascism?,"
    Truthout, January 16, 2018, https://truthout.org/articles/as-the-alt-right-strays-from
    -its-roots-will-it-turn-to-open-fascism.

11 John Muir, *Steep Trails* (Boston: Houghton Mifflin, 1918), 264.

12 Tim Dickinson, "The Sky Thief," *Rolling Stone*, July 8, 2021, https://www.rollingstone .com/culture/culture-features/beebo-russell-seattle-plane-theft-true-story-1187023/.

13 "Mumble Call Until 8:30pm," Unicorn Riot, August 31, 2021, https://vault.unicornriot .ninja/patriotfrontleaks/2021-transcripts/2021-08-31_Mumble_Call_Until_8_30pm .pdf.

14 Shane Burley, "Opinion | What Patriot Front's Embarrassing 'Flash Mob' Says About Anti-fascist Resistance," NBC News, July 22, 2021, https://www.nbcnews.com/think /opinion/philadelphia-bystanders-ran-patriot-front-out-town-it-won-t-ncna1273283.

15 "Project Blacklisted," Task Force Butler, September 9, 2022, https://www.taskforcebutler .org/blacklisted.

16 "Seattle's Patriot Front Couple: James Julius Johnson and Amelia Watts."

17 Austin Jenkins, "New Gun Restrictions Take Effect July 1 in Washington," OPB, July 1, 2022, https://www.opb.org/article/2022/07/01/new-washington-gun-restrictions -take-effect-july-1/.

18 Alain Stephens, "The Feds Are Increasingly Worried About Extremists Acquiring Ghost Guns, Leaked Report Shows," The Trace, August 6, 2021, https://www.thetrace.org/2021 /08/ghost-gun-government-report-3d-print-extremism-terrorism/.

19 Justin Rohrlich, "NJ National Guardsman Charged in Neo-Nazi 'Ghost Gun' Conspiracy," *Daily Beast*, July 2, 2021, https://www.thedailybeast.com/new-jersey-national -guardsman-joseph-maurino-charged-in-neo-nazi-ghost-gun-conspiracy/.

20 Alain Stephens, "They Planned to Start a Race War. DIY Gun Kits Allowed Them to Build an Arsenal," The Trace, January 23, 2020, https://www.thetrace.org/2020/01 /white-supremacists-the-base-fbi-virginia-diy-ghost-gun/.

21 Sandra E. Garcia, "White Man Gets 10 Years in Prison for Trying to Hire Hit Man to Lynch Black Neighbor," April 15, 2019, https://www.nytimes.com/2019/04/15/us/hit -man-lynching.html.

22 Ali Winston, "Atomwaffen Division's Washington State Cell Leader Stripped of Arsenal in U.S., Banned from Canada," *Daily Beast*, September 21, 2024, https://www.thedaily beast.com/kaleb-james-cole-atomwaffen-divisions-washington-state-leader-stripped -of-arsenal-in-us-banned-from-canada/.

23 "Hate symbol: Othala rune," Anti-Defamation League, n.d., https://www.adl.org /resources/hate-symbol/othala-rune.

24 David Crossland, "New Exhibition Explodes Myth of SS Castle Wewelsburg," *Der Spiegel*, April 6, 2010, https://www.spiegel.de/international/germany/confronting-the-nazi -perpetrators-new-exhibition-explodes-myth-of-ss-castle-wewelsburg-a-687435.html.

25 "Seattle's Patriot Front Couple: James Julius Johnson and Amelia Watts."

26 Melissa Chan, "Facing Rising Crime, Biden Implements New Federal Regulations for Ghost Guns," NBC News, August 24, 2022, https://www.nbcnews.com/news/us-news /ghost-gun-retailers-agree-stop-selling-kits-parts-new-york-city-reside-rcna43913.

27 Camille Jackson, "The Turner Diaries, Other Racist Novels, Inspire Extremist Violence," Southern Poverty Law Center, October 14, 2004, https://www.splcenter.org/resources /reports/turner-diaries-other-racist-novels-inspire-extremist-violence/.

28 John Ross, "Frequently Asked Questions," John-Ross.net (archived blog), n.d., https://web.archive.org/web/20141204021131/http://john-ross.net/faq.php.

29 John Williams, "A Reader's Hunting Guide," *New York Times,* February 14, 2014, https://www.nytimes.com/2014/02/16/books/review/a-readers-hunting-guide.html.

30 Camille Jackson, "The Turner Diaries, Other Racist Novels."

31 Lou Michel and Dan Herbeck, *American Terrorist: Timothy McVeigh and the Oklahoma City Bombing* (New York: HarperCollins, 2001), 278.

32 "Justin O'Leary, aka 'Ethan-WA,'" *Washington Nazi Watch* (blog).

33 Nelson George, "Angela Davis Still Believes America Can Change," *New York Times,* October 19, 2020, https://www.nytimes.com/interactive/2020/10/19/t-magazine/angela-davis.html.

34 Alberto Toscano, "The Long Shadow of Racial Fascism," *Boston Review,* October 28, 2020, https://www.bostonreview.net/articles/alberto-toscano-long-shadow-racial-fascism/.

35 Angela Davis, *Angela Davis: An Autobiography* (New York: Random House, 1974), 107–8.

36 Simon, "READER REPORT: White Nationalist Group Resurfaces in West Seattle with Mural Vandalism," *West Seattle Blog* (blog), November 27, 2021, https://westseattleblog.com/2021/11/reader-report-white-nationalist-group-resurfaces-in-west-seattle-with-mural-vandalism/.

37 "Alexi Guthrie, 27, of Simi Valley: Neo-Nazi and Patriot Front Director."

38 "Patriot Front Destroys Olympia Pride Mural (Leaked Meeting Excerpt, 10/17/2021)," Unicorn Riot, June 13, 2022, YouTube video, 5:16, https://www.youtube.com/watch?v=zRrF9UfiMlk.

39 Chris Schiano and Dan Feidt, "Patriot Front Meetings Spell Out Racist Network's Plans & Hateful Operations."

40 Andy Hobbs, "Downtown Olympia: Taking Back the Streets," *The Olympian,* September 28, 2014, https://www.theolympian.com/news/local/article26080879.html.

41 Jennifer Sullivan, "Performer Known as 'Drag King' Attacked in Olympia," KOMO, September 6, 2016, https://komonews.com/news/local/drag-king-says-she-was-attacked-near-olympia-tavern-sunday.

42 Chris Schiano and Dan Feidt, "Patriot Front Meetings Spell Out Racist Network's Plans & Hateful Operations."

43 Shaun Goodwin and Genevieve Belmaker, "Restored Olympia Pride Mural Survived Hate Vandalism, But Now It Needs a New Home," *The Olympian,* August 2, 2022, https://www.theolympian.com/news/local/article264088456.html.

44 "Colton Michael Brown, aka 'Network Director John-WA.'"

45 "Message from PF-327302," Unicorn Riot Discord Leaks, November 18, 2021, https://discordleaks.unicornriot.ninja/rocket-chat/message/715bd933-86ed-42c9-84b7-8213c92165e2.

46 "Jacob Stephen Sundt, aka Clark-WA," *Washington Nazi Watch* (blog), December 15, 2021, https://wanaziwatch.com/jacob-stephen-sundt/.

47 "Message from PF-3194," Unicorn Riot Discord Leaks, December 3, 2021, https://discordleaks.unicornriot.ninja/rocket-chat/message/846c4afc-9d13-4c2d-a763-8d1044770087.

CHAPTER 5   A Brief History of Punching Nazis

1   Adam Johnson, "In Month After Charlottesville, Papers Spent as Much Time Condemning Anti-Nazis as Nazis," FAIR, September 13, 2017, https://fair.org/home/in-month
-after-charlottesville-papers-spent-as-much-time-condemning-anti-nazis-as-nazis/.

2   Marc A. Thiessen, "Yes, Antifa Is the Moral Equivalent of neo-Nazis," *Washington Post*,
August 8, 2017, https://www.washingtonpost.com/opinions/yes-antifa-is-the-moral
-equivalent-of-neo-nazis/2017/08/30/9a13b2f6-8d00-11e7-91d5-ab4e4bb76a3a_story
.html.

3   Editorial Board, "'Antifa' Groups Only Help the Hateful Forces They Claim to Oppose,"
Washington Post, August 7, 2017, https://www.washingtonpost.com/opinions/antifa
-groups-only-help-the-hateful-forces-they-claim-to-oppose/2017/08/29/d7c900b4
-8cca-11e7-8df5-c2e5cf46c1e2_story.html?utm_term=.d551e7da3dad.

4   Mark Bray, "Foreword," in *The Antifa Comic Book: 100 Years of Fascism and Antifa Movements*, by Gord Hill (Vancouver: Arsenal Pulp Press, 2018), 7–12.

5   Natasha Lennard, *Being Numerous: Essays on Non-Fascist Life* (New York: Verso,
2019), 21.

6   David A. Love, "Why Malcolm X Said White People Should Be Like Abolitionist John
Brown," TheGrio, May 19, 2023, https://thegrio.com/2023/05/19/why-malcolm-x-said
-white-people-should-be-like-abolitionist-john-brown/.

7   Twin Cities PBS, "Anti-Racist Skinheads Fighting Nazis: The Baldies | Full-Length
Documentary," Twin Cities PBS, March 7, 2022, YouTube video, 51:44, https://www
.youtube.com/watch?v=8BSDZ1DIEIQ.

8   Mark Bray, *Antifa: The Anti-Fascist Handbook* (Brooklyn, NY: Melville House Publishing,
2017), 47.

9   Wes Enzinna, "The Long History of 'Nazi Punching'—and the Return of the 'Antifas'
in the Time of Trump," *Mother Jones*, January 27, 2017, https://www.motherjones.com
/politics/2017/01/video-richard-spencer-punch-antifa-fascism/.

10 Martin Sprouse and Tim Yohannan, "Interview with Anti Racist Action (Minneapolis)," *Maximum Rocknroll*, Issue no. 78, November 1989, https://libcom.org/article
/interview-anti-racist-action-minneapolis-maximumrocknroll-1989.

11 Twin Cities PBS, "Anti-Racist Skinheads Fighting Nazis."

12 Shannon Clay, Kristin Schwartz, and Michael Staudenmaier, *We Go Where They Go:
The Story of Anti-Racist Action* (Oakland: PM Press, 2023), 22.

13 Nigel Copsey and Samuel Merrill, "Understanding 21st Century Militant Antifascism,"
Centre for Research and Evidence on Security Threats, April 14, 2021, https://crest
research.ac.uk/resources/understanding-21st-century-militant-anti-fascism/.

14 Mow Bowseter, Mic Crenshaw, Alec Dunn, Celina Flores, Julie Perini, and Erin Yanke,
It Did Happen Here: An Antifascist People's History (Oakland: PM Press, 2023).

15 Christopher Mathias, "The Anti-Abortion Movement Killed People. Now Victims' Families Face a Post-Roe World," *HuffPost*, June 13, 2022, https://www.huffpost.com/entry
/anti-abortion-violence-murdered-families-roe-v-wade_n_62a37f2ae4b0cdccbe4fa969.

16 Shannon Clay, Kristin Schwartz, and Michael Staudenmaier, *We Go Where They Go*, 152.

17 Shannon Clay, Kristin Schwartz, and Michael Staudenmaier, *We Go Where They Go*, 264.

18 Luke O'Brien, "The Nazi-Puncher's Dilemma," *HuffPost*, December 20, 2017, https://www.huffpost.com/entry/nazi-punch-antifa_n_59e13ae9e4b03a7be580ce6f.

19 "Extremist Files: Matt Hale," Southern Poverty Law Center, n.d., https://www.splcenter.org/resources/extremist-files/matt-hale/.

20 "Church of the Creator Timeline," Southern Poverty Law Center, September 15, 1999, https://www.splcenter.org/resources/reports/church-creator-timeline/.

21 Bill Dedman, "Midwest Gunman Had Engaged in Racist Acts at 2 Universities," *New York Times*, June 6, 1999, https://www.nytimes.com/1999/07/06/us/midwest-gunman-had-engaged-in-racist-acts-at-2-universities.html.

22 William Claiborne, "Supremacist Group Grows Nationwide," *Washington Post*, June 28, 2000, https://www.washingtonpost.com/archive/politics/2000/06/29/supremacist-group-grows-nationwide/1d4dff39-e362-4d07-aa6b-e15c001506b4/.

23 Ed Vulliamy, "'Kill All the N***ers You Can,' Said the Cop. So They Made Him Mayor," *Guardian*, October 5, 2002, https://www.theguardian.com/world/2002/oct/06/usa.edvulliamy.

24 William Bunch, "Handcuffed by History," *New York Times*, September 2, 2001, https://www.nytimes.com/2001/09/02/magazine/handcuffed-by-history.html.

25 Tomas Rothaus, "January 2002: The Battle of York," CrimethInc., January 11, 2023, https://crimethinc.com/2023/01/11/january-2002-the-battle-of-york-anti-fascism-then-and-now.

26 Francis Dupuis-Déri, "How Black Blocs Have Changed Protest Movements Around the World," The Conversation, August 24, 2017, lack-blocs-have-changed-protest-movements-around-the-world-80856.

27 Staff Report, "Anti-Hate Groups Showed Up to Counter Racists at Martin Memorial Library," *York Daily Record*, January 14, 2002, https://www.ydr.com/story/archives/2017/08/13/2002-protests-prompted-hate-groups-visit-turned-violent-york-streets/563511001/.

28 Luke O'Brien, "The Nazi-Puncher's Dilemma."

29 Tomas Rothaus, "January 2002: The Battle of York."

30 Francis X. Clines, "York Journal; Racial Adversaries Converge on City Hall," January 16, 2002, https://www.nytimes.com/2002/01/16/us/york-journal-racial-adversaries-converge-on-city-trying-to-heal.html.

31 Mark Potok, "Racial Battle Breaks Out in York, Pa.; Points to Larger National Problem," March 5, 2002, https://www.splcenter.org/resources/reports/racial-battle-breaks-out-york-pa-points-larger-national-problem/.

32 "ARA Research Bulletin, Issue no. 3, Winter/Spring 2002," Chicago Anti-Racist Action, https://issuu.com/randalljaykay/docs/araresearchbulletinissue3winterspri.

33 P. J. Huffstutter, "40 Years for Plot to Murder Judge," *Los Angeles Times*, April 7, 2005, https://www.latimes.com/archives/la-xpm-2005-apr-07-na-hale7-story.html.

34 Jeffrey Gettleman, "William L. Pierce, 68; Ex-Rocket Scientist Became White Supremacist," *Los Angeles Times*, July 24, 2002, https://www.latimes.com/archives/la-xpm-2002 -jul-24-me-pierce24-story.html.

35 Shannon Clay, Kristin Schwartz, and Michael Staudenmaier, *We Go Where They Go*, 252.

36 Tomas Rothaus, *Another War Is Possible: Militant Anarchist Experiences in the Antiglobalization Era* (Oakland: PM Press, 2025).

37 Natasha Lennard, *Being Numerous*, 22.

CHAPTER 6 I'm Gonna Be Famous, Boys

1 "DC_12_4_21," Unicorn Riot – The Vault Server, n.d., https://vault.unicornriot.ninja /patriotfrontleaks/2021/Mega.nz%20Files%20A-M/DC_12_04_21/.

2 Terence McArdle, "The Day 30,000 White Supremacists in KKK Robes Marched in the Nation's Capital," *Washington Post*, August 11, 2018, https://www.washingtonpost .com/news/retropolis/wp/2017/08/17/the-day-30000-white-supremacists-in-kkk -robes-marched-in-the-nations-capital/.

3 "DC_12_4_21/Speech/," Unicorn Riot – The Vault Server, n.d., https://vault.unicornriot .ninja/patriotfrontleaks/2021/Mega.nz%20Files%20A-M/DC_12_04_21/Speech/.

4 Ellie Silverman, "A White Supremacist March in D.C. Was Pushed by a Fake Twitter Account, Experts Say," *Washington Post*, December 6, 2021, https://www.washingtonpost .com/dc-md-va/2021/12/06/white-supremacist-dc-march-patriot-front/.

5 "Message from PF-3527," Unicorn Riot Discord Leaks, November 29, 2021, https:// discordleaks.unicornriot.ninja/rocket-chat/message/be8abda6-25a6-4e59-a3e6 -a6ab6f6570c2.

6 "Tech-team," Unicorn Riot Discord Leaks, November 16, 2021, https://discordleaks.unicorn riot.ninja/rocket-chat/room/97f5b993-3c92-434d-a0ff-9a6afa764218?page=1#msg -9fdfd277-a76f-4e47-8ac9-8c983a929d64.

7 "ND - Carter MO," Unicorn Riot Discord Leaks, November 25, 2021, https://discord leaks.unicornriot.ninja/rocket-chat/user/55620bb2-b119-4bc3-8952-49f74737dc d9?&page=4.

8 "Dec 4th DC Demo from Benjamin MI," Unicorn Riot – The Vault Server, n.d., https:// vault.unicornriot.ninja/patriotfrontleaks/2021/Mega.nz%20Files%20A-M/Dec_4th _DC_Demo_from_Benjamin_MI/.

9 Harvey Eisner, "HERE'S THE NAZIS WHO TOPPLED THAT MONOLITH," Left Coast Right Watch, January 8, 2021, https://leftcoastrightwatch.org/articles/heres-the -nazis-who-toppled-that-monolith/.

10 Joan Braune, "Extremism, Fascist Voids and Antifascist Hope with Joan Braune," February 25, 2024, in *Final Straw Radio Podcast*, podcast, 1:13:48, https://thefinalstrawradio .noblogs.org/post/2024/02/25/extremism-fascist-voids-and-antifascist-hope-with -joan-braune/.

11 "Patriot Front Neo-Nazis Exposed in Parking Lot Clusterf*ck," Unicorn Riot, September 20, 2022, YouTube video, 1:01:37, https://www.youtube.com/watch?v=MGq4hpIchRY.

12 Chris Schiano, "Patriot Front Members Exposed in Parking Lot Clusterf*ck," Unicorn Riot, September 20, 2022, https://unicornriot.ninja/2022/patriot-front-members-exposed-in-parking-lot-clusterfck/#mcclain.

13 "Nw9," Unicorn Riot Discord Leaks, November 24, 2021, https://discordleaks.unicornriot.ninja/rocket-chat/room/5ec0851b-a7f3-4911-b632-f6f726251e25?page=3#msg-1d86b024-f575-4118-872c-6535974e4beb.

14 Dean Mershahi, "Patriot Front Members Settle Civil Suit over Defaced Arthur Ashe Mural," VPM, December 28, 2024, https://www.vpm.org/news/2024-12-18/patriot-front-members-settle-civil-suit-arthur-ashe-mural-noyce-gancarz.

15 "Message from PF-3194," Unicorn Riot Discord Leaks, December 11, 2021, https://discordleaks.unicornriot.ninja/rocket-chat/message/74f3dd53-9330-46ab-a3b1-cfa95ce7f9fc.

16 "(DM) David WA & ND - John WA," Unicorn Riot Discord Leaks, December 7, 2021, https://discordleaks.unicornriot.ninja/rocket-chat/room/6f8e42a7-ff13-49f9-85a0-c387f48b958f?page=2#msg-e7652745-24ac-4568-a7bb-f2c541590c9b.

17 Thomas Rousseau, "Patriot Front National Call, December 10, 2021," Atlanta Antifascists, December 10, 2021, Vimeo video, 53:01, https://vimeo.com/655596125.

18 Philip Oltermann, "Bella Ciao: A Brief History of the Resistance Anthem Sung to Viktor Orbán," *Guardian*, October 11, 2024, https://www.theguardian.com/world/2024/oct/11/bella-ciao-resistance-anthem-history-meps-strasbourg-viktor-orban.

CHAPTER 7 **A Brief History of Unmasking**

1 Randal Rust, "Ku Klux Klan | Tennessee Encyclopedia," Tennessee Historical Society, October 8, 2017, https://tennesseeencyclopedia.net/entries/ku-klux-klan/.

2 Michael Newton, *White Robes and Burning Crosses: A History of the Ku Klux Klan from 1866* (Jefferson, NC: McFarland & Company Inc., Publishers, 2014), 7.

3 "Extremist Files: Ku Klux Klan," Southern Poverty Law Center, n.d., https://www.splcenter.org/resources/extremist-files/ku-klux-klan/.

4 "Extremist Files: Ku Klux Klan."

5 Bryan Greene, "Created 150 Years Ago, the Justice Department's First Mission Was to Protect Black Rights," *Smithsonian Magazine*, July 1, 2020, https://www.smithsonianmag.com/history/created-150-years-ago-justice-departments-first-mission-was-protect-black-rights-180975232/.

6 "White Supremacy & Terrorism | Themes | Slavery by Another Name," PBS, n.d., https://www.pbs.org/tpt/slavery-by-another-name/themes/white-supremacy/.

7 Allen C. Guelzo, "Reconstruction Didn't Fail. It Was Overthrown," *Time*, April 30, 2018, https://time.com/5256940/reconstruction-failure-excerpt/.

8 Ida. B Wells, "Southern Horrors: Lynch Law in All Its Phases," Encyclopedia Virginia, 1892, https://encyclopediavirginia.org/primary-documents/southern-horrors-lynch-law-in-all-its-phases-by-ida-b-wells-1892/.

9 The Red Record: Ida B. Wells, "The Red Record: Tabulated Statistics and Alleged Causes of Lynching in the United States," Project Gutenberg, 1895, https://www.gutenberg.org/files/14977/14977-h/14977-h.htm.

10 Julianne McShane, "President Biden Signs Emmett Till Anti-Lynching Act into Law," April 11, 2022, https://www.nbcnews.com/news/nbcblk/ida-b-wells-pushed-7-presidents-pass-anti-lynching-legislation-now-s-f-rcna23596.

11 "Exposing the 'Thread-Bare Lie': How Ida B. Wells Used Investigative Journalism to Uncover the Truth About Lynching," WTTW, n.d., https://www.wttw.com/chicago-stories/ida-b-wells/exposing-the-thread-bare-lie-how-ida-b-wells-used-investigative-journalism-to-uncover-the-truth-about-lynching.

12 Alison Kinney, "How the Klan Got Its Hood," *New Republic*, January 8, 2016, https://newrepublic.com/article/127242/klan-got-hood.

13 Scott Jaschik, "Mississippi Will Rename Building, Add Context to Others," Inside Higher Ed, July 6, 2017, https://www.insidehighered.com/quicktakes/2017/07/07/mississippi-will-rename-building-add-context-others.

14 *Forgotten Hero: Walter White and the NAACP*, directed by Michelle Smawley (2025, WGBH), PBS, https://www.pbs.org/wgbh/americanexperience/films/forgotten-hero-walter-white-and-naacp/#film_description.

15 Walter F. White, "I Investigate Lynchings," *American Mercury*, January 1929, https://nationalhumanitiescenter.org/pds/maai3/segregation/text2/investigatelynchings.pdf.

16 Walter F. White, "The Work of a Mob," *The Crisis*, Vol. 16, No.5, September 1918, https://www.marxists.org/history/usa/workers/civil-rights/crisis/0900-crisis-v16n05-w095.pdf.

17 Tanasia Kenney, "Historical Marker at Site of Pregnant Woman's Lynching Is Removed, GA Officials Say," *Columbus Ledger-Enquirer*, October 12, 2020, https://www.ledger-enquirer.com/news/state/georgia/article246404680.html.

18 Katherine J. Lennard, "Uniform Threat: Manufacturing the Ku Klux Klan's Visible Empire, 1866–1931," PhD diss. (University of Michigan, 2017).

19 Alexis Clark, "How 'The Birth of a Nation' Revived the Ku Klux Klan," History, August 14, 2018, https://www.history.com/articles/kkk-birth-of-a-nation-film.

20 Robert A. Kahn, "Cross Burning," Free Speech Center at Middle Tennessee State University, August 7, 2023, https://firstamendment.mtsu.edu/article/cross-burning/.

21 Richard Corliss, "D.W. Griffith's *The Birth of a Nation* 100 Years Later: Still Great, Still Shameful," *Time*, March 3, 2015, https://time.com/3729807/d-w-griffiths-the-birth-of-a-nation-10/.

22 Charles Alexander, "Kleagles and Cash: The Ku Klux Klan as a Business Organization, 1915–1930," *Business History Review*, Vol. 39, No. 3 (Autumn 1965), 352. https://www.jstor.org/stable/3112145?mag=the-kkk-as-big-business&seq=5.

23 Linda Gordon, *The Second Coming of the KKK: the Ku Klux Klan of the 1920s and the American Political Tradition* (New York: Liveright Publishing Corporation, 2017), 71.

24 Kami Horton, "A Look Back at How White Supremacists Sowed Seeds of Hate in Oregon in the 20th Century," OPB, March 14, 2022, https://www.opb.org/article/2022/03/14/rise-of-klan-white-nationalism-hate-racism-oregon/.

25 Linda Gordon, *The Second Coming of the KKK*, 164.

26 Norman D. Brown, *Hood, Bonnet, and Little Brown Jug: Texas State Politics, 1921–1928* (College Station, TX: Texas A&M Press, 1984), 51.

27 Shawn Lay, *Hooded Knights on the Niagara: The Ku Klux Klan in Buffalo, New York* (New York: New York University Press, 1995), 45–6.

28 Shawn Lay, *Hooded Knights on the Niagara*, 48–9.

29 "Pastor, Home Bombed, Again Aids Raiders: Buffalo Officers Seek Trail of Foes of Liquor Violations Witness," *New York Times*, April 19, 1924.

30 Shawn Lay, *Hooded Knights on the Niagara*, 122–3.

31 Shawn Lay, *Hooded Knights on the Niagara*, 124–5.

32 Shawn Lay, *Hooded Knights on the Niagara*, 134–8.

33 "Buffalo Ku Klux Klan Chapter: List of Members," Buffalo History Museum, n.d., https://nyheritage.org/index.php/collections/buffalo-ku-klux-klan-chapter-list-members.

34 Shawn Lay, *Hooded Knights on the Niagara*, 133–42.

35 Linda Gordon, *The Second Coming of the KKK*, 166–7.

36 Linda Gordon, *The Second Coming of the KKK*, 169.

CHAPTER 8 **Patriot Fail**

1 "Colton Michael Brown, aka 'Network Director John-WA,'" *Washington Nazi Watch* (blog), January 24, 2022, https://wanaziwatch.com/colton-michael-brown/.

2 "Transcript: Last Mumble Before Dec Event," Unicorn Riot, November 28, 2021, https://vault.unicornriot.ninja/patriotfrontleaks/2021-transcripts/2021-11-28_Last_Mumble_Before_Dec_Event.pdf.

3 *Gancarz vs. Capito*, Complaint, W.D. Wash. (2023) https://www.documentcloud.org/documents/23902610-patriot-front-lawsuit/.

4 "Spencer Thomas Simpson, aka 'David-WA,'" *Washington Nazi Watch* (blog), June 17, 2022, https://wanaziwatch.com/spencer-thomas-simpson/.

5 "Transcript: Casual Mumble with Lawrence FL Et Al," Unicorn Riot, October 3, 2021, https://vault.unicornriot.ninja/patriotfrontleaks/2021-transcripts/2021-10-03_Casual_Mumble_with_Lawrence_FL_et_al.pdf.

6 "Seattle's Patriot Front Couple: James Julius Johnson and Amelia Watts," *Washington Nazi Watch* (blog), December 5, 2021, https://wanaziwatch.com/james-julius-johnson/.

7 *Gancarz vs. Capito*, Complaint.

8 *Gancarz et al. vs. Capito*, Complaint.

9 "Message from PF-3194," Unicorn Riot Discord Leaks, December 7, 2021, https://discordleaks.unicornriot.ninja/rocket-chat/message/1416eed7-8a33-4bd7-b985-2eb739d3457d.

10 "Justin O'Leary, aka 'Ethan-WA,'" *Washington Nazi Watch* (blog), February 28, 2022, https://wanaziwatch.com/justin-oleary/.

11 "Alexi Guthrie, 27, of Simi Valley: Neo-Nazi and Patriot Front Director," *Pacific Antifascist Research Collective* (blog), March 23, 2022, https://pacantifa.is/people/alexi-michael-guthrie-27-simi-valley-neo-nazi-director-patriot-front-socal/.

12 "Southern Oregon's Patriot Failure: Lawrence Alexander Norman Is Frederick OR," *Corvallis Antifascists* (blog), December 14, 2021, https://cvantifa.noblogs.org/post/2021/12/14/fred/.

13 "Jacob Stephen Sundt, aka Clark-WA," *Washington Nazi Watch* (blog), December 15, 2021, https://wanaziwatch.com/jacob-stephen-sundt/.

14 "Message from PF-327302," Discord Leaks, December 15, 2021, https://discordleaks .unicornriot.ninja/rocket-chat/message/69db8524-d262-4917-aa97-1a4012090f9e.

CHAPTER 9 American Antifa

1 "Introducing the Torch Network, an Antifascist Network," *Torch Antifa Network* (blog), December 14, 2013, https://torch-antifa.org/introducing-the-torch-network-an-anti fascist-network/.

2 Rocky Mountain Antifa and the TORCH Antifa Network, "Confronting the Trump Regime," in *Turning the Tide: The Journal of Anti-Racist Action*, Volume 20, No. 16, December 2016, https://archive.org/details/turning_the_tide_2006-2016/page/n307 /mode/2up?q=%22shit+show%22.

3 Charles Joughin, "10 Things You Should Know About Focus on the Family," Human Rights Campaign, November 13, 2014, https://www.hrc.org/press-releases/10-things -you-should-know-about-focus-on-the-family.

4 Samantha Michaels, "More Trans People Have Been Killed in 2015 Than Any Other Year on Record," *Mother Jones*, November 20, 2015, https://www.motherjones.com /politics/2015/11/more-transgender-people-have-been-murdered-2015-any-other-year -record/.

5 Abigail Edge, "Two Nights on Milo Yiannopoulos's Campus Tour: As Offensive as You'd Imagine," *The Guardian*, January 28, 2017, https://www.theguardian.com/world/2017 /jan/28/milo-yiannopoulos-campus-speaking-tour-colorado.

6 Joseph Bernstein, "Here's How Breitbart and Milo Smuggled White Nationalism into the Mainstream," BuzzFeed News, October 5, 2017, https://www.buzzfeednews.com /article/josephbernstein/heres-how-breitbart-and-milo-smuggled-white-nationalism.

7 "Forming an Antifa Group: A Manual," It's Going Down, February 16, 2017, https:// itsgoingdown.org/forming-an-antifa-group-a-manual/.

8 Michael Edison Hayden, "A Guide to Open Source Intelligence (OSINT)," *Columbia Journalism Review*, June 7, 2019, https://www.cjr.org/tow_center_reports/guide-to -osint-and-hostile-communities.php.

9 Aaron Gell, "Anti-Fascists Are Waging a Cyber War—and They're Winning," Medium, September 9, 2019, https://gen.medium.com/antifas-keyboard-warriors-254f62be2a95.

11 Abner Hague, "Make Journalism Antifa Again," in *No Pasaran! Antifascist Dispatches from a World in Crisis*, ed. Shane Burley (Chico, CA: AK Press, 2022), 435.

12 "Nate Marshall Is a Dumb Ass," *Rocky Mountain Antifa* (blog), March 17, 2014, https:// rockymountainantifa.blogspot.com/2014/03/nate-marshall-is-dumb-as-hell.html.

13 George Orwell, "What is Fascism?," *Tribune*, 1944, https://www.orwell.ru/library /articles/As_I_Please/english/efasc.

14 Olivia Nuzzi, "How Pepe the Frog Became a Nazi Trump Supporter and Alt-Right Symbol," *Daily Beast*, May 26, 2016, https://www.thedailybeast.com/how-pepe-the -frog-became-a-nazi-trump-supporter-and-alt-right-symbol/.

15 Anonymous Comrades Collective, "The Anonymous Comrades Collective would like to introduce you . . . ," X, July 13, 2021, https://web.archive.org/web/20210713153253/https://twitter.com/anonymouscommie/status/1414962918148513802.

16 "About Unicorn Riot," Unicorn Riot, n.d., https://unicornriot.ninja/about-unicorn-riot/.

17 Niko Georgiades, "Scarsella Trial – Part One: Jury Selection, Unicorn Riot Subpoenaed, Opening Statements," Unicorn Riot, January 27, 2017, https://unicornriot.ninja/2017/scarsella-trial-part-one-jury-selection-unicorn-riot-subpoenaed-opening-statements/.

18 David D. Kirkpatrick, "Infiltrating the Far Right," *New Yorker*, August 18, 2024, https://www.newyorker.com/magazine/2024/08/26/infiltrating-the-far-right.

19 "Minnesota Man Who Shot 5 Black Lives Matter Protesters Found Guilty," CBS News, February 3, 2017, https://www.cbsnews.com/news/minnesota-man-who-shot-5-black-lives-matter-protesters-found-guilty/.

CHAPTER 10 Very Fine People

1 Julia Carrie Wong, "'I Refuse to Be Like Them': Why the Man Shot While Protesting Milo Yiannopoulos Doesn't Want Revenge," *Guardian*, April 4, 2017, https://www.theguardian.com/world/2017/apr/04/man-shot-milo-yiannopoulos-protest-seattle-trump-interview.

2 David Rising, "Nazi Death Squads Focus of Latest War Crime Cases in Germany," Associated Press, June 6, 2018, https://apnews.com/article/01ca23bc045743ed962e668a94e25f11.

3 Chris Schiano, "Anticom Discord Server Shows Months of Neo-Nazi Incitement," Unicorn Riot, October 18, 2017, https://unicornriot.ninja/2017/anticom-discord-server-shows-months-neo-nazi-incitement/.

4 "Robert E. Lee Sculpture," Encyclopedia Virginia, n.d., https://encyclopediavirginia.org/entries/robert-edward-lee-sculpture/.

5 Second Amended Complaint, *Sines v. Kessler*, Civil Action 3:17–cv–00072 (W.D. Va.), 29–30.

6 "Sines v. Kessler Rush Transcript – Day 11: Dillon Hopper, Michael Tubbs, Marissa Blair, Thomas Rousseau," Unicorn Riot, November 8, 2021, https://unicornriot.ninja/2021/sines-v-kessler-rush-transcript-day-11-dillon-hopper-michael-tubbs-marissa-blair-thomas-rousseau/.

7 Expert Report of Kathleen M. Blee, PhD, and Pete Simi, PhD, *Sines v. Kessler*, Civil Action 3:17–cv–00072 (W.D. Va.), 53.

8 Expert Report of Kathleen M. Blee, PhD, and Pete Simi, PhD, *Sines v. Kessler*, 55–6.

9 Christopher Mathias, "Go Back to Your Country, They Said," *HuffPost*, November 4, 2019, https://www.huffpost.com/feature/go-back-to-your-country.

10 Paul Abowd, "Neo-Nazi 'Tyrone' Exposed as US Marine," Al Jazeera, April 17, 2018, https://www.aljazeera.com/news/2018/4/17/neo-nazi-tyrone-exposed-as-us-marine.

11 Jeremy Berke, "'Sieg Heil' and Assault Rifles: The President of Charlottesville's Synagogue Described a Harrowing Scene Outside the Temple," Business Insider, August 16, 2017, https://www.businessinsider.com/charlottesvilles-synagogue-president-scene-white-nationalists-neo-nazis-2017-8.

12 Second Amended Complaint, *Sines v. Kessler*, 49–50.

13 "1000 Clergy and Faith Leaders urged to come to Charlottesville for August 12," Congregate C'Ville, July 31, 2017, https://congregatecville.com/press-release-for-clergy-call.

14 Nora Neus, *24 Hours in Charlottesville: An Oral History of the Stand Against White Supremacy* (Boston: Beacon Press, 2023), 33.

15 Second Amended Complaint, *Sines v. Kessler*, 50–1.

16 Edna Friedberg, "Why Neo-Nazis Parade by Torchlight," *Atlantic*, August 21, 2017, https://www.theatlantic.com/politics/archive/2017/08/why-they-parade-by-torchlight/537459/.

17 "'Wade in the Water' Was Coded Message to Slaves," aired on April 27, 2016, on NPR, https://web.archive.org/web/20160701010159/https://www.mprnews.org/story/2016/04/21/marvis-staples-song-once-helped-slaves-escape.

18 A. C. Thompson, Ali Winston, and Jake Hanrahan, "Ranks of Notorious Hate Group Include Active-Duty Military," ProPublica and *Frontline*, May 3, 2018, https://www.pbs.org/wgbh/frontline/article/ranks-of-notorious-hate-group-include-active-duty-military/.

19 "*Sines v. Kessler* Rush Transcript –Day 5: Natalie Romero and Devin Willis Testimony," Unicorn Riot, October 29, 2021, https://unicornriot.ninja/2021/sines-v-kessler-rush-transcript-day-5-natalie-romero-devin-willis-testimony/.

20 Second Amended Complaint, *Sines v. Kessler*, 55.

21 Joe Heim, "A Stark Contrast Inside and Outside Church During Torch March, *Washington Post*, August 19, 2017, https://www.washingtonpost.com/local/a-stark-contrast-inside-and-outside-a-charlottesville-church-during-the-torch-march/2017/08/19/a2311a7a-847a-11e7-902a-2a9f2d808496_story.html.

22 Amir Vera, "James Fields, Who Plowed His Car into Crowd at 2017 Charlottesville Rally, Gets Second Life Sentence," CNN, July 15, 2019, https://www.cnn.com/2019/07/15/us/charlottesville-james-fields-life-sentence.

23 Second Amended Complaint, *Sines v. Kessler*, 61.

24 "Extremist Files: Michael Tubbs," Southern Poverty Law Center, n.d., https://www.splcenter.org/resources/extremist-files/michael-ralph-tubbs.

25 Second Amended Complaint, *Sines v. Kessler*, 65.

26 Nicole Hemmer, host, "The Summer of Hate," *A12: The Story of Charlottesville* (podcast), Miller Center, University of Virginia, https://millercenter.org/A12.

27 Nora Neus, *24 Hours in Charlottesville*, 127.

28 "Cornel West & Rev. Traci Blackmon: Clergy in Charlottesville Were Trapped by Torch-Wielding Nazis," *Democracy Now!*, August 14, 2017, https://www.democracynow.org/2017/8/14/cornel_west_rev_toni_blackmon_clergy.

29 Nora Neus, *24 Hours in Charlottesville*, 131.

30 Nora Neus, *24 Hours in Charlottesville*, 147.

31 David Straughn, "I Witnessed Terrorism in Charlottesville from a Foot Away," *Scalawag*, August 16, 2017, https://scalawagmagazine.org/2017/08/i-witnessed-terrorism-in-charlottesville-from-a-foot-away/.

32 Yesha Callahan, "Interview: How Corey Long Fought White Supremacy with Fire," The Root, August 14, 2017, https://www.theroot.com/interview-how-corey-long-fought-whitesupremacy-with-f-1797831277?rev=1502737785317.

33 Ian Shapira, "Fourth Man Sentenced in Charlottesville Parking Garage Beating of Black Man," *Washington Post*, August 27, 2019, https://www.washingtonpost.com/local/fourth-attacker-sentenced-in-charlottesville-parking-garage-beating-of-black-man/2019/08/27/42b7c5a2-c82b-11e9-a1fe-ca46e8d573c0_story.html.

34 Callahan, "Interview: How Corey Long Fought White Supremacy."

35 Maggie Mallon, "Elizabeth Sines and Leanne Chia Were in Charlottesville When White Supremacists Descended—This Is What They Saw," *Glamour*, August 18, 2017.

36 Nora Neus, *24 Hours in Charlottesville*, 174.

37 Nora Neus, *24 Hours in Charlottesville*, 181.

38 Rachel Langlitz and Kelsie Metzgar, "Medical Examiner: Heather Heyer Died of Blunt Force Injury During 'Unite the Right' Rally," WSET, December 3, 2018, https://wset.com/news/local/medical-examiner-heather-heyer-died-of-blunt-force-injury-during-unite-the-right-rally.

39 Andrew Buncombe, "Heather Heyer Was Buried in Secret Grave to Protect It from neo-Nazis After Charlottesville, Reveals Mother," *Independent*, December 15, 2017, https://www.independent.co.uk/news/world/americas/heather-heyer-grave-secret-hide-nazis-charlottesville-attack-mother-reveals-a8113056.html.

40 Nora Neus, *24 Hours in Charlottesville*, 184.

41 Nora Neus, *24 Hours in Charlottesville*, 194.

42 Ashley Curtis, "Helicopter Footage Shows Troopers' 2017 Pursuit of Charlottesville Murderer," WSLS, July 17, 2019, https://www.wsls.com/news/2019/07/18/helicopter-footage-shows-troopers-2017-pursuit-of-charlottesville-murderer/.

43 Chris Suarez, "Rally Raises Issues of Military Members Involved in White Supremacy," *Daily Progress*, May 11, 2018, https://dailyprogress.com/news/local/rally-raises-issue-of-military-members-involved-in-white-supremacy/article_642fd8ce-5576-11e8-ab8a-374269c6fdfe.html.

44 Politico Staff, "Full text: Trump's Comments on White Supremacists, 'Alt-Left' in Charlottesville," Politico, August 15, 2017, https://www.politico.com/story/2017/08/15/full-text-trump-comments-white-supremacists-alt-left-transcript-241662.

45 Glenn Thrush and Maggie Haberman, "Trump Gives White Supremacists an Unequivocal Boost," *New York Times*, August 15, 2017, https://www.nytimes.com/2017/08/15/us/politics/trump-charlottesville-white-nationalists.html.

46 Second Amended Complaint, *Sines v. Kessler*, 83–5.

47 Hawes Spencer, "Court Orders Unite the Right Planners Pay Millions in Damages," *Daily Progress*, July 2, 2024, https://dailyprogress.com/news/local/crime-courts/article_d536851c-37f2-11ef-85ec-935cccfd98a7.html.

48 "James Alex Fields Jr. Sentenced: Man Gets Life Plus 419 Years in Deadly Charlottesville Car Attack," CBS News, July 15, 2019, https://www.cbsnews.com/news/james-alex-fields-jr-charlottesville-car-attack-sentenced-life-plus-419-years-today-2019-07-15/.

49 A. C. Thompson, Ali Winston, and Jake Hanrahan, "Ranks of Notorious Hate Group."

50 Paul Abowd, "Neo-Nazi 'Tyrone' Exposed as US Marine," Al Jazeera, April 17, 2018, https://www.aljazeera.com/news/2018/4/17/neo-nazi-tyrone-exposed-as-us-marine.

51 Kelly Weill, "Alt-Right Charlottesville Marcher Brandon Higgs Accused of Trying to Kill Black Men," *Daily Beast*, February 12, 2019, https://www.thedailybeast.com/alt-right-charlottesville-marcher-brandon-higgs-accused-of-trying-to-kill-black-men/.

52 Christopher Mathias, "White Supremacist Sentenced to 25 Years for Maryland Hate Crime Shooting of Black Man," *HuffPost*, September 23, 2020, https://www.huffpost.com/entry/brandon-higgs-sentenced-hate-crime-shooting-baltimore_n_5f6b6fadc5b6718910f4270b.

53 Christopher Mathias, "Go Back to Your Country, They Said," *HuffPost*, November 4, 2019, https://www.huffpost.com/feature/go-back-to-your-country.

54 Michael Edison Hayden, "U.S. State Department Official Involved in White Nationalist Movement, Hatewatch Determines," August 7, 2019, https://www.splcenter.org/resources/hatewatch/us-state-department-official-involved-white-nationalist-movement-hatewatch-determines/.

55 Chris Schiano, "Exposed: State Department Official Posted in Charlottesville Nazi Chats," Unicorn Riot, August 7, 2019, https://unicornriot.ninja/2019/exposed-state-department-official-posted-in-nazi-charlotteville-chats/.

57 "MakePals, Tim Manning, Columbia, SC," *Firestorm on Fascism* (blog), June 6, 2020, https://firestormonfash.noblogs.org/files/2020/06/Sanitized_Tim-Manning-Columbia-SC-%E2%80%93-Firestorm-On-Fascists.pdf.

58 Adam Mintzer, "Columbia Charter School Teacher Fired After Accusations of Writing Racial Slur on the Board," WIS10, October 22, 2021, https://www.wistv.com/2021/10/22/columbia-charter-school-teacher-fired-after-accusations-writing-racial-slur-board/.

60 (@IdentifyDixie), "CONTENT WARNING: This thread contains descriptions of murder and language used by racists.1) Identity Dixie member James Lee Ginther III committed . . . ," July 1, 2020, 8:18pm, https://web.archive.org/web/20200703184718/https://twitter.com/IdentifyDixie/status/1278513350511603713.

61 "Next Bond Hearing for Ex-Husband Charged with Kidnapping and Murdering Sumter Woman," ABC Columbia, November 29, 2017, https://www.abccolumbia.com/2017/11/29/bond-denied-for-ex-husband-charged-with-kidnapping-and-murdering-sumter-woman/.

62 Ken Bell, "Woman's Ex Guilty of Her Murder, Gets Life," *Sumter Item*, April 14, 2019, https://eta.creativecirclecdn.com/sumter/files/20190413-211032-041419.pdf.

63 Shane Burley, "Why Charlottesville?," *Protean Magazine*, August 12, 2020, https://proteanmag.com/2020/08/12/why-charlottesville/.

CHAPTER 11 **Good Night White Pride**

1 Stephanie Mencimer, "Does Kris Kobach Have White Nationalists on His Campaign Payroll?," *Mother Jones*, August 4, 2018, https://www.motherjones.com/politics/2018/08/does-kris-kobach-have-white-nationalists-on-his-campaign-payroll/.

2 Hatewatch Staff, "'10,000 of Us Can Be James Allsup': White Nationalists Are Getting Involved in Local GOP Politics," August 28, 2018, https://www.splcenter.org/resources

/hatewatch/10000-us-can-be-james-allsup-white-nationalists-are-getting-involved-local
-gop-politics/.

3 "Message from @Reinhard Wolff," Unicorn Riot Discord Leaks, October 24, 2017,
https://discordleaks.unicornriot.ninja/discord/view/1356365?q=GOP#msg.

4 "Panic in the Discord of Identity Evropa," *Panic! In the Discord* (blog), March 10, 2019,
https://panicinthediscord.noblogs.org/post/2019/03/10/ciao-mondo/.

5 Chris Schiano and Freddy Martinez, "Neo-Nazi Hipsters Identity Evropa Exposed
in Discord Chat Leak," Unicorn Riot, March 6, 2019, https://unicornriot.ninja/2019
/neo-nazi-hipsters-identity-evropa-exposed-in-discord-chat-leak/.

8 Alex Kotch, "Koch Network Alums Are Going Full-On White Nationalist," Sludge,
May 30, 2019, https://readsludge.com/2019/05/30/koch-network-alums-are-going
-full-on-white-nationalist/.

9 "Kevin Pummill: The 'Undercover Academic' Exposed," *Washington Nazi Watch* (blog),
April 19, 2019, https://identifyevropa.org/kevin-pummill-undercover-academic/.

10 Howard Packowitz, "Teacher Accused of Making Racist Posts Has Twin-City Ties,"
WJBC AM 1230, April 24, 2019, https://www.wjbc.com/2019/04/24/teacher-accused
-of-making-racist-posts-has-twin-city-ties/.

12 "Howard J. Fezell, Former NRA Director, Exposed as Member of Identity Evropa,"
March 15, 2019, https://panicinthediscord.noblogs.org/post/2019/03/15/howard-j
-fezell-former-nra-director-exposed-as-member-of-identity-evropa/.

13 "Message from @Singleton Mosby WV," Unicorn Riot Discord Leaks, October 24,
2019, https://discordleaks.unicornriot.ninja/discord/view/1717956#msg.

14 Kelly Weill, "Cop Working at High School Revealed as White Nationalist Organizer,"
Daily Beast, March 18, 2019, https://www.thedailybeast.com/virginia-cop-daniel-morley
-revealed-as-identity-evropa-member/.

15 "Virginia Police Officer Fired After White Nationalist Probe," Associated Press, April 18,
2019, https://apnews.com/article/79470ff7f8b949b58744df27795c9baf.

17 Christopher Mathias, "After HuffPost Investigation, 4 White Nationalists Out of U.S.
Military—but Others Allowed to Remain," *HuffPost*, August 7, 2019, https://www.huff
post.com/entry/white-nationalists-military-kicked-out-huffpost-investigation_n_5d4b
0f83e4b0066eb70b9945.

18 Chris Schiano, "Identity Evropa Struggles to Gain Footing After Rebranding as Patriot
Group," Unicorn Riot, April 15, 2019, https://unicornriot.ninja/2019/identity-evropa
-struggles-to-gain-footing-after-rebranding-as-patriot-group/.

19 Chris Schiano, "Identity Evropa, Rebranded: Six Months Later," Unicorn Riot, September 30, 2019, https://unicornriot.ninja/2019/identity-evropa-rebranded-six-months
-later/.

20 Patrick Casey, "Building Upon Our Success: The Disbanding of AIM," *American Identity
Movement* (blog), November 2, 2020, https://archive.is/9bOvN.

21 "Master Sergeant Cory Reeves Exposed as White Supremacist Organizer (CO),"
Colorado Springs Anti-Fascists (blog), April 8, 2019, https://cospringsantifa.noblogs
.org/post/2019/04/08/master-sergeant-cory-reeves-exposed-as-white-supremacist
-organizer/.

22   Christopher Mathias, "Exposed: Military Investigating 4 More Servicemen for Ties to White Nationalist Group," *HuffPost*, April 27, 2019, https://www.huffpost.com/entry /white-nationalists-military-identity-evropa_n_5cc1a87ee4b0764d31dd839c.

23   David Roza, "Air Force Finally Kicks Out Senior NCO Demoted for White Nationalist Ties," Task & Purpose, September 10, 2020, https://taskandpurpose.com/news /air-force-white-nationalist-discharged/.

24   Michael Roberts, "Fascist Groups' Propaganda War on Denver and the Front Range," *Westword*, September 5, 2018, https://www.westword.com/news/fascist-groups-identity -evropa-and-patriot-front-and-their-propaganda-war-on-colorado-10729624.

25   "Identity Evropa and Patriot Front," *Colorado Springs Anti-Fascists* (blog), August 18, 2018, https://cospringsantifa.noblogs.org/post/2018/08/18/identity-evropa-and-patriot -front/#more-1858.

26   Michael Roberts, "Alt-Right Impersonating Antifa in Disinformation Campaign, Activist Says," *Westword*, August 31, 2018, https://www.westword.com/news/colorado-springs-anti -fascists-decry-alt-right-antifa-disinformation-campaign-9461780.

27   Heidi Beedle (@jsphnthsngr), "So I guess it is time to come clean. They are kinda right. You know what they say about broken clocks. I did start the @COSAntifa account," Twitter, October 14, 2019, 7:51pm, http://web.archive.org/web/20191015040141/https:// twitter.com/jsphnthsngr/status/1183938325033304067.

28   Dan MacGuill, "Did a Dominion Voting Systems Employee Brag About Rigging the Election Against Trump?," Snopes, November 20, 2020, https://www.snopes.com /fact-check/eric-coomer-dominion-trump/.

29   Tierney Speed and Katelyn Polantz, "Trump Allies Did Little to Investigate Election Fraud Claims, Court Documents Show," CNN, October 7, 2021, https://www.cnn.com /2021/10/07/politics/giuliani-powell-voter-fraud-claims-vetting-eric-coomer.

30   Alan Feuer, "Trump Campaign Knew Lawyers' Voting Machine Claims Were Baseless, Memo Shows," *New York Times*, September 21, 2021, https://www.nytimes.com/2021 /09/21/us/politics/trump-dominion-voting.html.

31   Sworn Statement of Joseph Oltmann, *Coomer v. Trump*, Civil Action cv–34319 (Denver Dist. Ct., 2020), https://www.courts.state.co.us/userfiles/file/Court_Probation/02nd_Judicial _District/Denver_District_Court/Cases%20of%20Interest/20CV34319/003/1283.pdf.

32   Lewis Pennock, "Activist Who Founded Banned Antifa Twitter Account Is Trans Former Teacher," *Mail Online*, December 20, 2022, https://www.dailymail.co.uk/news/article -11558861/Left-wing-activist-founded-banned-Antifa-Twitter-account-former-teacher.html.

33   "Colorado Springs Gay Club Shooter's Case Heads to Trial," Associated Press, February 23, 2023, https://www.kttc.com/2023/02/23/judge-finds-evidence-try-suspect-attack-gay -club/?outputType=amp.

CHAPTER 12   **A Little Army**

1   Chris Schiano and Dan Feidt, "Patriot Front Fascist Leak Exposes Nationwide Racist Campaigns," Unicorn Riot, January 21, 2022, https://unicornriot.ninja/2022/patriot -front-fascist-leak-exposes-nationwide-racist-campaigns/.

2   Renee Bracey Sherman and Lizz Winstead, "Anti-abortion Rally Draws Thousands in D.C.," NBC News, January 25, 2022, https://www.nbcnews.com/think/opinion /patriot-front-s-anti-abortion-advocacy-march-life-sends-clear-ncna1287952.

3   Michael Edison Hayden, "Prolific Alt-Right Propagandist's Identity Confirmed," Hatewatch, May 1, 2019, https://www.splcenter.org/resources/hatewatch/prolific -alt-right-propagandists-identity-confirmed/.

4   Megan Squire, Jeff Tischauser, and Michael Edison Hayden, "One in Five Patriot Front Applicants Claim Military Ties," Hatewatch, February 1, 2022, https://www.splcenter .org/resources/hatewatch/one-five-patriot-front-applicants-claim-military-ties/.

5   Christopher Mathias and Ali Winston, "Inside Patriot Front: The Masked White Supremacists on a Nationwide Hate Crime Spree," *HuffPost*, February 10, 2022, https:// www.huffpost.com/entry/patriot-front-white-supremacist-group-hate-crime-vandalism _n_620293abe4b0725faad01783.

6   Dan Goodin, "A White Supremacist Website Got Hacked, Airing All Its Dirty Laundry," *Ars Technica*, January 24, 2022, https://arstechnica.com/information-technology/2022 /01/data-leak-from-neo-nazi-site-shows-members-conspiring-in-hate-crimes/.

7   Tess Owen, "Leaked Chats Reveal Fascist Group Patriot Front Shames Members About Their Porn, Junk Food Habits," *Vice*, January 26, 2022, https://www.vice.com/en/article /patriot-front-leaked-chats-porn-habits/.

8   Sunny South Dallas AFA (@pegasusAFA), "For those keeping score at home, anti-fascists are stacking up the count of Patriot Front membership identified. We person-ally didn't know you could stack shit," Twitter, February 23, 2022, 4:50am, https:// web.archive.org/web/20220223045535/https://twitter.com/PegasusAFA/status /1496346777234120706.

10 Henry Larson, "CU Boulder Enrolled Alleged White Supremacist with Knowledge of His Past," *CU Independent*, March 9, 2023, https://www.cuindependent.com/2023/01 /30/cu-enrolled-alleged-white-supremacist-with-knowledge-of-his-past/.

11 Megan Squire, Jeff Tischauer, and Michael Edison Hayden, "One in Five Patriot Front Applicants."

12 The Activated Podcast (@activatedpod), "ICYMI: Yesterday we identified a Patriot Front prospect as San Diego local Victor Krvaric. Victor is corporal in the Marine Corps Reserve," Twitter, February 2, 2022, 9:30am, https://twitter.com/TheActivatedPod/status /1488882551393374211.

13 Bella Ross and Brendan Tuccinardi, "College Republicans Lean into Right-wing Rebrand in Return to Campus," *Daily Aztec*, October 30, 2019, https://thedailyaztec.com/96610 /news/college-republicans-lean-into-right-wing-rebrand-in-return-to-campus/.

14 Jason Hopkins, "'I Find It Unconscionable': College GOP Leader Urges Trump to End Guest Worker Programs Amid Record Job Losses," Daily Caller, May 26, 2020, https:// dailycaller.com/2020/05/26/college-republican-guest-worker-tucker-carlson-trump -immigration/.

15 Gary Warth, "San Diego County GOP Head Explains Old Video Showing Him with Nazi Images," *Los Angeles Times*, August 25, 2020, https://www.latimes.com/california /story/2020-08-24/old-video-shows-local-gop-head-with-images-of-hitler.

16 Amita Sharma, "Marine Investigation Finds Former GOP Chair's Son Engaged in Misconduct," KPBS Public Media, March 28, 2022, https://www.kpbs.org/news/local /2022/03/28/marine-investigation-former-gop-chairs-son-engaged-misconduct.

17 Will Carless, "Ex-GOP Student Leader's Links to Jan. 6 Capitol Riot and a neo-Nazi Web Site," *USA Today*, December 28, 2023, https://www.usatoday.com/story/news/ investigations/2023/12/28/oliver-krvaric-jan-6-capitol-riot/71971697007/.

18 David Gotfredson, "Report: Victor Krvaric Posted 'Racist' Messages, Suggested Fire-bombing Homeless Encampments," Cbs8.Com, December 26, 2024, https://www.cbs8 .com/article/news/local/report-victor-krvaric-posted-racist-messages-homeless -encampment-damage/509-14178f7b-ac67-4460-9519-2b050fbda0b5.

19 City News Service, "Son of Ex-county GOP Chair Pleads No Contest to Assault Weapon Possession," Cbs8.Com, November 26, 2024, https://www.cbs8.com/article /news/local/son-of-ex-county-gop-chair-pleads-no-contest-to-assault-weapon -possession/509-e574cda0-4c6d-49e2-a33a-2ef28273c9b9.

20 Wikipedia contributors, "Amy Freeze," Wikipedia, n.d., https://en.wikipedia.org/wiki /Amy_Freeze.

21 "Students Put Cheer in Their Marriage," Church News, February 4, 1995, https://www .thechurchnews.com/1995/2/4/23255899/students-put-cheer-in-their-marriage/.

22 Federal Trade Commission and Food and Drug Administration, "Warning Letter," FDA.gov, November 28, 2011, https://web.archive.org/web/20120107194130/https:// www.fda.gov/ICECI/EnforcementActions/WarningLetters/ucm281554.htm.

23 Amy Freeze, "America the Beautiful: Fox Weather's Amy Freeze Shares Love for Family and Country," Fox Weather, June 19, 2023, YouTube video, 0:59, https://www.youtube .com/watch?v=ZSJjij26x6s.

24 "Tyler Russell Arbuckle of Utah Identified as Member of Neo-Nazi Organization Patriot Front," *Texas Against Fascism*, February 23, 2022, https://texasantifa.noblogs.org/tyler -russell-arbuckle-utah-united-states-air-force-emt-patriot-front-member/.

25 "Message from PF-520619," Unicorn Riot Discord Leaks, November 16, 2021, https:// discordleaks.unicornriot.ninja/rocket-chat/message/7e7dac53-f4b6-4178-804f -cf42a18144c4.

26 "Logan Plank aka Patriot Front Member Clarke IL, an STL-area, Sheet Metal Union (SMART 36) Applicant, Son of Wood River, IL Councilman Jeremy Plank and Bethalto Teacher Tiffany Plank," *Chicago Anti-Fascists* (blog), January 22, 2022, https://antifascist chicago.noblogs.org/post/2022/01/22/logan-plank-stl-area-a-sheet-metal-union-smart -36-member-son-of-wood-river-il-councilman-jeremy-plank/.

27 "Wood River," History and Social Justice at Tougaloo College, n.d., https://justice .tougaloo.edu/sundowntown/wood-river-il/.

28 Jeff Tischauser, "Patriot Front Linked to Accused St. Louis Mural Vandal," April 14, 2022, https://www.splcenter.org/resources/hatewatch/white-nationalists-linked -accused-st-louis-mural-vandal-identified/.

29 Chris Schiano, "Patriot Front Neo-Nazis Tied to Springfield, IL Hate Crime," Unicorn Riot, August 23, 2022, https://unicornriot.ninja/2022/patriot-front-neo-nazis-tied-to -springfield-il-hate-crime/.

30 Aliana Mediratta, "Man Who Vandalized South 40 Underpass Receives Two Years Probation," *Student Life - The Independent Newspaper of Washington University in St. Louis*, October 25, 2024, https://www.studlife.com/news/2024/10/23/man-who-vandalized-south-40-underpass-receives-two-years-probation.

31 Case Supplemental Report, *City of Olympia v. Simpson*, Case No. 2022424, (Olympia Municipal Court, 2022), https://unicornriot.ninja/wp-content/uploads/2022/07/2022424_Documents-Redacted.pdf.

32 "White Nationalists Convicted of Planning to Riot at Idaho Pride Event," Associated Press, July 21, 2023, https://www.nbcnews.com/nbc-out/out-news/white-nationalists-convicted-planning-riot-idaho-pride-event-rcna95493.

33 Christopher Mathias, "The Far-Right's Assault on an Idaho Pride Event Was Meticulously Planned," *HuffPost*, June 20, 2022, https://www.huffpost.com/entry/groomer-panic-idaho-white-supremacists-lgbtq_n_62acc960e4b06594c1d6348b.

34 Garfield but Antifascist (@AntifaGarfield), "We can now confirm that arrested and humiliated neo-Nazi and Patriot Front member Jared Boyce goes by 'Logan UT' in Patriot Front chats," Twitter, June 28, 2022, 2:14pm, https://x.com/AntifaGarfield/status/1538223748171579394.

35 Kate Briquelet and Justin Rohrlich, "'Pack Your Stuff and Get Out of My House,' Says Patriot Front Member's Mom," *Daily Beast*, June 13, 2022, https://www.thedailybeast.com/pack-your-stuff-and-get-out-of-my-house-says-patriot-front-members-mom/.

36 Mack Lamoureux, "Why Do Neo-Nazis Keep Getting Arrested for Child Sexual Abuse Material?," *Vice*, July 20, 2023, https://www.vice.com/en/article/why-do-neo-nazis-keep-getting-arrested-for-child-porn/.

37 "Branden Mitchel Haney, neo-Nazi Flight Student," *Utah Antifascists* (blog), July 15, 2022, https://utah161.noblogs.org/post/2022/07/15/branden-mitchel-haney-neo-nazi-flight-student/.

38 William L. Spence, "Idaho Patriot Front Member Arrested in Coeur D'Alene a National Guard Member with a WSU Scholarship," *Spokesman Review*, June 16, 2022, https://www.spokesman.com/stories/2022/jun/16/idaho-patriot-front-member-arrested-in-coeur-dalen/.

39 Chris Schiano, "Two Patriot Front Members Charged for Defacing Gay Pride Mural," Unicorn Riot, July 17, 2022, https://unicornriot.ninja/2022/two-patriot-front-members-charged-for-defacing-gay-pride-mural/.

40 Western States Center et al., "Letter Requesting the DOJ Investigate Patriot Front," Western States Center, July 28, 2022, https://www.westernstatescenter.org/request-to-investigate-patriot-front.

41 Brandi Buchman, "Black Musician Sues White Supremacist Group for 'Coordinated, Brutal, and Racially Motivated Attack' That Left Him Injured, Traumatized," Law & Crime, August 10, 2023, https://lawandcrime.com/lawsuit/black-musician-sues-white-supremacist-group-for-coordinated-brutal-and-racially-motivated-attack-that-left-him-injured-traumatized/.

42 "Lawyers' Committee Files Lawsuit Against Patriot Front Members for Vandalism & Intimidation," *Lawyers' Committee for Civil Rights Under Law* (press release), October 18,

2022, https://www.lawyerscommittee.org/lawyers-committee-files-lawsuit-against -patriot-front-members-for-vandalism-intimidation/.

43 Bret Pallotto, "PA Man Facing Hate Crime Charge After Striking a Woman at Downtown State College Store," *Centre Daily Times*, June 27, 2022, https://www.centredaily .com/news/local/crime/article262921618.html.

44 Patriot Front Neo-Nazis Exposed in Parking Lot Clusterf*ck," Unicorn Riot, September 20, 2022, YouTube video, 1:01:37, https://www.youtube.com/watch?v=MGq4hpIchRY.

45 12 On Your Side Digital Team, "Richmond Man Faces Charges in 2021 U.S. Capitol Breach," 12 On Your Side, April 22, 2024, https://www.12onyourside.com/2024/04/22 /richmond-man-faces-charges-2021-us-capitol-breach/.

46 "Daniel Turetchi is Grand MD," *Antifa Seven Hills* (blog), January 21, 2022, https://web .archive.org/web/20221001004204/https://torchantifa.org/daniel-turetchi-patriot-front/.

47 "Daniel Turetchi," *Sedition Hunters* (blog), April 27, 2024, https://seditionhunters.org /daniel-turetchi/.

48 Antifa Seven Hills and NYC Antifa, "Paul Michael Gancarz," *Antifa Seven Hills* (blog), January 20, 2022, https://web.archive.org/web/20220612020751/https://torchantifa .org/paul-gancarz-patriot-front/.

49 "HRBT Expansion Project," Virginia Department of Transportation, n.d., https:// hrbtexpansion.vdot.virginia.gov/.

50 "Message from PF-327302," Unicorn Riot Discord Leaks, December 8, 2021, https:// discordleaks.unicornriot.ninja/rocket-chat/message/d050d74c-dab1-4b3f-af3b -0467512306ee.

51 "Message from PF-3194," Unicorn Riot Discord Leaks, December 5, 2021, https:// discordleaks.unicornriot.ninja/rocket-chat/message/1ab35ea8-a2d7-4b0c-9ef9 -f7d204d25f18.

52 "Message from PF-3194," Unicorn Riot Discord Leaks, December 12, 2021, https:// discordleaks.unicornriot.ninja/rocket-chat/message/cb28bbdd-1464-4b81-ac32-b79b f16cb3d9.

CHAPTER 13 **Antifa Supersoldiers**

1 Shawn Musgrave, "White House 'Antifa' Petition Written by Pro-Trump Troll," Politico, August 24, 2017, https://www.politico.com/story/2017/08/24/antifa-white-house -petition-trump-troll-241990.

2 KTNV Staff, "LIST: Guns and Evidence from Las Vegas Shooter Stephen Paddock," KTNV, January 20, 2018, https://www.ktnv.com/news/las-vegas-shooting/list-guns -and-evidence-from-las-vegas-shooter-stephen-paddock.

3 Detective Trevor Alsup et al., "LVMD Preliminary Investigative Report: 1 October / Mass Casualty Shooting," Las Vegas Metropolitan Police Department, January 18, 2018, https://www.lvmpd.com/home/showpublisheddocument/132/638298568303630000.

4 Michael Edison Hayden, "Las Vegas Shooter Stephen Paddock Was 'Antifa,' According to Persistent Alt-Right Conspiracy," *Newsweek*, October 3, 2017, https://www.newsweek .com/alt-right-conspiracy-theories-blame-antifa-mass-shooting-las-vegas-677075.

5 Saranac Hale Spencer, "No Evidence Linking Vegas Shooter to Antifa, FactCheck.org, October 5, 2017, https://www.factcheck.org/2017/10/no-evidence-linking-vegas-shooter-antifa/.

6 Brett Barrouquere, "Las Vegas Shooter Went on Antigovernment Rant Before Massacre: 'Sometimes Sacrifices Have to Be Made,'" May 18, 2018, https://www.splcenter.org/resources/hatewatch/las-vegas-shooter-went-antigovernment-rant-massacre-sometimes-sacrifices-have-be-made/.

7 Anna Merlan, "The Abortion Rights Group Other Activists Want Nothing to Do With," *Vice*, August 4, 2024, https://www.vice.com/en/article/the-abortion-rights-group-other-activists-want-nothing-to-do-with/.

8 David Neiwert, "Far-right Conspiracists Stir up Hysteria About Nonexistent 'Civil War' Plot by 'Antifa,'" November 14, 2017, Hatewatch, https://www.splcenter.org/resources/hatewatch/far-right-conspiracists-stir-hysteria-about-nonexistent-civil-war-plot-antifa/.

9 Michael Edison Hayden, "'Antifa Supersoldiers' Are Coming to Kill White People Within Days: Right Wing Conspiracy," *Newsweek*, November 2, 2017, https://www.newsweek.com/antifa-supersoldiers-coming-kill-white-people-right-wing-conspiracy-699037.

10 Ashley Feinberg, "This Is MSNBC's De Facto Ombudsman," *HuffPost*, December 7, 2017, https://www.huffpost.com/entry/cernovich-sam-seder-msnbc-twitter-rape_n_5a26bb8fe4b06d807b4f6557.

11 Patrick Strickland, "Far Right Pushes Conspiracy Theories After Texas Attack," Al Jazeera, November 8, 2017, https://www.aljazeera.com/news/2017/11/8/far-right-pushes-conspiracy-theories-after-texas-attack.

12 Saranac Hale Spencer, "Texas Shooting Unrelated to Antifa," Factcheck.org, November 8, 2017, https://www.factcheck.org/2017/11/texas-shooting-unrelated-antifa/.

13 Corky Siemaszko and Alex Johnson, "Texas Shooter Had a 'Purpose and a Mission' in Family Feud, Investigators Say," NBC News, November 6, 2017, https://www.nbcnews.com/storyline/texas-church-shooting/texas-church-shooter-may-have-been-targeting-his-mother-law-n817961.

14 Arun Gupta, "Portland's Andy Ngo Is the Most Dangerous Grifter in America," *Jacobin*, August 16, 2019, https://jacobin.com/2019/08/andy-ngo-right-wing-antifa-protest-portland-bigotry.

15 Andy Ngo, "A Leftist Mob 'Polices' Portland," *Wall Street Journal*, October 11, 2018, https://www.wsj.com/articles/a-leftist-mob-polices-portland-1539298766.

16 Shane Dixon Kavanaugh, "Bear Spray, Bloody Brawls at Patriot Prayer 'Law and Order' March in Portland," *Oregonlive*, October 13, 2018, https://www.oregonlive.com/portland/2018/10/patriot_prayer_flash_march_cal.html.

17 Alex Zielinski, "Undercover in Patriot Prayer: Insights from a Vancouver Democrat Who's Been Working Against the Far-Right Group from the Inside," *Portland Mercury*, August 26, 2019, https://www.portlandmercury.com/news/2019/08/26/27039560/undercover-in-patriot-prayer-insights-from-a-vancouver-democrat-whos-been-working-against-the-far-right-group-from-the-inside.

18 "Patriot Prayer Members Gets 3 Days Jail for Riot Conviction," Associated Press, August 2, 2022, https://www.seattletimes.com/seattle-news/patriot-prayer-member-gets-3-days-in-jail-for-portland-riot-conviction/.

19 Alex Zielinski, "Patriot Prayer's Joey Gibson Faces Felony Charge for May Day Brawl," *Portland Mercury*, August 15, 2019, https://www.portlandmercury.com/news/2019/08/15/26978277/patriot-prayers-joey-gibson-faces-felony-charge-for-may-day-brawl.

20 Mike Brest, "Journalist Describes Police Not Intervening When Antifa Assaulted Him," Daily Caller, May 2, 2019, https://dailycaller.com/2019/05/02/ngo-antifa-assualt-tucker-carlson-portland/.

21 Hannah Gais, "The Making of Andy Ngo," *Jewish Currents*, October 18, 2022, https://jewishcurrents.org/the-making-of-andy-ngo.

22 Madeleine Ngo, "Ted Cruz Demands Federal Inquiry of Portland Mayor After Antifa Attack on Conservative Journalist," *Dallas News*, July 1, 2019, https://www.dallasnews.com/news/politics/2019/07/01/ted-cruz-demands-federal-inquiry-of-portland-mayor-after-antifa-attack-on-conservative-journalist/.

23 Bill Cassidy and Ted Cruz, "Cassidy, Cruz: Antifa Is a Domestic Terrorist Organization," Office of Senator Bill Cassidy (press release), July 18, 2019, https://www.cassidy.senate.gov/newsroom/press-releases/cassidy-cruz-antifa-is-a-domestic-terrorist-organization/.

24 Joshua Nelson, "Journalist Attacked by Antifa: 'Criminal Cartel' Wants Violent Revolution, Should Be Designated as Terror Organization," Fox News, July 29, 2019, https://www.foxnews.com/media/andy-ngo-attacked-trump-should-designate-antifa-terror-organization.

25 Christopher Mathias and Andy Campbell, "Proud Boys, Outnumbered by Anti-fascists, Get Police Escort After 30-Minute Rally," *HuffPost*, August 20, 2019, https://www.huffpost.com/entry/proud-boys-portland-rally_n_5d59390ee4b0eb875f2539c4.

26 Sarah Taddeo, "75-year-old Buffalo Man Shoved by Police Speaks Out on Incident After Month in Hospital," *USA Today*, August 30, 2020, https://www.usatoday.com/story/news/nation/2020/08/31/buffalo-man-martin-gugino-talks-recovery-after-police-shoved-him/3445610001/.

27 "'His Brain Is Injured': Lawyer Updates on 75-Year-Old NY Protester Shoved by Police," NBC New York, June 11, 2020, https://www.nbcnewyork.com/news/local/75-year-old-buffalo-protester-hospitalized-after-cop-shove-suffered-brain-injury-lawyer/2457512/.

28 Maki Becker, "One Year Later Martin Gugino Looks Back and Hopes He Made a Difference," June 4, 2021, https://buffalonews.com/news/local/crime-courts/one-year-later-martin-gugino-looks-back-and-hopes-he-made-a-difference/article_a8aeed9a-c47d-11eb-8ad7-73d2819f95f9.html.

29 Jeremy Varon, "Martin Gugino – the 'Buffalo Protestor' and Our Friend," Witness Against Torture, June 20, 2020, https://witnessagainsttorture.com/2020/10/07/martin-gugino-the-buffalo-protestor-and-our-friend/.

30 Mike Desmond and Omar Fetouh, "GRAPHIC VIDEO: Two Buffalo Police Officers Suspended After Elderly Man Shoved and Injured," Buffalo Toronto Public Media, June 10, 2020, https://www.btpm.org/local/2020-06-04/graphic-video-two-buffalo-police-officers-suspended-after-elderly-man-shoved-and-injured.

31 Investigative Post Staff, "Police Assault Injures Protester," Investigative Post, June 5, 2020, https://www.investigativepost.org/2020/06/04/police-protesters-give-peace-a-chance/.

32 "President Trump Tweets 'Antifa' Conspiracy Theory that Originated on Anonymous Blog," NBC News, June 9, 2020, https://www.nbcnews.com/tech/social-media/president -trump-tweets-antifa-conspiracy-theory-originated-anonymous-blog-n1228356.

33 Robert Mackey, "Trump's New Favorite Channel, OAN, Keeps Lying About Buffalo Protester Assaulted by Police," *The Intercept*, June 19, 2020, https://theintercept.com/2020/06 /16/trumps-new-favorite-channel-oan-keeps-lying-buffalo-protester-assaulted-police/.

34 Larry Buchanan, Quoctrung Bui, and Jugal K. Patel, "Black Lives Matter May Be the Largest Movement in U.S. History," *New York Times*, July 3, 2020, https://www.nytimes .com/interactive/2020/07/03/us/george-floyd-protests-crowd-size.html.

35 Sam Jones, "US Crisis Monitor Releases Full Data for 2020," ACLED, February 5, 2021, https://acleddata.com/press/us-crisis-monitor-releases-full-data-2020.

36 Christopher Mathias, "The Real Looters of the Bronx," *HuffPost*, June 24, 2020, https://www.huffpost.com/entry/real-looters-bronx-protest-racial-justice_n_5eec c6bfc5b6722102268262.

37 Tobi Haslett, "Magic Actions," *N+1*, August 20, 2021, https://www.nplusonemag.com /issue-40/politics/magic-actions-2/.

38 Geoff Kelly, "Scant Proof of 'Outside Agitators,'" Investigative Post, June 5, 2020, https://www.investigativepost.org/2020/06/05/scant-proof-of-outside-agitators/.

39 Alfred A. Brophy, *Reconstructing the Dreamland: The Tulsa Riot of 1921* (New York: Oxford University Press, 2002), 70.

40 "Negroes Beware / Do Not Attend Communist Meetings," Alabama Department of Archives and History, 1930–1930, https://digital.archives.alabama.gov/digital/collection /voices/id/2020.

41 David Neiwert, *The Age of Insurrection: The Radical Right's Assault on American Democracy* (Brooklyn, NY: Melville House, 2023), 331–60.

42 scott crow, "Anarchists Respond to Accusations of Violence at Justice for George Floyd Demonstrations," Agency, June 1, 2020, https://anarchistagency.com/anarchists-respond -to-accusations-of-violence-at-justice-for-george-floyd-demonstrations/.

43 Davey Alba, "Misinformation About George Floyd Protests Surge on Social Media," *New York Times*, June 1, 2020, https://www.nytimes.com/2020/06/01/technology /george-floyd-misinformation-online.html.

44 Ben Collins and Brandy Zadrozny, "In Klamath Falls, Oregon, Victory Declared over Antifa, Which Never Showed Up," NBC News, June 6, 2020, https://www.nbcnews .com/tech/social-media/klamath-falls-oregon-victory-declared-over-antifa-which-never -showed-n1226681.

45 Ben Collins and Brandy Zadrozny, "Antifa Rumors Spread on Local Social Media with No Evidence," NBC News, June 2, 2020, https://www.nbcnews.com/tech/tech-news /antifa-rumors-spread-local-social-media-no-evidence-n1222486.

46 Christopher Mathias, "Living with the Far-Right Insurgency in Idaho," *HuffPost*, May 19, 2022, https://www.huffpost.com/entry/far-right-idaho_n_628277e2e4b 0c84db7282bd6.

47 Claire Galofaro and Michael Kunzelman, "Trump, Social Media, Right-Wing News Stir Up Antifa Scares," Associated Press, September 3, 2020, https://apnews.com/article

/race-and-ethnicity-media-social-media-kentucky-racial-injustice-97624252a276dea5c
fe2e79381df0248.

48 Scottie Andrew and Hallie Silverman, "Oregon Residents are Illegally Stopping Drivers
at Gunpoint During Wildfire Evacuations, Sheriff Says," CNN, September 14, 2020,
https://www.cnn.com/2020/09/14/us/oregon-armed-checkpoints-wildfires-looting
-trnd.

49 Luke Mogelson, "In the Streets with Antifa," *The New Yorker*, October 25, 2020, https://
www.newyorker.com/magazine/2020/11/02/trump-antifa-movement-portland.

50 Harmeet Kaur, "5 Reasons Why Experts Say We Should Be Wary of 'Outside Agitator'
Narrative," CNN, June 4, 2020, https://edition.cnn.com/2020/06/04/us/outside
-agitator-label-history-trnd/index.html.

51 Christopher Mathias, "White Vigilantes Have Always Had a Friend in Police," *HuffPost*,
August 30, 2020, https://www.huffpost.com/entry/white-vigilantes-kenosha_n_5f
4822bcc5b6cf66b2b5103e.

52 Patrick Strickland, "Antifa and America's Revamped Red Scare," Al Jazeera, November 17, 2021, https://www.aljazeera.com/features/2020/9/29/antifa-hysteria-americas
-revamped-red-scare.

53 Sam Jones, "US Crisis Monitor Releases Full Data for 2020," ACLED, February 5, 2021,
https://acleddata.com/press/us-crisis-monitor-releases-full-data-2020.

54 Christopher Mathias, "57 GOP State and Local Officials Were at the Capitol Insurrection," *HuffPost*, February 15, 2021, https://www.huffpost.com/entry/57-gop-officials
-at-capitol-insurrection_n_6026e5e2c5b6f88289fb90a6.

55 Michael M. Grynbaum, Reid J. Epstein, and Davey Alba, "How Pro-Trump Forces Pushed
a Lie About Antifa at the Capitol Riot," *New York Times*, March 1, 2021, https://www
.nytimes.com/2021/03/01/us/politics/antifa-conspiracy-capitol-riot.html.

56 Meg Anderson, "Antifa Didn't Storm the Capitol. Just Ask the Rioters," NPR, March 2,
2021, https://www.npr.org/2021/03/02/972564176/antifa-didnt-storm-the-capitol
-just-ask-the-rioters.

57 Christopher Mathias, "Tucker Carlson's Jan. 6 'Documentary' Is His Most Nakedly
Fascist Piece of Propaganda Yet," *HuffPost*, November 18, 2021, https://www.huffpost
.com/entry/tucker-carlson-patriot-purge-is-fascist-january-6-revisionism_n_6192b4a9e
4b05e93cbb3c1d7.

CHAPTER 14 **To Catch an Anti-Fascist**

1 Tim Dickinson, "He Infiltrated a Notorious White Nationalist Group. Now, He's
Being Sued for Exposing Them," *Rolling Stone*, August 10, 2023, https://www.rolling
stone.com/politics/politics-features/white-nationalist-patriot-front-antifa-lawsuit
-1234804251/.

2 Kim Kelly, "'If Others Have Rifles, We'll Have Rifles': Why US Leftist Groups Are Taking
Up Arms," *Guardian*, July 22, 2019, https://www.theguardian.com/us-news/2019/jul
/22/if-others-have-rifles-well-have-rifles-why-leftist-groups-are-taking-up-arms.

3 Hannah Allam, "'I Am Antifa': One Activist's Violent Death Became a Symbol for the Right and Left," NPR, July 23, 2020, https://www.npr.org/2020/07/23/893533916/i-am-antifa-one-activist-s-violent-death-became-a-symbol-for-the-right-and-left.

4 CrimethInc. Ex-Workers Collective, "On Willem Van Spronsen & His Final Statement," It's Going Down, July 14, 2019, https://itsgoingdown.org/on-williem-van-spronsen/.

5 Hannah Allam, "'I Am Antifa': One Activist's Violent Death Became a Symbol for the Right and Left," NPR, July 23, 2020, https://www.npr.org/2020/07/23/893533916/i-am-antifa-one-activist-s-violent-death-became-a-symbol-for-the-right-and-left.

6 John Sherwood, "Vyacheslav a. Arkhangelskiy: Violent Anarchist in Seattle," Flarelight, May 14, 2022, https://web.archive.org/web/20220514010836/https://flarelight.org/vyacheslav-arkadyevich-arkhangelsky-avenir-david-capito/.

7 David D. Kirkpatrick, "Infiltrating the Far Right," *New Yorker*, August 18, 2024, https://www.newyorker.com/magazine/2024/08/26/infiltrating-the-far-right.

8 Heidi Beirich, "Neo-Nazi Lawyer Represents Baltimore in Suit Over Wrongful Arrest and 19-Year Imprisonment of Black Man," Hatewatch, August 17, 2016, https://www.splcenter.org/resources/hatewatch/neo-nazi-lawyer-represents-baltimore-suit-over-wrongful-arrest-and-19-year-imprisonment/.

9 Michael Edison Hayden, "Leaked Emails Name Shadow Lawyer in Charlottesville Case," Hatewatch, October 21, 2021, https://www.splcenter.org/resources/hatewatch/leaked-emails-name-shadow-lawyer-charlottesville-case/.

10 Shea Davis, "White Nationalists Sued an Infiltrator. They Still Can't Find Him in Tacoma or Elsewhere," *News Tribune*, October 2, 2024, https://www.thenewstribune.com/news/local/article293324984.html.

11 Kim Kelly, "The 3-D Printed Gun Isn't Coming. It's Already Here," *GEN*, August 13, 2020, https://gen.medium.com/the-3d-printed-gun-isnt-coming-it-s-already-here-6855fd394a47.

12 Conrad Wilson, "Suspect in Fatal Shooting of Portland Right-Wing Protester Killed by Law Enforcement," NPR, September 4, 2020, https://www.npr.org/2020/09/04/909515885/protester-suspected-in-portland-shooting-death-killed-by-law-enforcement.

13 Vice News, "Man Linked to Killing at a Portland Protest Says He Acted in Self-Defense," *Vice*, September 3, 2020, https://www.vice.com/en/article/man-linked-to-killing-at-a-portland-protest-says-he-acted-in-self-defense/.

14 Bryan Denson and Conrad Wilson, "New Eyewitness Accounts: Feds Didn't Identify Themselves Before Opening Fire on Portland Antifa Suspect," ProPublica and OPB, October 14, 2020, https://www.propublica.org/article/new-eyewitness-accounts-feds-didnt-identify-themselves-before-opening-fire-on-portland-antifa-suspect.

15 Mike Baker and Evan Hill, "Police Say an Antifa Activist Likely Shot at Officers. His Gun Suggests Otherwise," *New York Times*, April 10, 2021.

16 Tim Dickinson, "Trump Claims—and Celebrates—Extrajudicial Killing of Antifa Activist," *Rolling Stone*, October 15, 2020, https://www.rollingstone.com/politics/politics-news/trump-celebrates-law-enforcement-killing-antifa-activist-we-got-him-1076384/.

CHAPTER 15 **Ignite the Right**

1 "Dismantling the Fortress Pt. 2," *Maichaira Action* (blog), May 30, 2023, https://machaira action.noblogs.org/post/author/machairaaction/.

2 "The Official Guide to DezNat | Deseret Nationalism," *DezNat Exposed* (blog), May 22, 2021, https://exposedeznat.noblogs.org/official-guide-to-deznat-deseret-nationalism/.

3 Jason Wilson, "Revealed: Assistant Attorney General in Alaska Posted Racist and Anti-semitic Tweets," *Guardian*, July 21, 2021, https://www.theguardian.com/us-news/2021 /jul/21/alaska-assistant-attorney-general-twitter-far-right.

4 "Iron March Dossiers," n.d., https://ironmarch.noblogs.org/.

5 Tess Owen, "ICE Detention Center Captain Was on a Neo-Nazi Website and Wanted to Start a White Nationalist Group," *Vice*, March 13, 2020, https://www.vice.com/en /article/ice-detention-center-captain-was-on-a-neo-nazi-website-and-wanted-to-start -a-white-nationalist-group/.

6 Christopher Mathias, "5 Years Later, the Hunt for White Supremacists Who Terror-ized Charlottesville Continues," *HuffPost*, August 11, 2022, https://www.huffpost .com/entry/charlottesville-rally-anniversary-ignite-the-right-database_n_62f5344a e4b095e7887e72f9.

7 "@Johnny O'Malley," Unicorn Riot Discord Leaks, n.d., https://discordleaks.unicorn riot.ninja/discord/user/1622.

8 Luke O'Brien and Jessica Schulberg, "This Neo-Nazi Speech Shows the Rally in Charlot-tesville Was Always Meant to Be Violent," *HuffPost*, February 24, 2018, https://www.huff post.com/entry/neo-nazi-video-charlottesville-violence_n_5a8ca5dce4b00a30a250606c.

9 Jason Wilson, "White Supremacist Richard Spencer Makes Racist Slurs on Tape Leaked by Rival," *Guardian*, November 5, 2019, https://www.theguardian.com/world/2019/nov /04/white-supremacist-richard-spencer-racist-slurs-tape-milo-yiannopoulos.

10 Christopher Mathias, "He Marched at the Nazi Rally in Charlottesville. Then He Went Back to Being a Cop," *HuffPost*, October 13, 2022, https://www.huffpost.com/entry /john-donnelly-police-officer-charlottesville-white-supremacist-woburn-massachusetts _n_634856a1e4b08e0e60812d63.

11 "Examination of Conduct: Woburn Police Officer John Donnelly," Middlesex County District Attorney's Office (press release), February 28, 2025, https://www.middlesexda .com/press-releases/news/examination-conduct-former-woburn-police-department -officer-john-donnelly.

12 "Ignite the Right: One Year Later," *Ignite the Right* (blog), August 11, 2023, https:// ignitetheright.net/ignite-the-right-one-year-later/.

13 Christopher Mathias, "An Elementary School Teacher's Secret Life as a White Nationalist Writer," *HuffPost*, May 26, 2021, https://www.huffpost.com/entry/benjamin-welton-white -nationalist-elementary-school-teacher-writer_n_60ae5e89e4b0d45b753140fb.

16 "The 'Dissident Homeschoolers' of Upper Sandusky: Katja and Logan Lawrence," *Anon-ymous Comrades Collective* (blog), January 23, 2023, https://accollective.noblogs.org /post/2023/01/23/dissident-homeschool/.

17 "'Vic Mackey' of the 'Bowl Patrol' Identified as Andrew Casarez of Orangevale, California," *Anonymous Comrades Collective* (blog), July 7, 2020, https://accollective.noblogs .org/post/2020/07/07/vic-mackey-of-the-bowl-patrol-identified-as-andrew-casarez -of-orangevale/.

18 Sebastian Murdock and Christopher Mathias, "Leader of Dylann Roof-Worshipping Neo-Nazi Group Under Police Investigation," *HuffPost*, July 27, 2020, https://www .huffpost.com/entry/andrew-casarez-neo-nazi-police-investigation_n_5f1f510cc5b 638cfec48ba47.

19 Jason Wilson, "'No-Fly' List Named Base, Bowl Patrol Members Prior to Public IDs," February 2, 2023, https://www.splcenter.org/resources/hatewatch/no-fly-list-named -base-bowl-patrol-members-prior-public-ids/.

20 Ian Shapira, "Charlottesville Mystery: Who Are the Last Two Attackers of a Black Man in a Parking Garage?," *Washington Post*, March 3, 2019, https://www.washingtonpost .com/local/charlottesville-mystery-who-are-the-last-two-attackers-of-a-black-man -in-a-parking-garage/2019/03/03/9b27629c-3550-11e9-af5b-b51b7ff322e9_story.html.

21 David Swanson, "Scenes from a Bloody Weekend in Charlottesville," *Village Voice*, August 15, 2017, https://www.villagevoice.com/charlottesville-unite-right-rally-protest/.

22 Ian Shapira, "Charlottesville Mystery: Who Are the Last Two Attackers of a Black Man in a Parking Garage?," *Washington Post*, March 3, 2019, https://www.washingtonpost .com/local/charlottesville-mystery-who-are-the-last-two-attackers-of-a-black-man -in-a-parking-garage/2019/03/03/9b27629c-3550-11e9-af5b-b51b7ff322e9_story.html.

23 "Red Beard and Sunglasses, We Have Not Forgotten," *Ignite the Right* (blog), October 13, 2022, https://ignitetheright.net/red-beard-and-sunglasses-we-have-not-forgotten/.

24 Natasha Singer and Cade Metz, "Many Facial Recognition Systems Are Biased, Says U.S. Study," *New York Times*, December 19, 2019, https://www.nytimes.com/2019/12 /19/technology/facial-recognition-bias.html.

25 Luke O'Brien, "The Far-Right Helped Create the World's Most Powerful Facial Recognition Technology," *HuffPost*, April 9, 2020, https://www.huffpost.com/entry/clear view-ai-facial-recognition-alt-right_n_5e7d028bc5b6cb08a92a5c48.

26 Mike Haskey, "President George W. Bush Greets Fort Benning Soldiers in Fort Benning, Georgia," *Columbus Ledger-Enquirer* via Alamy Images, January 11, 2007, https:// www.alamy.com/no-film-no-video-no-tv-no-documentary-president-george-w-bush -greets-fort-benning-soldiers-in-fort-benning-georgia-thursday-january-11-2007-photo -by-mike-haskeycolumbus-ledger-enquirermctabacapresscom-image386764808.html.

27 Catherine Rampell, "A History of College Grade Inflation," *New York Times*, January 14, 2011, https://archive.nytimes.com/economix.blogs.nytimes.com/2011/07/14/the-history -of-college-grade-inflation/.

28 "Christopher Andrew Healy – Professor from Pickens, SC Identified as Unite the Right Attendee #PoloHatUTR," *Sunlight Anti-Fascist Action*, September 30, 2022, https://sunlight161.noblogs.org/polohatutr-as-professor-christopher-andrew-healy-of -greenville-sc/.

29 Tara McKelvey, "Charleston Manifesto: Controversial Blogger 'Hates Violence,'" BBC News, June 22, 2015, https://www.bbc.com/news/world-us-canada-33228707.

30 Macon Atkinson, "Furman Professor Says He Exercised Free Speech at 'Unite the Right' Rally in 2017," *Greenville News*, October 6, 2022, https://www.greenvilleonline.com/story /news/local/2022/10/06/furman-professor-says-he-exercised-free-speech-at-infamous -rally/69545302007/.

31 Asia Wilson, "Civil Liberties Group Calls for Professor's Return to Furman Classroom," WSPA, October 6, 2022, https://www.wspa.com/news/local-news/civil-liberties-group -calls-for-professors-return-to-furman-classroom/.

32 Anisa Snipes and Amanda Shaw, "'He's Not a Nazi': Attorneys Dispute Facts Surrounding Fired Furman Professor," FOX Carolina, September 5, 2024, https://www.foxcarolina .com/2024/09/05/he-is-not-white-supremacist-attorneys-disagree-facts-surrounding -fired-furman-professor/.

33 Q&A on 4chan: /pol/ News Network (Levi Smith), "I wanted to start this thread to clear the air, and answer any questions, regarding my Twitter account: @polNewsForever . . . ," 4chan, July 4, 2017, https://archive.is/5fTDt.

34 /pol/ News Forever (@polnewsforever), "Antifa caused a car accident . . . ," Twitter, August 12, 2017, 10:51pm, https://web.archive.org/web/20170813134913/https://twitter.com /polNewsForever/status/896429045981872129.

35 "Logan Michael Smith of Clarksville, Tennessee: The White Supremacist Behind '/Pol/ News Network,'" *Sunlight Anti-Fascist Action*, September 10, 2024, https://sunlight161 .noblogs.org/logan-michael-smith-of-clarksville-tn-white-supremacist-behind-pol-news -network/.

36 "Logan Michael Smith of Clarksville, Tennessee."

37 Eli Motycka, "Assistant Professor Leaves Austin Peay After White Supremacist Allegations," Nashville Scene, September 23, 2024, https://www.nashvillescene.com/news /pithinthewind/apsu-white-supremacist-professor-allegations/article_60f3c6e6-79e3 -11ef-aa07-6fd03080bb81.html.

38 Chris Smith, "APSU to Revamp Hiring Practices Over Accusation of Professor's Involvement with Hate Site," ClarksvilleNow.Com, September 17, 2024, https://clarksvillenow .com/local/apsu-to-revamp-hiring-practices-over-accusation-of-professors-involvement -with-hate-site/.

39 Abigail McKenna, "APSU Community Rallies Online and on Campus Against Alleged White Supremacist Among Faculty," *All State*, September 20, 2024, https://theallstate .org/58087/ap-wire/breaking-news-ap-wire/apsu-community-rallies-online-and-on -campus-against-alleged-white-supremacist-among-faculty/.

40 Chris Smith, "APSU to Pay Embattled Psychology Professor $56,000 in Severance Agreement," ClarksvilleNow.Com, October 4, 2024, https://clarksvillenow.com/local /apsu-to-pay-embattled-psychology-professor-56000-in-severance-agreement/.

41 Chris Smith, "Psychology Professor, APSU 'Mutually Agree' to End His Employment Over Hate Group Accusations," ClarksvilleNow.Com, September 23, 2024, https:// clarksvillenow.com/local/psychology-professor-apsu-mutually-agree-to-end-his -employment-over-hate-group-accusations/.

42 Christopher Mathias, "He Didn't Deny Being a White Supremacist. Then He Was Elected to City Council," *HuffPost*, March 14, 2024, https://www.huffpost.com/entry

/oklahoma-enid-councilman-judson-blevins-white-supremacist_n_65f09c63e4b02ad
7de1a9376.

43 Matt Kennard, "Neo-Nazis Are in the Army Now," Type Investigations, June 5, 2009, https://
www.typeinvestigations.org/investigation/2009/06/15/neo-nazis-are-in-the-army-now/.

44 "Racist Extremists Active in U.S. Military," Southern Poverty Law Center, June 7, 2006,
https://www.splcenter.org/resources/stories/racist-extremists-active-us-military/.

45 Matthew Kennard, "The U.S. Military's History of Recruiting and Retaining Neo-Nazis,"
August 9, 2012, in *Takeaway*, produced by WQXR, radio interview, https://www.wqxr
.org/story/228802-us-militarys-history-recruiting-and-retaining-neo-nazis/.

46 Kathleen Belew, *Bring the War Home: The White Power Movement and Paramilitary
America* (Cambridge, MA: Harvard University Press, 2018), 20.

CHAPTER 16 **The Fire Rises**

1 Jay Heilman, Facebook, https://web.archive.org/save/https://web.archive.org/web
/20240612004528/https://www.facebook.com/jay.heilman.98.

2 Alice Herman, "'They're Eating the Cats': Trump Rambles Falsely About Immigrants
in Debate," *Guardian*, September 11, 2024, https://www.theguardian.com/us-news
/article/2024/sep/10/trump-springfield-pets-false-claims.

3 Brandy Zadrozny, "Trump's Baseless Allegations During Debate Put New Focus on
Ohio City," NBC News, September 13, 2024, https://www.nbcnews.com/tech/internet
/trump-neo-nazis-pushed-false-claims-haitians-part-hate-campaign-rcna170796.

4 Christopher Mathias, "JD Vance Is the GOP's Next-Gen Authoritarian," *HuffPost*, July
16, 2024, https://www.huffpost.com/entry/jd-vance-authoritarian-rnc_n_66969677e
4b0e5ea1d600462.

5 Alissa J. Rubin, "Ahmad Chalabi and the Legacy of De-baathification in Iraq," *New York
Times*, November 3, 2015, https://www.nytimes.com/2015/11/04/world/middleeast
/ahmad-chalabi-and-the-legacy-of-de-baathification-in-iraq.html.

6 Ava Kofman, "Curtis Yarvin's Plot Against America," *New Yorker*, June 2, 2025, https://
www.newyorker.com/magazine/2025/06/09/curtis-yarvin-profile.

7 Kris Maher, Valerie Bauerlein, and Tawnell Hobbs, "How the Trump Campaign Ran
with Rumors About Pet-Eating Migrants – After Being Told They Weren't True," *Wall
Street Journal*, September 18, 2024, https://www.wsj.com/us-news/springfield-ohio
-pet-eating-claims-haitian-migrants-04598d48?mod=hp_lead_pos7&mod=wknd_pos1.

8 Armando Garcia, Jeremy Edwards, and Hannah Demissie, "Vance Kept up False Claims
About Haitian Migrants After Aide Was Told They Were Baseless," ABC News, September 18, 2024, https://abcnews.go.com/Politics/vance-false-claims-haitian-migrants
-after-aide-told/story?id=113821189.

9 Brandy Zadrozny, "Trump's Baseless Allegations During Debate Put New Focus on
Ohio City," NBC News, September 13, 2024, https://www.nbcnews.com/tech/internet
/trump-neo-nazis-pushed-false-claims-haitians-part-hate-campaign-rcna170796.

10 "Extremist Files: Nick Fuentes," Southern Poverty Law Center, n.d., https://www
.splcenter.org/resources/extremist-files/nick-fuentes/.

11   Christopher Mathias, "They Were Not Tourists: The Radicals at the Heart of the Capitol Riot," *HuffPost*, July 4, 2021, https://www.huffpost.com/entry/capitol-insurrection -six-month-anniversary_n_60e07bf3e4b03f72964accc0.

12   Sebastian Murdock, "Elon Musk Says He'll Reinstate Twitter Account of Hitler-Loving White Supremacist," *HuffPost*, May 2, 2024, https://www.huffpost.com/entry /elon-musk-reinstates-nick-fuentes-twitter-account_n_6633e432e4b00b1eab529f92.

13   Christopher Mathias, "White Nationalists with Lanyards: Orlando Showed the Ugly Future of the Republican Party," *HuffPost*, March 4, 2022, https://www.huffpost.com /entry/cpac-afpac-white-nationalists-republicans-maga_n_6217fd24e4b0ef74d72d36d1.

14   Alan Feuer and Maggie Haberman, "Trump's Latest Dinner Guest: Nick Fuentes, White Supremacist," *New York Times*, November 25, 2022, https://www.nytimes.com/2022/11 /25/us/politics/trump-nick-fuentes-dinner.html.

15   Christopher Mathias, "Daily Wire CEO Tells White Supremacist Nick Fuentes He's 'Talented' and 'Very Funny,'" *HuffPost*, April 2, 2024, https://www.huffpost.com/entry /daily-wire-ceo-praises-white-supremacist-nick-fuentes-jeremy-boreing_n_660c28bde 4b0328a72be11a7.

16   Mollie Reilly, "Trump Insists He's 'Not a Student of Hitler' While Defending 'Poison-ing the Blood' Comments About Immigrants," *HuffPost*, December 22, 2023, https:// www.huffpost.com/entry/donald-trump-poisoning-blood-hitler_n_6585ba0ee4b 04da98426f6c2.

17   Matt Shuham, "Trump: Immigrants Have Brought 'Bad Genes' into the Country," *HuffPost*, October 7, 2024, https://www.huffpost.com/entry/trump-immigrants -bad-genes_n_67040a34e4b0924ce9db0b0e.

18   Christopher Mathias, "Trump's Alarming Use of a Word with a Deep Fascist History," *HuffPost*, September 20, 2024, https://www.huffpost.com/entry/trump-remigration -fascist-martin-sellner-europe_n_66ed912be4b07a173e51416d.

19   Christopher Mathias, "Trump's Alarming Use of a Word."

20   Christopher Mathias, Matt Shuham, and Jennifer Bendery, "How Did Laura Loomer Finally Earn a Spot at Donald Trump's Side?," *HuffPost*, September 17, 2024, https:// www.huffpost.com/entry/laura-loomer-donald-trump_n_66e8a3b0e4b0b7fef8324373.

21   Amanda Moore (@noturtlesoup), "Nick Fuentes and Laura Loomer cheersing to 'the hostile takeover of the Republican Party,'" Twitter, April 7, 2023, 1:26pm, https://x.com /noturtlesoup17/status/1644391255223173146.

22   Laura Loomer (@LauraLoomer), "Send those savages back to where they came from and tell them 2A was created for the sake of protecting our pets," Twitter, September 9, 2024, 7:08pm, https://x.com/LauraLoomer/status/1833281442278723598.

23   Laura Loomer (@LauraLoomer), "If Kamala Harris wins, she will allow third world invaders to kill your pets," September 9, 2024, 9:03am, https://x.com/LauraLoomer/ status/1833129057111752831.

24   Melissa Alonso, Jeff Winter, and Chelsea Bailey, "Vance's Team Was Told Haitian Immigrant Rumors Were False Before Debate, Springfield Mayor Confirms," CNN, September 21, 2024, https://www.cnn.com/2024/09/20/politics/springfield-ohio -vance-campaign-wsj-report.

25 William Brangham and Mary Fecteau, "How Life in Springfield Has Been Disrupted by Lies About Its Haitian Community," PBS News, September 18, 2024, https://www .pbs.org/newshour/show/how-life-in-springfield-has-been-disrupted-by-lies-about-its -haitian-community.

26 Miriam Jordan, "Many Haitians Prospered in Springfield, Ohio. Then Came the Hate," *New York Times*, October 11, 2024, https://www.nytimes.com/2024/10/11/us/haitians -springfield-ohio-pets.html.

27 Nathan Hart, "Springfield Cancels CultureFest as Immigration Controversy Stokes Threats, Safety Concerns," *Columbus Dispatch*, September 16, 2024, https://www .dispatch.com/story/news/local/2024/09/16/springfield-ohio-culturefest-canceled -threats-safety-concerns-haitian-immigrants/75246731007/.

28 Rashard Rose and Kate Sullivan, "Trump Says He Would Revoke Temporary Protected Status for Haitian Immigrants if Elected," CNN, October 3, 2024, https://www.cnn .com/2024/10/03/politics/trump-revoke-status-ohio-haitian-migrants.

29 Robert O. Paxton, "I've Hesitated to Call Donald Trump a Fascist. Until Now | Opin- ion," *Newsweek*, January 11, 2021, https://www.newsweek.com/robert-paxton-trump -fascist-1560652.

30 Taylor Lorenz, "Meet the Woman Behind LibsOfTikTok, Secretly Fueling the Right's Outrage Machine," *Washington Post*, April 19, 2022, https://www.washingtonpost.com /technology/2022/04/19/libs-of-tiktok-right-wing-media/.

31 Matt Laviates, "LibsOfTikTok Creator Accused of Inspiring School Bomb Threats Named to Oklahoma Library Board," NBC News, January 23, 2024, https://www.nbcnews.com /nbc-out/out-news/libs-tik-tok-bomb-threats-oklahoma-library-committee-rcna135369.

32 Will Carless, "When Libs of TikTok Tweets, Threats Increasingly Follow," *USA Today*, November 5, 2023, https://www.usatoday.com/story/news/investigations/2023/11/02 /libs-of-tiktok-tweets-death-bomb-threats/71409213007/.

33 Christopher Wiggins, "LibsOfTikTok Creator Seems Overjoyed at Report Highlighting Her Dangerous Posts," *Advocate*, November 7, 2023.

34 Christopher Mathias, "Richard Hanania, Rising Right-Wing Star, Wrote for White Supremacist Sites Under Pseudonym," *HuffPost*, August 7, 2023, https://www.huffpost .com/entry/richard-hanania-white-supremacist-pseudonym-richard-hoste_n _64c93928e4b021e2f295e817.

35 Parker Molloy, "HuffPost's Story on Rising Right-Wing Star Richard Hanania Is Really About Culture Rot," *Present Age* (blog), August 8, 2023, https://www.readtpa.com/p /huffposts-story-on-rising-right-wing.

36 "'StoneToss' Tossed: Hans Kristian Graebener of Spring, TX," *Anonymous Comrades Collective* (blog), March 12, 2024, https://accollective.noblogs.org/post/2024/03/12 /stonetoss-redpanels/.

37 "Goodbye 2024, Hello 2025 and the Story of Musktoss," *Anonymous Comrades Collective* (blog), December 31, 2024, https://accollective.noblogs.org/post/2024/12/31/goodbye -2024-hello-2025-and-the-story-of-musktoss/.

38 David Ingram, "Elon Musk's X Bans Revealing the Names of Anonymous Users After Scrutiny of Antisemitic Cartoonist," NBC News, March 21, 2024, https://www

.nbcnews.com/tech/social-media/elon-musk-x-bans-revealing-names-anonymous-users -cartoon-rcna144486.

39 Miles Klee, "Elon Musk All but Endorses the Great Replacement Conspiracy Theory," *Rolling Stone*, January 5, 2024, https://www.rollingstone.com/culture/culture-news /elon-musk-great-replacement-conspiracy-theory-1234941337/.

40 Sareen Habeshian, "Musk Endorses Far-Right German AfD Party," Axios, December 20, 2024, https://www.axios.com/2024/12/20/musk-germany-afd-party.

41 Maximilian Bornmann, "Geheimplan Gegen Deutschland," correctiv.org, January 10, 2024, https://correctiv.org/aktuelles/neue-rechte/2024/01/10/geheimplan-remigration -vertreibung-afd-rechtsextreme-november-treffen/.

42 "Neo-Nazi Comic Illustrator 'JinjerZilla': Joshua Thayer LeGoff of Cranston, Rhode Island," *Anonymous Comrades Collective* (blog), January 28, 2022, https://accollective .noblogs.org/post/2022/01/28/jinjerzilla/.

43 Christopher Mathias, "He Didn't Deny Being a White Supremacist. Then He Was Elected to City Council," *HuffPost*, March 14, 2024, https://www.huffpost.com/entry /oklahoma-enid-councilman-judson-blevins-white-supremacist_n_65f09c63e4b02ad 7de1a9376.

44 Christopher Mathias, "He Didn't Deny Being a White Supremacist."

45 Christopher Mathias, "Judson Blevins, City Councilman with Neo-Nazi Ties, Loses Recall Election," *HuffPost*, April 3, 2024, https://www.huffpost.com/entry/judson -blevins-recall-election-enid-oklahoma_n_660c9597e4b0328a72be47d9.

46 "Chicagoland-based Back the Blue & Protest the Protesters Organizer Emily Cahill Goes to Knox County Jail," *Anne Frank Army* (blog), n.d., https://annefranksarmy .noblogs.org/emily-cahill-goes-to-jail/.

CHAPTER 17 **Fire Brigades**

1 John Sherwood, "Decentralized Activism: Pros and Cons," Flarelight, March 23, 2022, https://web.archive.org/web/20220517013030/https://flarelight.org/decentralized -activism-pros-cons/.

2 "Change Your Life for the Better in 2024: Leave the White Nationalist Movement," *Atlanta Antifascists* (blog), January 1, 2024, https://atlantaantifa.org/2024/01/01 /change-your-life-for-the-better-in-2024-leave-the-white-nationalist-movement/.

3 Sam Levin, "Border Patrol Agents Jump Out of Rental Truck and Ambush People at LA Home Depot," *Guardian*, August 7, 2025, https://www.theguardian.com/us-news /2025/aug/06/ice-border-patrol-home-depot-los-angeles.

4 Austin Hornbostel, "Sen. Marsha Blackburn Introduces Bill Making It Illegal to 'dox' Federal Law Enforcement," *Tennessean*, June 5, 2025, https://www.tennessean.com /story/news/local/davidson/2025/06/05/blackburn-bill-criminalizing-doxxing-federal -law-enforcement-oconnell-ice/84048878007/.

5 Gerardo del Valle, Alejandro Bonilla, SuárezEdwin, and Corona Ramos, "Families of Vene-zuelans Sent to CECOT Open Up About Their Ordeal," ProPublica, August 7, 2025, https:// www.propublica.org/article/venezuelans-cecot-el-salvador-trump-families-video.

6 José Olivares, "Human Rights Groups Rebuke Kristi Noem's Visit to El Salvador Prison: 'Political Theater,'" *Guardian*, March 28, 2025, https://www.theguardian.com/us-news/2025/mar/27/kristi-noem-el-salvador-prison-visit-trump-admin.

7 Kate Connolly, "'The Gesture Speaks for Itself': Germans Respond to Musk's Apparent Nazi Salute," *Guardian*, January 22, 2025, https://www.theguardian.com/technology/2025/jan/21/the-gesture-speaks-for-itself-germans-divided-over-musks-apparent-nazi-salute.

8 Diane Adame, "Judge Rules Neo-Nazi Group to Pay $2.7 Million to Black Musician Attacked in Boston," GBH, January 13, 2025, https://www.wgbh.org/news/local/2025-01-13/judge-rules-neo-nazi-group-to-pay-2-7-million-to-black-musician-attacked-in-boston.

9 Jeff Tischauser, "Patriot Front Is Hidden Hand Behind Dozen Active Clubs," Hatewatch, May 9, 2025, https://www.splcenter.org/resources/hatewatch/patriot-front-active-clubs-network-influence/.

10 Tim Dickinson, "This 'Violence-Ready' Militia Is Hiding in Plain Sight," *Rolling Stone*, September 9, 2023, https://www.rollingstone.com/politics/politics-features/white-nationalist-active-clubs-1234835015/.

11 "The Return of Racial Fascism," in *For Antifascist Futures: Against the Violence of Imperial Crisis*, ed. Aloysha Goldstein and Simon Ventura Trujillo (Brooklyn, NY: Common Notions, 2022), 244.

12 Bill V. Mullen and Christopher Vials, editorial introduction to Penny Nakatsu, "Speech at the United Front against Fascism Conference (1969)," in *The US Antifascism Reader*, ed. Mullen and Vials (New York: Verso, 2020), 271.

13 Kit O'Connell, "Everyday Antifascism & the Limits of Antifa: Scott Crow on Movement Building Under Trump," PM Press, February 1, 2018, https://blog.pmpress.org/2019/07/24/everyday-antifascism-the-limits-of-antifa-scott-crow-on-movement-building-under-trump/.

14 Emily Gorcenski, "Antifascism Through the Lens of Transgender Identity," in *No Pasaran: Antifascists Dispatches from a World in Crisis*, ed. Shane Burley (Chico, CA: AK Press, 2022), 309–11.

15 Shane Burley, "Building Communities for a Fascist-Free Future," in *No Pasaran: Antifascists Dispatches from a World in Crisis*, ed. Shane Burley (Chico, CA: AK Press, 2022), 49.

Image Credits

Index

About the Author

Christopher Mathias is a journalist covering the far right. Previously a senior reporter at *HuffPost*, he's done work for MSNBC, Zeteo, and WNYC. His reporting chronicled the rapid radicalization of the GOP, and has helped unmask white supremacist cops, soldiers, teachers, and politicians. Mathias was a Deadline Awards finalist for feature writing. He lives in New York and goes by @LetsGoMathias on BlueSky and X.